GEORGE III

A Biography

George III painted by Ramsay.

Reproduced by Gracious Permission of Her Majesty the Queen.

GEORGE III

A Biography by

J. C. LONG 1892

MACDONALD : LONDON

First published in Great Britain in 1962 by
Macdonald & Co. (Publishers) Ltd.
London, W.1
Made and printed in Great Britain by
Purnell and Sons, Ltd.
Paulton (Somerset) and London

To
J. M. LARKIN

ACKNOWLEDGMENTS

Any writer on historical subjects is indebted to a host of predecessors without whom his work could not have come into being. Where I have made acknowledgment in the Bibliography, I do not need to repeat it here, as in the instances of H. Butterfield, J. H. Plumb, the late L. B. Namier, and the late R. Pares.

First, I have to acknowledge the gracious permission of her Majesty Queen Elizabeth II to reproduce extracts from the school papers of King George III before his accession. These papers are in the Royal Archives, Windsor Castle.

In addition, I am particularly indebted to:

In England: Robert Mackworth-Young, Librarian, Windsor Castle; the Public Record Office; the British Museum; S. Gordon, Librarian, House of Commons; the Society of Friends, London; John Fisher and Mrs. Sylvia Brittenden of London.

In Princeton, New Jersey: W. S. Dix and the staff of the Princeton University Library (Firestone); Dr. Kenneth Gapp and the staff of the Princeton Theological Seminary Library (Speer); Mrs. Meredith Knowlton, for research and secretarial aid; and my wife, Mary P. Long.

In New York: Mark Kiley, Librarian, the University Club; the New York Historical Society; and the New York Public Library. Also for research assistance, Mrs. Erma Green Gold, Harry Gold of the Aberdeen Book Company and Mrs. Alice B. Rypins (now of Santa Barbara, California).

In Washington, D.C.: Henry J. Dubester, Robert H. Land, and David C. Mearns of the Library of Congress.

In Bethlehem, Pa.: James Mack, Librarian, Lehigh University; Miss Jean Wesner, Librarian, Charles M. Schwab Memorial Library.

CONTENTS

Acknowledgments   vii

Part I. STEPS LEADING TO THE THRONE

1. Contract for the Crown   15
2. Prenatal Influences   20
3. The Happy Years   24
4. Boyhood Days   31
5. Struggle to Control Young George   38
6. New Leaders in the Kingdom   47
7. Ascendancy of Bute   52
8. Accession to the Throne   64
9. George III and Sarah Lennox   69
10. Sad, Regretful Coronation   78
11. Dilemma for a Young King   86
12. Honeymoon with the City   94

Part II. MISTAKES OF AN AMATEUR KING

13. George III versus Free Speech   105
14. "Firmness and Resolution"   115
15. Hardening of the Shell   119
16. Downfall of Bute   126
17. Grenville's Legacy of Errors   133
18. "Mr. Greenville" Rides High   140

Part III. MATURING YEARS

19. George III Comes of Age   147
20. The Stamp Act as Symbol   153

21. No Giants   159
22. Scandal Singes the Throne   162
23. The Testing of George III's Dream   167
24. George III's Wider Horizons   176
25. Twilight of the Constitution   184
26. A Period of Transition   189

Part IV. ORDEALS OF A TYRO TYRANT

27. The Gathering Storm   197
28. Thunder on the Left   200
29. "A Kind of Destiny"   206
30. Last Phases of the Colonial Era   211
31. Gauntlet at Philadelphia   215
32. 1778—A Year of Crisis   224
33. George Again Takes Charge   234
34. Revolt in England   242
35. "The Thought Was My Own"   254
36. The King Alone   259
37. The King in Crisis   263
38. Abasement of the King   267

Part V. FINAL RECKONING

39. A New Unwelcome Role   277
40. Home Life of a Monarch   284
41. The Mad Years   288
42. Actions in the Interludes   294
43. Hail and Farewell   302

     Notes   307
     Bibliography   319
     Index   325

LIST OF ILLUSTRATIONS

George III painted by Ramsay *frontispiece*

George as a boy *facing page* 48

Princess Augusta 49

John Stuart, third Earl of Bute 49

Hannah Lightfoot 49

Elizabeth Chudleigh, Duchess of Kingston 49

George and Charlotte by Reynolds 64

William Pitt, Earl of Chatham 64

George III by Benjamin West 64

Lord North 65

Lady Sarah Lennox 65

Elizabeth, Countess of Pembroke 96

Engraving of Queen Charlotte 96

George III by Gainsborough 97

PART I

Steps Leading to the Throne

I

CONTRACT FOR THE CROWN

George the Third, at the age of twenty-two, ascended the throne of Great Britain in October 1760. He was handsome, he was in love, and he offered new hope for an England which for many years had endured the ill-tempered reign of his grandfather, George II.

His father Frederick had been the heir apparent but had died untimely nine years earlier. Frederick was beloved by all classes of society except the Court, by most of the nobility, by the merchants of London, by the masses and by his son. Frederick was a wit, a musician of note and a man who had an awareness of the need for social reform. Many hoped that George III would emulate Frederick.

Time and circumstance, however, affect the life of everyone, and George III during his lengthy reign became a diverse character of contradictory elements, sometimes seeming possessed of the Devil. He early was the victim of a jealous possessive mother who plotted against his romances. For some years he was dominated by the scheming Lord Bute, a mentor in his household and his mother's confidant.

Though George III is remembered chiefly for his ill-fated conflict with the American colonies, the American period was but a small segment of his life—only sixteen years from the Stamp Act to the defeat at Yorktown, out of a reign of fifty years.

George III had the longest reign of any English king, exceeded only by that of Queen Victoria. He accordingly had a profound influence on British destiny both for good and for ill. His total career was a phantasmagoria, not alone in respect to the status of the Crown, but also in the internal convolutions and struggles of his complex personality.

George III in his royal office was a hired man, for his dynasty had been appointed by Parliament under specified contractual conditions. He tried to enhance the authority of the throne while giving lip service to what he called the Constitution, and he regarded the office of the king and his chosen ministers as the fountainhead of government.

It is not surprising that the young monarch was confused as to his real rights and duties. Until the bloodless Revolution of 1688 the powers and limitations of the Crown had been interpreted in various ways—witness the extremes of Charles I and Oliver Cromwell. After 1688, when Parliament spelled out the limits in written documents, many of the traditional honours of royalty remained, though in form rather than substance.

For example, the king ostensibly had the right to choose his own ministers to run the government, by whim or favouritism if he preferred. He created peerages and conferred knighthoods. Orders to the navy and army went forth in his name. The great William Pitt, the elder, would write to his commanders saying "the King has judged proper that" or "it is his Majesty's pleasure that". To George II Pitt often wrote, "I lay myself at your Majesty's feet", and at an audience with the king he bowed like a jackknife until his hawk nose was bent down between his tall thin legs.

An earlier long-term prime minister, Sir Robert Walpole, who had ruled virtually every act of George II, had tried to define the seeming inconsistency between form and fact when addressing the Parliament one day: "A seat in this House is equal to any dignity derived from posts or titles, and the approbation of this House is preferable to all that power, or even Majesty itself, can bestow: therefore when I speak here as a minister, I speak as possessing my powers from his Majesty but as being answerable to this House for the exercise of those powers."

The Ministry recommended all major appointments at the disposal of the Crown, including peerages. Men would not accept ministerial office unless they felt sure of support in Parliament. The manifold orders sent out by Pitt and others in the king's name were probably never seen by George II.

George III was the first of the Hanoverian kings who had any possibility of restoring the authority of the throne in ancient terms. George's great-grandfather, George I, crowned October 1714, never mastered the English language. George II, crowned October 1727, regarded England as a juicy plum and preferred to spend long vacations in Hanover. He was happy to have Sir Robert Walpole to manage all government affairs for him. When Walpole was forced out, George II had no close acquaintance with other chief persons in the realm. Sir Robert had seen to that.

An odd chain of circumstances had brought the Hanoverian Georges to the English throne. James II, the last ruling Stuart, had tried to govern England by personal rule in defiance of Parliament. Furthermore, he had become a Roman Catholic, largely at the instigation of Louis XIV. As a result of these two issues Parliament in 1688 forced him to abdicate. He fled to France with an infant son, James Francis Edward, later known as "the Old Pretender". The infant could have been named to the succession under a regency and Louis XIV had the audacity to proclaim the boy as king of England.

However, England had found that there was nothing "divine" in the principle of direct inheritance of the kingship; and past acceptance of that doctrine had been disastrous, as in the cases of Charles I and James II. Parliament now pursued the policy of appointing a succession by invitation under specified conditions which lent emphasis to the fact that the throne was a constitutional one. On the other hand, the inheritance theory (without the "divine") had the sanction of tradition and popular appeal. Hence Parliament had the problem of finding a prospective ruler who had acceptable religious and constitutional beliefs, and also the benefit of royal blood.

There were two persons of royal descent who were stoutly allied to the Protestant cause and not under the influence of Louis XIV. One was Mary, eldest daughter of James II, who was an ardent communicant of the Church of England and had broken with her father when he had tried to insist upon her conversion to Rome. The other was Mary's husband William, Prince of Orange, who was a grandson of Charles I and a fighter in the Protestant cause for Holland against France. In 1689 Parliament decided to invite William and Mary to the throne to rule jointly.

Lest there be any misunderstanding about the conditions, a parliamentary committee drew up a paper, the Declaration of Rights, also called the Bill of Rights, which was adopted by both houses. The paper began by reciting the faults of James II, including his establishment of an ecclesiastical commission, his raising of an army without parliamentary sanction, his suspension of certain laws, and his practice of levying money without the consent of Parliament. The document declared that such practices violated the original contract between the king and the people and would

B

not be tolerated. It affirmed that the subject had a right to petition and to a pure and merciful administration of justice. It declared that both houses of Parliament should have liberty of debate. It demanded protection for the free exercise of their religion by all Protestants and bound the king to maintain the Protestant religion.

"We do claim and insist on the premises," said the Declaration, "as our undoubted rights and liberties." The Declaration was publicly read to William and Mary at a banquet of the House of Lords and the House of Commons on February 13, 1689. In response to the reading, William formally accepted the offer under those conditions for himself and his wife and declared that he would maintain the laws and govern by advice of Parliament.

The Parliament expected that the document would establish permanently a constitutional throne. The succession was defined: first the children of William and Mary, if any. If they had no issue, the throne was to descend to Anne, Mary's sister, and her children. However, by 1701 it became clear that a new line of succession soon must be found. William was seriously ill, Anne was in poor health, and all of her children had died in infancy. Though Anne reigned until 1714 the Parliament did not wish to risk another period of confusion should the queen die suddenly.

James Francis Edward, son of James II, was still the most direct heir, but Parliament held that as the boy had been raised a Catholic and had been brought up in France where absolute monarchy was the rule, he was unfit to be the king of a Protestant nation. The next person in line was Anna, the only living granddaughter of Charles I and niece of James II, who had married the Duke of Savoy. The house of Savoy, however, was Catholic and therefore unacceptable.

The next possibility was to consider descendants of James I, father of Charles I. James I's daughter Elizabeth had married the Elector Palatine and her only surviving child Sophia had married the elector of Hanover, the chief ruler of a minor German state. Sophia and her husband and their heirs were a Protestant line. Accordingly negotiations were opened with her to accept the throne of England for herself and her descendants after Anne should die.

As in the case of the Declaration of Rights in 1701, the terms were set forward clearly in writing in a document called the Act of Settlement. This employment contract was even more stringent than the one which had been put before William and Mary. The Parliament had become perturbed at the way that the country was involved in the foreign politics of William, because of his Dutch connections. Hence, the new contract for the throne provided that all future kings were forbidden to leave England without the consent of Parliament. Furthermore, foreigners were excluded from all public positions, military or civil. The contract demanded that the sovereign must be a communicant of the Church of England.

It strengthened the provision that the king could act only through his ministers and that the ministers were responsible to Parliament. It affirmed that all public business should be formally done in the Privy Council and all its decisions signed by its members. It added that no judge should be removed from office save on an address from Parliament to the Crown. The house of Hanover accepted these terms. Sophia herself died before Queen Anne, but the latter was succeeded by George I, son of Sophia.

Hence, when George III, great-grandson of George I, came to the throne the principles on which he should operate and his responsibility to Parliament had been clearly and repeatedly defined.

At times it has been asserted that the Protestant succession, including the Hanoverians, had been called to office by an oligarchy who did not necessarily represent the popular will; but such a revolution, accomplished without bloodshed, would have been impossible if it had not reflected the independent temper of the British people. A Rev. Samuel Johnson, not related to his famous namesake, wrote a pamphlet in 1692 which intrinsically reflected the attitude of the commoners. He wrote: "All civil power is originally in the people. . . . The nation must make their King, for I am sure the King cannot make the nation. And as Sir William Temple very well observes, the basis of Government is the people, though the king be at the top of it; and to found the Government upon a king is to invert the pyramid and set it upon the pinnacle, where it will never stand." This comment was a pungent distillation of the views of John Locke (1632–1704), a contemporary of the reverend. Locke was the famous English philosopher who had drafted documents justifying the expulsion of James II by Parliament, and for generations thereafter he was regarded as the chief exponent of constitutional doctrine.

George III was the first of his line who possibly could challenge the group of prominent families, known as Whigs, who held the chief offices in the government. He was the first of the Georges to be British-born. He, through his father's wide acquaintanceship, through the numerous entertainments and conferences held in his boyhood home, knew many of the important men in the realm. The story of Frederick before and after George's birth, the circumstances of George's childhood until and following the death of his father help provide an understanding of George III's difficult character.

2

PRENATAL INFLUENCES

George III's father, Frederick Lewis, and his mother, Augusta, had begun their marriage under ill-starred circumstances. George II, King of Great Britain and the ruler of Hanover, hated and feared his eldest son, Frederick Lewis. The hostility was traditional as well as personal. In Hanover, a small German state, the ruler (called elector) was absolute. The subjects could only hope that a successor might be more tolerant and hence the eldest son was regarded jealously by the father and as far as possible deprived of public honours.

When the future George II and his wife Caroline went to live in England in 1714, they left their seven-year-old son Frederick in Hanover. On coming of age, however, Frederick insisted that he be allowed to live in the kingdom to which he was now heir. On arrival Frederick was received by his parents with cool politeness. He was formally appointed Prince of Wales and admitted to the Privy Council, as custom required; but otherwise he was kept in official obscurity.

Frederick in his initial years in England had time on his hands. He enjoyed convivial companions, though he was a teetotaller. He spent hours at the card table profitably whereat his sobriety doubtless helped. Frederick's involvement with women was the expensive phase of his debauchery, though there he seemed to carry off his losses with a certain gaiety and appreciation of value received. He would have preferred marriage, for he was basically a romantic as his later years proved, but state policy kept blocking his way.

At the age of four Frederick had been betrothed to Wilhelmina, daughter of the king of Prussia. George II disliked the Prussian monarch who was his cousin and his rival in the power politics of the various German states. George II delayed approving the marriage even though the event was definitely expected by the Parliament.

Frederick, when of age, thought he had a solution to this impasse. He was ardently eager to marry Wilhelmina. Her mother was agreeable to the idea and her father offered no objection. Frederick negotiated with Wilhelmina's mother for a secret wedding, believing that once this was accomplished all parties must recognize it. Unfortunately the mother talked too much. The British ambassador, though favourable, thought it his duty to report the intended event to his master. George II was incensed at this duplicity and it gave him the excuse to refuse his consent to the match then and permanently.

Frederick's next attempt was to seek the hand of Lady Diana Spencer, a granddaughter of Sarah, Duchess of Marlborough. The duchess was agreeable—some say it was her idea originally—and a dowry of £100,000 was fixed upon. This time Robert Walpole, the prime minister, intervened. The duchess had enormous wealth and prestige and was respected by all parties in or out of the Government. Compared to her lineage and history, Sir Robert Walpole was an upstart; but Sir Robert had the prevailing influence over George II and wished that no person of consequence other than himself be close to the royal family. The king forbade the proposed marriage.

Here Frederick again had doubly hard luck. Sarah, the duchess, was a strong-willed and persistent woman. She had no innate regard for these imported German kings and she was accustomed to refer to His Majesty as "neighbour George". She would not fear to tackle Walpole either, given time and opportunity. Alas for the prince, time ran against him, for soon after this thwarting of plans, in October 1731, Diana married the fourth Duke of Bedford, and died four years later.

Frederick, now nearing thirty, had reached years of discretion. He wished to settle down and had demanded of his father to select a suitable wife for him. It was obvious that anyone whom Frederick might choose would be opposed by George II and it was customary for royal marriages to be arranged by the parents. George II could not refuse the demand, much as he disliked having his hand forced, for the nation was restive over the fact that Frederick was unmarried and that hence there was no provision for continuation of the line. Further, there still was criticism of the king for annulling the betrothal to Wilhelmina.

George II was in a dilemma, for there were few ranking Protestant princesses. He finally settled on the sixteen-year-old Augusta of the unimportant court of Saxe-Gotha, little realizing what a power she ultimately would prove to be.

At the outset George II undertook to show his son and the prospective bride that they were not to expect any public attentions except those which he would permit. On the prospective bride's arrival at Greenwich, George II ordered that there be no demonstrations and after a delay of two or three days (accounts vary) the coach was directed to approach the Palace by back streets.

Augusta was shrewd enough not to show offence. When presented to the king and queen she prostrated herself flat on the floor before each in turn. She knew power when she saw it and could bide her time.

The wedding took place that evening in St. James's Chapel. Frederick and his bride continued to live at St. James's for the time being with little attention being paid to them in any quarter.

At the same time, however, Frederick was being plotted against by his father. That obtuse monarch planned to have his second son, William, Duke of Cumberland, succeed him in England, while Frederick must be content with the electorship at Hanover. The plan was preposterous, as Parliament had established the line of succession, but George II did not understand either English or the English. For his own reasons of spite and jealousy, he aimed to debar Frederick and his heirs, if any, from the succession.

If Augusta should have a child, the nation would rejoice in the fact that Frederick and his heir would assure a direct line for two generations. Queen Caroline had a plan to frustrate that. She conceived the hope that Frederick might be proved to be impotent, even though Augusta soon was pregnant. Also, Frederick had had an illegitimate son by a Miss Vane (mother and child both were now dead); but Caroline urged Lord Hervey, one of her favourites, to claim that Frederick's child by Miss Vane was Hervey's own. But Hervey baulked at that.

Caroline had an additional string to her bow. She invited Frederick and Augusta to stay with the king and herself at the summer palace at Hampton Court, the calendar now being June when the height of the London season was over. Frederick and Augusta accepted. Augusta, however, feared for the safety and future of her unborn child, and gave evasive answers to Queen Caroline's repeated questions as to just when the baby was due.

The very history of Hampton Court Palace was ominous. It was a vast and frightening structure of several hundred rooms, in grounds of over fifty acres, somewhat over a dozen miles west-south-west from London. Cardinal Wolsey had built the palace and given it to Henry VIII, who destroyed him. Henry's states-man, Thomas Cromwell, lodged there for a time. There Jane Seymour was courted by Henry and became his third wife. There Jane gave birth to Edward VI and died there twelve days later. Charles I was imprisoned there. Added to all that was the known hostility of George II and Caroline to Frederick.

Augusta perhaps did not know about all of these historic tragedies, but she had a sure instinct that the birth should not take place at Hampton Court. Anything could happen there including the charge that the infant was a changeling, or that it had not lived; and at Hampton Court there would be no witnesses favour-able to Frederick and herself. She wanted desperately for the child to be born elsewhere, but that would require surreptitious and skilful arranging.

In this crisis Frederick proved his manhood and his ingenuity. He arranged for lying-in accommodation at St. James's Palace. He and Augusta went there on July 25th, 1737, and again July 29, only to find that her time was not yet. They returned to Hampton Court after each of these trips. On Sunday evening, July 31, Augusta's labour pains increased sharply. She and the prince with some servants drove hastily the hour-and-a-half journey to London. Frederick alerted certain members of the cabinet to witness the genuineness of the birth, as was customary. The Lord President of the Council (Wilmington) and the Lord Privy Seal (Godolphin) arrived in time. Before midnight the first child of the prince and princess, a little girl, was born.

A message was rushed back to the king and queen at Hampton Court. They were asleep, but when awakened to the news they were greatly incensed at having been kept in the dark. The king raged at Caroline, saying that everything was due to her mis-management, and that a changeling doubtless had been wished upon them. The queen dressed, summoned companions, including her faithful Lord Hervey, and set forth for St. James's. When they arrived in London, and found the government witnesses at the palace, they realized that the surmise of a changeling was untrue. Further, Caroline's womanly heart melted at the sight of the infant and she was temporarily reconciled.

Though Caroline abandoned her hope that Frederick was impotent, the fact remained that he had no male heir. A princess could succeed to the throne, but a male heir would be doubly popular; and popularity for Frederick was what his parents still wished to prevent.

Yet oddly the king and queen, seemingly by Divine Providence, were thwarted further. Some months later Augusta was pregnant again. This time there were no plans for a secret confinement, for the need was not expected soon. However, on June 4, 1738, Augusta gave birth to a boy, George William Frederick, the future George III. He was a seven-months baby.

3

THE HAPPY YEARS

The future George III was born not at St. James's Palace, nor at Hampton Court, but at Norfolk House, a dwelling near the Palace which his father Frederick had acquired recently under turbulent circumstances.

Ever since the surreptitious midnight birth of the baby girl George II had pursued Frederick with a savage vindictiveness. The king's desire was to dismiss Frederick and his family from the Palace and cut off all communication with them; but he could not do this immediately, as some of the cabinet felt it would be a public scandal to have an open break of relationships in the royal family.

His parents' sentiments about their eldest son verged on the hysterical. One was quoted as saying: "My dear first-born is the greatest ass, the greatest liar, the greatest *canaille* and the greatest beast in the whole world and I heartily wish he was out of it."

In spite of cabinet disapproval, George II still wished to disgrace Frederick publicly. The king had fumed all through the month of August 1737 and had enlisted Sir Robert Walpole on his side. The latter was in favour of any move which would destroy the influence of the prince and believed that the king's programme would accomplish the purpose. Accordingly, he asked Lord Hervey to draft a proclamation of expulsion, which concluded:

My pleasure is, that you and all your family remove from St. James's as soon as ever the safety and convenience of the princess will permit.

To this I will receive no reply. When you shall, by a consistency in your words and actions, show that you repent of your past conduct and are resolved to return to your duty, parental affection may then and not till then induce me to forgive what parental justice now obliges me to resent.

Walpole then presented the document before a cabinet meeting, but two of his powerful associates did not agree. The Duke of Newcastle said "for God's sake" not to let such a paper be given out. Hardwicke, the Lord Chancellor, likewise was opposed. Sir Robert, however, argued that the king had the right to command obedience in his own household. Hardwicke reluctantly consented, provided that the order was couched in more gracious language. In September a notice dated September 10 was served on Frederick and family to leave St. James's Palace forthwith. He was not allowed to take any furniture from his suite, nor any trunks. "A clothes-basket is good enough for them!" said the king.

Sarah, Duchess of Marlborough, ever loyal to Frederick, expressed the popular view in saying:

The Prince in all this affair has shown a great deal of spirit and sense and the intolerable treatment which he has had for so many years will no doubt continue him to be very firm and to act right . . . I am never very sanguine and for a long time could not imagine which way the liberties of England could be saved. But I really think now there is a glimmering of light.

The obdurate George II notified all foreign ambassadors at Court and English embassies abroad that any attention whatsoever to Frederick Lewis, even social calls on him or his family, would be offensive to His Majesty. He sent similar notices to the peerage, employees of the government, officers in the armed services, and any in attendance on the Court. He removed the guards who

normally attend the Prince, he ordered soldiers not to salute
Frederick, and reduced his financial resources so that the prince was
obliged to incur debts to friends and usurers.

While dullness had cast a pall over the Court after the dismissal
of Frederick, he had become a popular hero. When the prince and
family left St. James's, there was a mob about his coach who cried
out "God bless you!" to which Frederick responded "God bless the
King and God bless the poor!"

Frederick, soon after the birth of young George, became bored
with London society and in 1739 he leased from Lady Orkney the
lavish estate of Cliveden on the Thames about 30 post road miles
north-west from London and 4 miles upstream from Maidenhead.
There Frederick enjoyed a dozen happy years regaled by his
princess, his children and an entourage of brilliant companions.

The physical prospect was entrancing. The house sat on a high
terrace sloping down to the river. The gardens replete with butter-
cups, daisies, lilies and pinks in season and framed with yew trees
formed a natural amphitheatre. At the foot of the slope near the
river Frederick built a stage out of a chalk cliff. Here he produced
many shows for his house guests and the countryside. He brought
down an orchestra from London for occasional performances, which
he himself conducted. He played the 'cello in a village musical
group.

Here in 1740 Dr. Arne presented his opera *Alfred* of which the
concluding hymn, "Rule, Britannia", entered forever into British
lore:

> *Britons proceed, the subject deep command,*
> *Awe with your navies every hostile land.*
> *Vain are their threats, their armies all are vain—*
> *They rule the balanced world, who rule the main.*

Prince Frederick was devoted to his Augusta and never seemed
to doubt her loyalty, which probably was unquestionable at this
stage. Lord Stair, ambassador to France and a frequent visitor at
Cliveden, said that "the Prince always made the Princess be present
at all their conversations", and that she showed her approbation
always in the right place; that she desired to be informed and
"has a great deal to say with the Prince".

Frederick continued to like the ladies, but after his marriage his
interests seemingly were on an intellectual plane. Lady Archibald
Hamilton, a loyal friend of long standing, was some years older

than he. Lady Middlesex had a lively brain but was "short and dark as a winter's day and yellow as a November morning". Lady Huntingdon was a religious zealot and a patroness of Wesley.

Cliveden teemed with children. Aside from George and his older sister (named for her mother), there were Edward, born 1739, William, born 1743, and Henry, born 1745. A young Frederick and Caroline Matilda were born several years later.

Frederick, the father, was devoted to outdoor life as well as to music, particularly when in the company of the youngsters. He hunted, caught salmon in the Thames, gardened, played cricket, tennis and "baseball", a simpler forerunner of the later American game but embodying similar principles.

Frequently at Cliveden were William Pitt, the elder, then just at the start of his fiery career; also two sons of Lord Egmont; two sons of the Earl of Marchmont; Lord Lyttelton, Lord Chesterfield, Lord Stair, the Grenville brothers, and intermittently Viscount Boling-broke.

Bolingbroke was the most influential of the group, and he had a part in the education of the future George III from his early boy-hood, but his major task currently was in the political field, aim-ing to teach the fledglings and to give them a programme whereas the main idea of the opposition hitherto had been to get rid of Walpole and his associates.

Bolingbroke was a man who had most of his career behind him. He had been one of the chief figures in government in the days of Queen Anne and had supported the Stuart succession. Hence he was *persona non grata* to the current government.

Bolingbroke advised the formation of a "Country Party" which should rally around a "Patriot King". He realized the need of some symbol which would unite the disparate opposition forces. The concept of "Country Party" was that of a body who would have the national interest as their chief concern. *The Idea of a Patriot King*, which Bolingbroke wrote and published, was a set of principles to guide the new party. His doctrine later was to be twisted and misrepresented by Princess Augusta when instructing her son George. She bore down on these words: "He must begin to govern as soon as he begins to reign." And further:

"His first care will be, no doubt, to purge his court, and to call into the administration such men as he can assure himself will serve on the same principles on which he intends to govern." Those were excerpts from the Bolingbroke text, but failed to convey his meaning unless they were accompanied by numerous qualifying thoughts. Bolingbroke presumably had in mind the guidance of Frederick Lewis, expected to be the next successor, as he wrote, "A new people will seem to arise with a new King . . . when the new King is a patriot coming after a bad King."

Bolingbroke had started his thesis by affirming that "the office of kings is then a right divine" (which, by inference, defended his former support of the Stuart succession) but immediately qualified this by saying "God is a monarch, yet not an arbitrary but a limited monarch limited by the rule which infinite wisdom prescribes to infinite power". After this bit of theology and sophistry, the author leaped promptly to an endorsement of constitutional limitations to the throne.

Bolingbroke said that the Patriot King will regard his rights as a trusteeship. In fine, the Constitution will be reverenced by him as the law of God and of man, the force of which binds the king as well as the meanest subject. The author also recognized that "the people had an original right to the whole by the law of nature". This last doctrine was consistent with Frederick's view of himself as a people's prince, his gratitude to England, and his regard for the untitled citizens of the City of London.

The prince had an active sense of social justice. His favourite slogan was "liberty and property", and he believed that the second was necessary to the security of the first. This view endeared him to the merchant class and also to the poor who wished to rise in the world.

The new Country Party in 1741 started off with a flourish, winning a majority in Parliament, driving Walpole from office in 1742 and setting up a new cabinet, mostly of their own followers. Wilmington nominally was chief minister, but Newcastle was the real power. Parliament voted the prince a substantial income and restored all his honours, and George II was obliged to accept the change.

The victory, however, was disappointing to the public. The new men in office seemed to forget about pushing for the reforms which had been expected. Two bad mistakes were made: Pitt was left out of the ministry at the insistence of George II. The other error was to retain the Duke of Newcastle, whose chief policy was to rule through bribery. Newcastle seemingly was continued in the ministry because of the inexperience and laziness of the newcomers. Newcastle was a tireless worker. He liked to meddle in every phase of government and his new colleagues apparently were satisfied to let him assume much of the burden of administration.

Prince Frederick apparently did not realize the significance of what had taken place. His debts were cleared, his party had won, and now his days were more free from care than ever. This era of peace at home lasted for him for about five years; for as long as England was at war on the Continent the prince felt it his duty to abstain from politics.

However, the supposed succession of Frederick to the throne was threatened in 1745–1746 by a chain of unforeseen events in which he feared that his younger brother, Cumberland, ultimately might be awarded the crown, as George II had always desired. The occasion of such uncertainty was the invasion of Great Britain in 1745 by the Young Pretender, "Bonnie Prince Charlie", a grandson of James II. The expedition which landed in Scotland and was joined by several thousand adherents was poorly organized and the Young Pretender himself seemed to have little gift of leadership. Nevertheless, the initial stages of the uprising were successful because the organization of the British forces was even less efficient.

The Stuart army advanced as far as Derby, within two weeks' march of London. Panic seized London. The Bank of England staved off depositors by paying out only sixpence on the pound. Gangs of labourers were ordered to throw up sandbags on the Thames. George II shipped the royal gold plate service to Hanover, whence it was never returned.

Cumberland was in charge of the British armies on the Continent, and Frederick sought permission to command the British forces at home and lead them against the Pretender; but the king would have none of that and appointed his favourite son, Cumberland. Cumberland on this assignment rapidly proved his ability. He reorganized the plan of campaign, gave confidence to the troops, even though he still spoke English with a German accent, and chased after Charlie, catching up with him at Culloden. Here Cumberland won a decisive victory. This time the Stuart army retreated at full speed while the British pursued them mercilessly, hunting them down like dogs and slaughtering several thousand men.

Cumberland returned to London as a conquering hero, where he was greeted by the huzzahs of the multitude and was voted an annual pension of £25,000; but soon public opinion turned against

him when word began to come back about the savage nature of
his victory.

Frederick, on the other hand, had shown toleration. He managed
to block legislation aimed to punish Oxford University for having
harboured Stuart sympathizers; and he obtained the release of
Flora MacDonald, a young woman who had been committed to
the Tower for aiding Prince Charles to escape.

It seemed that Providence had destined Frederick rather than
Cumberland to be a great and tolerant king and that his personal
troubles were at an end; but one day when he was attending the
horse races at Egham there was a chance meeting with a stranger
which was due to have a strong influence on his life, and even more
so on the life of his son, the future George III. The stranger was
Lord Bute, son-in-law of Lady Mary Wortley Montagu, due to
inherit great wealth, but Bute was not yet able to get his hands
on his wife's fortune. His father had been a Whig party manager
for Scotland, but the party had done nothing for the son. The
Earl of Bute was a slender, handsome man, noted for his well-
shaped legs. He could act, he could dance, and he had a way with
the ladies. He was handsome in the style of Mephistopheles, whose
nature he resembled.

On this race day—it was in 1747—he had been driven to the
track in a carriage owned by an apothecary, a rather unusual
companion for one of the peerage. The prince in his bachelor days
had had an affair with an apothecary's daughter; it is conceivable
that the meeting of Bute and Prince Frederick might not have
been so chance after all. At any rate, a rainstorm occurred, the
prince retired to his tent to play cards and needed a fourth at whist.
Someone had seen Lord Bute in the offing, and invited him to
participate. When the game was over, Bute found that the apothecary had left, so the prince invited his lordship to his own home.

The snake had entered the garden.

4

BOYHOOD DAYS

Frederick initially was entertained by the talents of Lord Bute.
The earl had been active in amateur theatricals, was familiar with
dramatic literature past and present and was a clever costume
designer. This all fitted in with Frederick's interest in the stage
and in the theatrical performances which he liked to produce at
Cliveden. Bute apparently was able to be charming when he wanted
to, judging by Frederick's original friendliness towards him and
the influence he ultimately exerted over both Frederick and the
young Prince George.

In general, men did not like him. Chesterfield called him "pomp-
ous, slow and sententious". Lord Shelburne said he had a "gloomy
kind of madness". Again he was called "unconciliatory and sullen,
with a great mixture of pride". Apparently Bute did not exhibit
those unpleasant characteristics in his relationship with Frederick.
Nevertheless the latter saw through Lord Bute in some respects for
he spoke of him as "a fine showy man, who would make an excellent ambassador in a Court where there was no business".

In spite of that comment Frederick appointed the Scotsman to
a sinecure post on his household staff which had few specific duties,
but it enabled Bute to be frequently at Cliveden; and the opportunity to be on intimate terms with the heir apparent was not to
be scorned. Bute, moreover, had several positive qualities. During
the first seven years of his married life, before he came into his
father-in-law's money, he had lived on an island off the coast of
Scotland. There he had occupied himself with the study of agriculture, botany, mathematics, architecture and with extensive
reading.

When finances at last permitted the family to move to London,
his lordship made up for lost time and cut a fine social swath. He
organized parties, amateur dramatics and acquired a reputation
as a popular "ladies' man". Frederick had particular use for him
in that last capacity. He encouraged Bute to take walks with
Augusta and also used him as part of a foursome for a stroll
or card game made up of Lady Middlesex (or some similar

guest), the Scots earl, Augusta, and himself. Lady Bute is rarely mentioned, and she apparently remained in London with their children.

George was only nine when Bute first appeared at Cliveden, and he did not come under the man's direct tuition until several years later; but the Scotsman was repeatedly in the family circle. As an organizer of amusements he represented fun, and as a man-about-town he symbolized sophistication.

All that was building well for Bute's future, as the children's daily routine was fairly rigid and unspectacular. When the future George III was twelve, he and his eldest brother, Edward, were scheduled to get up at seven o'clock and from eight in the morning until eight in the evening the royal children had an extensive pro-gramme of study, relieved only by a three-hour recess at noontime followed by a dinner period of an hour and a half. In addition to the usual schoolday subjects of mathematics, languages, and his-tory, the young princes had instruction in violin, fencing, and riding. Also at some point George learned to play the harpsichord and flute, accomplishments which he enjoyed throughout his mature life.

The character of George as a boy has been damned by a tutor who came into the household staff when the pupil was in his late teens. The tutor was Lord Waldegrave, who in his *Memoirs* refer-red to George as stupid, sullen, lazy, obstinate, and lacking in "that frank and open behaviour which makes honesty appear amiable". Unfortunately for George's reputation that description frequently has been repeated without the qualifying remarks made by Walde-grave who gave George credit for certain virtues, including self-control and freedom from hypocrisy.

Waldegrave in general was an amiable and honourable man, but he had tried earnestly not to be appointed as tutor and had accepted only upon the insistence of George II. As Waldegrave had no taste for his office and admitted his own incapacity for it, it is not strange that his royal pupil was unresponsive. Further, if Prince George at times was moody and obstinate, some of that may be attributed to the growing pains of adolescence.

As a matter of fact, the education of the boy was extraordinarily thorough. At Windsor Castle there are seven large boxes filled with the school papers of the future George III. They cover English history, European history, essays on the history of taxation methods, Greek, Latin vocabularies and translations, grammar, musical criticism, mathematics and natural history. Some of the papers are meticulously dated even as to the hour of the day, but the majority are undated and the particular years can be surmised only by the gradually maturing handwriting and the quality of thought.

George's long account of the history of England from the time of Alfred through the reign of George I is particularly stimulating because of various of his observations. Obviously there is no way of knowing how much of the paper represented the boy's original thinking and how much help he may have had from his tutors; but even if he were merely giving back to teacher teacher's own ideas, here is evidence that his mind at least was exposed to a quite spacious knowledge of English history. He idealizes the Saxons and looks upon the Normans as an influx of barbarians. He does not wholly accept the stories of the villainies of Richard III and qualifies his recital of them with the words "most authors seem to say". He further acknowledges the weakness of Henry VII's title.

Considering George III's later attachment to royal prerogative, his youthful criticism of Charles I is noteworthy: "He did not regard the laws but violated them when they thwarted his interest or inclination," and George recited at length the abuses of Charles. Naturally the prince had no affection for Oliver Cromwell and dismissed him with the succinct comment that he was "more arbitrary than anything". All in all, George's curriculum including the history of taxation methods by reigns, indicates an impressive preparation for a prospective ruler.

In the more standard subjects such as languages and mathematics the studies have a refreshing similarity to modern times. The following problem is one of many in young George's handwritten notebook on Fractions and Equations: "Qu. 28. Some persons agreed to give 6d. each to a Waterman for carrying them from London to Gravesend, but with this condition: that for every other person taken in by the way 3d. should be abated in their joint fare; now the Waterman took in 3 more than a 4 part of the number of the first passengers, in consideration of which he took of them but 5d. each. How many passengers were there at first? Answ. 36."

The intensive study programme of the children was relieved by masques and plays fostered by Frederick and Lord Bute. When the future George III was only ten, he played in a production of

c

Addison's *Cato*. Young Frederick North, the future prime minister, was also in the cast. (North's father, Francis, Earl of Guilford, was a chief tutor of the royal children at this time.) James Quin, the actor, coached the boys in public speaking. When Quin was told years later that the king had read well his address to the Parliament, Quin pointed out proudly that it was he who had instructed His Majesty on how to speak.

There was a considerable amount of gaiety at Frederick's Court which continued even after his demise. One of the brighter lights at Cliveden was Miss Elizabeth Chudleigh. She had become maid of honour to the Princess Augusta in 1740 at the age of twenty and was eighteen years older than George. She took a kindly interest in him and years later gave him a birthday ball when he came of age. The very fact that he accepted so public a demonstration from her was an indication of her favourable status in the household.

Elizabeth Chudleigh became one of the most notorious characters of the age but never involved Prince Frederick or others of his family in her scandals. One of her most sensational performances was to appear at a masked ball at Somerset House in a state of considerable undress. There are various accounts of the matter by the gossips of the day. Mrs. Elizabeth Montagu, a notable bluestocking, a friend of Pitt and not given to sensationalism, wrote to her sister: "Miss Chudleigh's dress, or rather undress, was remarkable; she was Iphigenia for the sacrifice, but so naked the high priest might easily inspect the entrails of the victim. The maids of honour (not maids the strictest) were so offended they would not speak to her." George's mother likewise was shocked and threw a veil over Miss Chudleigh. Possibly Mrs. Montagu exaggerated, though there are others who corroborated her story. Some said that she wore a dress of skin-tight pink silk embroidered with fig leaves. However that may be, she created a sensation.

After a childhood of genteel poverty, through good social connections she was received at Court where her vivacious personality charmed George II and many others. The nineteen-year-old sixth Duke of Hamilton proposed to her and they became secretly engaged shortly before he started off on the customary Grand Tour of Europe. In his absence their correspondence was intercepted by a maiden aunt of Elizabeth's whose house served as a mail address. Hence neither Hamilton nor Miss Chudleigh heard from each other.

Elizabeth, stung by the apparent perfidy of Hamilton, was married on the rebound to Augustus John Hervey, a naval lieutenant who was a member of the eminent Hervey family. However, he had very limited financial means. Hence the marriage was kept secret as Elizabeth could not afford to give up her salary as maid of honour.

When the Duke of Hamilton returned from his journeys he immediately sought out Elizabeth, demanded why she had not written to him and again proposed marriage. Elizabeth was in an agonizing position. She had no assurance that Hervey would divorce her, and if she told Hamilton the truth he might very well lose all interest in her. Hamilton obviously could not understand the situation at all and embarked on a career of dissipation. He finally in 1752 married the famous beauty Elizabeth Gunning. Elizabeth Chudleigh in turn indulged in a frenzy of social activity. She became popular with many of the leading nobility of the time with whom her name was frequently connected in a scandalous way, whether justly or not.

How much young George knew of Miss Chudleigh's adventures in the social realm is uncertain. His mother has maintained that he was brought up innocent of the wickedness of the world and his brother Edward also said that they knew nothing of what the outside world was like. That may have been true as to sex, but George's home was riddled with political intrigue in which Princess Augusta participated.

By 1747 England had had repeated defeats in the Continental war and was about to sign an unfavourable treaty at Aix-la-Chapelle. It was clear that a change in most of the cabinet offices would be essential. Frederick thought that the time was ripe to start organizing an opposition which would get rid of the old-school Whigs, most of whom had remained in power after the failure of the Country Party to effect any reforms.

Before the election of June 1747, in reference to the current ministry, he wrote to one of his political lieutenants: "Pray God they have not a strong majority, or adieu to my children, the Constitution and everything that is dear to me. My upright intentions are known to you; my duty towards my father calls for it. One must redeem him out of those hands that have sullied the Crown and are very near to ruin all. I will endeavour it and I hope with all my friends' assistance to rescue a second time this kingdom out of wicked hands."

Frederick was correct in believing that George II was unpopular, in part because the nation had lost face and had incurred a staggering debt, though actually the king had had little part in British policy. Frederick's observation that he must redeem his father "out of those hands that have sullied the Crown" was reminiscent of Bolingbroke and was part of the philosophy which George III later adopted.

Enters now the Duke of Newcastle, chief minister of George II. Newcastle always could smell trouble in the wind and took pains to keep himself informed by an elaborate spy system. At this time he sent a female agent to Princess Augusta. The woman's reports are still in existence in the British Museum in the diplomatic correspondence of the Pelham Papers. She reported that Augusta told her that the prince had hopes of enlisting 225 members of Parliament and would be thus able to force a change of administration during the year. Frederick was not seeking Tories, but his idea was similar to that of the Country Party which had been tried before. Some of the opposition leaders urged the prince to work with the Tories, as that obviously would bring in a number of votes; but Augusta stated that she had prevailed upon Frederick not to do so.

There were five different meetings between Augusta and Newcastle's agent, between April 27 and June 17. These took place at Ranelagh Gardens where the princess could be seen talking with another woman without necessarily arousing suspicion. Augusta's chief purpose apparently was to keep in the good graces of the king. She was reported by the spy as deploring this move to form an opposition party, which Newcastle did not desire nor would it be pleasing to His Majesty. Frederick was gaining in political strength, for it was assumed that George II, now sixty-seven years of age, would not reign for many years longer.

One day in April 1749 Frederick held an after-dinner meeting at Carlton House, his London headquarters. The purpose was to draw up plans to be put into effect after his accession. He planned to change the ministry and dissolve the existing Parliament. He wished to exclude both Pitt and Henry Fox from the Commons. Pitt after earlier affiliation with Prince Frederick had recanted his opposition views and thrown in his lot with George II.

Some profitable job would be found to persuade Fox to retire from political life; and it was decided to appoint Pitt as Ambassador to Turin. It was quite unlikely that Pitt would have accepted such an appointment, as he had secure tenure in Parliament from the borough of Old Sarum. Frederick probably knew that this was an impractical project, but the possibility of exporting the troublesome Pitt was humorous to contemplate.

The year before this event, when George III was not quite eleven, Frederick prepared a paper, "Instructions for my son George, drawn by my-self, for his good, that of my family, and for that of his people, according to the ideas of my grandfather, and best friend, George I." (His ideas were far more in keeping with the times than those of George I, but the reference was a slap at George II.)

The document began, "As I allways have had the tenderest paternal affection for you, I cannot give you a stronger proof of it, than in leaving this paper for you in your mother's hands, who will read it to you from time to time and will give it to you when you come of age or when you get the Crown." He apparently had no distrust of Augusta, for he said, "I know that you will have allways the greatest respect for your good mother, as I have already exhorted you in my will."

He recommended a policy of peace with honour. "If you can be without war, let not your ambition draw you into it. A good deal of the National Debt must be pay'd off, before England enters into a war: At the same time never give up your honour nor that of the nation. A wise and brave prince may oftentimes, without armies put a stop to the confusion, which the ambitious neighbours endeavour to create."

He urged George to keep a balanced budget, to reduce the national debt, to lower the interest rate if possible, and to keep in touch with the monied men and the business interests, to show them that "it is your earnest desire to support the credit of the nation".

He advised George to test the trueness of his friends by encouraging them to tell him the truth, even if it sometimes ran contrary to his prejudices, and Frederick put stress on one thought that George himself adopted in his first address to the Parliament: "Convince this nation that you are not only an Englishman born and bred, but that you are also this by inclination."

He recommended a separation of the thrones of Hanover and Great Britain, a connection which had caused so much criticism of George I and George II, though he advised that a military alliance be maintained which would be mutually beneficial.

"I conclude," Frederick wrote, "with recommending you, the Princess, the rest of my children and all your subjects to the protection of God Almighty; which, depend upon it my son, you will have, if you fear and obey Him."

And in the testament of Frederick, Prince of Wales, heir apparent, was this singularly prophetic sentence, as if he had a premonition that he might die untimely: "I shall have no regret never to have wore the Crown, if you do but fill it worthily."

5

STRUGGLE TO CONTROL YOUNG GEORGE

In March 1751, when playing tennis, Frederick was hit in the eye by a ball. An abscess resulted. From that or other neglected causes, Frederick contracted pneumonia and died on March 31, 1751. Though the death of Frederick was an event of profound importance to the future of the kingdom, George II still harboured resentment against his oldest son and saw to it that the funeral was a meagre one with only a few attendants, a fact which shocked even the callous commentators of that era.

There were many who mourned the Prince. Tobias Smollett, the novelist and historian, wrote:

> This excellent Prince who now died in the forty-fifth year of his age was possessed of every admirable quality which could engage the affection of the people—a tender and obliging husband, a fond parent, a kind master, liberal, generous, candid and humane; a munificent patron of the arts, an unwearied friend to merit; well disposed to assert the rights of mankind in general and warmly attached to the interest of Great Britain.

In Frederick's own household the effect of his death was overwhelming. When Prince George, the future George III, now thirteen, heard the news he turned pale, laid his hand on his breast, saying, "I feel something here just as I did when I saw two workmen fall from the scaffold at Kew," and he wept inconsolably the whole day through.

Any parent will realize the tragic suffering caused to a thirteen-year-old boy by the death of his father. With Prince George the change in his life was more than a personal one, for George now became a property. Since Frederick had been only forty-four at the time of his death and since the Hanoverian kings had been long-lived, there had been no expectation that George III would be heir to the throne at least for another generation.

Now, however, all the sources of power in the kingdom tried to get control of the young prince or of those who could influence him. Granting that a constitutional monarch was governed by the ministry, the throne at most times had considerable weight in naming the principal members of a cabinet and also had under its control the appointment of many of the best jobs in Court and government service.

The first situation in which Prince George was the centre of a tug of war was the appointment of a regent. George II was nearly seventy and if he should die several years would elapse before George III would be old enough to reign. Hence in May 1751 a regency bill was brought into Parliament and immediately caused strenuous debate. All agreed that the Princess Dowager Augusta should be a regent in the event of George II's death, but Henry Fox, abetted by the Duke of Cumberland and the king, argued that there should be a regency council with strong executive powers. On the other hand, Pitt argued eloquently that there should be no restrictions on the rights of the dowager except such as might have her approval. When the bill was passed, the princess was provided with ample powers and the regency council was largely advisory. As a sop to the throne the Duke of Cumberland was named as chairman of the council. One month later Pitt's favourite sister Ann was named Keeper of the Privy Purse in the household of Augusta, which gave Pitt a convenient political entrée to the prince and his mother.

Another person who seized upon George as a property was Augusta. As the years rolled on she tried to dominate him in a pathological fashion which became a public scandal. One time in later years when George was walking from St. James's Palace to his mother's house nearby, a voice from the darkness cried out, "Are you going to suck?" During George's early teens, however, Augusta seemed mostly concerned about his financial value to her, according to her conversations with George Bubb Dodington, a long-time friend of Frederick and herself. Since potentially she was a future regent she had valid claims upon George II for the support of her family, apart from whatever moral claims she might have as Frederick's widow. Young George was Augusta's ace card in dealing with His Majesty.

While she and the king were on the best of terms outwardly, privately there was dissension between them. More than a year after Frederick's death when Dodington congratulated Augusta on the kindness and civility of George II to herself and her children, she replied that she wished the king "was less civil, and that he put less of *their* money in his pocket." She pointed out that George II had saved £30,000 a year through the prince's death and that he ought to pay Frederick's debts. The king continued to be evasive on money matters and she admitted that she had to speak to His Majesty "in strong terms" many times. She was worried lest Prince George marry in the near future, because she had eight other children to be provided for, whereas if Prince George began to have children of his own his first financial care would be for them.

Augusta's attitude toward her oldest son certainly seemed to be more practical than affectionate when he was in his teens. When he was fourteen she referred to him as "very honest", but she wished that he was "a little more forward and less childish at his age". She also affirmed that he did not seem to take very much to anybody except his brother Edward. By the time George was seventeen she was complaining that he should mingle more with older people and that he was "shy and backward".

Like all of the strong supporters of Frederick, Dodington now was out of favour with the Court and the cabinet. He sought the good wishes of the king and Newcastle, without success; and over a period of several years Bubb attempted to use the young George as a figurehead around whom he might build a party which could win the support of Parliament.

Dodington could reasonably hope to accomplish this if he could get the firm support of Augusta. The cabinet was irresolute and seemingly had no understanding of how to extricate the country from its troubles. Dodington said that the ministry of late years "had been like children round a fire, telling stories of spirits, till they frightened one another, that they dared not look behind them".

As early as March 9, 1754, Dodington in calling upon Augusta assured her that he would always be loyal to her interests and said that she should take some kind of a stand so that the ministry would have a policy and that the people would see that she would have some share in it. Augusta had complained previously that the ministers did not come near her, that she had seen the Duke of Newcastle only twice, and had had but one formal call from the Archbishop and the Lord Chancellor. All this was a singular lack of courtesy to her status as princess dowager.

Dodington kept pressing Augusta to get some influential people around her, but she replied that to get things into the hands of certain people (probably meaning Bute) was impossible "and for anything else what did it signify?" Dodington kept urging his point, but Augusta refused to take the hint that he might be a leader in some such movement. He wanted to know what were her plans in the event of the king's death. She said *"alors, comme alors"*—we shall see what we shall see.

Dodington returned to the subject on May 27, 1755, with the suggestion that she negotiate a settlement with Newcastle and the king which would protect the interests of them both and also assure a continuity of ministry. Augusta agreed in principle but said that there were one hundred good reasons that tied her hands from interfering with the king, those of her children being obvious enough, and if she were to stir it would make things worse.

By August sixth of 1755 Dodington was about ready to give up his effort to persuade Augusta to action and in fact began to suspect that there was more to the situation than she was telling him. She again complained to him bitterly that no one kept her informed on national affairs, that she felt that the war was being outrageously mismanaged, and that there was disgraceful dissension in the cabinet. Further, Dodington said, "She took serious pains to convince me that she had no fixed settlement or connections at all. She may deceive me; but I am persuaded, she has no fixed digested political plan, or regular communication in politics, with anybody, except Mr. Cresset" (the household treasurer whose political influence was negligible).

Dodington's fear that Augusta might be deceiving him was well founded, for the letters of Bute show that he was already at work preparing to cut a figure in a new administration when George succeeded to the throne, but not until that event took place did Bute approach Dodington with the offer of a cabinet post, and all through the latter's visits with the princess dowager there is no record that Bute was mentioned by name.

Another force seeking domination over Prince George was his grandfather, George II, who saw an opportunity to assert himself by controlling the education of Prince George. The tutors currently in the household were Bute, North, a Colonel Robinson, Stone and Scott. They had various titles but all were supposed to have some part in the education of the boy. The king now appointed two new men in senior authority; one was Lord Harcourt and the other was the Bishop of Norwich. Harcourt apparently felt it to be his duty to minimize the influence of Augusta. He was pointedly rude to her when they met. She saw him only three times during an entire summer. When he came for Prince George, Harcourt would stay in the hall and decline to enter the drawing-room. He spoke of the children's late father in so disrespectful a manner that they would come to Augusta almost in tears.

The bishop was a less obnoxious character but, in the opinion of Augusta, not well fitted to teach children. "His thoughts seem to be too many for his words," she said. He taught the children logic which Augusta thought a peculiar subject for youngsters of their age. Norwich, in contrast to Harcourt, treated Augusta politely, took the attitude of being an injured party and insinuated that there were those who were setting Prince George against him. He complained of not being shown the proper respect and asked Augusta to support him.

Harcourt and Norwich now plotted to get rid of Stone, Scott, and Cresset, claiming that they were teaching the youngsters Jacobite principles. Harcourt and Norwich threatened to resign their posts unless these three were dismissed. Augusta complained to Dodington that it was absurd to make charges against Cresset who had nothing whatever to do with the education of the children, and as to Jacobitism, she did not know what that meant. She had been satisfied with Stone and Scott though she was not sure how much the children were learning.

This threat of resignation by the two new tutors stirred up a public clamour and George II showed good sense by appointing a cabinet council to look into the matter. The council cleared the accused who were left in their posts and to the consternation of Harcourt and Norwich their resignations were accepted.

It was on this occasion that the king appointed Waldegrave and the other new tutor, the Bishop of Peterborough. Peterborough gave the children a religious education which Augusta supplemented by employing a Stephen Hales, a notable scientist who became famous for his experimental work on blood pressure.

Waldegrave, in addition to his dislike of Prince George, complained that the mother and the nursery ruled in everything, that Prince George showed the effects of adulation by the "bedchamber women, and pages of the back stairs." At the time when Waldegrave was employed in the household Augusta said that the children liked him, though George later in life referred to him as "a depraved, worthless man." Waldegrave after less than four years was ousted by Augusta and Bute was promoted to chief tutor.

In the midst of all this pulling and hauling, changing of tutors, political jockeying, domination of his mother, George found an emotional outlet in his devotion to Lord Bute. Though Bute in time used his influence for building up his own personal power at the expense of George's happiness, he appears to have been a thorough and conscientious teacher who cared for his pupil and had an interest in his personality. He taught him among other subjects the theories of government including Blackstone's *Commentaries* which he had in manuscript form. (Blackstone was yet to be published.)

Blackstone had strong views on the authority of the throne, but with qualifying limitations. He said, "I shall not, I trust, be considered as an advocate for arbitrary power, when I lay it down as a principle that in the exertion of lawful prerogative, the King is and ought to be absolute: that is, so far absolute that there is no legal authority that can either delay or resist him."

That statement is a noteworthy straddle, fit to flatter a king and yet keep him in bounds. Note the words "lawful prerogative". In short, if the king acts legally, there can be no legal redress against him.

Blackstone went on to recite numerous powers which he believed belonged to the throne, but again qualified this by saying "unless where the constitution hath expressly, or by evident consequence, laid down some exception or boundary". It is understandable that Bute would emphasize the arbitrary principles in Blackstone's *Commentaries* and minimize the limitations.

As George approached maturity Augusta began to worry about the kind of friends he should have. When he was only fourteen she observed that the younger generation were so ill educated and so very vicious that they frightened her; and two years later she expressed the wish that the prince saw more company, "but who of the young people are fit?"

Then when George was seventeen she said to Dodington that George should associate more with men. She said that women "could not inform him". She did not know what friendships to suggest for she still held that the character and conduct of the "young people of distinction" were such that she really was afraid to have them near her children. She said that she would fear for her own daughters if they were not protected by being royalty, because the current behaviour of women was "indecent and low" and she commented on the immoral habits of George II.

If Augusta was worrying about George making an undesirable marriage, she might have taken comfort from the regency bill which provided "if the minor marries without the consent of the Regent and Council, such marriage shall be void and all persons concerned guilty of high treason".

Further, in June 1753 Parliament passed a Marriage Act which provided for the prevention of clandestine marriages. Hitherto no publication of banns had been required. Any clergyman, in any place, might marry a couple without license, consent of parents, or other preliminary condition, though it was customary to sign a marriage register with witnesses.

A notorious marriage mill was conducted by a Rev. Dr. Keith, known as the Mayfair Chapel, also as the Curzon Street Chapel, which was in the neighbourhood of St. George's Church, Hanover Square. Here were performed several thousand clandestine marriages by Keith or his associates. Among these were the following notable entries in registers which are still preserved at St. George's:

1748, March 23	Hon. George Carpenter and Frances Clifton
1749, September 14	William, Earl of Kensington, and Rachel Hill, Hempstead
1751, May 25	Henry Trelawney, Esq., and Mary Dormer, St. Margaret's
1751, July 21	Edward Wortley Montagu[1] and Elizabeth Ashe, St. Martin's Fields
1752, June 30	Bysshe Shelley[2] and Mary Catherine Michell, Horsham
1751, May 25	Hon. Sewallis Shirley and Margaret, Countess of Oxford

[1] A relative of Lord Bute.
[2] Grandfather of the poet.

1752, February 14   James, Duke of Hamilton,[1] and Elizabeth Gunning

1753, March 15   James Stewart Stewart, Esq., and Catherine Holoway, of St. Matthew's, Friday Street

Augusta may well have been alarmed, even though George's isolation from the society of young people outside of the royal household may have been complete. His brother Edward in later years implied that the children were cloistered, though his exact words were "No boys were ever brought up in greater ignorance of evil than the King and myself." Various contemporary writers maintained that George was confined to the company of his mother and Lord Bute.

Nevertheless, there was a recurring rumour that George had had an affair with a beautiful Quaker girl by the name of Hannah Lightfoot. No concrete proof has been found that he married her and the probabilities against it are strong. Even if he did so, the provision of the Regency Act would have made such a marriage void. Hannah was the first girl to have her name associated with that of George, and there were only three or four others; but she was not the only romance in his life.

The linking of George's name with Hannah was persistent. There was a reference to the matter in *The Public Advertiser*, September 7, 1770. The paragraph dealt primarily with a scandal involving an affair of one of George's brothers with a commoner whom he subsequently married. It then alluded to a proposed new publication entitled *The Letters of an Elder Brother to a Fair Quaker*. Also *The Citizen* on February 26, 1776, threatened to publish "*The History and Adventures of Miss L-ght-f--t, the Fair Quaker,* wherein will be faithfully portrayed some striking pictures of female constancy and princely gratitude." Mrs. Hester Thrale Piozzi, a patroness of Samuel Johnson, in correcting various alleged errors in the *Memoirs* of Sir N. W. Wraxall, wrote that a son of George III and Hannah Lightfoot was still alive. However, Mrs. Piozzi was a romantic who was inclined to accept current gossip uncritically.

That there was a Hannah Lightfoot and that she disappeared under mysterious circumstances is thoroughly established in documents extant today in the possession of the Society of Friends, Euston Road, London. Hannah was a member of the Westminster

---

[1]Mentioned earlier as suitor of Elizabeth Chudleigh.

Monthly Meeting of Friends. She had been born in the East End of the metropolis, but was living with an uncle Wheeler, a linen draper, and was assisting in his shop. Both the shop and the Wheeler home were located near St. James's Palace. George easily could have met her and had friendly conversations as he walked to or from St. James's to see grandfather. An "affair" would have been difficult to arrange, but not an informal acquaintanceship.

In 1754 Hannah, who had been a regular attendant at meeting, no longer appeared. At the January session, 1755, the Minute Book states that it was currently reported that Hannah was married by a "priest" (probably Church of England) and not by a Quaker cere- mony and that she had "absconded from her husband". Thereupon a committee was appointed to visit her and bring back a report. At the September meeting the committee said that they had visited Hannah's mother who couldn't or wouldn't tell them where Hannah was. The mother confirmed that Hannah had been married by a clergyman, but "was not fully satisfied she was absented from her husband".

At the meeting in January 1756 the committee said that they had been continuing to make inquiry about Hannah and could not learn where she was or could be spoken with. Those present voted to draw up a "testimony of denial against Hannah Lightfoot" for marrying against the known rules of the society. This resolution was reaffirmed at the March 1756 meeting and was elaborated to say that the meeting would disown her and could have no "fellow- ship" with her "until from a penitent mind and true contrition of heart she shall be induced to signify her unfeigned sorrow for her offence and that this may be her case is what we truly desire".

Hannah did not repent nor was her place of residence disclosed to the Society of Friends. She was married to an Isaac Axford, at the Curzon Street marriage mill. The record is extant today in a register of St. George's parish. It was rumoured that Axford was spirited away then or shortly afterwards. That gave colour to the theory that Prince George was enamoured of Hannah and that this marriage with Axford was hastily arranged. There was a reference to Hannah in the will of a Robert Pearne probated April 4, 1757, leaving a trust fund to "Mrs. Hannah Axford, formerly Miss Hannah Lightfoot" and identifying her as a niece of "the late John Jeffrys, a watchmaker in Holborn". Jeffrys was a member of the committee from the Westminster meeting assigned to locate Hannah.

Though no conclusive proof exists, it seems probable that George had met Hannah and deeply loved her, as a young man can idealize and worship a young woman slightly older than himself. We know that Hannah had financial protection from some source, that a portrait alleged to be she was painted by Sir Joshua Reynolds and is to be seen at Knole, seat of the Sackville family. Most impressive, moreover, is the devotion of George III to the Quaker "persuasion" throughout his life. At one point he said that were it not for his coronation oath, which bound him to support the Church of England, he could have been a Quaker. Frequently he gave audience to leaders from the Society of Friends and permitted them to lecture him on his duties, an attitude much at variance with his usual authoritarian behaviour. Something obviously had made him tender toward the Quakers. Hannah seems the most plausible explanation.

The story of such an affair, no matter how much or little truth there may have been in it, must have been frightening to Augusta. Not long after that she received a still greater shock, for she learned that George II was interviewing German princesses with the idea of choosing one as a wife for her son, and was recommending a Princess Caroline of Brunswick-Wolfenbüttel, all without Augusta's knowledge or consent.

6

NEW LEADERS IN THE KINGDOM

The Princess Dowager Augusta, indeed, was frantic at the thought of Prince George suddenly involved in matrimony at the hands of George II; and she changed her tune about the advisability of her oldest son being kept sheltered from society.

"The Prince ought to mix with the world," she said. "He is shy and backward. The match would shut him up forever, with two or three friends of his, and as many of hers (the proposed bride)." Augusta agreed that Princess Caroline was said to be handsome, had good qualities, and abundance of wit, but if she should take after her mother, "She will never do here. . . . Her mother is the most satirical, sarcastical person in the world and will always sow mischief wherever she comes. Such a character would not do with George; it would not only hurt him in his public, but make him uneasy in his private situation."

By the time that George was reaching his majority his mother had a much better opinion of him than formerly, saying that he was "not a wild dissipated boy, but good-natured and cheerful . . . not quick, but with those he was acquainted, applicable and intelligent". Waldegrave recorded that "the Prince of Wales was taught to believe that he was to be made a sacrifice, merely to gratify the King's private interest in the Electorate of Hanover", a charge which was not without considerable truth. Waldegrave said of George II's Brunswick nominee, "The young Princess was most truly misrepresented—his Royal Highness implicitly believing every idle tale and improbable aspersion, till his prejudice against her amounted to aversion itself."

Whatever the merits of the Princess Caroline, the future George III was not inclined to let others, especially George II, settle his marital destiny. He said in a note to Bute, "I can never agree to alter my situation whilst this old man lives; I will rather undergo anything ever so disagreeable than put my trust in him for a single moment in an affair of such delicacy."

The future George III had a romantic streak in him which was covered up by his austere public behaviour of later years, but his prominent pale blue eyes always were alert to notice female beauty. The impression made on him by the charms of lovely women was revealed in future spells of insanity when he raved about one or another. He apparently became deeply enamoured of Elizabeth, Countess of Pembroke about this time. She was a great granddaughter of Sarah, Duchess of Marlborough, and niece of Lady Diana Spencer whose hand had been sought by his father. The duchess and her connection had been friendly to Frederick and to opposition leaders throughout the years.

Elizabeth became a part of Prince George's household when he was eighteen. In 1756 Elizabeth's husband, the tenth Earl of Pembroke, was named Groom of the Bedchamber to George, a post which he held for many years. Within three years a son was born to the Pembrokes, who became the eleventh Earl. Elizabeth's husband, however, was away on military duty for months at a time and after six years of marriage he eloped with a Miss Hunter, though no divorce ensued and ultimately the Pembrokes were reconciled. Meanwhile George had ample opportunity to sym-

George as a boy, painted by the French artist Jean Etienne Liotard. Note the alert
expression which belies the charges of boyhood stupidity.

Reproduced by Gracious Permission of Her Majesty the Queen.

Princess Augusta, mother of George III, painted by J. B. van Loo.

John Stuart, third Earl of Bute, painted by Ramsay.

Hannah Lightfoot, portrait by Sir Joshua Reynolds (about 1756).

Elizabeth Chudleigh, Duchess of Kingston, painted by Sir Joshua Reynolds.

pathize with Elizabeth, probably innocently, though in one of his later mad spells he imagined that he had made her his queen.

George was beginning to spread his wings. In June 1756 Miss Chudleigh held a magnificent birthday ball in his honour, referred to earlier. From then on he attended numerous Court levees and dances, at one of which he fell in love with Lady Sarah Lennox, an incident that had many consequences to his career.

George II now on his grandson's birthday offered him an income of £40,000 a year and his own apartments in St. James's Palace and Kensington Palace. The offer was a stingy one by royal standards, since in times past the Prince of Wales was allowed £100,000 out of the monarch's £800,000 income, the Privy Purse as voted by Parliament.

Prince George accepted the money offer, but declined the proposal to set up separate apartments, holding that it was his duty to remain with his mother. In the same letter he made a request which was galling to George II. The prince asked that Lord Bute be appointed Groom of the Stole in the prince's household, a mark of signal rank. Now the king had already promised this honour to Waldegrave in recognition of his services as tutor and his loyalty to the royal policies. His Majesty was inclined to be obdurate but Newcastle and Henry Fox, at the moment his chief advisers, persuaded George II to yield. He did so, but personally refused to give the gold key, badge of the office, to Bute, handing it to the Duke of Grafton who was on the Prince's household staff. Grafton in turn slipped the key into Bute's pocket, suggesting that he take no notice of the insulting manner with which it had been conferred.

This instance of ill will on the part of George II exemplified the confusion of state affairs which existed from the death of Henry Pelham in March 1754 until Pitt finally became head of the government in July 1757. During the interim there were just four men of chief consequence in the kingdom—Newcastle, Fox, Pitt and Bute.

The Duke of Newcastle was born Thomas Pelham, older brother of Henry, in 1693. He became enormously wealthy through his marriage and through the death of several relatives, including his father, who left him their properties. He became duke at the age of twenty-two. Newcastle was in many ways a ridiculous man, indecisive, timid, devious, with a high-pitched squeaky voice; yet he had a great flair for political management and a personal honesty which led him ultimately to leave office poorer than when he entered it. Moreover, he had given his brother Henry one half of the property inherited from their father, though the latter as a younger son could not have claimed it. Pelham and his brother had made an efficient working team, for Henry Pelham was a direct solid administrator, whereas Newcastle could deliver parliamentary majorities. When Pelham died, Newcastle, who had been Secretary of State, took over his brother's office at the Treasury and named Henry Fox to the Secretaryship. Newcastle also held the trump card of having the confidence of the king and for a time was the only person in the cabinet who communicated directly with His Majesty.

Henry Fox had abilities as a debater, practical judgment, a wide knowledge of the politicians of his day, and an understanding of the workings of Parliament. He was unhampered by political idealism, often agreeing with Pitt, but refusing to stand with him on occasions which might have cost Fox the sinecures which he enjoyed from the Crown. Pitt, nevertheless, had a reluctant admiration for the forthrightness of Henry Fox. He held that Newcastle was "a very great liar" and when Fox told a different tale than Newcastle, Pitt believed Fox. Fox had accumulated a considerable fortune and had married a daughter of the influential Duke of Richmond. He therefore was comfortably situated, and was able to take the ups and downs of his political career with equanimity, which gave him a considerable advantage over more emotional and less secure rivals.

William Pitt (later Lord Chatham) was the stormy petrel of the four, an outsider who could not be ignored. He was the most brilliant orator of his day. No one could stand against him in parliamentary debate. When an administration was responsible for a disaster, such as the slaughter of General Braddock and his troops at Fort Duquesne in 1755 and the unjust execution of Admiral Byng (for alleged cowardice at Minorca) in early 1757, Pitt's thunderings in Parliament were terrifying. More than that, his integrity and independence won him the adulation of the public, including the powerful mercantile interests of the City of London.

The lowest man on the totem pole at this time, but a real source of power, was Lord Bute who by this time had extraordinary control over the personality of the heir apparent, Prince George.

Bute hovered over the political scene like a buzzard waiting for the death of the old king, and he let the three other men know that he was going to be a force which must be recognized.

Each of the four men had one quality in common, great diligence in their attention to government, and no one of them during the period 1754–1757 could gain ascendancy without consideration of the others. The result was an intermittent stalemate which George II and Waldegrave, of all persons, made an almost farcical attempt to resolve.

Henry Pelham had described Waldegrave as a man "totally surrendered to his pleasures". It is certain that Waldegrave did not seek office, had not wanted the job of teaching Prince George, and sought no favours from the king. His Majesty, however, conceived the impractical idea that Waldegrave could be his personal agent and stir up dissension between Fox and Pitt.

Waldegrave was only forty years of age and had given no evidence of ability or desire for political experience. Nevertheless, with the king's backing, he was able to add to the confusion. The details are unimportant. Suffice it to say that during the period of about a year preceding mid-1757 Pitt, Fox and Newcastle were out of the cabinet at one time or another. The Duke of Devonshire and Pitt formed a government early in 1757 and were dismissed in March of the same year. Several weeks followed in which there was no cabinet, despite the efforts of Waldegrave to put one together.

Then to Waldegrave's great concern, the king insisted on appointing him First Lord of the Treasury and prime minister, on June 8, 1757. It took the unhappy earl only four days (the shortest prime ministership in English history) to find out, what he already knew, that he was unable to rally a cabinet to his leadership. George II at last realized that he must accept Waldegrave's resignation and that a cabinet must be acceptable to the parliamentary leaders, even if it meant assenting to ministers for whom he himself had a profound distaste. Otherwise the functions of government, including the voting of the Privy Purse, would be at a standstill.

7

ASCENDANCY OF BUTE

In July 1757 George II, alarmed at the domestic state of the nation and the repeated defeats of the British navies and armies abroad, called Pitt to the helm. Pitt was named Secretary of State and leader of the House of Commons. He was in fact the premier and so regarded by the public, though Newcastle remained as First Lord of the Treasury and the nominal head of the cabinet, with residence at 10 Downing Street. Pitt had full charge of policy while Newcastle took care of the political jobbery, an area in which Pitt had neither the aptitude nor the desire to act.

The Pitt administration changed the morale of the nation and the effectiveness of British arms within a matter of months. Victory followed victory and it could be assumed that Prince George, the future George III, would be elated at the prospect of the kingdom being restored to greatness, but it was not so. In a letter to Bute following a notable British conquest the future George III wrote, "I can't help feeling that every such thing raises those I have no reason to love" (meaning Pitt). He added that England's "popular man is a true snake in the grass".

That was a pregnant statement showing how successfully Bute had poisoned the mind of George against any leaders in government who might in the future have a greater influence than Bute. He constantly instilled suspicion in the mind of the young man, a belief that all ministers were corrupt and desirous of depriving the Crown of its rightful powers. Indeed, from his late teens until he ascended the throne at the age of twenty-two George's letters to Bute are almost abject in tone.

In earlier written instructions to George, Bute had advised him to be guided by his mother and resist all other advice: "When I survey this whole nation I see no one person who can come in competition with your royal mother in your breast. She alone can wish you great and happy for your own sake. All others must have interested views, riches, ambitions, honours, will contaminate every advice they give, hers alone you can without the least suspicion and with the utmost safety follow."

Bute also warned George about enemies that might try to wean George away from him: "As to me, should secret malice paint me to you in a villain's dress . . . I am certain several attempts will be made of this kind, and tho' you may think at present they would have no effect yet you little know the various arts that will be made use of to gain this single point, and if once gained you are, Sir, infallibly ruined and undone."

George in turn gave his mentor the most ardent reassurances, writing to Bute: "I am young and unexperienced and want advice. I trust in your friendship which will assist me in all difficulties. . . . I do hope you will from this instant banish all thoughts of leaving me, and will resolve, if not for my sake for the good of your country, to remain with me. I have often heard you say, that you don't think I shall have the same friendship for you when I am married as I now have. I shall never change in that, nor will I bear to be in the least deprived of your company. And I shall expect that all my relations shall show you that regard which is due to the Friend of the whole family."

And the prince further swore: "I will by my behaviour show that I know if I in the least deviate from what I here promise and declare, I shall lose the greatest of stakes, my Crown, and what I esteem far beyond that, my Friend. I hope this will persuade you not to leave me when all is at stake, when nobody but you can steer me through this difficult, tho' glorious path."

Such expressions tempted Bute to hope for any prize. Even before George II died, he was eager to insure his own future and asked Pitt to promise him Newcastle's place as First Lord of the Treasury, a request which Prince George approved.

This was an appalling piece of gall, but Pitt replied in polite terms, through an intermediary, that it was not feasible, because of Bute's inexperience and the fact that he was only a Scottish peer. Further Pitt said, "I cannot bear the touch of command . . . I cannot be dictated to," which would be the case with Bute at the Treasury and in the chief confidence of the future king. Pitt added graciously that when the time came Prince George should choose between them and that he would be willing to retire to some honourable post on the sidelines, without responsibility, but available for counsel if called upon.

Both Bute and young George were furious, for they had hoped to use Pitt's talents under their direction and Bute realized he could not conceivably run the government without Pitt's abilities at his

command. The adoring prince wrote to his tutor, "I owe everything to you", praised Bute for his "invariable uprightness and
disinterestedness", and said of Pitt, "He has shown himself the
most ungrateful and in my mind most dishonourable of men, I
can never bear to see him in any future Ministry."

George promised Bute that regardless of official position he would
be the real chief minister, "for all men will find the only method
of succeeding in their desires will be by first acquainting you with
what they mean to request before they address themselves to me."
He added that Bute would be able to name any ministerial slate
provided it did not include Pitt, "the blackest of hearts".

Even Bute became somewhat frightened at the thoroughness
with which his teaching had taken hold, and for a time he discouraged George's urgings that he think about public office. However, Bruce vacillated between fear of office and his further demands
upon the ministry that he be given first place. Bute's chief personal
ambition for the immediate future was to become an English peer,
for he realized that his Scottish title would never qualify him for
high cabinet rank as long as the present ministerial system
prevailed.

It was all very well for Bute and Augusta to adjure George to
be a man, to "be a king", but the boy's current outburst showed
an alarming naïveté about the constitutional history of the nation,
as if all the powers except those of the Crown could be brushed
aside by mere assertion. After all, if a monarch had an unrestricted
right to name his cabinet, why had Bute bothered to apply to Pitt?

Bute himself, even had he been less ambitious, had been an unfortunate choice as chief tutor, for he had a narrow mind incapable of a spacious concept of government. His letters to his charge
and others dealt mainly with the manipulations of offices, the petty
prejudices and shifting alliances of party factions. George was
brought up to believe that the government was a kind of jungle
dominated by wild malodorous political beasts in human form. He
dreamed, probably sincerely, that he would clean up the whole
place, bring in good men and a brighter, better day. But how to
do that effectively? He had little coherent instruction beyond the
testament of his father, and even that concerned goals rather than
techniques.

George, dominated by an abject devotion to Bute, looked upon
him as a miracle man who would carry him through all troubles
and triumphs. "If I should mount the Throne without the assist-

ance of a friend [Bute], I should undoubtedly be in the most dreadful of situations," George wrote to Bute in December 1758. Bute did not disabuse his pupil of that view. A day of reckoning, when such trusting hopes would be called to account, was inevitable, but the day was not yet.

Meanwhile, Pitt for several years (1757–1761) had an unchallenged command of England's government, taking no orders from Parliament or cabinet, but directing all. His strength was in consummate oratorial skill which swept away any opposition, in a noble concept of England's destinies, indefatigable labour, a vast grasp of the problems of administration, showmanship, essential selflessness, and absence of personal fear.

The people raised no cry against him, for unlike most personal governments, he was always for the "liberty of the subject". He tolerated no repressive measures, sought to free minorities, such as Jews and Huguenots, from discriminatory laws and ignored personal attacks by pamphleteers and cartoonists. He was a public hero. The young prince might call Pitt names, but to the nation he was "the Great Commoner".

In the few years of Pitt's first administration he changed the map of the world. He raised Great Britain from a nation of negligible influence to a leading world power. Prince George might rail, but the rebirth under Pitt's direction was due to have a bearing on the policies and acts of George III for most of his life. Hence it may sharpen a knowledge of the problems, opportunities and blindnesses of this badly tutored young prince to describe briefly the England that was in 1757 and the England that Pitt left him as a legacy for a potentially glorious reign.

A fundamental problem which Pitt faced at the outset was the small population of England compared with her rivals. There were only seven million persons in Great Britain compared with ten million in Spain, five million in Prussia, twenty-nine million in Austria, and twenty-seven million in France. Only marked superiority in leadership and tactics could offset such a disadvantage. England had had neither quality in evidence for many years. Its armies and navies were manned mainly through political appointment and were crippled by the tradition of seniority. The result of these defects had been a long series of defeats on sea and land. England had been saved from even worse disasters by the fact that the various European nations were frequently quarrelling among themselves and that favouritism was even ranker in France than in the British Isles. The fact that Great Britain was an island kingdom had been and was to be a protection under normal circumstances but the current mobility of the French and Dutch fleets removed that advantage.

The dark aspect of England's affairs was further deepened by a severe defeat of Frederick of Prussia on June 18, 1757, at Kolin. Pitt, normally against subsidies to foreign allies, had approved substantial aid to Prussia in the hope that her armies would be able to hold France in check; but now Chesterfield was moved to write to a friend, "The King of Prussia, the only ally we had in the world, is now, I fear, *hors de combat*. The French are masters to do what they please in America. *We are no longer a nation. I never yet saw so dreadful a prospect.*"

Pitt's courage did not fail him, for he believed that he saw various means by which England could be rescued from her ignominious position. In Parliament he had repeatedly pointed to the two or three million subjects in America as a vital integral part of the empire, adding nearly a third to the home population, supplying trade, skilful manpower and limitless potential wealth. Pitt's goal therefore was the extension of the British colonial influence throughout all of North America including Canada, and all this was to be done with earnest regard for "the liberty of the subject". As an evidence of his intent, Pitt, shortly after he became premier, had these words included in George II's address to Parliament: "The succour and preservation of my dominions in America have been my constant care. And, next to the security of my kingdom, they shall continue to be my great and principal object: and I have taken such measures, as I trust, by the blessing of God, may effectually disappoint the designs of my enemies in those parts."

The address also promised "to prevent our true friends, and the liberties of Europe, from being oppressed or endangered by any unprovoked and unnatural conjunction". In short, Pitt gave warning that he had not deserted Prussia and that England would not ignore any coalition of enemies such as the Bourbon states of France and Spain. That warning, of course, could have little effect unless backed up by effective striking forces; nevertheless, it served notice on the world that England still was in the running in any international race.

In the early weeks of the Pitt administration England suffered further reverses. Lord Loudon, commander of British forces in

North America, had been allocated a considerable force to recapture Louisbourg, the major French fort on Cape Breton Island,
which guarded the entrance to the St. Lawrence River. A colonial
army previously had captured the fort for England, but the
ministry had traded it back to France in the treaty of Aix-la-
Chapelle. The French subsequently had rebuilt the fortress on
stronger lines. Hence Loudon had been authorized to use his best
troops for the Louisbourg campaign.

Such a conquest would have had a tonic effect on the morale of
England at the start of the Pitt administration, but on August 30,
1757, Pitt received the incredible news from the general that
Loudon had abandoned the project, because he had heard that the
French had sufficient troops to defend the fort and that it was too
late to do anything further in America that season.

Meanwhile the Duke of Cumberland, "Butcher" Cumberland of
Culloden, had been in charge of the army of observation allied
with Frederick of Prussia. On July 25, 1757, while Cumberland was
asleep, his forces were surrounded by the French at Hastenbeck in
Germany. He was able to make a personal escape thanks to an
aide-de-camp, Colonel Jeffery Amherst, who organized a rear-guard
action. Cumberland soon afterward was compelled to sign a humiliating treaty at Closter Seven, agreeing to disband the Hanoverian
and Hessian troops and deliver Hanover to the French.

The Earl of Bute who at this stage was currying favour with Pitt
wrote to him commiseratingly on August 5, 1757: "Oh, my dear
friend, what dreadful auspices do we begin with! And yet, thank
God, I see you in office. If even the wreck of this Crown can be
preserved to our amiable young Prince, 'tis to your efforts, your
abilities, my dear Pitt, that he must owe it." Bute went on to say
that he had full confidence that Pitt would rise above these adver-
sities. Bute concluded by calling the minister "my dearest friend"
and signed the letter "most affectionately".

Pitt was looking for able young men, men of daring and enterprise. Beckford, the Lord Mayor, agreed with Pitt's view that
Louisbourg had critical importance. He was confident that Great
Britain was capable of taking this objective "provided a commander
can be found that has courage and capacity equal to the under-
taking". Pitt was determined to find such a man and turned for
advice to Sir John Ligonier, a professional soldier who had succeeded Cumberland as commander of the British forces. Ligonier
offered three names for consideration, all younger officers who had

served with distinction. They were Colonel Jeffery Amherst, Major General Henry Seymour Conway, and Colonel James Wolfe. Amherst was then aged forty, Wolfe was thirty, and Conway was thirty-seven. All three of these then virtually unknown men subsequently had an influence on the affairs of George III. Amherst and Conway were close to the throne through most of George III's life, though when in the ministry they served with firm outspoken reservations; and Conway much of the time was openly in opposition to the Crown policies.

Pitt recommended Amherst for the Louisbourg command, and George II's nominal approval was required. His Majesty, however, was opposed to the radical procedure of elevating a colonel to such an important post. Pitt preferred not to run counter to the wishes of the king for as yet Pitt had little evidence to back his military judgment. Hence he took the more tactful route of outlining the problem to the king's mistress, the Countess of Yarmouth, and she, in turn, convinced His Majesty.

Given that encouragement, Pitt recalled Amherst from the Continent and in secret orders appointed him a major-general for the Louisbourg campaign only. At the same time Pitt removed Loudon from all operations in North America. However, the king insisted that Loudon's replacement be old General Abercromby who had seniority, for George II was unhappy at Pitt's novel practice of promoting by merit.

Pitt provided Abercromby with fifteen thousand regulars and an excellent staff, with the youthful and enterprising Lord Howe as second in command. Abercromby's assignment was to take Fort Ticonderoga which was located near the northern border of New York. If the British could capture it the way would be open to the advance on Montreal. Further, if Amherst could take Louisbourg, he and Abercromby could then co-operate in a pincer movement which could conquer eastern Canada including the two chief cities of Montreal and Quebec.

A third element in the campaign was an expedition to attack two forts on Lake Ontario which, if successful, would cut off communications of the French with their western outposts and also protect Abercromby's left flank. Pitt appointed a Colonel John Bradstreet of Maine for this project, and authorized him to raise provincial troops, giving them the novel privilege of equal status with the British regulars.

At home Pitt effected a drastic change in navy policy. Instead of sending out the fleet to engage the enemy in formal battles on a large scale, he dispatched many ships to operate individually or in small squadrons. The objective was to pounce upon the French coast many times from many quarters and keep the Bourbon forces in a constant state of uncertainty. Within a short time, day after day, frigates could be seen sailing down the Thames for unknown destinations, a sight which aroused the populace to great enthusiasm. The destinations were unknown except to Pitt and the naval officers involved, for Pitt knew that the ministry and Court were riddled with spies and intrigue. "Sealed orders" was the rule. As the result of his caution the attacks remained surprise attacks.

During the summer of 1758 ten thousand mobile British marines kept diverting the movement of some ninety thousand of the French forces who expected an invasion now here and now there as the British struck repeatedly. This activity was particularly useful to Frederick of Prussia who had now reorganized his forces and was helpful in keeping France in check. Since Frederick again had become a real force, Pitt was ready to renew military aid for him; and as a sop to George II he consented to make an effort to recapture Hanover.

Immediately there was a great clamour among the aristocracy seeking to receive commands in the European campaigns. Pitt finally appointed the young Duke of Marlborough in charge of the British forces and named Lord George Sackville as second in command. Both were to serve under the general direction of Prince Ferdinand of Brunswick. Lord George Sackville, whose career to date had been inconspicuous, nevertheless moved in the highest circles and was a close friend of Prince George. Sackville's father was the first Duke of Dorset and his oldest brother, Lord Middlesex, was due to be the second Duke. Lady Middlesex was in the household of the Princess Augusta.

By the middle of August 1758 reports began to come in from various fronts. Captain William Amherst, brother and aide-de-camp to the general, arrived in London with the welcome news that Louisbourg had been captured. The aide-de-camp called on Prince George who happened to be in London. The future king said to the captain that he had expected great things of General Amherst but this news even exceeded his expectations. Bradstreet sent word that he had taken his objectives and was pressing westward to attack Fort Niagara. In India Robert Clive won additional victories.

But two days after the triumphal reports from Louisbourg Pitt learned that Abercromby's forces had been slaughtered before Ticonderoga, including Lord Howe, who was killed in a skirmish before the main attack. The doddering old general had remained at his base camp twelve miles from the fort and had sent his best battalions to make an ill-conceived frontal attack against the ramparts. Now the general was retreating southward and had abandoned all further action for the season.

Hence the year ended with missions yet to be accomplished and Newcastle went to George II to complain that the nation could not bear the expense of these world-wide campaigns; but His Majesty had been caught up in the hopes of victory and gave Pitt his full support.

Then followed the year of 1759, one of the most glorious in British military and naval history, *annus mirabilis,* as Horace Walpole called it; but it was a distressing period for the young Prince George. Late in the summer of 1759 the future George III suffered the loss of a beloved sister Elizabeth. He was now twenty-one and she eighteen. Her passing affected him deeply. It was the first serious break in the family circle since the death of his father. George at this time showed sensitivity and depth of feeling. He wrote to Bute that he was unable to concentrate on his studies. "I have attempted this morning to read but find it impossible as yet to do anything except think of that dear sister I have lost, who was a friend as well as relation; with whom I had flattered myself to live till Heaven thought it proper to take me out of this world."

Elizabeth's symptoms suggest that she had died of appendicitis and in her last days she had begged George that her body should not be subjected to an autopsy. George asked Bute to make sure that the request would be observed. He was fearful that it might be refused, for he said, "My mother bears our common loss surprisingly," a significant comment on that harsh enigmatic woman, Princess Augusta.

Prince George, following some minor reverses on the European scene and a gathering of French ships on the Normandy coast which threatened invasion, applied to be a captain-general of the army. "I really cannot be immured at home like a girl whilst all my countrymen are preparing for the field and a brother younger than me allowed to go in quest of the enemy." Further, George said he was willing to go as a volunteer if he could not have top rank.

The request, which Bute advocated to both George II and Pitt, was an old political gambit, though sincere on the part of the young prince. Previously in times of crisis the opposition had urged the current heir apparent to offer his military services, as a move to embarrass the ministry.

Young George's suggestions were obviously naïve though courageous. His proposals to be captain-general of the army was fantastic and it was not feasible for the heir to the Crown to enlist as a volunteer soldier. Both George II and Pitt dealt with the request tactfully, expressing great appreciation of the loyalty evidenced by the request, but promising nothing specific. Prince George was not at all satisfied and referred to the answers as "puts off", as indeed they were, and resolved that he would use "puts off", too, when people came to him after his succession.

In 1759 there was a black spot on British honour in the battle of Minden. Prince Frederick of Brunswick was in charge. Lord George Sackville headed the British forces. At some point Prince Frederick ordered him to advance. Sackville did not. Six times came the order and Sackville did not move. One theory is that he was drunk and another that he would not take orders from a foreign officer. In either case, his conduct was indefensible. In the court-martial, which Sackville himself requested, he was cashiered.

Then followed a most singular procedure. In the opinion of Prince George it was necessary that Sackville, his close friend and the brother-in-law of Lady Middlesex in the household of Augusta, be cleared. Bute was assigned the unpleasant task. He went to Pitt who gave the matter serious attention. Pitt held that if Sackville was guilty of insubordination the verdict must stand, for all discipline in the army would fail if influence could overrule it. Pitt, after a personal review, supported the verdict of the court-martial which was approved by George II, and from then on Sackville (later Lord George Germain) was Pitt's implacable enemy.

Bute took a very stiff line in the matter and wrote to Pitt: "I am extremely concerned to observe by your letter that all endeavours have proved hereto unsuccessful, in regard to a business which the Prince has so much at heart." He said that "All the prudential reasons and arguments will not prevent . . . very pernicious consequences. . . . I will not be responsible for the consequences of this treatment." Pitt was unmoved by these threats and the verdict stood.

A new plan obviously was needed for the conquest of Canada. General Amherst had observed that the French Canadians could retreat to the westward for infinite distances from which no foreign army could overtake them. Thomas Pownall, then royal governor of Massachusetts, had recommended to Pitt a three-way campaign, assuming that Ticonderoga could be taken, that troops could move up from that point and Louisbourg, and thirdly that the British troops at Fort Niagara (which had been captured by Bradstreet and Sir William Johnson the prior year) would move down from the west, joining the other two armies. These troops were in charge of a General Gage.

Pitt was impressed by the plan, but in naming Amherst as commander-in-chief in America he allowed the general a free hand in strategy. Wolfe, however, was given a special assignment to take Quebec in a drive up the St. Lawrence River, though responsible to Amherst in the overall campaign.

Amherst decided to undertake personally the capture of Ticonderoga and Crown Point, then move on to the outskirts of Montreal to be joined by Wolfe from the east and by General Gage advancing from western forts—in short the Pownall plan, which Amherst may have had a part in framing. Amherst took Ticonderoga early in August of 1759. Wolfe, as the world knows, in the same period scaled the Heights of Abraham outside of Quebec and died in the moment of British victory.

As far as the public knew in 1759 the North American campaign had been concluded successfully and news from India and the West Indies was favourable; but the end was not yet. The dispatches between Amherst and Wolfe had been intercepted by the French. Hence neither Amherst's troops nor those of Wolfe's army could effect a juncture. Wolfe's successors had all they could do to hold on at Quebec. Gage had not moved eastward from Niagara, on the excuse that the season was too late. Canada, in fact, had not surrendered, despite Wolfe's victory at Quebec.

While Pitt was able to coast on the popular acclaim, he knew that his goals had not yet been accomplished. Pitt knew that Canada was still under French rule unless the capital Montreal could be captured and the governor thereof sign articles of capitulation. Amherst was kept in America for still another season, 1760. This time the commander-in-chief took upon himself the approach from the west. The thrust toward Montreal from Ticonderoga and Crown Point, already in British hands, was given to a Colonel

Haldimand. Wolfe's successor, Murray, was due to move in from Quebec. All advanced according to plan.

Amherst had assembled three armies from points about a thousand miles distant and all arrived within forty-eight hours of the appointed juncture. J. S. Corbett, the historian, called it "one of the most perfect and astonishing bits of work which the annals of British warfare can show" and Fortescue, historian to George V, described General Amherst as "the greatest military administrator produced by England since the death of Marlborough; and he remained the greatest until the rise of Wellington".

Amherst had said to the French governor, "I have come to take Canada and I will take nothing less". The terms were unconditional surrender; but Amherst drew up particulars which allowed the French the exercise of their Roman Catholic religion (not permitted to British Catholics at that time) and their customary courts of law, military honours of war for the surrendering regiments, and the same privileges of trade as accorded to other British subjects. All of this, as Amherst wrote to Pitt on October 14, 1760, was subject to "the King's pleasure". That really meant Mr. Pitt's pleasure.

Pitt approved; but he had an immediate objective on the European front with which he was concerned. He desired to seize and fortify the island of Belle Isle at the mouth of Quiberon Bay. The location was about the centre of the west coast of France and would give England an observation post whereby she could detect any hostile assembly of forces by France.

Initially Pitt had obtained the agreement of George II for this new move; but Pitt's influence was beginning to wane, because of the high cost of war on a world-wide front and because of his tactless disregard of his colleagues. When Pitt had a further conference with George II on October 24, 1760, he found that military and naval authorities had planted doubts in the king's mind. His Majesty suggested that some other method might be undertaken, but William Pitt never again had the opportunity to meet George II face to face.

8

ACCESSION TO THE THRONE

George II, who for about twelve years had been expected to expire, died unexpectedly of a heart attack at about seven o'clock in the morning of October 25, 1760. He was seventy-seven years of age.

About eight o'clock the prince, the future George III, was taking his usual horseback ride in the Palace grounds at Kew when he was greeted by a messenger, one of the king's pages, who handed him a brown piece of paper on which was written that George II had had a serious accident.

Prince George, after glancing at these words, dismissed the messenger. He then turned to his groom, instructing him to say that they were returning to the Palace because his horse had gone lame and to say nothing else "as you value your employment". Upon reaching the Palace the new king walked by a back pathway to Lord Bute's house and alerted him. The circumstances indicate that Bute had bribed the Court pages (there was always someone on duty every hour day and night) so that he and George would have the first news of the king's demise and be ready to act. "Accident" was probably the code word.

At nine o'clock a courier arrived from George's aunt, the Princess Amelia, bringing a formal announcement that George II was dead. George III receipted for the document promptly, signing it "G.R." (George Rex). George III and Lord Bute promptly set out for London to pay respects to the deceased and to hold the customary initial meeting with the Privy Council.

George and Bute had been on the road but a short time when they were met by the blue and silver equipage of Pitt drawn by six horses. The famous minister had come to advise George that he was now king. Pitt said that there were certain formalities to be undertaken about which he would be glad to advise and he desired the new king's instructions. George III replied that he would come and give his own orders and was on his way to London to do so. The royal coach drove on with Pitt following on behind.

George's behaviour was a startling departure from precedent, for the king's ministers were supposed to advise the monarch on

Famous portraits of George and Charlotte painted in 1780 by Sir Joshua Reynolds as a condition of his accepting the first presidency of the Academy.

William Pitt, Earl of Chatham (*left*) and George III by the American, Benjamin West. In the background are, left to right, General Amherst and the Marquis of Lothian.

Reproduced by Gracious Permission of Her Majesty the Queen.

Lord North.

Lady Sarah Lennox, who would have been Queen of England if George III's mother had not intervened.

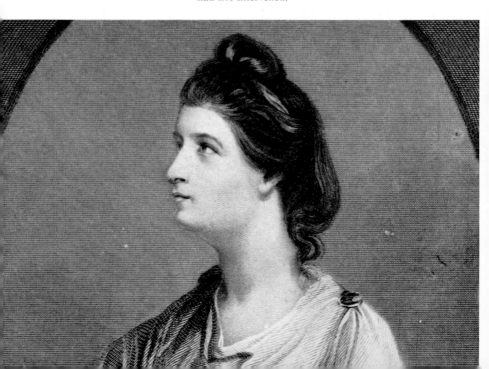

what to say in addressing the Privy Council. The Council in earlier times had been the chief administrative arm of the Crown. It was composed of the principal men in the kingdom, past and present chief officers of state, powerful private citizens from whatever cause, princes of the royal blood, and the two archbishops. When the king had a strong personality these men were his servants, and under a weak monarch the Privy Council was the *de facto* ruler of England.

Since the accession of the Georges, however, the cabinet system had become well established. As Georges I and II were frequently away in Hanover and had little grasp of the English system, the strengthened position of the cabinet as a means for getting government business attended to was inevitable. The cabinet officers were *ex-officio* members of the Privy Council and dominated it. The Privy Council became in effect an honorary club which met on certain state occasions. The king was at liberty to add a councillor or to strike a name from the list, but the Privy Council nevertheless had become a body without real power.

Pitt had been rudely rebuffed in his attempt to be the first person to take charge of the king, and there was a weakness in his situation which Lord Bute evidently understood. While Pitt rightfully was regarded by the public as the chief of the administration, directing the affairs of the nation as he saw fit, the nominal head of the ministry was the First Lord of the Treasury, the Duke of Newcastle.

Accordingly, while Pitt was arranging to have the Privy Council meet at Savile house, George III summoned Newcastle to Leicester House, treating him as first minister. There Pitt found the two, and Lord Bute who stayed throughout the entire conference. After much polite conversation George startled Newcastle and Pitt by saying, "My Lord Bute is your good friend; he will tell you my thoughts."

The remainder of the day was passed in considerable confusion, as no one seemed to be in charge of the arrangements. Some members were summoned to one house and some to another. At length, by late afternoon, the Council members were assembled at Carleton House where at six o'clock the Archbishop of Canterbury informed the group of the death of George II, which of course they all knew by that time, and the Council directed the archbishop to inform George III, who was waiting in another room, that they had signed a proclamation of His Majesty.

E

Thereupon George came before the Council and read his declaration. He expressed "the tenderest affection for my native country" and paid his respects to the experience and abilities of the councillors. Near the conclusion of his remarks he said, "As I mount the Throne in the midst of a bloody and expensive war, I shall endeavour to prosecute it in the manner most likely to bring on an honourable peace."

The king's declaration left the cabinet members dumbfounded. The drafting of the declaration properly was the business of the ministry, but it had been drawn up by Bute who had not consulted the cabinet. Furthermore, the words "bloody and expensive war" and the intention to make peace were words most embarrassing to the foreign relations of the country. England had no moral right to make a unilateral peace without consultation with her allies. Moreover, in the eyes of the nation the world-wide conquests of Pitt's expeditions were glorious. A repudiation of the war by the new monarch could have many damaging repercussions.

Pitt now saw that he would be obliged to struggle with Lord Bute as the real power behind the throne, distasteful as that was to him. He wrestled all the following day with the Scotsman and finally convinced him that the record should read, "As I mount the Throne in the midst of an expensive, but just and necessary war, I shall endeavour to prosecute it in the manner most likely to bring on an honourable peace in concert with my allies."

George did not like being made to change the wording, but since Bute advised it, he agreed. Accordingly it was the revised version which appeared in the record and was published to the world.

The body of George II had been lying in state throughout all these proceedings and on November 11 was interred in the Henry VII Chapel. There was pomp and ceremony in the rites, but there is little mention of the matter in contemporary accounts except for the report in the *Annual Registry*. George II had been a cipher in government for many years and everyone was interested in the new king and the new day.

George III reigned for so many years that the portraits and cartoons of his middle age have made the major impression—that of a fat man, stolid, heavy-faced, gross; yet when he ascended the throne, he was a handsome youth of twenty-two. He had the prominent blue eyes, long nose and the thick lips of the earlier Georges, but he was tall and well-built. Whereas his father Frederick with dark complexion was almost Moorish in appearance,

George had a fair skin and high colouring. Also, at this stage, the king's manner was gracious in contrast to that of his ill-tempered grandfather and he possibly owed these good manners to Frederick. Horace Walpole, the letter writer who was not generally disposed toward favourable comment about anyone, high or low, said of him:

For the king himself, he seems all good-nature, wishing to satisfy everybody; all his speeches are obliging. I saw him again yesterday, and was surprised to find the levee-room had lost so entirely the air of the lion's den. This sovereign don't stand in one spot, with his eyes fixed royally on the ground, and dropping bits of German news: he walks about and speaks to everybody. I saw him afterwards on the throne, where he is graceful and genteel, sits with dignity, and reads his answers to addresses well.

On the 18th of November the young king made his first speech before Parliament. The king's address is drawn up in advance by the cabinet and it is understood to be the official view of the government with the monarch simply acting as the official announcer. George III delivered the speech prepared for him, but he prefaced it with a paragraph of his own drawn from the testament left him by his father, who had said to him, "Convince this nation that you are not only an Englishman born and bred, but that you are also this by inclination."

George III's paraphrase which he stated to the Parliament was "born and educated in this country, I glory in the name of Briton".

The way in which George III had declared his loyalty robbed the declaration somewhat of its desired effect. The fact that the king had added an extemporary paragraph of his own was a dangerous precedent, for the ministry would never know to what it might be committed without its foreknowledge. Newcastle said to Pitt that "this would never do", but he assumed they would need to put up with it in this instance.

The choice of the word "Briton" was criticized in many quarters as being a definite attempt by George to declare himself part Scotsman. In fact, some said that the king had originally written the word "Englishman" and then the word "Britain" to express his loyalty to both England and Scotland, and finally changed it to "Briton" at Bute's insistence. Bute was pressing his luck, for Scotsmen in general were highly unpopular in England and Lord Bute was looked down upon as an opportunist, without proper credentials, who was exploiting his relationships with the king and the princess dowager.

While George's favouritism to Lord Bute was unpopular, his desire to kick over the traces of tradition were applauded by the younger generation. Lady Susan Fox-Strangways, niece of Henry Fox, said that if she were a young king, she would do "something every now and then that would make the Ministers stand aghast".

The king had already made his ministers aghast twice by disregarding precedent and now created a third and very touchy offence by appointing certain officers of his own household without consultation with the Whig party. He gave jobs to several Tories, namely George Pitt (a free-lance Pitt—not a follower of the minister), Norborne Berkeley (later Lord Botetourt and a future governor of Virginia), a Mr. W. Northey, the Earl of Oxford, and Lord Bruce.

The Whig connection at this period consisted of about seventy great families (including their immediate relatives) who in alliance or rivalry exercised the power and patronage of the state. They quarrelled among themselves, different factions got in or out of power, but control remained in the general pattern of the party.

The Tories had had to be content with local plums. The English villages and countryside were ruled by justices of the peace who were local landed gentry. Though the gentry were largely Tory, they had aided the Revolution against James II because of his attempt to rule all of England from London, but the Tories still found themselves virtually proscribed except for local office.

The term "Whig" was beginning to solidify into a party description indicating liberal tendencies. Originally, according to legend, the word "Whig" referred to a horse thief and then came by association of ideas in the English mind to mean a Scottish Presbyterian. Subsequently, it also meant a rebel, and finally it referred to the political group which supported the Protestant succession in deposing the Stuart line.

"Tory" also started as a slang term comparable to the word "harp", meaning an Irish Catholic. It was also applied to dispossessed Irish outlaws who plundered English settlers and finally in England it was understood to mean those who were excluded from government when James II was forced to abdicate. The term subsequently applied to Stuart sympathizers or those who were merely anti-Whig.

When Henry Fox heard of George III's Tory appointments he wrote in his diary, "I laugh". Those two words reveal the essential character of Henry Fox. He was a realist and at times a cynic. He had spent a long political life in the service of the Whig party. He had been a Lord of the Treasury, Secretary of War, a leader of the House of Commons, a Secretary of State, and was now Paymaster General, a job in which he made a fortune.

In spite of his ability to get employment for himself, or perhaps because of it, Fox repeatedly was denounced by various factions in his own party. Nearly every prominent man in the Whig connection, from Pitt down, had called him all sorts of names, but in the end they needed him, for he had skill in management of the Commons and great administrative sense. He had by now been in politics for a quarter-century and had no illusions. Hence he wrote, "The Duke of Devonshire is frightened about Tories; I laugh."

There was no doubt that the old order was changing; but Fox would have the ability to change with it, whichever way events should develop. One thing which he did not foresee was that his own family would become involved in a crisis in which he, George III, and Lord Bute would have a three-way struggle.

9

GEORGE III AND SARAH LENNOX

Though George III became king on the death of his grandfather on October 25, 1760, he delayed the coronation until September 22, 1761. Why the long delay? Because he was in love with Lady Sarah Lennox and wished to make her his queen. He had loved her even before he had ascended the throne.

Theirs was one of the most stirring romances in the eighteenth century because of its intrinsic significance. It was full of portent for history whether it succeeded or failed. The affair has had an atmosphere of mystery, because of its sudden ending; but the letters between George III and Lord Bute published for the first time in 1939 give the shocking explanation.

Lady Sarah Lennox, daughter of the second Duke of Richmond

and sister of the third Duke, was of royal blood, as her great-grandfather was Charles II and one might say that her great-grandmother
Louise de Quérouaille, Charles II's mistress, Duchess of Portsmouth, was of semi-royal status. Her son, the first Duke of Richmond, was a royal bastard, which then was a designation of some
distinction.

The Dukes of Richmond inherited highly valuable properties,
became one of the leading families of England and married into
other great houses. As an equal if not more valuable legacy, the
descendants of Louise inherited her wit, beauty and enterprise
which enabled them to become influential in affairs of state. Sarah's
father several times was a regent during the absence of George II
in Hanover.

Lady Sarah in her own right had the talents and prospective
fortunes of her family, and she also enjoyed the position of "a
princess" of various Whig families who frequently quarrelled with
one another. She was a favourite of her brother-in-law Henry Fox
and at the same time beloved by her brother Charles, the third
Duke of Richmond, who disliked Fox. She had the gift of extraordinary and original beauty described by Henry Fox in the following words:

Her beauty is not easily described, otherwise than by saying she had
the finest complexion, most beautiful hair, and the prettyest person that
ever was seen, with a sprightly air, a pretty mouth, & remarkably fine
teeth, & excess of bloom in her cheeks, little eyes—but this is not des-
cribing her, for her great beauty was a peculiarity of countenance, that
made her at the same time different from and prettyer than any other
girl I ever saw.

Fox understandably might have been biased by affection, but
Horace Walpole, whose nature was critical to say the least, frequently paid tribute to her. "Lady Sarah", he wrote, "was more
beautiful than you can conceive. No Magdalene by Correggio was
half so lovely and expressive." It is not strange that Prince George
had fallen in love with her at first sight, about a year before he
became king.

Lady Sarah as a child had been a favourite of George II and at
the age of five had been dandled on his knee. However, her parents
had died when Sarah was very young and the little girl was
brought up by relatives, living in Ireland and elsewhere until she
was fifteen. She returned to London in October 1759 where she

lived with her oldest sister and brother-in-law the Henry Foxes at Holland House.

Soon thereafter Prince George met her at a levee and stood like one thunderstruck by her charm and beauty. He promptly came over and spoke with her, and continued in conversation until obliged to pay some attention to the general company. Soon after the event Prince George avowed his love in a letter to Lord Bute: "What I now lay before you I never intend to communicate to anyone; the truth is the Duke of Richmond's sister arrived from Ireland toward the middle of November. I was struck with her first appearance at St. James's, my passion has been increased every time I have since beheld her; her voice is sweet, she seems sensible, has a thorough sense of her obligations to her sister Lady Kildare, in short she is everything I can form to myself lovely."

He began to see Sarah repeatedly at balls held at St. James's and at the suburban Palace of Kensington which was near to Holland House. It was probably the first time in his life that he had the companionship of a young girl who treated him sincerely and naturally. At one of these early meetings a dance "The Betty Blue" was the rage and Prince George asked her to teach it to him, which she did. On another occasion he took her aside and asked her about her stay in Ireland: "Tell me about your sister's household. Does Lady Emily, or Lord Kildare, govern? Either a husband or wife must take the lead."

"I think any husband who allowed his wife to govern would be very foolish," said Sarah. Then she added, "Everybody says you are governed by your mother."

George must have been somewhat disconcerted with this reply, but he went on, "And do you not think parents are the best people to govern?"

"Yes, sometimes," Sarah agreed, "but a German woman is not the best person to govern the King of England."

George was not offended and perhaps was even more attached to Sarah for having the courage and kindliness to speak so frankly, for presumably she would not have made the remark in any hostile manner.

George kept on with the conversation and finally tried to get her to say something with which she did not agree.[1]

"No," said Sarah, "it would be telling an untruth."

"But you would not mind telling a white lie?"

[1] Fox states this in his *Memoir* but does not recall what the subject was.

"Yes, I would, Sir."

George was getting in deeper and deeper. A letter to Bute said: "The other day I heard it suggested as if the Duke of Marlborough made up to her. I shifted my grief 'til retired to my chamber where I remained for several hours in the depth of despair, I believe this was said without foundation at least I will flatter myself so." And he also said: "I am daily grown unhappy, sleep has left me, which never was before interrupted by any reverse of fortune; I profess before God I never have had any improper thought with regard to her."

But the letter also contained an ominous sentence, "I don't deny having often flattered myself with the hopes that one day or another you would consent to my raising her to a throne."

The mere thought that Bute's consent was involved showed the extent to which the young man was under his lordship's spell. Bute was profoundly opposed to any such match for reasons of his own. Obviously with Sarah as queen all the elements of the Whig connection would have united sway in Court and ministry and the influence of Princess Augusta and himself would soon be at an end. Bute, however, could recognize the unwisdom of trying to drive George from his present state by a head-on collision and he wrote an equivocal reply:

My dear Prince's kind confidential letter is of too great consequence to return an immediate answer; not but God knows my dear Sir, I with the utmost grief tell it you, the case admits not of the smallest doubt; however I will carry your letter with me to the country, weigh every circumstance, and then like an honest man, a most devoted servant, and a faithful friend, lay the whole before you; think Sir in the meantime, who you are, what is your birthright, what you wish to be, and prepare your mind with a resolution to hear the voice of truth, for such alone shall come from me, however painful the office, duty and friendship and a thousand other ties, commands me, and I will obey tho' death looked me in the face.

George continued to make up to Sarah clumsily and hesitatingly, perhaps the more clumsily because he cared so much. He suggested to her that he might extend the grounds of Kensington Palace until they were connected with Holland House. He took frequent horseback rides past the fields of Holland House where he saw Sarah helping with the haying, which was doubtless a piece of play-acting on her part, enabling her to see and be seen as he was riding by.

As the months rolled on and after he had become king, George strove to bring the matter nearer to a head. On February 19, 1761, Sarah attended a ball with Lady Caroline Fox, her aunt Lady Albemarle and Lady Susan Fox-Strangways. Lady Albemarle and Susan sat on one side of the ballroom while Sarah and her aunt sat opposite.

George after a significant look at Sarah suddenly came toward Susan and asked her, "You are going into Somersetshire. When do you return?"

"Not before winter, Sir," Susan replied, "and I don't know how soon in winter."

"Is there nothing that will bring you back to town before winter?" the king continued.

"I don't know of anything."

"Wouldn't you like to see a Coronation?"

"Yes, Sir. I hope I should come to see that!"

"I hear it's very popular my having put it off. . . . Won't it be a much finer sight when there is a Queen?" the king asked.

"To be sure, Sir."

The king continued, "I have a great many applications from abroad but I don't like them. I have had none at home; I should like that better."

Susan was puzzled by this cryptic conversation, not knowing whether it was a proposal to her, a general comment or what the point was. "What do you think of your friend?" the king finally asked. "You know whom I mean. Don't you think her fittest?"

"Think, Sir?" Susan stammered, uncertain of his meaning.

"There will be no Coronation until there is a Queen," the king explained, "and I think your friend the fittest person for it. Tell your friend so from me."

George paused and then added, "I think none so fit."

He then went across the room to Sarah and bade her ask Susan what he had been saying. "Make her tell you, and tell you all," he added, which Sarah did.

Naturally the Fox family interpreted this as a definite declaration in spite of its informality of approach. "His Majesty is not given to joke," Henry Fox wrote in his *Memoir*, "and this would be a very bad joke, too. Is it serious? Strange if it is, and a strange way of going about it."

By this time Lord Bute, Princess Augusta and the king's uncle, the Duke of Cumberland, were on the war path. Bute had advised

George that it would be inadvisable for him to marry an English-woman. Bute's point, of course, was preposterous. Edward IV, Richard III, Henry VII and various other kings of England had married English subjects. Four of the six wives of Henry VIII were English girls, though their fates hardly could be called happy.

Augusta argued that royalty should marry royalty and she did not recognize the royal blood which flowed in the Richmond veins. Cumberland took an even franker stand, pointed out that the house of Hanover had always taken German wives and that there were plenty of royal princesses in the various German kingdoms. King George III despite his dependence on Bute was not to be dissuaded by mere argument. Only an arbitrary prohibition on the part of Bute could prevail and that was a risky thing for Bute to attempt, especially if he could accomplish his purpose otherwise. Luck for the moment played into Lord Bute's hands.

Sarah seemingly was by no means as interested in the king as he was in her, nor was she of the temperament to be dazzled by the thought of becoming a queen, a position in which her freedom would be limited. Furthermore the stumbling manner in which the king had made a proposal, if it were a proposal, was humiliating. Hence Sarah was in a mood to fall into a plan contrived by her brother Lord George Lennox and his wife. In short, they planned to make a match between Sarah and Lady Lennox's brother, a handsome fellow of six feet two whose name was William John Kerr, Lord Newbottle (sometimes spelled Newbattle), grandson and heir of the Marquis of Lothian. He moved in the same circles as the Richmonds, was already well acquainted with Sarah, and the fact that she was the object of George III's attention made her seem additionally desirable. Newbottle consented to have a clandestine tryst with Lady Sarah accompanied by the George Lennoxes. Sarah slipped out of the house early one morning while the Foxes were still sleeping and met the three in St. James's Park where Newbottle pressed his suit. Sarah was responsive and Newbottle said that he would promptly ask for his father's permission to marry.

Though this tryst was supposedly secret, it was observed by Lord Bute and His Majesty. Someone had tipped off Lord Bute and he apparently thought that the king would be disgusted if he saw Sarah's attitude, but apparently it had the opposite effect of fearing lest she be taken away from him. In a short time, however, Sarah unexpectedly received a letter from Newbottle

written at his parents' dictation saying that they refused their
consent.

On Sunday, February 22, 1761, the king held a drawing room.
Fox and his family insisted that Sarah attend even though she was
in a black mood and did not wish to go. The moment she arrived
the king took her aside and said, "Has your friend told you of my
conversation with her?"

"Yes, Sir."

"And what do you think of it?"

"Nothing, Sir."

"Nothing comes of nothing!" the king exclaimed indignantly
and walked away.

Fox, who was eager for the match to succeed, was greatly distressed at the way things were going and thought it best to ship
Sarah out of town to the Richmond estate, owned by her oldest
brother Charles, until she could have a chance to think things over.
Hence on February 23, 1761, she left in a carriage for Goodwood,
the Richmond estate in Sussex, near Chichester. Newbottle learned
of this, perhaps from his sister, set out in pursuit and overtook
Sarah on the road. There he "unsaid all he had wrote", Sarah
reported to Susan, and she agreed to see him further.

Goodwood was only a two days' ride from London and Newbottle
came down frequently to see Sarah. Her relatives urged her to put
an end to this affair but she refused. Hence they moved her to an
estate at Bruton in Somerset over a hundred miles from London
which was owned by Lord Ilchester, Henry Fox's brother. As
Sarah's chum Susan Fox-Strangways was visiting there at the time,
Sarah did not object to the move. Newbottle apparently was annoyed and did not make the longer journey to see her.

One day shortly after arriving at Bruton, when Sarah rode to
hounds her horse stumbled; she was thrown and broke a leg. She
was in bed for six weeks while the leg was healing and many
visitors came from London to see her, including her nephew
Charles James Fox, but not including Newbottle. Why he became
disaffected is not clear, but when he was told of Sarah's injury he
said, "It will do no great harm, for her legs were ugly enough
before."

George III on the other hand was distressed. He inquired repeatedly about her health from Connolly, a brother-in-law of Sarah,
expressing concern that she should be left to the care of a country
surgeon. His Majesty wished to go down to see her, but was finally

dissuaded on the grounds of impropriety, for according to custom the king must travel with a large entourage. Upon reflection on the differing attitudes of Newbottle and the king, Sarah began to be reconciled to the latter and was willing to accept His Majesty if he should renew his suit in a more definite manner.

Meanwhile, however, there was an ominous event, namely that Lord Bute on March 12 accepted the post of Secretary of State at George's express desire. The remainder of the cabinet at this stage were disposed to humour the young king's wishes. Hitherto Bute had been a dominating force behind the curtain, but now with official status he had power to negotiate with foreign countries on the possibility of finding a wife for George III. There were rumours that the king had chosen a Princess of Brunswick, but that proved to be false. However, Fox was worried, even though the king kept inquiring about Sarah. In writing to his wife on the matter (she was evidently visiting at Bruton) Fox said, "Don't tell Lady Sarah that *I am sure* he intends to marry her, for I am *not sure* of it. . . . *I am sure* that he loves her better than Lord Newbottle do's."

Sarah at last came back to Holland House on May 22, 1761. Her first meeting with George was on May 29, when she attended the theatre. He was in the royal box and expressed great pleasure in seeing her. On the following Sunday there was as usual a drawing room, this time at St. James's, and Sarah attended. The king greeted her heartily and engaged her in lengthy conversation.

The next significant event on the Court Calendar was George III's birthday ball, held the following Thursday, June 4, 1761. Because her leg was not quite mended Sarah was not dancing, but she sat at the head of the dancers' bench nearest the king's chair. He kept edging the chair more and more over toward Sarah and conversed with her all evening, even after the music had stopped. Everyone sat in suspense until about one o'clock, when the king remembered his duty and dismissed the assembly.

Among the subjects of this lengthy conversation was a remark to Sarah by George that he had urged his sister to dance the Betty Blue. "A dance, Madam," he said, "that you are acquainted with because it was taught me by a lady." Sarah pretended that she did not know whom he meant.

"A very pretty lady," he added, "that came from Ireland November was a twelvemonth."

"I am talking to her now," he continued, "she taught me the ball on Twelve Night."

"Indeed, Sir," Sarah replied, "I did not remember it."

"That may be," George went on, "but I have a good memory for whatever concerns that lady. I had got a pretty new country dance of my own for the late King's birthday, if he had lived to it and I named it, the *Twentyfifth of February*." (The date was Sarah's birthday.)

Princess Augusta now moved into the situation which seemed to be coming rapidly to a head. When Sarah went to Court again on June 15, George had little opportunity to talk to her because Lady Bute had been instructed by Augusta to place herself in the circle whenever the king came near to Lady Sarah. This was an effective manœuvre as His Majesty could not very well affront the wife of Lord Bute. George's oldest sister Augusta showed hostility by coming up to Lady Sarah and laughing in her face. It is reported that George's mother did the same.

For the next two or three mornings Sarah went through the motions of helping with the haying at Holland House, at the time when George took his morning horseback ride. Each time he stopped, dismounted and made a few remarks about the weather, but that was all. However, on June 18, when Sarah again attended a drawing room, the king said to her, "I was told you were to go out of town. If you had gone I should have been miserable. . . . For God's sake, think of what I said to Lady Susan Strangways before you went to the country!" Then he repeated the remark and added, "And *believe* I have the strongest attachment."

This declaration was made publicly where many persons could hear it. Nearly all the Court including Fox assumed that this was either a definite proposal or preliminary to one. Sarah herself was not quite so sure and thought that possibly a less honourable suggestion than marriage might be forthcoming. Meanwhile she was being coached by the Foxes on how to bring the king to a decisive statement, and she shrank from the ordeal.

"In short," she wrote to Susan, "I must show I wish it to be explained, without seeming to suspect any other meaning. What a task it is! God send that I may be able to go through with it. . . . I am working myself up to consider what depends upon it that I may *me fortifier* against it comes—the very thought of it makes me sick in my stomach already. I shall be proud as the devil but no matter . . ."

When she went to Court on Sunday, June 21, the stratagems of Princess Augusta again prevented any intimate conversation with the king. The same thing happened again on June 25 and Sarah wrote indignantly to Susan, "I won't go jiggitting forever if I hear nothing." On Sunday, June 28, she attended the Chapel Royal where the king's eyes were on her throughout the service.

On Thursday, July 2, Sarah with her sister Lady Caroline Fox once again was at Court, and again Princess Augusta and Lady Bute surrounded the king who spoke to Sarah, but said nothing in particular. Not until two days later did Sarah learn the explanation of George III not breaking away boldly from his mother and Lady Bute.

The fact was that on the day before, July 1, notice was sent to the members of the Privy Council to meet on July 8 to hear His Majesty declare his intended marriage with Princess Charlotte of Mecklenburg-Strelitz.

10

SAD, REGRETFUL CORONATION

Here followed one of the most poignant personal crises in the history of any monarch, painful for the jilted Lady Sarah, but devastating to the heart of George III.

Sarah wrote to her cousin Lady Susan a few days after she learned the astonishing news of the king's engagement. "Even last Thursday, the day after the orders were come out," she said, "the hypocrite had the face to come up and speak to me with all good humour in the world. . . . He must have sent to this woman before you went out of town; then what business had he to begin again? In short, his behaviour is that of a man who has neither *sense, good nature,* nor *honesty.*"

Sarah obviously could put only this interpretation on George's actions, not knowing the grievous struggles he had had with his mother and Bute. Anyone who has been deeply in love can see in George's behaviour the hope that even up to the last moment there might be some cataclysm which would make it possible for Sarah to be his queen. He "boiled" for Sarah Lennox, as he had written to Lord Bute. He had submitted to Bute's adverse ruling, but not willingly. His stumbling, awkward approaches to Sarah were not those of a skilful seducer, but of a young man overwhelmed by love. He stuttered, he feared rejection. His lips were thick with embarrassment and his knees could scarce support him.

"Sarah Lennox, Lady Sarah." Her name clamoured in his thoughts day and night—her beauty, her wit, her gaiety, her darling self. "Lady Sarah Lennox, Queen of England." Great God, it seemed intolerable to give her up! Such is the only way to account for those last days, because George with all of his faults of obstinacy, over-meticulousness, self-will, was rarely found guilty of deceit.

George also had some faint reason to hope that the plans of Bute and Augusta to marry him off might fall through. His proposed engagement to Princess Caroline of Brunswick had been kept alive for three years, despite his objections, by her father and George II and finally was terminated by her marrying somebody else. His father's engagement of several years to a Prussian princess ultimately had come to nothing. George for weeks had used delaying tactics with his mother. He had sat with her evening after evening reviewing the list of eligible Protestant princesses and he had found one objection after another.

Finally Augusta and Bute had settled on Princess Charlotte of Mecklenburg-Strelitz. She was a shy, rather homely girl of seventeen, whom George had never seen. Her good points physically were fine dark hair, pretty eyes, and a trim slender figure, but she had a rather flattish nose and a wide mouth which became the butt of cartoonists. Her Court was a minor one, hardly worthy to be considered by the English throne, yet more manageable in negotiations than a more powerful Court. Augusta had taken matters into her own hands, sending an emissary by the name of Graeme (or Graham). Even so there was still an improbable chance that Charlotte could refuse, that something could happen; but once the notice was sent to the Privy Council, the die was cast.

The possibility of Charlotte's refusing had not been quite as remote as one might think. When Graeme was introduced to her, she was lying between covers on a sofa, probably by prearrangement between her brother and Graeme. The latter, according to custom, as personal representative of the king, stripped one leg bare from the knee down and thrust it between the covers against Charlotte, flesh to flesh. She recoiled in horror and astonishment; but her brother admonished her, "Don't be a baby, you are going to be queen of England."

Lady Sarah Lennox, due to the eminent position of her family, was bound to mingle in the affairs of the Court, publicly and frequently, and was determined to keep a stiff upper lip. "I shall take care to show that I am not mortified to anybody," she said in a letter to Susan. ". . . Luckily for me I did not love him, nor did the title weigh anything with me. . . . The thing I am most angry at, is looking so like a fool . . ." Then she cautioned Susan to say nothing about the matter of her feelings to anyone, expressing a worldly wisdom beyond her years: "He will hate us all anyway, for generally one hates people that one is in the wrong with and that knows one has acted wrong."

The chief object for which George had delayed the coronation, namely Lady Sarah, had proved to be a mirage, and the delay had been extraordinary. Queen Anne had been crowned within six weeks after her accession to the throne, George I within seven months, George II within four months, and the date of September 22 for George III's coronation would make a gap of eleven months. Normally the only reason for delay between accession and coronation was the time necessary for preparation of the elaborate ceremony.

The engagement with Charlotte was not fully formalized until the approval of the Privy Council on July 8. Hence the time was short between then and the coronation date, considering that arrangements must be made to bring the bride-to-be to England and also for the holding of the royal wedding. George did not propose to have his bride treated in the rough fashion which had been accorded to Augusta and Frederick at their marriage. Hence George busied himself personally with a mass of details so that Charlotte might arrive several weeks ahead of time. He felt confident that this could be accomplished and wrote to Bute, "I must on this occasion make use of a favourite expression of the Man Mountain [one of George's epithets for Pitt] that 'willing minds overcome all difficulties'."

He also began to take a fussy concern in the management of his household and of Charlotte, a characteristic which grew upon him. He sent word to Germany that she should bring only one or two women attendants, preferably "quiet people", for he said that he had seen such women "meddle much more than they ought to do" and he was annoyed when he learned that his emissary on his own responsibility had agreed that Charlotte could bring over a male barber. Apparently Graeme's permission was allowed to stand, for the Duchess of Northumberland reports that Charlotte's entourage included two of her German women and the barber.

By early September George had become reconciled to his forth-coming marriage with Charlotte and in fact declared himself "very impatient for that minute that joins me to her, I hope for my life". In acknowledging thanks to the Creator for this blessing he said, "I have now but one wish as a public man and that is that He will make her fruitful." (George's wish was amply rewarded, for Charlotte, now seventeen, before the age of forty bore him fifteen children, namely in August 1762, August 1763, August 1765, September 1766, November 1767, November 1768, May 1770, June 1771, January 1773, February 1774, April 1776, November 1777, February 1779, September 1780 and August 1783.)

The king's mother was taking no chances of the marriage falling through. In August there had already been one threat of delay, for Charlotte's mother had died, but after a brief interim her brother consented that the plans should go ahead. Even so, it was September 7 before Charlotte arrived at Harwich, at eleven in the morning. The committee to receive her included the Duchess of Hamilton, the beautiful Elizabeth Gunning, whose husband was the one-time suitor of Elizabeth Chudleigh. When Lady Hamilton told Charlotte that the wedding was scheduled for that evening, the poor girl fainted and was brought to by having lavender water thrown in her face.

George was at the Palace gate to meet her on arrival and handed her from her carriage. Anticipating her attempt to kneel and kiss his hand, he embraced her and took her to the Palace where he introduced her to the Princess Dowager Augusta.

On the sea voyage to England Charlotte had shown high spirits, strumming on her guitar and jesting with the other passengers. She continued to show an independent spirit on her wedding day while she was dressing for dinner. One of her attendants said that the king preferred some particular manner of dress and she observed, "Let him dress himself, I shall dress as I please." When she was told that the king liked to retire early, she said that she did not care about going to bed with the chickens.

After dinner with the king, his oldest sister, and his mother, Charlotte and the family prepared for the procession to the Chapel Royal where the wedding was to be held about ten o'clock. The bride's dress was white and silver with a mantle of violet-coloured velvet fastened to one shoulder by a bunch of large pearls. She

F

wore a tiara of diamonds, said to be worth £60,000. The tiara caused Charlotte's first run-in with her mother-in-law, who was becoming more and more of a battle-axe now that her son was safely king. Charlotte said that she would remove her jewels including the tiara when taking her Communion, as a proper respect to the Lord's Supper. The princess dowager did not agree at all. Charlotte pleaded that her mother had brought her up that way, but Augusta was adamant and her will prevailed.

The wedding was a gala affair. The bridesmaids were daughters of dukes or earls and were dressed in robes of white and silver with diamond coronets on their heads. They carried the bride's mantle which was so heavy that it dragged the dress halfway down her back, causing Horace Walpole to say, "The spectators knew as much of her upper half as the King himself."

There were eleven bridesmaids, led by Lady Sarah Lennox, and it was said the king had difficulty keeping his eyes from her. She had been invited to this honour, to which she was entitled by rank, by the Lord Chamberlain whose duty it was to issue invitations. The invitation was not a command and some of Sarah's relatives thought that she should refuse, under the circumstances, but Sarah thought that a refusal would be far more conspicuous than to accept.

The Archbishop of Canterbury began the ceremony with the time-honoured words, "Dearly beloved, we are gathered together here in the sight of God, and in the face of this congregation . . ." The ceremony proceeded and came to the prayer, "Look, O Lord, mercifully upon them from heaven, and bless them as Thou did send Thy blessing upon Abraham and Sarah . . ."

At the mention of the name of Sarah the king was visibly confused, so much so that it was a subject for comment later; but this was the last instance in which his love for Sarah was shown conspicuously, though Charlotte in later years showed jealousy of Sarah or of her memory.

After the wedding the party returned to St. James's Palace where Charlotte sang and played the harpsichord until supper was announced. It was after three in the morning when the party broke up and the king and queen retired. At this point George set an example in modest public behaviour which was not typical of English monarchs until Victoria. It had been the custom for certain wedding guests to sit around the royal bedchamber while the king and queen were in bed, making obvious remarks.

George would have none of that and there was no levee whatsoever.

In the morning upon meeting Lord Hardwicke, George happened to observe that it was "a very fine day".

"Yes, Sire," Hardwicke leered, "and it was a very fine night."

The king was not amused.

A week before the coronation there was a royal ball attended by the king and queen, as well as by the Duchess of Northumberland, a close friend of the royal family and also of Bute. The duchess noted in her diary a clear description of the king at that time:

He was in his person tall and robust, more graceful than genteel tho' both in a remarkable degree when he danced, which he did better perhaps than anybody ever did and with an unparalleled air of majestic dignity.

There was a noble openness in his countenance, blended with a cheerful good-natured affability, he was fair and fresh coloured and now and then a few pimples out. His eyes were blue, his teeth extremely fine. His hair a light auburn, which grew very handsomely to his face . . . his voice was strong, melodious, and clear.

The coronation proved to be a mixture of impressive pomp and ludicrous errors. The procession formed at Westminster Hall where the banquet was to be held later. It had a new board floor covered with matting and three large galleries, under the first of which was a vast cabinet for crockery and other supplies. A raised wooden roadway with railings, and covered with blue cloth, led to Westminster Abbey.

The ceremony began with the Recognition. The Archbishop of Canterbury in a cope of white and gold addressed the assembly in a loud voice, saying, "I here present unto you George, the undoubted King of this realm," whereupon the congregation shouted, "God Save the King!" The same was repeated to the four points of the compass. Next came the oath. The king and queen each advanced to the altar, knelt down before the open Bible, placing the right hand on the Gospel. The archbishop then said, "Will you solemnly promise and swear to govern the people of this Kingdom of England and the Dominions thereto belonging according to the statutes in Parliament agreed on and the laws and customs of the same?"

The king and queen each replied, "I solemnly promise so to do."

Then the archbishop said, "Will you to your power cause law and justice in mercy to be executed in all your judgments?"

To which Their Majesties replied, "I will."

Finally came the Protestant affirmation on which George laid great emphasis later in his career. The archbishop said, "Will you to the utmost of your power maintain the laws of God, the true profession of the Gospel and the Protestant Reformed Religion established by law?"

The king and queen pledged their oath to observe all that which they had promised and then kissed the book in token of that pledge. They both retired, and the king moved to St. Edward's chair to await his anointing.

Finally the king and queen approached the altar to take Communion, and George inquired of the archbishop if he should not remove his crown when doing obeisance to the King of Kings. The archbishop did not know and asked the opinion of the Bishop of Rochester who was assisting him, and the latter did not know either. Thereupon the king removed his crown, saying that he felt certain that that was the proper thing to do and that the queen should remove her coronet.

The archbishop held that that would be a difficult and confusing thing for the queen to do because it would disarrange her hair and be difficult to replace the coronet. The king said, "Very well, but let the golden circlet be regarded merely as part of Her Majesty's costume, and not as a crown." And thus they took the Sacrament. Shortly after three-thirty the long ceremony was over, and those invited to the coronation banquet proceeded toward Westminster Hall.

From this point on there was a crescendo of mishaps. The queen rushed to a powder room which had been provided for her exclusive use and almost knocked down the Duke of Newcastle coming out of it, for he had not expected her to arrive so promptly. As the king was about to leave the Abbey a large jewel fell from his crown, an omen which was remembered in later years when England lost the American colonies. The jewel was immediately recovered.

When the throng reached the banquet hall, a vast auditorium which could accommodate several thousand persons, the place was in almost total darkness because someone, probably Lord Talbot, had the idea that the lighting effects which were planned would be more dramatic if brought on suddenly. About two thousand candles had been provided, connected by a series of flax fuses. At a signal the fuses were lit and did light the candles but gave an effect more startling than anticipated as flakes of burning flax fell on the crowd like a fiery snow flurry. The queen was terrified, but the incident passed without injury to anyone.

There was a great impatience for food on the part of everyone, for all were ravenous after the long ceremony and the appetites were sharpened further by the smell of roasting venison and other hot meats. The only persons who obtained food quickly were the princess dowager and the royal children who ate in a separate room. The main throng by courtesy could not eat until Their Majesties had been served, but there was no place for the king and queen to sit. A dais had been provided at one end of the hall and a table, but someone had forgotten to provide chairs. Therefore the king and queen were obliged to stand until this omission was remedied. The king complained to the deputy earl marshal, Lord Effingham, that there seemed to be a lack of efficiency in the arrangements.

"It is true, Sir," the marshal replied, "that there has been some neglect, but I have taken care that the *next Coronation* will be regulated in the exactest manner possible."

George was vastly amused at this excuse. Effingham's remark struck the king as so funny that he insisted that the unhappy earl repeat it several times to others present.

Lord Talbot, who was Lord Steward of the Household and therefore in charge of the banquet, now found himself in the position of a harassed headwaiter, as there were about seventy more guests than there were places. No table had been provided for the Lord Mayor and Aldermen of the City of London. Talbot at first took a high tone to these commoners indicating that nothing could be done about their plight, but the Lord Mayor was having none of that. He said that the City would soon be giving a banquet to Their Majesties, which would cost £10,000, and it was intolerable that they should be asked to the Court and be given nothing to eat.

Talbot broke down and gave the Aldermen the table which had been reserved for the Knights of the Bath, who were extremely resentful at this move. However, places were found for them and their ladies by crowding them into the table which had been reserved for the law lords, an arrangement which caused much grumbling. The Lord Steward also had been too economical in his supply of food, not having allowed for the extra guests. The

Duchess of Northumberland complained in her diary "instead of profusion of geese, etc., not wherewithal to fill one's belly".

Lord Talbot was due to suffer one more mishap before the evening was over. The incident was actually the fault of Lord Talbot's horse, rather than of his lordship. There was a place in the banquet protocol where it was Talbot's duty as Lord Steward to ride up to the dais and pay his respects to the king and queen. Talbot had had the bright idea that it would be a gracious thing after the obeisance to ride his horse backing down the hall. He had practised with the horse repeatedly when the hall was empty, but when the occasion came, the animal, instead of moving forward in the first instance, remembered the second part of his lesson and tried to advance rear end first toward Their Majesties. Talbot tried vainly to straighten him out with bit and bridle while the diners roared with laughter.

The affair passed into history, for Wilkes celebrated it in No. 12 of the *North Briton*. There, quoting Milton, Wilkes said that the horse "danc'd about in various rounds his wand'ring course".

I I

DILEMMA FOR A YOUNG KING

Now that the coronation had been accomplished and George III felt himself to be a dedicated and consecrated monarch, he began to take policy into his own hands.

It will be recalled that George III had had no occasion to think about the responsibilities of kingship until his father's unexpected death in 1751. From then on George, who was only thirteen at the time, was confronted with what kind of king he should be. Should he be relatively passive, a figurehead, not interfering with the ministerial quarrels of various functions and not attempting to make policy? That had been the attitude of George I and George II. During most of those reigns the government had been firmly administered by Sir Robert Walpole or Henry Pelham. The monarch in each case felt occasional resentment at the need to knuckle under to the ministry, but there was little room in the system whereby a king could direct the affairs of the country unless he had far more diligence and understanding than was enjoyed by either of the first two Georges.

In the years following the death of Pelham in 1754, however, the ministry was weak, irresolute, shaken by internal quarrels and frequent changes in personnel. There was a vacuum that cried aloud for leadership. Here was a situation which justified the Princess Dowager Augusta and Lord Bute in training George to be a king who would rule as well as reign. Opinion both at home and abroad held that the glory of England was sinking. Augusta herself feared that to be the case.

However, unluckily for Augusta, Bute, and George's will to power, a champion had emerged. We have reported the British victories achieved under Pitt's brilliant ministry. "I know that I can save England and that no one else can," he truthfully had said. He had accomplished the greater part of his mission before George III succeeded to the throne, had raised England to new heights of power and prestige. As long as Pitt or another minister of substantial merit held the chief direction of the cabinet, there was little room for a strong king to direct the affairs of the country.

Bute was shrewd enough to see this and even before George became king he poisoned the young man's mind against the strongest men in government. Pitt was painted as an obnoxious, arrogant, deceptive, scheming, vain man. Newcastle was corrupt and corrupting, indecisive, lying, touchy, undependable. Fox was a self-seeking, money-hungry opportunist; and the king's conscience, as Lady Sarah Lennox had predicted, made him welcome an excuse to hate Henry Fox, her brother-in-law.

There was enough truth in Bute's characterizations, biased as they were, to lend some plausibility in the mind of the young monarch. These prejudices, however, were dangerous to himself and the country, for the Whig party through years of experience had the ablest leaders. The Tory minority was considerable, holding 110 seats in Parliament. There were able men among them, but it would take time to build an effective cabinet from their ranks, and even Bute himself recognized that he could not operate the government singlehanded.

George in his first year, accordingly, had indulged in relatively trivial changes; and he continued to lean on Bute as his mentor. He set a commendable example in the conduct of the society of the day and insisted on certain reforms at Court. He abolished Sunday dances at St. James's Palace and put a limit on gambling stakes there. He required the Archbishop of Canterbury to abolish the elaborate balls which had been given at Lambeth Palace, the archbishop's residence, on the indisputable grounds that the palace was the property of the Church and intended solely for religious purposes.

George did not, however, have the Puritan view that "worldly pleasure" was a sin (a view evident in the disciplinary theories of the Wesleys). The king attended horse races, but did not bet; played cards for low stakes; and declined to agree to the remonstrances of the Bishop of London who asked him to abolish Sunday driving and discontinue Sunday concerts.

We have seen how George shocked the old guard and amused the younger generation, such as Lady Susan Fox-Strangways, by shattering precedent. We recall that he had made his initial declaration to the Privy Council and altered his address to the Parliament without consulting the ministry. Further, he had appointed Tories to his household staff without consulting any cabinet member. Nevertheless, these were acts directed by Bute and not real evidence of the king's initiative.

Bute in fact treated George in his first year as though the king were still a pupil in the schoolroom and this attitude was deepened by the fact that the king had not helped Bute on something very dear to the Scotsman's heart. Bute ardently desired to be made an English peer and made application within a month after George III had succeeded to the throne, asking Newcastle and the Lord Chancellor to grant his wish. He told them that they could do it if they pleased and put it as a test of their friendship with him. Newcastle said that by a rule of the House of Lords in 1711 the sovereign could not confer upon a peer of Scotland a peerage of Great Britain entitling him to the privileges of the House of Lords. Bute held that this proviso could be overruled if the Lords so chose. A second appeal was made to Newcastle two days later who said that to comply would be "absolutely impossible" and that even if he were to attempt it personally, he did not think that his associates would go along with it.

Bute then rebuked George III for not having taken "a more spirited part". It is conceivable that had the king been a mature and experienced monarch, he might have been able to persuade the House of Lords to change its ruling; but under the circumstances and since the existing cabinet knew that Bute was ravenous for power at their expense, Newcastle was correct. The rule indeed was rescinded in 1782, but much too late for it to be of any use to Bute. Meanwhile he gave up the attempt and entered Parliament in the only way open to him, by being elected as one of the sixteen peers of Scotland.

At the very outset of the new reign Bute continued to hold the dominating position of teacher to his pupil. On one occasion in November 1760, less than a month after the accession, Bute was engaged in a conversation with Pitt when the king sent for the Scotsman, who did not stir. George sent several more times but Bute did not condescend to come for about an hour. Devonshire made the comment that this was rather extraordinary treatment of a king, especially one that Bute had represented to be so tender about being treated with the proper respect.

Even this degree of rudeness on the part of Bute did not at that time alienate him from the monarch, who still was apologetic in response to any rebuke by Bute. When Bute regretted that the king had not been more aggressive, George replied, "Let him with justice say whether I have not from the first day of my mounting the Throne wished for his consent to get rid of those who are unwilling to do their duty." The time would come when the king would not care a fig for Bute's consent, but at the present George was still in his apprenticeship.

In referring to those "who are unwilling to do their duty" George III had reference to Pitt, whose independence was greatly offensive to the king. Pitt, in fact, always treated the Crown respectfully and was uniformly courteous to the monarch in personal audiences, in contrast to the occasional rudenesses of Bedford, Richmond, and others; but Pitt would not kowtow to Bute and at times denounced him in the presence of others, which was a mortal offence to the king. Since Pitt was the real power in the government at this time, having the prestige of victories on land and sea, the ardent support of the Whigs, the Parliament and the City, the king's chief resentment was directed against him.

In a letter to Bute criticizing Mr. Pitt's independence, George showed a naïve ignorance of the history and temperament of the English people. He expected that they would turn on Pitt and would look to the Crown to curb him. "I am happy enough to think I have . . . the real love of my subjects, and lay it down for certain that if I do not show them that I will not permit Ministers to trample on me, that my subjects will in time come to esteem me unworthy of the crown I wear."

The English people had customarily dealt severely with kings who tried to trample on Parliament or the ministry, but they gave their support to ministers who held the monarch to close constitutional limits. That had been evident in the cases of George I and George II. While George III had set out to change that situation, it was a youthful bit of wishful thinking to believe that his subjects would applaud such an attempt. For example, George III had no sympathy for free speech if directed against him or his favourites, yet he seemed to live in a world of vague idealism where he as a Patriot King would be the benevolent leader of his loving subjects. His character has sometimes been compared to that of a country squire, a valid comment if it suggests solidity, but not stolidity, for George suffered agonies of internal discontents. ·

It will be recalled that when George unhappily accepted Lord Bute's veto of the marriage with Lady Sarah Lennox, he promised to divert his mind and address his thoughts to his kingdom "with application". He adopted a regimen which left little time for vain regrets. He arose shortly before five o'clock to light a fire which had been laid the night before. He returned to bed for a few minutes until the room warmed up, then rose, washed, dressed, and went to his study where he wrote numerous memoranda until eight. These he locked in a cabinet, for he did not believe in discussing government affairs with Charlotte.

At eight o'clock he had breakfast with Charlotte where he limited himself to a cup of tea, possibly fearing the obesity which was characteristic of his family and overtook him in later years. For exercise he indulged in horseback riding and for diversion in various types of handicrafts, including button-making. The rest of the day was spent in the business of the Court and government. Here again he entered into minute details. For example, with reference to a small ball at Court he wrote out a list of eight male dancers to be invited with a caution that there should not be doubling up in the same families: "I own to me it appears very like a nursery when brothers and sisters, except where form requires it, dance together." He concerned himself with appointments in the army, navy and the Church in which the Crown had a voice.

In the evening he frequently attended Court functions, concerts, the theatre, or stayed at home where he played the flute, with Charlotte accompanying him on the harpsichord. He seemingly tried to keep busy every waking hour. Charlotte was relegated to domestic *hausfrau* accomplishments. George apparently did not desire a second Augusta in his household. While Charlotte had shown some spirit on her arrival in England, her incessant pregnancies, her vigorous mother-in-law, and the weight of being in a strange country reduced her to being a public cipher. Fanny Burney, the diarist, when later on Charlotte's staff, found the queen to be an inconsiderate petty tyrant in the home. Yet that could not be attributed to any innate viciousness on the part of Charlotte, for by Hanoverian tradition the convenience of the queen was to be served by the adoring subject.

While the earnest, auburn-haired young king was busying himself with details, foreign affairs were approaching a crisis in mid-1761. The French offered to negotiate for peace on the basis of the status quo. France thereby would be peacefully yielding all of North America and a large share of her interests in India, whereas her one gain would be the island of Minorca. The French offer nevertheless was highly embarrassing to Pitt. Both the opposition and most of his own cabinet felt that the French might be sincere and that the offer gave the opportunity to cease fire without loss of face.

Pitt did not agree, holding that it was necessary to consolidate gains further, that England should dictate her own terms of peace, not negotiate them, and that it was necessary to declare war with Spain due to information which he had in hand. He had learned that there was a secret treaty of mutual support between the Bourbon monarchs of Spain and France which, among other things, would permit Spain to attack Portugal which had been a British ally for several centuries.

The commercial interests in the City of London favoured continuing the war to a successful conclusion. It had created more business than the nation had ever known and had protected trade lines to all corners of the globe. The cabinet members whose wealth depended more on land and inherited wealth were groaning over the taxes and were threatening to resign.

Bute, in his influential office of Secretary of State, clamoured for peace and in this had the backing of the king. Pitt, deserted by all of the ministers except his brother-in-law Lord Temple, had no option but to resign, which he did to the pleasure of most of his colleagues. Lord Granville (the former Carteret) sneered, "I find the gentleman is determined to leave us, nor can I say I am sorry for it, since he would otherwise have certainly compelled us to leave him."

Oddly enough, the two persons most distressed at this turn of events were the Earl of Bute and His Majesty. Their intention had been to embarrass Pitt, to make him change his policy, to knuckle under, mistakenly thinking that he would care more about his job than his principles. There was an indignant outcry throughout the nation at the ousting of Pitt; and Bute and the king began to ponder how they might persuade him to resume office, for Bute realized that he lacked experience and knowledge to carry on suddenly in this crisis.

Hence George III summoned Pitt and asked him what terms would accommodate him. Pitt replied that he could form a cabinet if he could be sure of the unqualified support of Bute. That was more than the latter could swallow. It would mean the abandonment of the carping role which he enjoyed, the commitment of the king to Pitt, rather than to Bute. His Majesty and the favourite said that this would be unacceptable, but to come back in a few days with some other proposal.

On the second interview Pitt proposed a complete slate made up of his own proved friends. Lord Temple was to be First Lord of the Treasury, himself Secretary of State, Cumberland to be head of the army, the Duke of Newcastle to be in the cabinet (though not in first place), and those who voted for making the peace to be ousted.

George III understandably was outraged at what amounted to a demand for a complete surrender. "But you want to reduce me to the terms by disavowing my own act and what my soul proves," he said. "No, Sir, before I submit to these conditions, I will first put the Crown upon your head and next submit my neck to the axe."

Bute decided that he could put together some kind of a ministry, but he was terrified at his own unpopularity, at the popularity of Pitt and at the latter's eloquent ascendancy in Parliament, his ability to tear an opponent to shreds. Hence Bute's first move was to try to placate Pitt.

Bute and the king hit upon a bright idea, if it should work, of offering Pitt the governor-generalship of Canada at £5,000 a year, along with soft words about how Canada really had been his conquest and that a special bill could be introduced whereby he could retain his seat in Parliament. It was a fascinating idea for His Majesty to think of Pitt as three thousand miles away; but Pitt respectfully declined. George made Pitt another offer, namely the Duchy of Lancaster, a sinecure requiring no duties but providing revenues which amounted to being an outright gift from the throne. Such a favour obviously would have put Pitt under obligations; and he again declined. Then came the third proposal, to raise Hester Pitt, William's wife to the peerage and to pay him a pension of £3,000 a year to be continued "for two lives", presumably to son and grandson, or whomever he might name.

Just why Pitt accepted this offer, granting that there were no strings to it, always has been a puzzle. He had inherited a fortune from the Duchess of Marlborough, had had a modest inheritance from his own family and Hester had brought him a large dowry. Possibly Hester was fascinated with becoming a peeress and Pitt's devotion to her would have weighed in that situation. Probably Pitt also thought that this would be a moderate recognition of his services to the state; and it had come to him entirely unsolicited. Both Beckford, the Lord Mayor, and Edmund Burke (even then becoming a prominent Whig leader) held that the reward to Pitt was entirely fitting, erring if at all on the modest side.

The purpose of the gift to Pitt on the part of Bute and the king was evident in the manner of its announcement in the *Court Gazette* which led off with the appointment of Pitt's successor, the Earl of Egremont, and a brief statement of the favours conferred upon Pitt:

The Right Honourable William Pitt having resigned the Seals into the King's hands, his Majesty was this day pleased to appoint the Earl of Egremont, to be one of his Majesty's principal Secretaries of State. And, in consideration of the great and important services of the said Mr. Pitt, his Majesty has been graciously pleased to direct, that a warrant be prepared for granting to the Lady Hester Pitt, his wife, a Barony of Great Britain, by the name, style, and title, of Baroness of Chatham to her heirs male; and also to confer upon the said William Pitt Esq. an annuity of three thousand pounds sterling, during his own life, and that of Lady Hester Pitt, and their son John Pitt, Esq.[1]

There were two peculiar circumstances about this announcement. First, such intimate details in a public statement were unusual; but second and doubtless more important, a chief minister made his own public statement about retirement, if he chose to do so.

As Bute had anticipated, the acceptance of the honours and a pension from the Crown was highly unpopular among the people

---

[1] John Pitt was the eldest son; William, the brilliant son and future prime minister, was younger.

who had looked upon Pitt as their defender and now felt that he had sold out. The word "pension" was distasteful to the masses, probably more offensive than if Pitt had accepted the chancellorship of the Duchy of Lancaster, for few among the commoners would know whether the office was a sinecure or not.

Pitt was immediately conscious of the interpretation which had been placed on this incident and wrote to Beckford that his resignation had been grossly misrepresented, that the honours were not "a bargain for my forsaking the public", and that he had been overruled by his colleagues because of "a difference of opinion with regard to measures to be taken against Spain". The *Gazette,* of course, had mentioned none of this.

Both Beckford and Burke came immediately to Pitt's support, the former in a public letter and the latter in an article in the *Annual Register*. This soon calmed the tide of disapproval, much to the chagrin of Bute and his associates who now included Henry Fox. Fox in referring to Beckford and his loyalty to Pitt called Beckford "toad-eater to a mountebank".

Pitt was far from dead politically, he had not abandoned his principles; but it was clear that for the time being there was no way for him to have a place in the cabinet. For four years he had been all-powerful and before that had outstanding influence either in or out of office. Now that was changed. An attempt by Pitt to defeat the ministry on the peace issue failed by a vote of 364 to 65, and Augusta exclaimed, "Now my son is King of England!"

12

HONEYMOON WITH THE CITY

It was customary for the Corporation of the City of London to give a large banquet to a new monarch shortly after his accession to the throne. There were various ceremonies, many floats on the Thames and a great parade, on the streets leading from St. James's Palace to the Guildhall.

Repeatedly in the past there had been bad blood between the City of London and the reigning monarch. The royalty and nobility who lived for the most part in the West End of London looked down upon the merchants and other members of the middle and lower classes who lived within the confines of the City proper. Yet it was the Londoners, especially the merchants and manufacturers, who paid a very substantial share of the taxes which supported the royal family. However, persons engaged in trade, even exporters, importers and merchant adventurers, were not considered quite the best butter unless they had acquired great wealth or had married into families of the nobility.

It will be recalled that at the coronation banquet of George III Lord Talbot had had difficulty in finding a place for the aldermen of the City. Now the time for the banquet at the Guildhall had arrived. The occasion gave promise of being a happy one, because George III still was having a honeymoon with the City. He had not yet become embroiled in any of the controversies of his later life in which he and the London authorities disagreed. Since he himself was a bridegroom of less than two months, since he was good-looking, auburn-haired, blue-eyed, a fine figure of a fellow, he appealed to the romantic nature of the masses and indeed was fairly popular with all sets.

Some of the older Whig politicians sniffed trouble in George's general attitude about the authority of the Crown; but any unpopular acts or attitudes of George at this time were blamed primarily on Bute, his Scottish favourite. Hence the Guildhall banquet was looked upon with favour and anticipation by everyone.

The day was November 9, 1761. The morning was foggy, but toward noon the sun shone brightly and the weather continued fair. This in itself was considered a good omen, because in November it was more usual to have heavy yellow fog.

The dinner was to be in the evening, but there were processions all day long beginning around noon. Even before that, there were many gaily decorated barges sailing on the Thames, and there were celebrations from one dock to another, so that many were in a rather exuberant mood by the time they arrived at the Guildhall. For example, according to custom, the barge belonging to the Stationers Company stopped at Lambeth Palace, the home of the archbishop, where His Grace saw to it that hampers of the best claret were put aboard. This was supposedly the tribute of the Church to learning, for the Stationers were made up of publishers and booksellers.

The king and his entourage decided to proceed to the banquet hall by highway. There were two reasons for this. One was that the royal procession was due to stop at St. Paul's Square where they were to be honoured by a concert of choirboys and by an address to Their Majesties. Secondly, they were to review a parade from a balcony at the home of David Barclay (1682-1769), a leading Quaker and one of the family which founded Barclay's Bank.

Barclay had a magnificent home at 108 Cheapside, probably the largest in the City proper. It was near the church of St. Mary-le-Bow, so called because of the bow-shaped arches in the belfry of the church. This location was at the very heart of the large City population. (It was said that anyone born within sound of the Bow-bells was a true Cockney.)

The Barclay house had large balconies, which from time to time had been used by royalty and other dignitaries watching the famous parades of the Lord Mayor's Day. On this occasion the whole front of the establishment was draped in crimson damask silk, over one hundred yards of material.

As in the case of the coronation dinner, the various events of the day were marred from time to time by lack of management. This probably was due to the fact that the top officials delegated their duties to underlings and cared more about displaying themselves in prominent positions than in making things work.

The first trouble came with traffic. The distance from St. James's Palace to the Barclay house was less than three miles; nevertheless, it took from twelve noon to four in the afternoon to traverse this route. The highway was jammed with carriages and people far more than had been anticipated. In the king's party alone there were between twenty and thirty carriages. First came the king's uncle, the Duke of Cumberland, in a coach drawn by six horses preceded and followed by guards. Then his aunt, Amelia, had a similar coach. Next came a second uncle, the Duke of York, also accompanied by a numerous retinue. The next carriage contained George's three brothers, William, Henry and Frederick. The Princess Dowager of Wales, George's mother, shared a coach with two of the king's sisters, the younger Augusta and the Princess Caroline Matilda. These ladies were attended by twelve footmen and a company of guards. The state coach, containing George and Charlotte, was accompanied by two officers of state in another chariot, by the Grenadier Guards, by the Yeomen of the Guard and by a corps of the Horse Guards.

Elizabeth, Countess of Pembroke, who was in George III's household both before and after he became king. He clamoured to make
her his mistress or his queen in his mad spell of 1788.

Engraving of Queen
Charlotte from *George
III and His Family*,
written anonymously
and published in 1824.
This engraving seems
realistic, portraying her
Germanic origin and
her somewhat homely
yet friendly appearance.

George III as painted by Thomas Gainsborough.

Reproduced by Gracious Permission of Her Majesty the Queen.

The royal entourage proved to be much larger than the City authorities originally had expected, and the Aldermen had quietly, several days in advance, sent word to the Lord Chamberlain asking if the royal family could not reduce the number. But George III resented the suggestion, saying: "Now this is only for to have more of their sugar casks." The phrase "sugar casks" referred to the fact that Alderman Beckford, a great friend of Pitt and one of the wealthiest men of the kingdom, owned large sugar plantations in Jamaica and may have invited various West Indian friends to the banquet.

George III and his ancestors had been notorious "free-loaders" on the public till and the king saw no reason why he should not include at the City banquet as many of his following as he chose, and therefore the original acceptance list remained unchanged. In short, the king's party included some fifty or sixty dignitaries in addition to which there were scores of retainers. The latter, of course, did not get into the main banquet hall; nevertheless, food for them had to be provided.

The ceremonies at St. Paul's took place as scheduled, without mishap, and then the royal party, consisting, however, of only the immediate relatives of the king, proceeded to the Barclay home. This visit, in contrast to other confusions of the day and evening, was well arranged. The Court several days ahead of time had sent an official to instruct Mr. Barclay in how his family should conduct themselves in the presence of majesty. However, Mr. Barclay said that in certain matters the principles of his religion must govern. Barclay had a total of four sons and ten daughters, some of the latter still being children. He affirmed courteously that the family would wear the official garb of the Society of Friends, in other words, the girls would be in plain habit and would not have special gowns for the occasion. To the credit of George and Charlotte, they accepted these arrangements.

When Their Majesties arrived at the Barclay home, they were greeted by three of the younger daughters who kissed the king's hand, but did not kneel. For the Quakers held that they should kneel only to the King of Kings and that to kneel to any mortal man would be bowing the knee to Baal. George, who usually was prone to take quick offence at anything that failed to pamper his dignity, accepted this all in good spirit and he obviously had a love and respect for Quakers.

Then, quite extraordinarily, George III kissed his hostess and all of the grown daughters. Perhaps not all seven of the young ladies were present, though contemporary reports say that the house was thronged by relatives. Possibly there wasn't the same emotional satisfaction that there might have been from kisses of Hannah Lightfoot, if indeed George had known them, or of Sarah Lennox. But, quantitatively, it was obviously a satisfying experience. What is more, the king's three brothers thereupon followed suit, as did the queen. The princess dowager, in turn, pleased with the charm of a five-year-old daughter, smothered her with kisses.

The whole procedure was quite un-royal, but George himself carried it off with graciousness, according to all accounts. He may have been a little overwhelmed, for during the afternoon he withdrew in conversation with Mr. Barclay, while the queen and the rest of the party went into the back parlour and kitchen, where a large buffet was served. George declined any refreshment and continued to talk at length with his host, primarily on religion. Barclay, in turn, presented His Majesty with a copy of the *Apology* which was a textbook of the Quaker faith.

The Quaker daughters dutifully wore their plain clothes and adhered to their prescribed manners, but humanly they were dazzled by the royal display. One of them wrote of Queen Charlotte:

She is vastly genteel with airs ... truly majestic. Her hair, which is of light colour, being in what is called Coronation ringlets, has a circle of diamonds.

Her clothes, which were as rich as gold and silver and silk could make them, were a suit from which fell a train supported by a little page in scarlet and silver.

The luster of her stomacher was inconceivable . . . on which was represented, by the vast profusion of diamonds placed upon it, the magnificence attending so great a Prince, who, I must tell you, I think a fine personable man. I doubt not that the novelty of our appearance aroused her curiosity, for amidst such a profusion of glitter, we must look like a parcel of nuns.

From time to time the king and queen appeared on the Barclay balcony to receive the greetings of those in the procession. There were two striking incidents, the first of which was comic. When the Lord Mayor's coach passed by, the Lady Mayoress stuck her head out of the window to pay her obeisance to Their Majesties. She had on a huge headdress which became jammed in the window sash when she tried to withdraw her head; and the procession was obliged to stop until a footman could come along and restore the lady's head back into the carriage.

A less pleasant incident occurred which involved Lord Bute, Pitt and the latter's brother-in-law, Lord Temple. Beckford had urged Pitt that he and Temple should attend this banquet. Pitt at the time and again afterwards said that he did not think it a good idea. Pitt had said that the banquet was in honour of George III and Queen Charlotte and he did not wish to do anything that would in any way detract from the respect being given to Their Majesties. Beckford held, however, that since Pitt had incurred unpopularity with the City, due to his accepting a pension and a title for his wife, he should show that he was still one of the people, and for him to be absent might be wrongly interpreted. Hence, Pitt consented and he and Temple rode in a chariot in the procession.

As the Pitt vehicle approached the Guildhall it was greeted by the huzzas of the multitude. Men surrounded the equipage, some even kissing the horses and shouting the praises of the late prime minister. Bute later claimed that Beckford had hired a claque to show the popularity of Pitt.

Conversely, Pitt's attorney, Thomas Nuthall, alleged that Lord Bute had hired a number of bruisers to accompany his chariot for his own protection and that they had engaged some of the Pitt followers to march along with them.

When the king and queen left Barclay's, they acted like normal social guests, saying they hoped they had not caused too much trouble and that they had greatly enjoyed the visit. The queen expressed her sentiments in German, for she did not yet know any English, but an interpreter translated her words.

George III at this stage of his career exhibited a gentility and graciousness which were seldom evident in his later days. He directed that a company of guards stand by to protect the house, because those hundred yards of silk damask were valuable and marauders might well try to tear them down and make away with them. Further, when George and the queen returned from the banquet at two o'clock in the morning, he saw that some of the family were still seated on the balcony watching the goings-on (for the whole City stayed awake that evening) and as the royal coach passed, the king waved a greeting. Later, he offered a knighthood to Mr. Barclay, who said that it was adequate satisfaction to him to have the privilege of entertaining the king and queen. And when

George offered to give one of the boys a handsome job at Court, Mr. Barclay is said to have declined, saying that he "hoped to bring the boy up in honest trade". (As the boy later became a partner in Barclay's Bank, that doubtless was more advantageous than anything that might have been provided at Court.)

The Lord Mayor and the Lady Mayoress arrived at the Guildhall at 6.30 p.m. and shortly thereafter they sent an escort to Mr. Barclay's house for George and Charlotte. Various ceremonies followed, including public addresses, and finally at nine o'clock Their Majesties were seated in the big hall to receive the dinner.

A special platform had been erected for George and Charlotte at the front of the hall, over which there was a canopy. As an initial gesture, the Lord Mayor acted as chief butler to serve the king, and the Lady Mayoress waited on the queen. This lasted just for a few minutes, however, and then the management of the dinner was taken over by the caterers, Messrs. Horton and Birch, who were able to handle the banquet with more efficiency.

There was a special table for the Lord Mayor and the Aldermen. Then to the right of them were more tables for the Privy Councillors, the ministers of state, and the leaders of the nobility. On the left there was a table for the foreign envoys. Scores of persons of lesser rank were seated in the balconies and the retainers referred to earlier were fed in the basement. There were perhaps two thousand in the main hall and another thousand of retainers, soldiers and humbler folk fed below stairs.

The king was in excellent spirits and, considering the fact that he had had nothing to eat or drink since noon and that it was now nine o'clock, he must have had a rugged and untiring constitution. A contemporary authority says that there were placed on the tables four hundred and fourteen dishes, hot and cold, not including desserts.

The dinner was accompanied by various wines, including champagne and burgundy, and according to reports "nothing was so scarce as water". After the dinner the royal party retired to the Council Chamber "where they had their tea". A host of servants then carried the tables out of the main hall and relaid the floor with fresh carpeting where everything was made ready for the ball.

Etiquette did not require that George and Charlotte should dance at the ball, but the initial minuet was led by the Duke of York, a symbol of the friendship between Court and City. After that, other members of the royal family danced with "ladies of distinction", and finally the floor was open to the entire party.

By midnight, even the rugged George thought that he had had enough and asked to have the state coach brought to the door. That was easier said than done, for a wild party had been going on below stairs and the royal coachman was drunk. It was nearly two o'clock before he could be found and put into shape to drive. The princess dowager was furious, for her carriage also was delayed and she insisted on waiting impatiently in the vestibule; but George and Charlotte accepted the situation good-humouredly. George assured the Lord Mayor that this had been a most delightful affair and that he appreciated the good wishes of the City.

The evening had a semicomic conclusion because as Their Majesties' coachman tried to drive his vehicle through the gateway of St. James's Palace he did not quite make the turn and knocked over one of the posts. The roof of the coach was broken by collision with the sentry box; but there were no injuries, not even a cut from broken glass.

There have been various reports of this Lord Mayor's banquet by eyewitnesses and none have recorded any displeasure on George's part, even over the final incident. His graciousness and good humour were significant. If his later career was soured by frustrations and his own unfortunate temperament, he was at this period a warm human being.

PART II

Mistakes of an Amateur King

13

GEORGE III VERSUS FREE SPEECH

King George III in the first several years of his reign became involved in unfortunate situations which shaped his character and ultimately sullied his reputation. He cannot escape responsibility for his errors, as they arose in part from his will to power, yet it should be remembered that he was only twenty-two when he came to the throne. He was virtually an amateur king, both amateur and immature, and made some of his critically serious mistakes well before he reached the age of thirty.

History has shown that in monarchy as well as in other walks of life there is no guarantee that ability will be inherited. Where a king is chiefly a symbol of the state, having little if any administrative functions, the requirements of ability are not severe. George III, unfortunately, tried to assume a wide range of authority. That, coupled with his poor tuition by a Scotsman who did not understand the English temperament, soon led the king into a series of troubles.

One of his most unpopular moves was his attempt to throttle the freedom of the press in the affair of the *North Briton* in the several years beginning with 1762. The Crown's opposition to this anti-government paper was due not primarily to a hatred of free speech as such, but to collateral issues.

The *North Briton* was a magazine founded by John Wilkes, who became known as "a friend to liberty" and an ardent supporter of the cause of the American colonies. In fact, in America Wilkes has been remembered chiefly as a champion of freedom, as has Wilkes's friend, Isaac Barré. Barré was an ambitious extrovert who made his chief fame by speeches in Parliament supporting American "independency". The high regard in America for these two men was such that a settlement in Pennsylvania was named for them, now the city of Wilkes-Barre.

The repute of Wilkes began before his espousal of America, for he was persecuted at home on issues involving a free press. His troubles, however, were aggravated by the fact that he was not only a libertarian but also a libertine.

There was nothing novel in being a profligate in the upper levels of British society in the eighteenth century; but Wilkes, as in everything else which he did, was a flamboyant, conspicuous, and aggressive rake who possibly was not as outrageous as he painted himself. He was the son of a prosperous distiller. His mother was a straight-laced Calvinist who placed her son in the hands of stern Presbyterian tutors. He spent a brief time at the University of Leyden and at the age of twenty-two he was married, at the urging of his parents, to a woman ten years his senior who had a considerable fortune. The couple were never compatible and Wilkes, now supplied with ample funds, began to seek his pleasure in the company of young bloods of the day.

Though Wilkes fathered two illegitimate children, his chief forms of excess were drinking and blasphemy. Along with eleven other boon companions he rented a former monastery known as Medmenham Abbey and supposedly made this the scene of orgiastic rites. The group were sometimes known as the Hell Fire Club, or again as the Order of St. Francis in honour of their president, Sir Francis Dashwood (later Lord Despencer). Just what went on is not clear, as the members would reveal nothing, while throwing out dark hints of their wickedness. It was said that on one occasion they administered Communion to a baboon. Wilkes later maintained that he and his colleagues had shown no disrespect for the Almighty, but admitted that they satirized various sacraments and practices of religion which, he held, had become mere formalisms and needed to be exposed as such.

The mystery surrounding the Abbey was enhanced by the fact that the members employed no servants who might tattle about their affairs, but were waited on by probationers who were sworn to secrecy. There seems to be no doubt that there was a vast amount of wine and hard liquors consumed. On one occasion when Wilkes thought he had had enough and had gone to bed, his colleagues followed him and forced him to drink a quart of claret before they would allow him to go to sleep.

The twelve members were a talented group. Wilkes was a tall, dashing figure with a face of almost incredible ugliness, having a bad squint which was caricatured by Hogarth. Along with this striking appearance Wilkes had a ready wit and a vivacity which made him socially acceptable even to those who disapproved of him, such as non-member Samuel Johnson. Of Hell Fire elect were Lord Sandwich who also became a cabinet member and in due course a prosecutor of Wilkes; Thomas Potter, son of the Archbishop of Canterbury; Charles Churchill, poet and curate who seduced a stonecutter's daughter; and the ubiquitous George Bubb Dodington who seemed to have a faculty for turning up everywhere.

Wilkes ultimately became bored with this roistering, which did not give adequate scope to his talents, and he decided to go into publishing and politics. In 1757 he was elected to Parliament, but the foundation of his fame was laid in publishing. The Whig factions and the Court party, the latter generally known as Tory, had carried on a battle of pamphlets, especially after the accession of George III. Bute told the king that the other side began it and that he was going to hire a group of writers to support the king's cause, and of course to defend himself. He followed through with this intention and engaged several men, the best known of whom was Tobias Smollett, novelist and historian.

Wilkes addressed himself to Pitt and Lord Temple, offering to be a pamphleteer for the Whigs, as a volunteer, not for pay. This offer seemingly was sincere, nor was it altered; but Wilkes, frequently in debt, repeatedly "touched" Temple for mortgage money or unsecured loans.

Wilkes's earlier writings anonymously had appeared in a publication *The Monitor*, which attacked the government so violently that one printer after another declined to work for him. Thereupon Wilkes, against the advice of Lord Temple, set up a private printing plant in his own house and it was there that he started the *North Briton*. The magazine originally was intended to last for only three issues, but its popularity was such that it continued until the authorities suppressed it.

The *North Briton* supported "the liberty of the subject" and exposed the errors of the government, but it was also a scandal sheet indulging in personalities, and Lord Bute was a particular target. Wilkes repeatedly with innuendo and satire attacked Bute and his alleged affair with the king's mother. George III understandably was outraged. Since his teen-age years he had heard adverse gossip about Augusta and Lord Bute and had threatened that some day he would punish the scandalmongers, and now the ugly charges were appearing in print. The effrontery was intolerable. Whatever might be said for free speech, George hardly could be expected to take this passively, and he ordered his ministers to do something about it.

While ways and means were being sought to destroy Wilkes, he unwittingly gave a powerful weapon to his enemies. He composed and printed privately a pamphlet entitled *Essay on Woman,* ostensibly a satire on Pope's *Essay on Man,* as to title and general form. Wilkes always maintained that he never intended the work for general publication and that he had instructed the printer employed in his shop to make twelve copies only, presumably one for each of the Hell Fire members.

The *Essay* as printed consisted of only ninety-four lines, though there were other brief pieces in the pamphlet. The text was incredibly foul, making frequent use of unprintable words, at least not printable in any reputable paper. Libellous footnotes were sardonically and falsely attributed to Bishop Warburton, who had annotated Pope's poem; and there were satirical passages on religious themes. Particularly offensive was a lewd couplet about Lord Bute referring to his prowess in bed. Wilkes very likely was taking a respite from his serious work and composed the piece solely for his colleagues as a bit of dirty fun.

How the government learned of this publication is uncertain, as testimony was conflicting; but Wilkes's printer, unauthorized, had made an extra copy for himself. It soon came into the hands of the authorities and Wilkes's reputation was badly compromised.

Lord Sandwich, First Lord of the Admiralty, rose in the House of Lords with a copy of the *Essay on Woman* in his hands and began to read passages from it in a grave tone of self-righteous disapproval. When he came to the notes attributed to Bishop Warburton, the latter interrupted in a fury, possibly feeling that some persons might believe that he actually was the author. The cleric shouted that the very fiends of Hell would refuse to keep company with Mr. Wilkes and that he would apologize to the Devil for comparing them.

Sandwich resumed his reading and at the conclusion the House of Lords voted the *Essay* to be a blasphemous libel. The action had no legal force though it raised prejudice against Wilkes in some quarters, but there was considerable criticism of Sandwich for acting in a way that was "not done". It was well known that he had been a member of the Medmenham group and hence not entitled to take a holier-than-thou attitude toward Wilkes.

Wilkes probably would have been ignored except for the embarrassment to the administration and the king caused by issue after issue of the *North Briton* which emphasized weaknesses of the government. The paper, for example, bore down on the bribery of Parliament members by Henry Fox. This was a touchy subject with King George. He had pledged himself to bring in a new day in Parliament free from corruption. He had made that position conspicuous by ostentatiously depriving the Duke of Newcastle of royal funds for political purposes. At the same time Bute had access to the king's revenues and made use of them to buy votes, though possibly at the outset without the royal knowledge.

Bute, however, found that money alone could not gain control of the House of Commons, for management was needed. He convinced the king that in order to be his faithful servant and carry out his policies he needed an effective party whip. Otherwise he could not continue with the responsibilty of being prime minister. Further, he designated that the man he needed was Henry Fox.

George groaned at having Fox forced upon him. He had personal reasons to hate Fox, Lady Sarah's brother-in-law, and the man was known as a cynical political manager. The Whigs reviled Fox as a turncoat for entering the king's service, though Pitt and other Whig leaders had not hesitated to denounce Fox from time to time when he was in their camp.

Fox entered into his new role with great diligence. Newcastle had had most of the better government jobs at his disposal and he also had had the appointment of many lesser positions. Fox proceeded to root out all of the Newcastle following, even to minor clerks. There was virtually a complete overturn of personnel in most branches of the government, extending in a less drastic degree to the army and navy. Obviously this activity, while making new friends for the government, made hundreds of enemies throughout the whole Whig connection, and the incessant attacks on Fox in the *North Briton* brought Wilkes the continuing support of Newcastle, Temple and Pitt.

It was difficult, however, for the government to find a cause against the *North Briton* until No. 45 appeared. This issue dealt with the highly unpopular Peace of Paris which had been signed on February 10, 1763. England had been outmanœuvred in the negotiations and it was the general opinion that the nation gained nothing more in the settlement than could have been obtained a year previously.

The king's Address to Parliament dealt chiefly with an attempt to justify the treaty of peace. The *North Briton* No. 45 tore into the alleged fallacies and hypocrisies of the claims which were made. The king's speech had declared, "My expectations have been fully answered by the happy effects which the several allies of my crown have derived from this salutary measure *of the definitive Treaty.* The powers at war with my good brother, the King of Prussia, have been induced to agree to such terms of accommodation, as that great prince has approved; and the success which has attended my negotiation, has necessarily and immediately diffused the blessings of peace throughout every part of Europe."

This claim was particularly dubious because the public believed that the king of Prussia had virtually dictated the terms and had deserted the British cause. There was reason for that scepticism as Prussia followed the policy of balance of power and did not look with favour upon the extraordinary rise of England during the past several years. Gratitude for subsidies previously received was forgotten.

George III's speech had boasted that the government policy had "the entire approbation of Parliament" but, said the *North Briton*, "the world knows how that was obtained. The large debt on the civil list . . . shows pretty clearly the transactions of the winter". Namely, the majority vote had been obtained by bribery.

Another point which gave great offence to the Crown was the jeering of the paper at the claims of economy on the part of the administration, though the extravagance and waste had been notorious. Said the *North Briton,* "Let the public be informed of a single instance of *economy,* except indeed in the household." That last phrase was a nasty thrust, for the thriftiness of the king was well known. He forbade his servants to take tips; he personally inspected the kitchen department to see that there was no stealing or waste of provisions. At one point upon learning that the daughter of a woman who had been his wet nurse was now facing poverty he wanted to do something handsome for her, and gave her a job in the royal laundry!—a practical, if modest, solution, for the mother had been a laundress.

Another offensive note in No. 45 was its emphasis on the fact that "the King's Speech has always been considered by the legislature, and by the public at large, as the Speech of the Minister". That was true, but the editorial continued, "Every friend of his country must lament that a Prince of so many great and amiable qualities, whom England truly reveres, can be brought to give the sanction of his sacred name to the most odious measures, and to the most unjustifiable public declarations, from a Throne ever renowned for truth, honour, and unsullied virtue."

The observation was a double jab at His Majesty. George III was proud of the fact that the sentiments in the king's speech were his own and he did not submit to being a mere mouthpiece. Yet the words for which he would accept responsibility were declared to be "odious".

The king now told Halifax, one of the Secretaries of State, to take action against Wilkes and the attempt was made to charge him with treason. The government cried "treason" because on most charges a member of the House of Commons was privileged to express his views, but that sanction did not extend to treason.

The government's case, however, was weak because it did not have any evidence that Wilkes personally was the author of No. 45. Most of the articles were unsigned. The paper had as co-editor the notorious Charles Churchill. The name of George Kearsley (who acted as business manager) was listed as publisher, and there was no actual proof as to which articles, if any, were written by Wilkes. The only circumstantial evidence was that the paper was printed in Wilkes's home, against the previously mentioned strong advice of Lord Temple.

Halifax somehow or other had to find evidence and he issued a general warrant "against the authors, printers and publishers of the *North Briton* No. 45", but naming no one. A general warrant was admittedly illegal, but it had been used from time to time, and Halifax apparently felt that it might be successful in intimidating Wilkes.

Early one morning Wilkes was taking a walk along Great George Street, in which his home was located, when he was accosted by one of the king's messengers who said that he had a warrant of arrest for Wilkes which must be executed immediately and that Wilkes must accompany him to the home of Lord Halifax, which was only four doors away. Wilkes asked to see the warrant and noting its general terms, said that it did not apply to him.

The messenger replied that he had verbal orders "to arrest Mr. Wilkes". Wilkes cautioned the man to behave civilly, not to try any violence in the street, or to try to use force, or Wilkes would kill him instantly. On the other hand, if the man would come quietly to Wilkes's home he promised to convince the messenger of the illegality of the warrant and the injustice of the orders that he had received.

After the two had entered the house, Wilkes repeated that the warrant was absolutely illegal and void, "that it was a ridiculous warrant against the whole English nation". He suggested why not serve it on the Lord Chancellor, a Secretary of State, or Lord Bute, or his next-door neighbour. The man said stolidly, "I am to arrest Mr. Wilkes," but he made no move to do so physically.

After a while two other messengers and assistants arrived, all trying to persuade Wilkes to accompany them to Lord Halifax's, and Halifax himself sent over several polite messages inviting Wilkes to call. Wilkes sent back word that he had not previously had the honour of visiting his lordship and the initial invitation of the morning had been "rather rude and ungentlemanlike". While this was transpiring the co-editor, Mr. Churchill, appeared. Wilkes assumed that the messengers did not know Churchill by sight, but it had been rumoured that there was an order out to arrest Churchill also. Accordingly, Wilkes instantly said to Churchill, "Good morning, Mr. Thompson. How does Mrs. Thompson do today? Does she dine in the country?"

Churchill got the idea, said that his wife was waiting for him and that he had merely dropped by to pay his respects. He went home immediately, gathered up all the papers that were in his house, and went into the country where the government never was able to locate him.

This was a dramatic day on Great George Street in both of the houses such a short distance apart. The news spread rapidly around London and several friends of Wilkes dropped in to ask if they could be of help. He said they could and asked "two or three" to go to the Court of Common Pleas, make affidavit of his being made a prisoner in his own house under an illegal warrant and demand habeas corpus. Wilkes learned that the judge gave orders that the writ should be issued "immediately", but the office for issuing such writs was temporarily closed and therefore Wilkes was not instantly protected.

Lord Halifax, increasingly irritated by the delays, finally sent a constable to take Wilkes by force, together with several additional assistants. Wilkes, with a shrewd sense of his rights, demanded that all persons leave his house, saying, "I know and shall support the rights of an Englishman in the sanctuary of his own house." The constable then threatened him with violence and said that a regiment of the guards if necessary would be called out to take him to Lord Halifax, and the constable demanded his sword.

Wilkes said he would yield, but that if his visitors were not assassins, they must give him their names in writing and thirteen set their hands to the paper as being present. The demand for written evidence was a valid one on the part of Wilkes and respected by his visitors. They well knew the deep feeling of the public for the rights of an Englishman in his own home, which was a vital part of the unwritten Constitution. Far better to be on record merely as emissaries of Lord Halifax than to run the danger later of being prosecuted for forceful entry.

When the thirteen visitors had signed the paper, Wilkes got into his sedan chair for one of the most ridiculous parades in history. It would have been a simple matter to walk, of course, but Wilkes had a sense of the dramatic. Hence he was carried in state for the short distance to the house of Lord Halifax, accompanied by the constable, several messengers, and their assistants, including the thirteen signers.

On entering the Halifax drawing room he found that Egremont, the other Secretary of State, also was there and that they were all set to put him through a grilling. Wilkes began by saying that the king had no more loyal subject than himself, though His Majesty had the misfortune to be served by insolent and despotic ministers, a rather courageous comment considering that he was temporarily in their power, though also expecting the writ of habeas corpus to arrive at any moment.

Halifax had a list of prepared questions which he demanded that Wilkes answer, but the editor declined to fall into that trap and sat stubbornly noncommittal until the expected writ of habeas corpus arrived. Halifax and Egremont, however, were prepared for this move. For the moment they bypassed the general warrant and drew up a specific one charging John Wilkes, Esq., for being the author and publisher of a seditious libel, the *North Briton* No. 45, tending to inflame the people against His Majesty "and to excite them to traitorous insurrections against the Government".

This was a tactical move, based on no evidence whatever at the moment, but it temporarily negatived the particular habeas corpus which had applied to the general warrant and it was too late in the day for Wilkes to get relief from this new charge. Further, the Secretaries of State addressed a warrant of commitment to the constable of the Tower of London, or his deputies,

H

requiring that they confine the said Wilkes "until he shall be delivered by due course of law".

Customarily the political prisoners in the Tower had accommodations equivalent to those in a first-class hotel, plus gardens and outbuildings with various entertainment features. On a later occasion when Wilkes spent twenty-two months in the Tower, he enjoyed practically full liberty as long as he stayed on the premises, but now, for the first forty-eight hours, the government saw to it that he was not allowed to communicate with any of his friends. The purpose of this severity was to provide an opportunity for Halifax's agents to ransack Wilkes's home in the hope of finding proof that he personally had written certain articles in the *North Briton*. They entered the house, brought a locksmith to open drawers and boxes, carried off correspondence and other records, and took Wilkes's purse—all without finding the kind of proof they hoped for. Within several days a new habeas corpus writ for Wilkes was obtained and the government was forced to release him.

Though Wilkes survived to experience many ups and downs during a long life, his luck at present was running out, for George III was pursuing him relentlessly. The House of Commons voted by 258 to 133 that the privilege of a member did not extend to "seditious libel". A copy of No. 45 was ordered burned by the common hangman in front of the Royal Exchange.

When word of this became known in many quarters of London, a great mob gathered, shouting, "Wilkes and liberty!" Some hardy soul grabbed the magazine before it was half-burned. Someone else threw in a petticoat and jackboot, symbolic of Augusta and Bute. A jackboot was a large boot coming above the knee, frequently worn by fishermen. Though the pun on Bute's name was crude, it delighted the populace. Bute himself had become so unpopular that whenever he appeared in public he was accompanied by several bruisers to protect him from violence.

Wilkes was ordered to appear before the bar of the House to answer charges. George now took reprisals wherever he could against all who had supported Wilkes or voted against general warrants. He removed General Conway from command of his regiment and deprived Major Barré of his commission. He struck the name of Temple off the list of his Privy Councillors.

Wilkes pleaded illness for his non-appearance at the bar of the House and sent excuses signed by two doctors. He then fled to France on the pretence that he was going to visit his thirteen-year-old daughter for the Christmas holidays. That was true, for he did have a daughter, his only legitimate child, who was at school in Paris. The father and daughter were devoted to each other for many years and the letters of Wilkes to her reveal a tender and charming affection.

His visit presumably was a pleasant one, and it was conveniently prudent for him to make it at this time. After arrival he took the added precaution of sending certificates of his illness by two French doctors, even though he had been promised protection by French authorities if any attempt were made to extradite him. However, the persecution on the home front continued. He was expelled from the House of Commons in January 1764. In February he was tried *in absentia* before Judge Mansfield, was held guilty of "seditious libel and blasphemy", and declared an outlaw.

George III heard the news with approval; but now that Wilkes was an outlaw was the young king satisfied? Not at all. He wrote to his prime minister, "Firmness and resolution must now be shown, and no one's friend saved who had dared fly off; this alone can restore order, and save this country from anarchy." He promised that no one who had deserted him would go unpunished.

14

"FIRMNESS AND RESOLUTION"

Ever since Bute became Secretary of State in March 1761 the attitude of George III had become almost pathologically autocratic. He appeared to be trying to prove both to Bute and himself that he was a man of decision. His "firmness and resolution" comment was an echo of various of his letters to and from Bute.

The king's correspondence with his Scottish mentor is full of complaints about George's fancied ill-treatment by his ministers and other high officials at Court. He regarded any criticism of the government or of Bute as a personal affront and repaid it with a prompt irritability which indicated high nervous tension. George III had become suspicious, sniffing disloyalty in every corner. The Duke of Devonshire, for example, who was Lord Chamberlain,

one morning in October 1762 was seen by the king in the company
of Newcastle while His Majesty was en route from Kew to London.
Newcastle had been threatening to resign from the cabinet and
George suspected that the two were conniving at something or
other without his prior knowledge. When Devonshire called at the
Palace the same day the king sent word through a page that he
would not see him.

Devonshire realized that George considered himself insulted for
some reason and sent word back by the page to inquire where he,
Devonshire, should leave his wand—the symbol of his office. The
king replied, again by the messenger, that Devonshire would
receive his orders in due course. George III's attitude obviously
was adamant, and upon departing the Duke said to the page, "God
bless you, it will be very long before you see me here again."

Devonshire immediately turned over the wand to Egremont, one
of the Secretaries of State, without waiting for any further word
from the king. George III thereupon was furious at having been
deprived of the initiative. He wrote to Bute that this was "im-
pertinent conduct" and struck Devonshire's name from the list of
Privy Councillors, a gesture which had become a favourite one
with him.

Furthermore, George had a long memory for supposed wrongs.
Several months later the Duke of Bedford declined a post in the
cabinet because he would "deserve to be treated as a madman" if
he took part in the weak ministry that Bute was trying to put together. He urged Bute, "for God's sake", to let the Dukes of Newcastle, Devonshire and Grafton, and Earl Hardwicke be called again
into His Majesty's service.

Bedford was a shrewd man politically. He was the head of a
sizeable Whig faction, which sometimes united with the other
Whigs and sometimes did not, but he had commanded enough
respect among the various political groups to be sent to France to
collaborate on the peace preliminaries. He proved not to be a
successful diplomat, but he was one of the leading men of his
time. His forthrightness and bluntness had irritated the king and
this message recommending Newcastle and Devonshire enraged
George, who said that it proved the justice of the opinion that he
had held of Bedford's character, namely that "it contains nothing
but passion and absurdity". He said that Newcastle and Devonshire would have ruined Bute if they could and he would have
nothing whatever to do with them.

This air of distrust on the part of George III made it difficult for him to get a cabinet of able men. Cabinet members were spied upon. The king ordered Halifax, a Secretary of State, to send orders to the post office to continue examining the letters to and from Lord Temple. This, to be sure, was a practice not invented by George III. It had been done at times in prior ministries, but he carried it on intensively. He also was known to have private advisers other than Bute who sometimes were secretly instructed to oppose the policies of the ministry in Parliament. It seemingly gave George III satisfaction to keep all important personages uncertain as to their standing with him.

Bute himself was beginning to have his fill of the difficulties of government and in March 1763 offered to resign. His great unpopularity made his office burdensome. He pleaded ill health and said that he had achieved his major objective of restoring the country to peace. He told George that he felt that government affairs were in such shape he could turn them over to a successor.

George III at first received this news with reluctance, saying that it was "the most cruel political blow that could have happened to me". But worse was yet to come. Bute recommended to the king that Fox be the next prime minister. He was quite sincere in this proposal. He previously had said to Fox, "When you, Sir, with a spirit and a generosity that I can never forget, gave us your help, to save this poor country in its extreme peril, honour, gratitude, duty and affection made my stay necessary; but now, thanks to kind Providence, the vessel's safe in harbour."

The king protested violently. Why must Fox be elevated to the head of the government when everyone knew His Majesty's aversion to the man? George said to Bute, "In the case of Mr. Fox I fear we shall never think alike . . . seeing him at the head of the House of Commons was very unpleasant to me," and added that he had agreed to receiving Fox in any capacity only because Bute had insisted. George suggested various other expedients—possibly Fox and Newcastle jointly as Secretaries of State who would jealously keep an eye on one another. Finally the king was almost persuaded to accept Fox, if Bute said that there was no other way. Then to the relief of everyone Fox declined the opportunity.

Fox had been promised a peerage for his leadership in the House of Commons. He had always preferred wealth (which he had acquired) to political eminence; his service with the government had brought him abuse and hard work, and his wife wanted him to take things easier and enjoy life. George III accepted Fox's withdrawal with enthusiasm. Fox promptly was elevated to the peerage as Lord Holland and disappeared publicly from the political scene.

George III at this period was living in an era of discontent which he seemed not to understand. The nation was going through a period of postwar disillusion. There were no excitements of victory such as had existed during the Pitt administration, and, as has been said, the peace treaty had thrown away prizes such as those in the West Indies which had been won at the cost of British treasure and lives. The middle classes were resentful at the decline in prosperity and the rise in taxation. The masses for the most part lived in desperate poverty and had no orderly means for redressing their wrongs.

In this situation it was unfortunate that George III had not escaped from the thraldom of Bute, that he was still so immature in his outlook and that he was unable to provide the enlightened leadership which the nation needed. His instinct was correct when he declared for "firmness and resolution", but he directed that policy erroneously and wastefully in asserting the authority of the throne often in trivial matters, and in espousing unpopular causes, one of which was a proposed tax on cider.

In theory an excise tax is a just and efficient means of raising revenue, but customarily it is an unpopular method because it is visible. The customer is continuously aware that he is paying for the cost of the government, whereas in certain other types of levy, such as tariffs, the taxation in effect is hidden. There were taxes on beer, ale, porter and wine in this period. Much earlier there had been protests on the beer tax, but the public had become habituated to paying it. The high taxes on gin had been substantially lowered in 1740 as the higher rates had proved to be unenforceable.

The proposed tax on cider was especially obnoxious because that beverage had never been taxed before and because cider was the drink of the poor man and the farmer. Cider obviously could be enjoyed in the sweet form or allowed to ferment and ultimately converted to apple brandy. Cider customarily was made in the home and produced by an individual or family, an advantage which appealed to the English temperament.

The method of collection of this tax also was obnoxious. The visits of excise officers to individual homes were considered invasions of "the liberty of the subject" and it was proposed that defendants would be brought before commissioners instead of having trial by jury. Still further objections came from the apple growers supplying the city markets who feared that the tax would cause the public to turn to other beverages. The various objections were voiced strenuously in Parliament and George Grenville was the unfortunate minister assigned to push the legislation through. To the attacks of the opposition Grenville kept saying that if this tax were unacceptable they should say where else might a tax be laid.

"I say, Sir," he kept repeating in Parliament, in his high-pitched voice, "let them tell me *where*! I repeat it, Sir, I am entitled to say to them, tell me where." While he was saying this Pitt audibly began humming a popular song which was entitled "Gentle Shepherd, Tell Me Where". Grenville was infuriated and he shouted, "If gentlemen are to be treated with contempt——" Pitt merely turned to him, made a deep bow and departed. And the nickname "Gentle Shepherd" clung to Grenville for a long time afterwards.

Meanwhile the king from behind the scenes was urging "firmness" on the ministry. A certain Richard Glover had drafted a petition against the cider tax which the City of London presented to the House of Commons. Glover previously had been brought into Parliament through Bute's influence and the king now suggested that that support should be withdrawn.

After the cider bill had passed the third reading in the House of Lords, officials of the City hurried to St. James's Palace to present a petition against the bill asking George to veto the measure. His Majesty received the document without making any comment whatever. After the visitors had left, the king promptly wrote to Bute. "What times do we not live in, when a parcel of low shopkeepers pretend to direct the whole legislature." The following morning he signed the bill.

15

HARDENING OF THE SHELL

Though the king was consciously developing a resolute exterior for his personality, the inner man had a gentler and more flexible spirit. Inwardly he had a capacity to reason, he was capable of personal tenderness to family and friends (in addition to his extra-ordinary attachment to Lord Bute), and he exhibited numerous instances of personal courage during his lifetime.

His development may be compared to that of a snapping turtle who has a tender shell in its earlier stages. Gradually the shell hardens, the claws sharpen, and the jaw develops a vicious strength capable of inflicting punishment on the enemy. Finally the creature is withdrawn into its hard exterior which is all the public can see.

At this period George had been flexible about the cider tax behind the scenes and conceivably might have changed his attitude about it publicly if there had not been so much pressure and ill-will on the part of the opposition. A letter to Bute at the time of the second reading shows that the king had some doubts on the wisdom of forcing the measure through. Fox already had recommended to Bute that it would be wiser to abandon the tax in view of its unpopularity. His Majesty was inclined to go that far, if Bute could save face by not appearing to be driven into change. George suggested that Bute could say that he himself did not have objections to the tax, but that he would drop the proposal because of "his wish for public tranquillity". The king, however, was still placing too much reliance on Bute's judgment, for he said, "It is foolish to give my D. friend advice on such a subject; he knowing so perfectly what he ought and ought not to say." As we have seen, Bute ignored the advice both of Fox and the king and forced the issue through.

Though George had suffered considerable frustration in his government relationships during the first years of his reign, his domestic life was serene. His behaviour appears most charmingly at the time of the birth of his first child. There are numerous accounts of the event, as most of the cabinet were present, and Lady Northumberland (the future duchess) recorded some intimate details, which she knew as a Lady of the Bedchamber and an intimate friend of the royal family.

The queen was in labour on the afternoon of August 12, 1762. Lord Cantelupe, Vice Chamberlain to the queen, had been fore-warned of the expected event and had been appointed as the one to notify the birth to the king, and to have as a fee for delivering the message £500 if a girl, £1,000 if a boy! By late afternoon the accredited attendants were on hand: the midwife, of course; Charlotte's two German women; the Ladies of the Bedchamber; Egremont; Bute; Devonshire (who had not as yet incurred the king's wrath); George Grenville (at this time a Secretary of State); Halifax; Cantelupe; Lord Huntingdon; Lord Talbot (the horseman who was Lord Steward of the Household); the Archbishop of Canterbury; and others. The king awaited the news in his apartments nearby.

"The Queen scarce cried out at all," said Lady Northumberland, "and at twenty-four minutes past seven she was delivered."

Lord Huntingdon, though it was Lord Cantelupe's assignment, rushed to inform the king of the queen's safe delivery and told him erroneously that it was a girl. George replied that he was "but little anxious as to the sex of the child so the Queen was but safe". George went to the bedchamber, and soon after that the child was brought out and shown to all, "a strong, large, pretty boy".

In the days immediately following, the king and queen enjoyed great popularity, first of all because the nation welcomed the baby boy who would be heir to the throne. Lord Bath wrote to a friend, "There is a vast spirit of discontent in the City, but at our end of the town the mob follows the Coach . . . and the young Prince . . . as they are taking the air in Hyde Park, crying out 'God bless him, he is a lusty, jolly young dog, truly'."

Another cause of popularity with the multitude was the fact that the queen in celebration of the birth was supposed to provide free cake and caudle to all comers without need for any guest to have a special invitation. Caudle was a warm drink consisting of thin gruel, mixed with wine or ale, sweetened and spiced; it was a usual beverage for women after childbirth.

Lady Northumberland was in charge of the distribution on the evening of August 24, 1762. There she found a considerable throng pressing into the waiting room where the cake and caudle were served. The visitors included stablemen and general citizenry. Lady Northumberland, bewildered as to how to handle the situation, went to the king's apartment for advice. George assigned a troop of Yeomen of the Guard to attend her. After she had instructed the guard to admit only twelve persons at a time, she had the situation under control. The great number of visitors is indicated by the fact that during the week of these ceremonies the distribution amounted to £500 worth of cake and about eight gallons of caudle each day.

The next event in connection with the birth was the baptism, at which there were no mishaps. Attendance was limited to the royal family and household and the hour was about half-past six in the evening, in the queen's drawing room. At the head of the drawing room was a bed of state on which Queen Charlotte was lying. It had trappings of crimson velvet trimmed with gold and lined with white satin, and the counterpane was covered with Brussels lace. The queen had a jewelled stomacher adorned with diamonds and emeralds and her dress was white and silver. On a table at the foot of the bed was a large gilt baptismal bowl.

The royal family, including the king and his household, approached the queen first. Then Devonshire, as Lord Chamberlain, was sent to fetch the baby prince. Devonshire returned, preceded by the verger, followed by the governess of the infant, bearing the child on a white satin pillow embroidered with gold. The sponsors were the princess dowager, the Duke of Cumberland, and the proxy of the queen's brother.

The Princess Dowager Augusta then took the infant from the governess as the babe cried most lustily (tradition says this is the Devil being driven out of the child) and the Archbishop of Canterbury completed the ceremony, by which the king appeared much moved. (The prince, named George Augustus Frederick, succeeded to the throne as George IV, but unfortunately did not live up to this devout start.)

While George was readily disturbed to an unusual degree by political opposition, he was not frightened by physical force. On one occasion a mob of about two thousand unemployed silk workers approached Kensington Palace where he was residing and, not finding the king there, caught up with him at Wimbledon where he was horseback riding. The men were enraged because the House of Lords had vetoed a proposed protective tariff on silk. The king heard their protests without a flicker of fear and promised his influence in trying to help their case; and he did try to do so, as will appear later.

The chief bone of contention which ran through most of the king's trouble with his ministry and whatever opposition there was at any given time was solidified by George's persistent adherence to the idea of the authority of the throne. He clung to the doctrine of a Patriot King supported in some undefined way by his loving subjects, and George saw nothing unconstitutional in that principle.

Various authorities have pointed out the excellence of the English constitutional system for England, namely the combination of law and custom which permits adaptability to new conditions as the centuries roll on, but that very fluidity was a handicap to George III who felt that he was being entirely constitutional when in fact he was trying to turn back the clock.

However, except for the central issue, George III tried to get along with the various political figures of the times, who were a difficult lot. Even his "dearest friend", Lord Bute, was becoming an increasing handicap due to his unpopularity, political awkwardness, and arbitrary manner. Most of the men having any experience in political life at this time were double the king's age or older. George was born in 1738, Newcastle in 1693, Bute in 1713, Henry Fox in 1705, Halifax in 1716, and the men in the Grenville phalanx were in their fifties. There were no prominent younger leaders who might have reached a better mutual understanding with the king.

The Grenville connection may properly be referred to as a phalanx rather than a family, for the Grenvilles were related to virtually every important interest in the nation and felt themselves to be the appropriate administrators of the Kingdom. In fact, including sons and grandsons they were the most influential group in the ministry or Parliament during most of George III's reign. The hard core of this sphere of influence were the three Grenville brothers, Richard (Lord Temple), George, and James, and their sister Hester's husband William Pitt. The close connection may be visualized by the chart on the next page.

There were two other Grenville brothers who were not actively in politics, Thomas, a naval officer who was killed in action in 1747, and Henry, who was governor of Barbados and held other appointive posts. Lord Lyttelton (1709–1773), a first cousin, attended Eton, and generally voted with the Grenville phalanx. Egremont's father had been an early supporter of Pitt. Egremont was independent, changed sides from time to time, but usually sided with the Grenvilles as he was brother-in-law of George Grenville.

In the face of this formidable group the fact that George III had been privately and badly tutored, instead of associating with other boys in a sizeable school, was a great handicap. Note from the chart that Temple, George Grenville, and Pitt were all Eton boys (so were Lyttelton, Fox, and Bute). Egremont, George Grenville, and Pitt attended Oxford. The old school tie did not prevent various factions from quarrelling with each other, but there was a

GRENVILLE, RICHARD (Lord Temple) *1711–1779*
   Eton
   Tutor-travel 4 years
   M.P. '34
   M.P. '41
   Earl '52

GRENVILLE, GEORGE *1712–1770*
   Eton
   Christ Church, Oxford
   Law
   M.P.   '41
   Treasurer of Navy '54
   Treasurer of Navy '56
   Out with Pitt   '57
   In with Pitt   '57
   Cabinet   '61
   Secretary of State '62
   Prime Minister   '63–July 10, '65
   (m. Egremont's sister)

                              EGREMONT (born Wyndham) *1710–1763*
                                 Christ Church, Oxford
                                 Tory-Whig
                                 M.P.   '34
                                 M.P.   '41
                                 M.P.   '47
                                 Secretary of State '61–'63

GRENVILLE, JAMES *1715–1783*
   M.P.   '41
   Deputy Paymaster '46
   Treasury Board   '57

GRENVILLE, HESTER *1721–1803*
   m. William Pitt   '54
                              WILLIAM PITT (Chatham) *1708–1778*
                                 Eton
                                 Trinity, Oxford
                                 M.P.
                                 Secretary of State
                                 Prime Minister

community of background, experience of how to deal with one's associates, in contrast to the inexperience of the king.

Pitt was more Grenville than the Grenvilles, even before he married Hester. As a young man he was a protégé of the late Lord Cobham, an uncle of the Grenville boys. Pitt was a frequent visitor at Stowe, Cobham's estate, and in the Grenville home. His brilliance early won him an ascendancy in the family. His own forebears were persons of consequence and he was related to various eminent families, including the Villiers connection, but his attachment to the Grenvilles evidently was based on congeniality, similarity of viewpoint, and solidified by his marriage to Hester, which was an enduring love match.

Richard, as the oldest Grenville, inherited the bulk of the property and in 1752 had become Earl Temple. He was a handsome, somewhat stolid man, who was dazzled by the imaginative and eloquent Pitt. He was head of the Grenville family and as such gave the impression of considering himself the most important member of the clan, a feeling bolstered by his very considerable wealth, which was much greater than the comfortable circumstances of Pitt. However, in politics customarily Temple was an echo of Pitt.

James Grenville, who was the youngest of the quartet, voted steadily for the family interest, but took no aggressive part in Parliament, evidently content to bask in reflected glory.

In addition to Pitt, the other strong man in the combination was George Grenville. His accomplishments were solid and down to earth in contrast to the vaulting ideas of the Great Commoner. Furthermore, Grenville preserved his independence by living within his modest income.

Edmund Burke, who frequently was on the opposite side from Grenville, paid tribute to him in a speech dealing with American taxation four years after Grenville died, saying, "Undoubtedly, Mr. Grenville was a first-rate figure in this country. With a masculine understanding, and a stout and resolute heart, he had an application undissipated and unwearied." Burke added that Grenville had "a well-earned rank in Parliament, by a thorough knowledge of its constitution, and a perfect practice in all its business". Pitt had said of the man twenty years earlier, "Mr. Grenville is universally able in the whole business of the House."

Grenville, in short, had the favourable qualities of the country squire or the British middle class, moral, diligent, able in his daily work, and having a sense of responsibility. Conversely, he was fixed in his ideas, unable to see merit in opposing views, and he consequently was even less flexible than George III in his unpopular taxation measures.

Grenville was Treasurer of the Navy four times in the years 1754–1757 due to changes in the ministry and was accorded cabinet rank in 1761. When the Pitt administration fell in 1761 Bute had thought that he would protect the government against any attack by the Great Commoner through two moves. The first was to retain George Grenville in office and the second was to appoint Egremont (whose sister was married to George Grenville) as Secretary of State in the place of Pitt.

In Egremont Bute had found a man who was too inconsequential to cause him serious trouble, but from the outset it was seen that Bute's efforts to appease the Grenville-Pitt connection gave him no immunity from them.

16

DOWNFALL OF BUTE

The appointment of Egremont as a principal Secretary of State might have been a solution of the cabinet difficulties, at least for a time, for he was a tactful person, not prone to raise issues. However, he died in 1763 after less than two years in office.

George III's difficulties in government now came to a head, for Bute acted on his earlier threats to retire. On April 8, 1763, he resigned from the cabinet and ostensibly from all official connection with the government. He realized that his personal unpopularity was a handicap to George. Furthermore, the physical violence by which Bute had been threatened from time to time caused him continuous mental strain. His official excuse for his retirement was poor health, which doubtless was induced by public abuse and personal frustration.

George III accepted both the resignation and the reason offered, and said of Lord Bute, "I saw his health would not permit him to remain and that the only comfort that remained to me was that I should by this preserve my d. friend's company years the longer."

Again referring to Bute's retirement, the king said, "My heart is very full whenever I think of that most unhappy moment."

The most pressing problem for George III in 1763 obviously was to find a satisfactory prime minister to succeed Bute. George still was hampered by his inexperience and by his naïve idea that he could restore the authority of the throne, as though wishing would make it so. He had depended much too long on the guidance of Bute and there was no one in his cabinet that he desired to name as successor. Egremont might have been satisfactory, but after his death the king reluctantly sent for Pitt.

The method of approach was peculiar. Bute was the principal agent in the transaction, even though he was officially out of the government. He went to Alderman Beckford, Pitt's friend, and persuaded Beckford to go into the country where Pitt was then living and urge him to come into the Queen's House in London for a conference with the king. Pitt reluctantly agreed and in the conference set up a number of conditions. He said he must be loyal to the Newcastle Whigs, and that Chief Justice Pratt (who had signed the habeas corpus for Wilkes) should be legal adviser to the cabinet. He insisted on the exclusion of Bedford, who had been a chief cause of Pitt's resignation on the peace issue. George received these various conditions agreeably.

"There is pen, ink and paper," he said. "Make out a list of your administration at once." Pitt demurred, saying that he felt obliged to consult Temple and other associates before making any final commitments. George then invited Pitt to return the following Monday with his list. On Sunday Pitt conferred with Newcastle and Temple and prepared a list, but during the day Pitt received a secret message from a friend in the government saying that a hitch had developed. Bute had come to the view that he and his friends would be wholly out of power in any administration which Pitt proposed. Bute in turn convinced George III of Pitt's undesirability and on Monday the Great Commoner met with a cool reception. The king objected to proposals which he had accepted only two days before and finally said, "Well, Mr. Pitt, I see this won't do. My honour is concerned and I must support it."

Pitt, whose health was failing, realized the difficulty of dislodging the Bute influence, and accepted the decision without argument. He bowed low to the king and said, "Sir, the House of Commons will not force me upon your Majesty and I will never come into your service against your consent."

George was now really in trouble. The next man who might be available was the stolid George Grenville whom the king had always disliked. Other possibilities were even less acceptable to His Majesty. The hated Fox had retired to private life; Bedford and the Duke of Richmond had scolded the king on various occasions, which he deeply resented. Hence His Majesty regretfully approached Grenville.

The latter received the overtures in a sour mood. He had seen the equipages of Bute and of Pitt outside the Queen's House and realized that something was going on behind his back. Grenville had reason to be bitter over this distrust, for he had alienated himself from the other Grenvilles by agreeing to continue in the Bute administration, and the king had promised him that he would never call Pitt into the ministry. Hence Grenville himself laid down terms, the chief of which was that Bute must retire from all influence *and personally must leave the City of London.* Furthermore, the king must not give the office of Privy Purse to any one of Bute's friends.

"Good God!" George said. "Mr. Grenville, am I to be suspected after all I have done?"

Nevertheless, His Majesty agreed to the terms and Grenville accepted the office of prime minister.

Bute, however, except for taking trips into the country, did not leave London until two or three years later. On the contrary, he remained in town and continued his attentions to the princess dowager.

George tried to be ruler of the people, but he continually was being thwarted by a timid and sometimes hostile ministry, as in the case of the Spitalfields weavers. Following his promise to the weavers, the king instructed Grenville to get some relief through Parliament. Grenville, to George's surprise, said that the measure proposing a higher tariff on silk had been rejected and that nothing further could be done about it.

The king persisted in his demand and Grenville said that the session of Parliament was virtually over, and repeated that there was no opportunity for new business. His Majesty, however, ordered Grenville to bring up the subject with some of the leaders in the upper house. The inference was that Grenville should not depend on his own judgment as to what could or could not be done. Grenville stubbornly held that the only subject which remained to be considered was the speech to be given at the adjournment of Parliament and that he, Grenville, would like to discuss the matter.

"Mr. Grenville," George replied, "I will speak to you another time about that. I promise you I will speak to you; you may depend upon it I will speak to you," and turned away in wrath.

The situation became more acute because the mob of weavers now surrounded the Houses of Parliament. They accosted one lord after another, asking how they had voted on the bill; and they were particularly hostile to Bedford who had spoken against the tariff.

When Bedford left the session around five in the afternoon and got into his carriage to go home, the mob followed him, throwing stones. One sizable rock was hurled through the window right at Bedford's face. He partially warded it off with his forearm but received a bad cut on the forehead.

When he reached his residence on the north side of Bloomsbury Square a crowd of men were trying to storm the gates. Bedford with an undaunted courage which was typical of him emerged from his carriage, faced the mob, and invited any two of them to come into the house with him and discuss matters. The invitation was accepted and Bedford asked the spokesman if there was any justice in his being assaulted for having voted according to his convictions. This comment was not satisfactory, for seemingly the mob had hoped to terrorize Bedford into changing his vote. More and more men kept pouring into the courtyard.

The civil authorities attempted to disperse the crowd by a proclamation, but that did not work, and George sent a troop of cavalry to the rescue. The horsemen chased the mob out of the courtyard and the crowd scampered down the side streets around Bloomsbury Square. Seven persons were captured and brought before a magistrate where each one affirmed that he was not a weaver but had been paid a full day's wages to stir up disturbance. In short, they were paid agitators, and Horace Walpole, who came upon the scene while the disturbance was at its height, was told that the mob was directed by "four or five gentlemen in disguise who were not suspected".

The horseguards continued on duty while the Duke and Duchess of Bedford stayed up all night and received many callers who came through sympathy or curiosity. Bedford was convinced that the mob had been stirred up by Lord Bute, and the duchess expressed the same opinion to Horace Walpole "with warmth and acrimony". Bute was suspected on the theory that if the govern-

I

ment could not maintain order he would be recalled to take charge. The reasoning was dubious and Walpole said that he was not much inclined to believe that Bute was the instigator "nor thought a mob the tool with which Lord Bute would choose to amuse himself". The Bedfords remained fixed in their opinion, however, and when the Northumberlands, who were related to the Butes by marriage, arrived, the Duke of Bedford left the room and the visitors were not asked to sit, nor were they spoken to.

The resentment and suspicion of the Bedfords was fanned by the fact that the Duchess of Northumberland previously had offended the princess dowager and had openly shown her resentment to Lord Bute. The following day Bedford told his suspicion to the king and it was hinted several times in the House of Lords that Bute was responsible for the riots.

Walpole had a more plausible theory. He held that the disturbance had been stirred up by a Humphrey Cotes and other friends of Wilkes. Wilkes was still in exile, but Cotes had visited him recently in Boulogne, and the friends of Wilkes kept inciting the public against the government.

It was Almon, formerly a printer for Wilkes, who told Walpole about the "gentlemen in disguise" and hinted that he could disclose who they were.

"Name no names to me, I will not hear them," said Walpole.

Almon then gave Walpole a pamphlet published by Cotes against Lord Bute and Lord Holland (the former Henry Fox) and talked of "risings that would be all over England".

Walpole said, "I should be sorry to have the mob rise. It would occasion the army being quartered in London, and then we should all be enslaved."

The following morning there were still crowds about the House of Lords which indicated that the crisis was not yet over, a fact which greatly agitated George III and logically enough changed his policy toward the weavers' complaints, for to yield under duress would be regarded as a sign of weakness. On the contrary, he proposed that his uncle, the Duke of Cumberland, should take over the army and deal with any unruly persons. George was eager not to be charged with cowardice or lack of his cherished characteristic of "firmness". However, Cumberland had the good sense to say that there was no need for such an extreme step and that the disturbance would soon die down.

Lord Mansfield, legal adviser to the king and ministry, said that it would be inadvisable to change ministers now, as that would shake public confidence. Grenville took the same position, alleging that he did so not for the sake of holding onto his job which had become burdensome, but because a change at this point would reflect upon the capacity of the administration to keep order. The king was inclined to agree for the time being and he willingly accepted Bedford's proposal that Parliament should not be adjourned but should continue to sit, for if adjournment were taken at this time the full burden of dealing with the situation would be upon the ministry.

George III, still incensed at Grenville, again sent overtures to Pitt through his uncle the Duke of Cumberland hoping that Pitt and Temple would be pleased to come into office; but there had been an unforeseen reconciliation in the Grenville clan and they refused to have any part in displacing George Grenville. This was a bitter blow to the king who found the tactless arrogance of his prime minister virtually intolerable.

As a result the young and discouraged George III was afflicted with an intermittent nervous breakdown in the early part of the year 1765. There were days when he was unable to make any decision about anything, when he would spend hours at his desk with his head resting on his forearm. There were times when in conference with Grenville or other ministers his face would turn a fiery red and he would burst into tears. This was the first of several attacks.

Intermittently he had a fever and his pulse frequently was erratic. He felt that most of the cabinet were against him and were thoroughly unreliable. While a persecution complex is a symptom of insanity, in this instance it had a valid basis. The cabinet were not against the king, but most of them were against Bute and the influence of Bute, which in George's mind amounted to the same thing.

On one occasion he wrote to Bute, "Every day I meet with some insult from these people; I have been for near a week as it were in a fever. My very sleep is not free from thinking of the men I daily see. . . . Excuse the incoherency of my letters; but a mind ulcered by the treatment it meets with from all around is the true cause of it." This was the initial warning of the recurring threats to his sanity.

George III became increasingly worried about his mental condition. Accordingly, he decided that a new regency bill should be enacted since it would be many years before his son would be old enough to reign. Blackstone, the famous legal authority, and Lord Mansfield advised that a new act was not necessary, as the present one, enacted in the time of Prince Frederick, covered all contingencies, was still in force, and named the princess dowager as regent. Augusta, however, was now forty-six years old and might not live the full span of time until George III's successor would be of age. She did, in fact, die several years later.

The king told Grenville that he desired to have a new act introduced and he would prefer to have the name of the regent a secret to be decided by him in the future. It is possible that the king had in mind a regency council which would include his mother and Lord Bute, but he was told that a measure proposing unnamed persons would be resented by the Parliament and could not pass.

The king gave way gracefully on that point and the ministers then came up with another proposition. Halifax, Grenville and Sandwich proposed that the bill should name the queen, the royal family, or descendants of the late king if they were now and usually residing in England. Halifax proposed to George that it would be advisable to omit the name of the princess dowager specifically lest embarrassing opposition and discussion be created. George was reported to have agreed to this and he never denied subsequent assertions by Halifax to that effect; but as Lady Bute said later, if he did agree to it he did not understand the implications and doubtless assumed that the term "royal family" included his mother.

When the trio of ministers received the consent to use the king's name in favour of omitting mention of Augusta in the act they were delighted. Whatever interpretation the king had put on the proposed language, Halifax, Sandwich and Grenville had in mind that Augusta and Bute would be excluded by the wording. Since the king appeared to be in such poor health they were quite apprehensive about the appointment of a regent, and particularly they feared Augusta, as she presumably would be guided by Bute in all things.

The regency bill caused much discussion for many sessions in Parliament. A motion was made in the Commons supporting the king's original idea that the naming of a regent should be left to him, but that was defeated as Halifax had predicted. The debate raised the question of who were to be regarded as "in the royal family". All were agreed that the queen, though born a foreigner and not yet twenty-one, should be included. Time would soon remedy the age question, she was declared naturalized by her marriage, and it was said that to omit her would be a "slur".

Halifax hinted privately to the Lords that His Majesty would be willing to have his mother's name omitted. Thereupon the Duke of Richmond crossed up the ministry by moving that the princess dowager, the queen, and descendants of George II residing in England, should be eligible to be regents. Ever since Richmond's sister Sarah Lennox had been jilted by the king, Richmond delighted in opportunities to embarrass His Majesty. The ministers now were in an awkward position. They had the controlling votes in the Lords and defeated Richmond's bill, which placed the omission of Augusta's name squarely on their responsibility.

Halifax then moved the same words as Richmond, except for the princess dowager, and this bill, supported by the government-controlled votes, passed. Richmond was elated at the success of his strategy and Bute was dumbfounded. Walpole commented to Lord Hertford, "Open war seems to be declared between the Court and the Administration, and men are gazing to see which side will be victorious."

But worse was yet to come for the ministers. In the House of Commons a Judge Morton held that the omission of the princess dowager's name was an affront, whatever interpretation might be made of the wording of the bill, and therefore moved that her name be inserted after that of the queen. This caught the ministers flat-footed, and the Commons including many of the government votes passed this enthusiastically. Thereupon the ministers, not daring to insult the king's mother openly, endorsed the bill of the Commons up to the House of Lords where it finally was enacted into law.

17

GRENVILLE'S LEGACY OF ERRORS

During George's illness and after, Grenville's ministry left a legacy of errors which were due to plague the king for many years.

Such matters as general warrants, the continued persecution of Wilkes, the cider tax, and taxation of the American colonies were embarrassments that the king later could have disavowed, but did not. In fact, Grenville was so much in sympathy with the royal policies that he might have continued in office indefinitely, but for his rudeness, his love of personal power, and his jealousy of Bute.

A general warrant would be a powerful police weapon for king or ministry. The Wilkes case naturally had highlighted the issue and now that Wilkes was temporarily disposed of, the opposition, led by Pitt, proposed a resolution in Parliament condemning the principle of general warrants. Pitt, Lord Temple, the Duke of Grafton, and other liberals welcomed the opportunity to pursue the matter without the embarrassment of Wilkes, who rightfully at that time could be regarded as a "bounder". Gladstone, the nine-teenth-century prime minister, said, "The name of Wilkes, whether we choose it or not, must be enrolled among the great champions of English freedom." But Wilkes in his early years had not re-vealed his best qualities and the opposition was relieved to discuss the general warrants issue solely on the merits of the question.

George III, Grenville, and Sir Fletcher Norton (the Attorney-General) soon made their positions entirely clear by opposing the motion of condemnation of general warrants. The resolution said that "A General Warrant, for apprehending and seizing the authors, printers and publishers of a seditious libel together with their papers, is not warranted by law". That seemingly was a mild statement, but it drew the fire of the government at once. George III kept in touch with Grenville daily behind the scenes, asking for a prompt written account of the debate. According to Grenville, George III expressed great resentment at those who spoke in favour of the resolution, said that he would support his present ministry even if the opposition carried the question and that "firmness and steadiness" was what alone could get the better of the state of anarchy which seem to threaten the government, and that "it must be shown".

In the early part of the debate starting on February 13, 1764, reference was made to the Wilkes case by a government witness who stated that he had not intended that Colonel Wilkes be held a close prisoner in the Tower and that he had taken care that the prisoner was made comfortable while there. This was so obviously irrelevant that Grenville became uncomfortable and suggested an adjournment. In fact, he was alarmed at the attendance which exceeded 450 and feared what it might portend. Part of the large attendance was due to the widespread support of the opposition's statement on the issue and part was due to the desire to hear the eloquence of Pitt, who usually put on a brilliant performance.

Following Grenville's suggestion, a government M.P. moved to adjourn.

"I think we should not adjourn until we know whether we have a Constitution or not," said Pitt. The motion to adjourn was defeated by a substantial vote.

The strategy of the government now was to prevent a vote on the resolution itself which undoubtedly would have carried at that moment. Hence the speakers for the administration, seeing that they could not get an adjournment, tried to fill up time with numerous technical points such as holding that the resolution was a matter for the law courts, rather than Parliament. They repeatedly asked that the clerks reread their notes on what previous speakers had said.

This kept on until half-past four in the morning when another move to adjourn was defeated. Grenville, who knew that Pitt was in poor health, kept hoping that he would give up and go away; but the Great Commoner, in anticipation of such tactics, had arranged for the use of an adjoining room to which he retired from time to time but was constantly available to the opposition whenever needed. The discussion still dragged on until half-past seven, when everyone was too exhausted to continue.

The debate was resumed several days later when Grenville thought that he had an adroit solution by inserting the word "treasonable" in the resolution. He believed that he had Pitt on the hip by pointing out that the latter had twice used general warrants in time of war. One of Pitt's great gifts, however, especially as a debater, was that he was never afraid of inconsistency or of disavowing his conduct under past circumstances. He conceded that he had twice issued general warrants during his ministry for the seizure of suspected enemies. He agreed that he had done so illegally and was prepared to take the consequences, that he had been willing to risk his head because of "the real exigency of the time". He pointed out that the action of the government in the Wilkes case did not involve any crisis and further that a specific warrant could have been drawn in the first instance. The Parliament in supporting the ministry had voted away its own privileges, he alleged, "and laid the personal freedom of every representative of the nation at the mercy of his Majesty's Attorney-General.

"The extraordinary and wanton exercise of an illegal power in this case admits of no justification, nor even palliation. . . . If the House negatives the motion," he thundered, "they will be the disgrace of the present age and the reproach of posterity; who, after sacrificing their privileges, have abandoned the liberty of the subject upon a pretence that was wilfully founded in error and manifestly urged for the purpose of delusion."

Sir Fletcher Norton, who had become Attorney-General only a few months before, was furious at Pitt's reflections on his office and said that he should regard a resolution by members of the House of Commons no more than he would "the oaths of so many drunken porters". This observation plainly did not sit well with the members of Parliament. There were protests not only from the opposition but from many who were normally on the king's side.

Norton stepped into the argument repeatedly, citing legal cases and observing that general warrants had the prestige of past usage, that the validity had never been debated in the courts, and that persons apprehended had frequently been bailed by the court. Norton, in fact, spoke eloquently and a member complimented him sarcastically on his great talent for being able to hold the attention of a group of drunken porters.

George III became increasingly perturbed at the behaviour of the Commons. He told Grenville that they were "endeavouring to take away every power that was necessary toward carrying on the Government", and to tie his hands in such a manner as must prevent his being able to do his duty.

General Conway, who had spoken against the ministry, had been deprived of his commission in the army; but Grenville told His Majesty that he felt it would be unwise to dismiss more persons upon a question seemingly so popular. The king, in fact, did refrain from extensive dismissals but he continued to hold his ground against the resolution. When Bedford told the king that the opposition now was much elated and felt sure of a change in the ministry, the king said if that was their hope they would find themselves deceived.

George III was partly correct in his prediction, as the affair may be said to have ended in a draw. The opposition did succeed in passing the resolution, but they were unable to follow up the advantage because of Pitt's illness. Without his leadership they were unable to force new issues on the Grenville ministry which was able to survive this one defeat without retiring.

Unfortunately for George III's career and happiness both Grenville and Bute were made of more durable stuff than some of their more agreeable contemporaries. Within two or three years death had removed from the scene men who could have been helpful to the king by widening his understanding and making him more tolerant, instead of jealously keeping him from other contacts which was the policy of Bute and Grenville.

Egremont, who died in August 1763, had been an unselfish friend of the king. Devonshire died in October 1764 at the age of forty-five, a tragic loss. "There's a chapter for moralizing!" wrote Walpole: "but five and forty with forty thousand pounds a year, and happiness wherever he turned him! My reflection is, that it is folly to be unhappy at any thing, when felicity itself is such a phantom!" It will be recalled that Devonshire had been a close friend of the royal family, having a part in the baptism of the baby prince.

True, George III in a fit of temper had dismissed Devonshire from the Court and had struck his name from the list of Privy Councillors, but that did not necessarily signify a permanent estrangement. The king frequently denounced those about him and yet could accept reconciliation, Pitt being the most notable example.

As for removing a name from the list of Privy Councillors, this might almost be termed a favourite indoor sport with George III. As stated earlier, the Privy Council had become primarily an honour society, and membership was at the discretion of the sovereign. George III, who repeatedly was thwarted by one or another official, seemingly found a real pleasure in taking the book which listed the Privy Councillors and literally and physically striking out a name shouting, "Off with his head!" like the Queen of Hearts in *Alice in Wonderland*.

Hardwicke, who had been a solid member of the Pitt cabinet, had died in March 1764. He was Philip Yorke, Lord Chancellor, and first Lord Hardwicke. Waldegrave died in April 1763. Though trusted by George II and briefly a tutor to George III, he was *persona non grata* at Court as long as Bute was around; but Waldegrave had never gone into opposition and, significantly, shortly before his death, Cumberland tried to include him in a new ministry.

Along with the loss of familiar faces, circumstances were working against the young George. The discontent about the cider tax increased. There were protest meetings and resolutions in various sections of the country. Cumberland's negotiations with Pitt in May 1765 had broken down in part because Pitt made repeal of the cider tax one of his conditions. The apple crop had been poor, causing a sharp rise in the price of cider. The public blamed the tax and, absurdly enough, some blamed the shortage on the influx of Scotsmen whom Lord Bute had allegedly brought in to eat the fruits of England.

John Wilkes in France was keeping up a fusillade of correspondence with his sympathizers in England and at the same time building a favourable reputation. In a letter to Temple dated as early as August 2, 1763, he had written, "I trust that a very fair account from Paris will bear testimony to my discretion and reserve, two virtues I find growing upon me." He mastered the French language to the extent that he spoke it fluently and was able to compose *bons mots* which drew the applause of the intelligentsia, such as Diderot and other savants of the time. He was able to introduce his daughter into élite French society, and she had the personality to make lifelong friendships among "the best people". Wilkes also was shrewd enough to avoid any close ties with Bourbon sympathizers or Jacobites, so that there would be no question of his loyalty to the Protestant succession.

The most unfortunate situation, however, which George III now faced was Grenville's introduction of the famous or infamous Stamp Act which was due increasingly to alienate American feeling. Grenville prepared the way for this measure (which ultimately passed Parliament on March 22, 1765) as early as 1763 and did it in the most tactless manner. Whatever theoretical justification might be advanced for such a tax, it was bound to be unpopular.

The shrewd Sir Robert Walpole years before had declined to have any part in such a proposal. "I will leave the taxation of America," said he, "for some of my successors, who may have more courage than I have, and be less a friend to commerce than I am. It has been a maxim with me, during my Administration, to encourage the trade of the American colonies in the utmost latitude; nay, it has been necessary to pass over some irregularities in their trade with Europe; for, by encouraging them to an extensive growing foreign commerce, if they gain £500,000 I am convinced, that in two years afterwards, full £250,000 of their gain will be in His Majesty's exchequer, by the labour and product of this kingdom; as immense quantities of every kind of our manufacture go thither; and as they increase in their foreign American trade, more of our produce will be wanted. This is taxing them more agreeably to their own constitution and to ours."

Grenville, however, thought that the colonies should pay for part of the great war which had brought Canada into the British empire and thus removed the fear of invasion from French Canada. He ignored the fact that General Amherst had raised vast sums from the colonies to help finance the war (some part of which was returned by the British Treasury). Grenville approached the subject primarily as a moral issue, for even he estimated that the tax would yield only £100,000, out of some £2,000,000 revenue which needed to be raised.

In the winter of 1763–1764 Grenville had called in the agents of the leading colonies resident in London, said that he intended to have a stamp tax levied on the colonies by act of Parliament to be authorized in the forthcoming session, that they should acquaint their assemblies at home of this plan so that they might be prepared. He graciously added that if they would prefer to have some other tax equally productive, they could let him know about it.

The colonial legislatures were both surprised and incensed. The colonies frequently had made substantial contributions to the Crown, but these were in response to requisitional letters from the king in council, letters circulated by the Secretary of State as representing the Crown, but not imposed as a right by Parliament.

The assembly of Pennsylvania now passed a resolution expressing willingness to provide funds in the traditional manner, but not through an imposed tax. Other colonies followed suit. Benjamin Franklin, who was agent for Pennsylvania at this time, brought this resolution into the House of Commons, when Grenville was present, and before the Stamp Act had been introduced. Franklin said that he felt sure that more money would be obtained from the colonies by voluntary grants than Grenville himself expected from his stamps.

Franklin described the customary method of raising revenue from the colonies in this fashion: "The occasion was always first considered by their Sovereign in his Privy Council. . . . He directed his Secretary of State to write circular letters to the several Governors, who were directed to lay them before their Assemblies," requesting "such sums as should be suitable to their abilities, loyalty, and zeal." Franklin stated that colonial contributions to the war had been so substantial that for five years in a row the king had recommended to Parliament to return £200,000 a year to the colonies.

He held that by the "constitution" of the colonies, "their business was with the King, in matters of aid. They had nothing to do with any financier, nor he with them; nor were the agents the proper channels through which requisitions should be made.

"It was therefore improper for them to enter into any stipulation, or make any proposition to Mr. Grenville about laying taxes on their constituents by Parliament which really had no right at all to tax them." He denounced Grenville for sending the colonies "a menace that they should certainly be taxed, and only left them the choice of the manner". Franklin pointed out that the Pennsylvania resolution left the door open for raising funds in what he called "the usual constitutional manner", and he questioned whether Grenville made his proposal at the order of the king or even with the king's knowledge.

Franklin's suspicion was well founded. George III in due course was drawn into this issue and ultimately made to appear as the chief villain in the conflict, but Grenville had pursued this course on his own initiative. He introduced the stamp bill on February 6, 1765, and, as stated, it became an act on March 22, but the royal assent was given "by commission", for the king during that period was mentally ill.

The ministry were delighted. They had put the act through with a majority of nearly 250 votes. The opposition at this time was feeble as Pitt still was in retirement, bedridden with the gout, and the Whigs were divided into factions.

18

"MR. GREENVILLE" RIDES HIGH

The Right Honourable George Grenville, prime minister, First Lord of the Admiralty, Chancellor of the Exchequer, and plain "Mr. Greenville" to the king, as George III always called him, enjoyed his new-felt independence to the full as he conferred with his colleagues on terms for continuing his ministry. With the

Stamp Act victory established, with Pitt unable to replace him, and with no other strong man in sight, Grenville believed himself to be the indispensable man. Hence, he threatened to retire and leave George III without a ministry "unless"——

His Majesty on May 21, 1765, instructed Grenville to report to him that evening on certain cabinet matters, chiefly the question of what terms the cabinet would demand as conditions of continuing to serve. Grenville decided to take his own good time in complying.

The meeting of the prime minister and his colleagues was held significantly at the Bedford house in Bloomsbury Square. The great antagonism of Bedford to Lord Bute made it probable that Grenville would continue his policy of trying to eliminate the influence of Bute entirely. Those present included Halifax and Sandwich, in addition to Grenville and Bedford. The evening wore on and Grenville made no move to notify His Majesty until a messenger arrived with a tart note from the king dated "15 min. past 9 P.M." It said, "I am surprised that you are not yet come, when you know it was my orders to be attended this evening. I expect you therefore to come the moment you receive this." Grenville decided that he would do well to report at once. He did so, though only to advise the king that his confreres had not finished their discussions and would meet again on the morrow.

The next day the colleagues met at 10 Downing Street in official session which required the presence of the Lord Chancellor (Robert Henley, Lord Northington), whose daughter Bridget was in the royal household and reportedly a favourite of George III. Northington was not in sympathy with the Grenville group, but he was in the minority.

Following the meeting the ministers went to St. James's and said that they must ask three things. Grenville as prime minister naturally was the spokesman.

First, would His Majesty promise not to consult Lord Bute any more?

Second, would he dismiss Mr. Mackenzie (Bute's brother) from the direction of Scottish affairs?

Third, would he immediately declare Lord Granby to be Captain General of the armed forces?

George said that the last point would be a great affront to his uncle, the Duke of Cumberland, who had been considered for that post, which was currently unoccupied, that the demand obviously was a piece of revenge against Cumberland for having been the king's emissary in trying to persuade Pitt to form a ministry.

In reply to George III's comment, Grenville said insolently that he did not understand why Cumberland was so often at Court.

The king ignored the remark and said, "Are these questions or terms?"

"Questions," answered Grenville.

"But do you mean," said the king, "to adhere to them as *sine qua non*?"

"We do," Grenville replied.

George said that he would give them an answer that evening. Instead of that, however, he sent them a message by Northington agreeing that he would no longer see Lord Bute, that he would dismiss Mr. Mackenzie (though he must somehow recompense him), but that he would not yield to appoint Lord Granby as Captain General. The ministers were not satisfied with that answer and resolved to call upon the king the following morning.

The Lord Chancellor occupied a rather peculiar position in this cabinet. He was part of it by virtue of his office but was avowedly a king's man. He had been a loyal follower of Frederick Lewis and for several years from 1751 had been legal adviser to George. He had been the king's nominee for the Lord Chancellorship and he had no ties of obligation to any Whig, Tory, or Bute faction.

Northington was a handsome man of middle height, rather thin, with a fresh complexion, made the ruddier by excessive drinking in his youth, which had moderated somewhat because he was afflicted with gout. One day he was heard to murmur in the House of Lords, "If I had known that these legs were one day to carry a Chancellor, I'd have taken better care of them when I was a lad."

The duties of Lord Chancellor, aside from his membership in the cabinet, included presiding over the House of Lords, acting as head of the judiciary, and as guardian of orphans and lunatics. Such a post customarily inflated its occupant with pomposity, but not Northington. He was a bluff, noisy man, addicted to swearing, drinking, laughter, and hearty anecdotes.

When the ministers arrived for their second conference they had some new objections. Yielding on the Granby matter, they now demanded the dismissal of Lord Holland (Henry Fox) from the Paymaster's office. This was a piece of personal spite on the part of Bedford, for Fox had been out of politics ever since he had obtained his peerage. In view of his great wealth the Paymaster's office now meant little more than prestige, but to be ousted would appear as a public rebuke.

George III cannily turned to Lord Sandwich, who had been a close friend of Holland for several years and at one time had shared his office suite. "You write the letter of dismissal," said His Majesty. Sandwich, who rarely had feelings of delicacy, declined. The king, however, agreed that Holland would be removed, and he also accepted the dismissal of his friend Lord Northumberland from the government of Ireland.

There was one point, however, which stuck in His Majesty's craw, namely the dismissal of Mackenzie from every post of income or honour. He was willing to waive the salary which Mackenzie enjoyed as the Crown's agent in Scotland, but held that he should continue to have the title of Privy Seal of Scotland which was an honorary post.

Mackenzie had given up a lucrative position to serve the king; and George in turn had promised that he should have the title of Privy Seal for life. The king now said that his honour was involved and he did not see how he could go back on his word.

Grenville replied, "In that case, Sir, we must decline coming in" —in other words, the cabinet would resign.

George in great distress then said, "I will not, on that account, put the whole kingdom in confusion and leave it without a Government at all; but I will tell you how the matter stands; that he has my royal word to continue in office: and if you force me, from the situation of things, to violate my royal word, remember you are responsible for it and not I."

Grenville replied grudgingly and vaguely, "We must make some arrangement for Mr. Mackenzie."

"If I know anything of him," the king answered, "he will give himself very little trouble about your arrangements for him."

George III's estimate of Mackenzie's attitude about his dismissal was correct. Both verbally and in writing the Scotsman assured the king of his loyalty and of his gratitude for past favours. He said that he was relieved that His Majesty had yielded to the ministers; otherwise Mackenzie would have been "in the most disagreeable situation in the world", having distressed the king's affairs.

George Grenville had triumphed as of May 24, 1765, but his conduct proved him to be profoundly inept. He had solid virtues, of the sort that sound best in obituaries, but any person in any circumstance who considers himself indispensable is courting disaster. To humiliate the king was a major error in judgment and a lack of understanding of George III's character. While the king was temporarily dependent on Grenville, his potential weight was great and the public had a deep reverence for the Crown.

George III promptly after this galling experience authorized his uncle Cumberland to explore various avenues, now that aid from Pitt or Temple seemed impossible, whereby some kind of ministry could be found to replace the current one.

Cumberland prevailed on the Marquess of Rockingham to head a new ministry. Rockingham was a man of great wealth, high character, and considerable general influence; but he lacked political experience and did not care for office. The fact that Rockingham consented to serve was a tribute to Cumberland's persuasiveness, but Rockingham alone did not have the capacity to put together a functioning cabinet and hence a little time was required to work that out. Cumberland himself had mellowed since his military days. He was devoted to his nephew, George III, and now agreed to serve in the cabinet as an unofficial representative of the throne. Cumberland and Rockingham completed their slate by July 10, 1765, less than eight weeks after the Grenville victory. The Lord Chancellor had the satisfaction of addressing the following note to Mr. Grenville:

> I have this moment received his Majesty's commands to signify to you his pleasure, that you attend his Majesty at St. James's this day, at twelve o'clock, with the seal of your office.
>
> I am very unhappy in conveying so unpleasing commands, as I have the honour to be, with great respect, etc.,
>
> NORTHINGTON.

When George had authorized Northington to send Grenville the note of dismissal he was secure in the fact that Cumberland had a new cabinet in readiness. Hence the appointment set for noontime on July 10, 1765, was a firm date and the interview was fraught with tension on both sides.

PART III

Maturing Years

19

GEORGE III COMES OF AGE

George III at last came of age when he decided to get rid of "Mr. Greenville". Bute was on the Continent; Pitt had retired to the role of "village philosopher", as he called it; and the princess dowager was beginning to complain that she had no influence over her son any more. Hence Grenville was the only remaining cord that needed to be snapped.

Both the king and his prime minister apparently had a sense of the historic importance of the farewell interview to which Grenville had been summoned, because each wrote a memorandum on the subject, and each seemed to feel a need for self-justification.

The king was very sore over the humiliating way in which the ministry had laid down various conditions, including the banishment of Bute and his brother Mr. Mackenzie.

"Honest men will feel for me," wrote George III to Bute, "and will see that it was impossible for me either as a King or man to bear any longer the usage I met with and that necessity, not choice, has made me take several steps that cut me to the soul."

He reviewed the fact that Bute had been the person who originally had recommended Grenville and said that he had offered the latter "cordial support if he would act firmly and with that deference owed me".

The king did not mention the deceitfulness of the ministers on the regency act, but he did refer to numerous other grievances, including the fact that the cabinets blocked his constitutional right to nominate ministers. He had desired to nominate the late Lord Hardwicke to the administration, to which the cabinet at first agreed, but then opposed "lest it should lessen their personal weight from feeling his great superiority over them".

Grenville, according to the king, had become jealous even of Pitt. Formerly Grenville had urged that the Great Commoner be sought after, "giving him *carte blanche*", but now held that it was "the duty of every honest man to prevent his ever coming into the Administration".

"Whenever the Ministers were fearful of Opposition," wrote George III, "they were very cringing and fawning to me, but whenever released from that dread they gave way to their plans of being masters."

Grenville's self-serving account of his final conference with His Majesty does not contradict George III's memorandum in any essential particular. Grenville's tone was chiefly that of injured innocence, affirming that certain things which the king found obnoxious were the vote of the ministry rather than of Grenville personally.

George III stated that when the Duke of Bedford had offered to resign from Grenville's cabinet a short time before, the king had understood that Bedford was resigning on behalf of all of his colleagues. Grenville replied that he had heard that rumour, but that if he, Grenville, had intended to resign he would have done so personally.

Grenville urged His Majesty to tell him what he had done either by "omission or commission" to incur displeasure.

George III replied that he had found himself "too much constrained", and that when Grenville had proposed anything to him, it was no longer as advice, but what the king was to *obey*.

Grenville "started" at that word and completely disavowed any such attitude (apparently either through self-delusion or hypocrisy). He begged His Majesty to give any instance which could have given that impression. The king promptly obliged and Grenville changed the subject.

The prime minister, evidently seeing at last that his dismissal was absolute, begged the king to scotch a rumour allegedly circulated by Grenville's enemies that he had been ordered to "leave the Seals at the Closet door" without the opportunity of an interview.

George III readily agreed that this of course was a falsehood.

Then Grenville went into a long harangue about his own difficult relationships with Lord Bute and the king said that Bute had had no hand in advising the present change.

In conclusion, Grenville maintained that his service had been attended with great success, even though now found to be unacceptable, and he alleged that the plan of the new administration was "a total subversion of every act of the former . . . most particularly on the regulations concerning the Colonies". He said that he was going to continue to maintain his attitude on colonial policy both in Parliament and out of it and "if any man ventured to defeat the regulations laid down for the Colonies, by slackness in the execution, he should look upon him as a criminal and betrayer of his country".

As a final shot, referring to the new administration, Grenville said that in that new cabinet there were those "whose honour he should be sorry to trust"; and with that he withdrew from the royal presence.

Grenville had shrewdly appraised the incoming administration in believing that the colonial policy of these men would be quite different. The men whom the Duke of Cumberland had assembled stood for either a moderate toleration of individual rights or an active zeal for such rights, both at home and in the colonies.

The Marquess of Rockingham, the new prime minister, was a tall, inarticulate man with a curiously wedge-shaped profile. He had an affection for liberal-minded men, though lacking the capacity himself to advocate a cause effectively.

The two Secretaries of State were the Duke of Grafton for the Northern Department and Henry Seymour Conway for the Southern. The latter was the same Conway who recently had been deprived of his army commission by the king in a fit of temper. Conway was an American sympathizer and related to several of the great Whig families. Cumberland evidently felt that it was advisable to reconcile Conway with the throne. Northington, loyal to the king personally, was a holdover from the prior cabinet but did not carry great weight politically.

Augustus Henry Fitzroy, third Duke of Grafton, at first glance seemed a rather odd choice (though he later became a prime minister), for he was notoriously pleasure-seeking and lazy. He, too, was on the side of human rights. He had supported the cause of Wilkes though disliking the man personally. His mother was the daughter of a former governor of New York and the Jerseys (both under one administration at that time) and the family had colonial sympathies.

His personal life was checkered. The marriage with his first wife, by whom he had two boys, was happy at the outset, but she eloped with the Earl of Upper Ossory. By a second wife he had twelve children. In between these two marriages he supported a mistress, Nancy Parsons, daughter of a Bond Street tailor. She had been the common-law wife of a Jamaica merchant and ended by marrying a viscount. During this period Grafton neglected business while squiring the lady, riding to hounds, and betting at the race track, so much so that Horace Walpole deplored that public affairs were "postponed to a whore and a horse race".

Grafton, however, had his serious side. He was devoted to Pitt. He became a Unitarian, which was quite unconservative for those days, and even wrote tracts on the subject during his later years.

Another man in the group, at this time merely the political secretary to Rockingham, was a red-haired Irishman by the name of Edmund Burke. Burke soon distinguished himself in the House of Commons to the surprise of everyone, especially as he was not born in England and had little, if any, private means. An observer in Parliament wrote that he "astonished everybody with the power of his eloquence, and his comprehensive knowledge in all our exterior and internal politics, and commercial interests. He wants nothing but that sort of dignity annexed to rank and property in England, to make him the most considerable man in the lower house".

The unfortunate lack in this ministry was the fact that its creator, Cumberland, suddenly died. He had loyalty to the king yet sympathized with the newer politicians and commanded their respect. He might have been able to reconcile George III to the new views of the new men.

It was a young ministry. The king, who was now twenty-seven, had been surrounded by men twice his age or older; but Rockingham was only thirty-five, Burke thirty-six, Conway was forty-four, and Grafton was only thirty-four. Cumberland had included the ancient Duke of Newcastle in the sinecure office of Lord Privy Seal, but the doddering old duke took little active part.

Rockingham, without a Cumberland to run interference for him, was unable to have much influence with His Majesty and the ministry startled George III by its wholesale change of policy. It obtained the repeal of the cider tax. It sounded the death knell of general warrants. Though the resolution against general warrants had passed in the Commons, it had been thrown out in the Lords, but now the prohibition against general warrants was enacted into law.

George III secretly instructed Court favourites in Parliament that they were free to vote against measures of which he disapproved, even though they were advocated by his ministry. This was a habit which grew upon the king, which he pursued increasingly, even against his later favourite prime minister, Lord North. That conduct was a facet of his unshakable belief in the personal rule of a king, but it obviously was a procedure inconsistent with the English system of government and caused great confusion.

When the ministry sought the repeal of the Stamp Act and the king privately was against yielding, publicly he took a neutral attitude, for when the Duke of Bedford proposed that modification might be wiser than total repeal the king wrote, "I do not think it constitutional for the Crown personally to interfere in measures which it has thought proper to refer to the advice of Parliament." Nevertheless, he arranged for Conway to send him reports almost daily on the debates in Parliament stating who voted how. He also directed Rockingham to make similar reports.

One of these reports dealt with the vote of the caucus on the king's proposed speech to Parliament. George III had been insulted when the *North Briton* made fun of the fact that His Majesty's address was written for him, but the Rockingham report indicates that it was customarily passed upon by members of both houses before being officially delivered. On this occasion the advance draft was heard by sixty peers and by two hundred in the Commons, and Rockingham wrote, "There is some ground to surmise that there will be an attempt in both Houses of Parliament to add some words."

In spite of the king's restiveness, he was willing for the time being to retain his present ministers, for at least they treated him courteously. The situation in the colonies was getting worse, however. Some of those in Parliament held that the change of ministry had been an evidence of weakness which encouraged the colonies in their rebellious attitude, though others believed that the continuation of Grenville's and the king's "firmness" would have accelerated the difficulties.

It has been said occasionally that the American Revolution was not regarded as important in England, that the sympathizers with the American cause were a small minority, but the evidence does not support that view. Day after day and week after week, as early as 1765, American affairs had a major part in the transactions of Parliament. They were a prominent subject of comment in most of the correspondence of the time and the possible effects of the Stamp Act were of great concern to the commercial elements who suffered from the loss of American trade.

Virginia, as early as May 29, 1765, had voted that Parliament had no right to tax that colony and they based that position on their rights as British subjects which they held were confirmed by their charter. Massachusetts and other colonies passed similar resolutions. Several of the provinces met in congress in New York in October 1765. They formed committees of correspondence and threatened to discontinue use of British goods as long as the Stamp Act remained on the books.

In England, societies of manufacturers, merchants, shipowners, and guilds passed resolutions against the measure and forwarded petitions to the Parliament. Grenville and other proponents of the stamp tax had alleged that these petitions had been obtained "by artifice", that they were propaganda. Rockingham endeavoured to meet the situation by moderation and vagueness, probably hoping that the difficulties would blow over. He did not promise repeal, but took no steps toward enforcement.

This policy incensed Pitt, whose health had improved enough for him to appear again in the House. He said: "I was in town on Wednesday last, saw Lord Rockingham, and learnt nothing more than what I knew before; namely, that the Marquis is an honest and honourable man, but that 'moderation, moderation!' is the burden of the song among the body. For myself, I am resolved to be in earnest for the public, and shall be a *scarecrow of violence* to the gentle warblers of the grove, the moderate Whigs and temperate statesmen."

Rockingham, however, continued with his policy. He instructed Conway to write to the colonial governors to try to use lenient measures, without being specific as to just what was meant. When Parliament met in January of 1766 the speech from the throne reaffirmed the rights of Great Britain to govern, but did not threaten to use force.

When Benjamin Franklin appeared before the Parliament again, this time as a provincial agent for the colonies as a whole, he was treated cordially by the ministry and he in turn affirmed the loyalty of the colonies to Great Britain. He said that the new system of taxation and the Stamp Act were a violation of the right of British subjects to representation and that a conciliatory system beginning with repeal would re-establish harmony. The opponents of the Stamp Act in Parliament were divided into two groups, those who favoured repeal because it was expedient and those who believed in the colonial stand of "no taxation without representation".

Rockingham's reluctance to face the issue was bringing about increasing dissatisfaction and protests were made to the king, asserting need for a change. However, George said, "My own opinion I confess is if possible to keep this Administration," and there was indeed a question as to whom he could turn. As Northington wrote in a letter to the king, "Though I see around me in the world many dwarfs, I see no giant."

20

THE STAMP ACT AS SYMBOL

Grenville had been riding high when he had obtained the passage of the Stamp Act during the illness both of the king and of Pitt. Franklin had made the point that possibly the king had no knowledge that such an act would be imposed on the colonies.

The act, even though it was not enforced in the Rockingham ministry, had become an ever-increasing source of contention between the colonies and the mother country. It became a symbol far more potent than might be expected at first glance. The British Board of Trade previously had made rulings and Parliament had passed acts, such as the duties on molasses, which served the interests of Great Britain at the expense of the colonies. But there was something about the Stamp Act, maybe it was the tactlessness of Grenville or maybe it was an explosive moment in history, which made it the focus not only of the conflict between America and Great Britain, but also in England between those who championed the rights of the individual and the arbitrary attitude of the ministry and the throne.

In America, Patrick Henry had made an address on the Virginia resolutions which has rung down through the ages, declaiming against the injustice of the Stamp Act. Patrick Henry said, "Caesar had his Brutus, Charles the first his Cromwell, and George the third——"

The Speaker interrupted him with cries of "Treason! Treason!"

Henry with a grim smile finished his sentence with the words, "may profit by their experience! If this be treason, make the most of it."

When Parliament convened in January 1766 the ministry was

well aware that the Stamp Act was still the most troublesome issue on the horizon. Pitt had risen from his sickbed and was in attendance. Moreover, he had rented an apartment on Bond Street from the Duke of Grafton which was an indication that he intended to stay through the session. Pitt was unpredictable. In general terms he surely would be on the side of liberty, but no one could forecast just how he would declare himself on any particular stand. Both Rockingham and the throne were edgy, worrying over what position he might take.

The king's address opening the session, which had been approved in advance, was an attempt to satisfy everyone and to avoid any definite commitments, even though Rockingham and Conway had told the king privately that a bill for repeal of the Stamp Act seemed to be inevitable. The wording of the address was vague. Equally vague was the reply of the Commons.

Pitt rose to comment, saying that he had just come to town and was speaking solely for himself without alliance to any party, and asked that the addresses be read again. That was done, and then Pitt said that he commended the king's speech, and also the Commons' reply "as it decides nothing". He felt that this issue should have been faced up to much more promptly, namely as soon as Grenville had been dismissed. He turned to Grenville, saying, "As to the late Ministry, every capital measure they have taken has been entirely wrong."

He then gave qualified approval to the current ministry, conceding that they were men of good character and had been courteous to him, but he could not give them his confidence at this stage, a confidence which must be proved by performance. "Methinks I plainly discover the traces of an overruling influence," he said, indicating that the ministry may have been held back by the attitude of the throne or Bute.

He made it clear that he had no prejudice against Scotsmen, reminding the House that it was he who originally had employed Highland regiments in the British army. They had acquitted themselves valiantly, and he deplored prejudice against them. He said that when Bute retired "it was not the *country* of the man by which I was moved, but the *man* of that country wanted wisdom and held principles incompatible with freedom".

That observation relieved the mind of the ministry as to its own existence. Pitt now had declared himself against Bute as well as against Grenville. Hence the current cabinet was the only group left with whom he could affiliate and they were already sympathetic to him and his measures. Pitt then addressed himself to the act itself and to the views of some persons who felt that it was a point of honour to enforce the act. "If gentlemen consider it in that light," he said, "they leave all measures of right and wrong, to follow a delusion that may lead to destruction.

"It is my opinion, that this kingdom has no right to lay a tax upon the colonies.

"At the same time, I assert the authority of this kingdom over the colonies to be sovereign and supreme, in every circumstance of government and legislation whatsoever. They are the subjects of this kingdom, equally entitled with yourselves to all the natural rights of mankind, and the peculiar privileges of Englishmen: equally bound by its laws, and equally participating of the Constitution of this free country.

"The Americans are the sons, not the bastards of England.

"Taxation is no part of the governing or legislative power. The taxes are a voluntary gift and grant of the Commons alone. In legislation, the three estates of the realm are alike concerned; but the concurrence of the Peers and the Crown to a tax, is only necessary to close with the form of a law. The gift and grant is of the Commons alone."

As to Grenville's claim that the colonies in effect had representation, Pitt said, "There is an idea in some, that the Colonies are virtually represented in this House. I would fain know by whom an American is represented here? Is he represented by any knight of the shire, in any county in this kingdom? The idea of a virtual representation of America in this House is the most contemptible idea that ever entered into the head of man: it does not deserve a serious refutation.

"The Commons of America, represented in their several assemblies, have ever been in possession of the exercise of this, their Constitutional right, of giving and granting their own money. They would have been slaves if they had not enjoyed it. At the same time, this kingdom, as the supreme governing and legislative power, has always bound the Colonies by her laws, by her regulations and restrictions in trade, in navigation, in manufactures—in everything except that of taking their money out of their pockets without their consent. Here I would draw the line."

Pitt temporarily stopped at that point and the House sat silent for some moments, stunned by the vigour of his presentation.

Conway then rose and said that he was in agreement with virtually everything that Pitt had said and that he would gladly have
Pitt accept the leadership of the ministry and would serve under
him (a position which Rockingham already had tried to bring
about). Conway said that he personally would take the responsibility for the delay in notifying Parliament of American troubles as
the earlier reports were vague and uncertain.

"The excuse is a valid one, if justifiable," said Pitt ambiguously,
and without comment on the invitation to join the ministry.

Grenville now sailed into a lengthy defence of the Stamp Act,
citing numerous precedents. However, he weakened his logic by
ill-temper, declaring that Pitt preached insurrection. Grenville
described the Americans as "open rebels" and affirmed that Magna
Charta gave the right to tax the colonies.

Pitt jumped to his feet and tried to speak. Grenville shouted
back at him. The tall, hawklike Pitt and the squat, sturdy Grenville
stood facing each other, each clamouring for the floor, while other
members joined in the shouting until the Speaker called for order.

Pitt said that he merely wanted to finish his thought, but that if
the House objected he did not wish "to transgress against order.
I am content, if it be your pleasure, to be silent".

However, the House resounded with cries of "Go on! Go on!"

"I have been charged with giving birth to sedition in America,"
Pitt then said. "They have spoken their sentiments with freedom
again this unhappy Act, and that freedom has become their crime.
Sorry I am to hear the liberty of speech in this House imputed as
a crime. But the imputation shall not discourage me. It is a liberty
I mean to exercise. No gentleman ought to be afraid to exercise it.
It is a liberty by which the gentleman who calumniates it might
have profited. He ought to have desisted from his project. The
gentleman tells us, America is obstinate; America is almost in
open rebellion.

"I rejoice that America has resisted.

"Three millions of people so dead to all the feelings of liberty,
as voluntarily to submit to be slaves, would have been fit instru-
ments to make slaves of the rest."

Pitt was one of the greatest orators that ever appeared on the
Anglo-Saxon stage. He was aware of all the audiences whom he
wished to win, including posterity. At the moment he saved face
for the members who had voted for the Stamp Act by assuming
that they had been overwhelmed by Grenville's erudite speeches on

law and precedent. Pitt sagely acknowledged Grenville's legal scholarship.

"I come not here armed at all points, with law cases and acts of Parliament, with the statute-book doubled down in dog's ears, to defend the cause of liberty," Pitt said. ". . . I would not debate a particular point of law with the gentleman. I know his abilities. I have been obliged to his diligent researches: but, for the defence of liberty, upon a general principle, upon a Constitutional principle, it is a ground on which I stand firm; on which I dare meet any man."

As to the argument that Britain could and therefore should force the colonies to obey, Pitt said: "In such a case, your success would be hazardous. America, if she fell, would fall like the strong man. She would embrace the pillars of the State, and pull down the Constitution along with her."

The Great Commoner then urged a spirit of toleration, saying: "The Americans have not acted in all things with prudence and temper. The Americans have been wronged. They have been driven to madness by injustice. Will you punish them for the madness you have occasioned? Rather let prudence and temper come first from this side. I will undertake for America that she will follow the example. There are two lines in a ballad of Prior's, of a man's behaviour to his wife, so applicable to you and your Colonies that I cannot help repeating them:

> Be to her virtues very kind,
> Be to her faults a little blind."

Pitt still had not come quite clearly to the point, but he did so now: "Upon the whole, I will beg leave to tell the House what is really my opinion. It is, that the Stamp Act should be repealed, absolutely, totally, and immediately."

That was late in January. The debate rolled on, but the tide was turning toward repeal.

The auburn-haired, tremulous George III during all of this was standing in the wings, so to speak, being pulled and hauled both by the Rockingham ministry and adverse private advisers. As George was later blamed for supporting the Stamp Act, his memorandum to himself in 1766 (the exact date is uncertain) is important. Herein he wrote, "I thought the modifying the Stamp Act the wisest and most efficacious method of proceeding." But if the various factions would not agree to that, he said, "I thought repealing infinitely more eligible than enforcing, which could only tend to widen the breach between this country and America."

His Majesty obviously at this time was open to conciliatory counsel. Conway, desirous of appeasing the Crown and other conservative elements, moved a series of resolutions later known as the Declaratory Acts, which asserted the supremacy of Parliament over the American colonies. The resolutions were adopted by a large majority and aroused little comment outside the Commons. They were virtually unknown in the colonies at this time, for they involved no action and were merely a declaration of principle.

But Pitt and the other pro-Americans kept the Stamp Act issue alive. Burke in January had made his maiden speech for the American cause. Petitions for repeal kept pouring in from all the chief cities of England. Rockingham had told the king that in view of public opinion the Stamp Act should be removed from the books.

George III assured Rockingham that as between repeal or enforcement he favoured repeal and could be quoted to that effect. The prime minister and Conway, thus encouraged, now were able to declare their sympathies publicly and firmly.

In the Commons, Conway on February 22, 1766, at last moved a resolution that the government should bring in a bill for the repeal of the Stamp Act. His relief, his elation at being able to come out in his true colours, were described by Burke, who said, "I stood near him, and his face, to use the expression of the Scriptures of the first martyr, his face was as it were the face of an angel."

To the gratification and surprise of the ministry, the resolution passed by the large majority of 275 to 167, and the actual repeal followed on March 18, 1766. Rockingham in reporting the vote to George III said, "Lord Rockingham cannot nor ought not to disguise from his Majesty the pleasure he felt upon this event as he flatters himself . . . that it is a confirmation that the opinion he had humbly submitted to his Majesty was well founded in point of public opinion.

"The joy in the lobby of the House of Commons which was full of considerable merchants both of London and from different manufacturing parts of this country, was extreme."

2 I

NO GIANTS

Northington was correct in saying that he saw no giants about him, nor did he pretend to be one himself. Indeed he was a pygmy, if a pygmy is smaller than a dwarf, for he had not lived up to his supposed function in the Rockingham administration. He was a king's man, as has been said earlier, and the king's advocate. Cumberland had taken the unusual step of including him in the Rockingham ministry (for normally he would have gone out with the prior ministers) on the assumption that Northington would bring the support of the Crown to the Rockingham group and vice versa. Northington was either unable or unwilling to do anything of the sort. He voted against the ministry on most issues until his colleagues realized that he was not one of them at all and they ultimately ceased to notify him of cabinet meetings.

There were, in fact, just four men of outstanding potentials at that particular time and each at that time had fatal defects. George III by virtue of his office could have used his prestige for moral leadership, but he failed to do so. He was well intentioned and he had shown human traits that commanded sympathy and affection, but he was not prepared to lead the country out of its trying situation.

Lord Bute had power even when out of office because of his potential influence with the king, but his defect was selfishness. He had exploited the devotion of his pupil. He apparently, and of course quite absurdly, had believed that he, though a Scot unfamiliar with politics, could become the chief man in England. It was all sheer selfishness because he might have helped George to mature and administer the royal office intelligently.

The third powerful man was Grenville, full of political knowledge, details of economics, the structure of government, and all that, but we have seen that he had the fatal defect of egotism and insensitivity to the feelings of others. He had no flair.

Now the fourth man in this tarnished galaxy was William Pitt, who in his heyday had flair *par excellence,* a sure instinct for what was both popular and right. Pitt at this point had the weakness of vanity and ill health. The two were linked. Though Pitt always had a driving ego which probably helped him to rise to the top, it had not blinded him to realism as long as he had his health. Formerly, he could accommodate himself to the political machinations and the idiosyncrasies of Newcastle in the days when he, Pitt, was in his great administration.

For example, Newcastle called on Pitt early one day when the latter was in bed. The Duke, who was always afraid of catching cold, found the room chilly, and therefore fully clothed crawled into an adjacent bed where the two ministers discussed the affairs of the nation. Pitt was entirely willing to humour his colleague in this peculiar conference if it would forward the plans of his government. He did not stand on ceremony. Pitt's accomplishments at the height of his career have been described by Edmund Burke:

No man was ever better fitted than Mr. Pitt to be the minister of a great and powerful nation, or better qualified to carry that power and greatness to their utmost limits.

Under him Great Britain carried on the most important war in which she was ever engaged, alone and unassisted, with greater splendour, and with more success, than she had ever enjoyed at the head of the most powerful alliance. Alone this island seemed to balance the rest of Europe. In short, he revived the military genius of our people; he supported our allies; he extended our trade; he raised our reputation; he augmented our dominions.

But now that was all some years back. Pitt had drawn on his own strength unsparingly. Gout and melancholia, which were in part inherited from his father, kept growing upon him. Pitt brooded over the fact that his fellow ministers in 1761 had turned him down and had kept him from pursuing the war against Spain, especially since subsequent events showed that his policy had been right. Though he treated the young king with great reverence he resented the fact that His Majesty had not tried to stop the fall of the Pitt administration. The various appeals of George III to Pitt in the past several years seemingly did not salve his ego, as they obviously had come about only when Bute was at his wits' end as to where to turn. Pitt also was sour at various Whig factions who had failed to defend him from attacks in Parliament which had occurred in his absence, and he was displeased with Temple who no longer was willing to play second fiddle.

All things considered, Pitt was no longer the man who would

re-establish the glory of England. He could and did make several historic speeches against the Stamp Act and for the American position, but he seemingly did not have the strength to take on the full burden of government.

The failure of these four potential giants—George III, Bute, Grenville, and Pitt—to measure up to the needs of the hour tends to refute the "great man" theory of history. The need of England and the colonies cried aloud for a man of adequate stature, but perhaps it was the blessing of destiny that there was no one to be found.

George III was aware of the weakness of his ministry and yet he had learned how foolish he had been to quarrel with any cabinet until he had signed up a succeeding group. Hence he wrote to Northington, "I think if proper vigour is now shown, it will be the only means of preventing those constant changes of administration that have enervated the executive power," and he added, "it is not right to move until one knows what the subsequent step must be."

Throughout the first half of 1766 the American question was debated in both the House and the Lords, with the ministry almost constantly on the American side. However, Rockingham, having taken an equivocal position, did not know how to move off from it in any fashion which would not offend one side or the other. Therefore His Majesty as well as those sincerely friendly to the ministry looked around for a new man, someone who would have Rockingham's approval and yet be more articulate. The decision was to invite the Duke of Grafton to be prime minister, in spite of his devotion to horses, hounds, and so forth.

Grafton, as we have seen, had various charming qualities, in spite of his laziness in politics, and he also had the virtue of humility. He said that he would "use spade and mattock" in the service of Pitt, that he would follow the directions of the Great Commoner without question, but unless Pitt came into the ministry he, Grafton, was incapable of carrying on such a responsibility.

A proposal accordingly was sent to Pitt in his rural retreat and he at last responded favourably. The plan was that Grafton would be prime minister and accordingly First Lord of the Treasury. Pitt would take the job of Lord Privy Seal which involved no departmental work. That office normally was held by a peer and therefore it would be necessary for the Great Commoner to be elevated to the House of Lords.

L

This was done. William Pitt, the Great Commoner, became the Earl of Chatham. Another uproar in the City resulted from this move—similar to the criticism when Pitt's wife had become a baroness and he had accepted a pension; but this time Pitt was too ill and disconsolate for the criticism to have much effect on him or on public policy.

The Chatham-Grafton ministry took charge in July 1766.

22

SCANDAL SINGES THE THRONE

George III in the Stamp Act issue had tried to be flexible. He was willing to go along with repeal if that were necessary, even though his preference was for modification. He had not at this stage in 1766 solidified in his policy of "firmness and resolution" to a degree where his mind was closed to persuasion.

In his personal life, however, his desire to appear as a paragon of virtue was undermined by scandalous circumstances around the throne. Part of the idea set forth by Bolingbroke in *The Patriot King* was that the king would be virtuous, primarily in politics, yes, and personally also. George III, now in 1766, and for the two or three years which followed, had his personal reputation clouded by gossip and also by certain acts of those who had been close to him.

Several of the women in his life were indiscreet, or notorious, or unfortunate, or all three, nor was it possible to conclude precisely in which category certain ones belonged. The women reputed to be, or to have been, closely associated with George were his mother Augusta, Lady Sarah Lennox, Lady Pembroke, Elizabeth Chudleigh, Bridget the daughter of Lord Northington, and Hannah Lightfoot. To recapitulate:

Hannah Lightfoot's supposed acquaintance with George III probably was a reality and equally probably platonic.

Bridget, the eldest daughter of Lord Northington, whose father was a favourite of the king, had the run of the Palace. Hence Wraxall's claim, mentioned earlier, that the king had eyes for her, was a part of the gossip around the throne, though no specific charges were made.

What was the state of Queen Charlotte in all of this? She had had a succession of babies, usually less than a year apart. She also had been instructed to have nothing to do with discussion of government business, and she had virtually no social life apart from official functions.

Charlotte occasionally expressed jealousy of the king's female friends, but that was about all, for there is no evidence that she created any crisis. Why the king compelled her to a cloistered existence is not known, but it may have been his experience with his mother. It will be recalled that his father Frederick had brought Augusta into political discussions, and after he had died Augusta continued to interfere in government, especially in support of Lord Bute. The relationship of those two continued to be a national scandal.

Here again should be reviewed the case of Lady Pembroke, a great granddaughter of the Duchess of Marlborough. She was a Lady of the Bedchamber to Queen Charlotte. By her family connection she was one of the most important ladies of the realm. Her marriage to the tenth Earl of Pembroke could have been a normal affair, but in the mid-'60s, after the Pembrokes had had a child and after he had been spending several years on the Continent as a military officer, he had run off with a Miss Kitty Hunter. At one time, perhaps in his teens as suggested earlier, George III had fallen in love with Elizabeth. Pembroke left Kitty and became reconciled with his wife. Pembroke, despite all this, continued as a Lord of the Bedchamber in the royal household.

Miss Hunter promptly married a man by the name of Clarke. He seemingly was a complacent gentleman, satisfied, for a price it may be assumed, to provide a legitimate name for her. The assumption is reasonable as she very soon thereafter became the mistress of Augustus John Hervey, who secretly was the husband of Elizabeth Chudleigh.

No wonder that scandal singed the throne, and it came nearer and nearer.

Elizabeth Chudleigh, it may be recalled, was a maid of honour to Augusta, George III's mother. Augusta during George's boyhood had condoned various incidents in Elizabeth's behaviour, but many more incidents had occurred since.

Hervey had risen in life since his beginnings as a minor navy

officer. Due to a series of unexpected deaths it seemed probable in
the 1760s that he would inherit the title of Earl of Bristol. If so,
that obviously would make Elizabeth Chudleigh the Countess of
Bristol. With that expectation she took the step of digging up the
papers of her secret marriage and having them verified. Meanwhile
the expected demise of the current Earl of Bristol was delayed and
Elizabeth became mistress of the very wealthy Duke of Kingston.

Augustus Hervey desired to be free to marry again and Elizabeth
desired to be free also. Therefore Augustus approached her with
the idea of their getting a divorce. Divorce was disapproved by the
Church of England and a barrier to the holding of any office about
the Court. Hence Elizabeth did not like the word and she sought
a decree of "jactitation" from the ecclesiastical authorities. Jactitation was the equivalent of annulment.

It was rumoured that Hervey was paid £14,000 for such an agreement. In any case he did not contest the action. It is reasonable to
assume that various sums must have been paid to somebody, for
Elizabeth obtained the decree from the Church tribunal and
thought herself free to marry the Duke of Kingston. She did so
(though she later was tried for bigamy), and was presented officially
at the Court of George III as Duchess of Kingston. Hervey also
attended in the background, saying that he wished to see this
honour paid to his widow.

George III, of course, knew all these persons intimately. Lady
Pembroke continued to live at the Court, and in his later years in
various times of his madness George imagined that he was married
to Elizabeth Pembroke, that she was the real queen and that she
had displaced Charlotte. Elizabeth, who moved in a dissolute,
wealthy society, having many friends who regarded themselves as
above moral restrictions, was notable for her beauty, her serenity
and dignified conduct. Hence while George admired and "burned",
his infidelity probably was only mental.

Sarah Lennox, who might have been queen if George had had
the courage of his heart's desire, had fallen on unhappy days. And
since she was in the very top rank of the social world George's
previous attention to her was well known. She had married a handsome and eligible young man by the name of Sir Charles Bunbury
within a few months after she had been jilted by the king. Bunbury
had been devoted to her after his fashion; but he was primarily a
sportsman, kept a stable of horses at Newmarket, and neglected
her.

She fell in love with a first cousin, Lord William Gordon, had a child by him, and after two months left Bunbury to live with her lover, taking the baby with her. Bunbury for several years after urged Sarah to return to him and always gave the child the protection of his name. Sarah finally left Gordon, but declined to rejoin Bunbury and instead accepted the support of her disapproving brother Richmond. She occupied a modest cottage on his estate and withdrew completely from society. Richmond meanwhile due to political circumstances was a Secretary of State in a compromise cabinet. George was not obliged to see any of his ministry except the prime minister face to face, but the proximity of Richmond was uncomfortable.

Scandal kept coming nearer home.

The king's eldest brother William Henry (Edward had died), five years younger than George, now Duke of Gloucester, had married the widow of Lord Waldegrave. This was obnoxious to George III on two scores: firstly, though Waldegrave had refrained from opposing George III's politics, he had been a particular friend of the grandfather George II and George III had disliked Waldegrave as a tutor. Secondly, the widow Waldegrave was a natural child of Sir Edward Walpole and therefore not only one of the hated Whig connection, but an illegitimate one. Several years later George III moved to have an act passed whereby he could regulate the marriage of his relatives, but it was too late for this one.

Coming still nearer was the continuing gossip about his mother, and she apparently now threw discretion to the winds. Lord Bute came back to London. Even though the king in late 1766 and 1767 adhered to his promise not to see Lord Bute, the Princess Dowager Augusta remained loyal to him. He fell ill in London and every day she sent to inquire about the state of his health and publicly sent him roses and fruits.

All of the Court, all of London society, were aware that the princess dowager still was devoted to Bute. Those who had always believed in the scandal were obviously reinforced. On the other hand, it may be said that she was a lonely woman who had less and less influence over her son and she probably felt that this man who had been her support in his days of eminence was entitled to consideration now.

There was another scandal in the royal family, world-wide in its notoriety and profoundly embarrassing. George III's sister Caroline

Matilda had been married to the king of Denmark, had been accused of adultery and kept a prisoner in Elsinore, Hamlet's castle. This sister was the victim of a plot by the dowager queen of Denmark. The charges at any rate were never proved. George had sent a warship to rescue Matilda who was released without protest by the Danish authorities. Under her brother's protection, Matilda was established in a sanctuary at Zelle in Germany. There she died in 1775 while still in her twenties.

There was a further embarrassment which touched the king himself. George had assured Grenville and succeeding ministers that he would have nothing to do with Bute. That promise had been made as early as 1763 and George had not kept it. He had not succeeded in fooling Grenville or other political wiseacres. At this point, somewhere in the summer of 1766, the king had decided that at last he would break with Bute, who obviously had failed repeatedly as a mentor, and increasingly was a liability. Known records do not produce the letter which George III wrote cutting off all relationship with Bute, but Bute's reply, which was written somewhere around August 1766, is in his published correspondence.

George III evidently had dismissed Bute in the most uncompromising terms. He apparently held the Scotsman responsible for corruption of the Parliament, which, after all, Bute had done on George III's behalf. He accused Bute of ambition and trying to get up a party of his own.

Bute replied, "I protest. I could scarcely believe my eyes when I read this. Is it possible that you should not see the total difference between men setting up to be leaders of a party, for seditious or ambitious purposes, and me?"

Bute went on to say that he would never again be in politics in any way, that he would not ask any men to follow him since he had lost the royal favour, and concluded by assuring George III that he was everlastingly devoted to him. "And thus I end as I began, entreating my dear Prince to forgive me for troubling him with so tedious a letter. . . . I hope . . . it will induce him to believe me . . . devoted to him in another manner than any other man is or ever was in this country."

George III was at last freed from the major personal embarrassment to his reign.

The scandals in and around the royal family added to George III's problems as a monarch, to his compulsions to appear as a strong man. It may be fairly surmised that the moral insecurity about the throne increased George III's determination to take an inflexible stand against the rebellious colonies, a righteous stand according to his dim lights . . . uninformed, lacking in vision, but honestly conceived.

23

THE TESTING OF GEORGE III's DREAM

When the Chatham-Grafton cabinet was formed, it was temporarily the kind of administration without party of which George III had been dreaming. The king at last had been willing to accept the magic name of Pitt at any price in order to have a secure ministry, but he was determined not to be "in the chains", as he put it, of a Whig connection or of any other faction.

Before obtaining Pitt's consent, George had been negotiating with Rockingham and Grafton to form what His Majesty called "a comprehensive administration". He desired Rockingham to write out a list of proposed cabinet officers. The marquess, however, sought to talk the matter over in person with the king before being committed in writing to specific names.

When Pitt's participation was assured, however, George III dropped the correspondence with Rockingham and instructed Conway to send "the usual letters of dismission" to the Duke of Richmond, Newcastle, Rockingham, and other cabinet members who were not continuing under the new auspices. He also said that Mackenzie should be notified that he was being restored to his prior office in Scotland. That was a real triumph for George III and enabled him to look upon his new cabinet with great amiability.

Furthermore, happily for the king, Lord Temple had declined to serve. Temple was willing to agree with Chatham's demand that Grenville should not be included, even though there had been a reconciliation in the family, but he had demanded the right to take part in deciding what persons should be included in the new ministry. When the former Mr. Pitt did not agree to that, Temple declined to serve as a messenger boy and wrote to his sister, Lady Chatham, "I received the proposition of being stuck into a Ministry as a great cipher, at the head of the Treasury, surrounded with other ciphers. . . . I told the King . . . *I would not go in like a child to come out like a fool.*"

In his days as Mr. Pitt, Chatham had declined to form a ministry unless the king would accept Temple as First Lord of the Treasury, on the ground that in the absence of Pitt the First Lord would be the person to have access to the king and to convey Pitt's ideas. Pitt held that he could not trust someone else to undertake that mission.

The situation had changed somewhat since Grafton had come into political prominence. It was Grafton who had urged that the presence of Pitt in the government was indispensable. Grafton, moreover, was steadfast in political loyalty. His devotion to Pitt had been unwavering and continued to be.

The new administration, sometimes called Grafton-Chatham because the First Lord of the Treasury usually was the chief minister, was more commonly referred to as the Chatham administration because of the prestige of the erstwhile Pitt. The situation was somewhat comparable to that of Pitt's great ministry when Newcastle was the First Lord of the Treasury, though actually subordinate to Pitt who then was Secretary of State. Newcastle's main strength then was in his indiscreet control over the House of Commons.

Now, however, Conway, not Chatham or Grafton, was manager of the House of Commons. Hence the power and leadership were divided three ways—Grafton, Conway and Chatham. Chatham, if health had permitted, might have been able to guide the policies and administer the general plan, but his health was continuously feeble and in taking the post of Privy Seal he had avowedly indicated that he could not be counted on for the day-to-day direction of affairs.

These unforeseen developments, such as the refusal of Temple, played directly into George III's hands. He nominally had surrendered to Pitt, but in raising him to the House of Lords the king had weakened that whole family connection and the axis of power was now in his own hands as he had long desired.

George III was thoroughly conscious of the meaning of the new dispensation in conferring the earldom upon Pitt. The king wrote to Chatham on January 29, 1766, "I know the Earl of Chatham will zealously give his aid to destroying all party distinctions and restoring that subordination to Government which alone can preserve that inestimable blessing, Liberty, from degenerating into Licentiousness."

It was true that party distinctions were destroyed in the composition of the new ministry. Burke referred to it as a mosaic, "a tessellated pavement," a mosaic without cement. Chatham though had described it as a ministry of "talents assisted by public opinion".

The roster included Conway, Grafton, and Northington, holdovers from the Rockingham days. Northington, a king's man and a second-time holdover, was moved to the post of President of the Council. Justice Pratt, elevated to the peerage as Lord Camden, replaced Northington as Lord Chancellor. Camden and Conway were staunch Whigs of the old school. There were two newcomers, Lord Shelburne and Charles Townshend.

There was no unifying policy. Shelburne, now twenty-nine years of age, one year older than the king, was added to the cabinet as a Secretary of State. There was a considerable difference of opinion about his character. Some of the Pitt-Chatham admirers have charged him with being an incorrigible liar and thoroughly untrustworthy. On the other hand, the historian Bisset, who lived 1759–1805 and was the author of an extensive history of the reign of George III, refers to Shelburne as "a nobleman of considerable abilities possessing a great extent of literary and political information, a warm admirer and zealous supporter of Mr. Pitt". Shelburne had been active in Parliament, had declined to come into the Bute ministry, had served briefly under Grenville, but had incurred the displeasure of the king by opposing the persecution of Wilkes. He had been out of office for two years and it was not clear just where he stood either as to his loyalties or on issues of the day.

Charles Townshend, the new Chancellor of the Exchequer, born in 1725, was an enigma. He had served in Parliament from 1745 to 1756, but without strong commitment to any faction beyond the fact that he was at times a protégé of Lord Halifax. He was Secretary of War in 1761 and in 1763 President of the Board of Trade. At one time he was friendly with George Grenville, but later opposed him. In 1765 Townshend had succeeded Henry Fox as Paymaster and was quite content to stay there, as the salary was excellent and it was customary for the head of the Pay Office to make considerable sums of money on the side, particularly in pocketing the interest on government funds before they were needed to pay bills. This practice was not regarded as a crime; in fact Pitt had been the only head of the Pay Office to refrain from profiting in this fashion.

The plan of making Townshend the Chancellor of the Exchequer was not at all pleasing to that gentleman. In protest, he sought an appointment with George III and pointed out that his present office had a salary of £7,000 annually, whereas the Exchequer paid but £2,500. He said that the proposed elevation was not his choice and that if he accepted it would only be because of the king's express commands. George III reported the conversation to Pitt (four days before he had become Chatham) and the latter held firm, affirming that Townshend's presence was necessary to strengthen the administration.

Townshend had certain qualifications which could be useful, which recent ministries had lacked. His manner was vigorous and vehement. He was tall and overbearing and talked in a loud voice accompanied by loud laughter. Rockingham had been a notoriously poor speaker, a weakness acknowledged by himself. Conway was an able talker and had a good mind, but he was a gentleman and gracious in manner, whereas Townshend could be a hatchet man for the ministry to shout down opposition in the sometimes rough-and-tumble debates which occurred in Parliament. He was said to have brilliant eloquence, but a lack of sincerity. His fluctuations, however, may have been due to a shallowness of mind and a fondness for devising expedients for their own sake, rather than because of any insincerity.

Bisset describes Charles Townshend at this time as "the most active member of the Ministry" and "taking a lead in the management of affairs. He was a personage of very considerable abilities . . . not, indeed, very select in the measures which he proposed or the arguments that he employed, but extremely happy in the art of giving the best colour to the sentiments and opinions which he happened to adopt". In support of this opinion Bisset pointed out that Townshend had voted for the Stamp Act when it was popular in the House and when it lost its popularity he voted for the repeal. In short, he was "more anxious about the currency of opinions than their weight; he was extremely inconsistent".

The looseness of this "mosaic without cement" soon became apparent. The theory that a ministry having no responsibility to a party would be a docile instrument executing the will of the king proved to be a fallacy. If George III had had more experience he might have been able to pull the group together, but that did not take place. Townshend immediately started plotting against Grafton, aiming to form an alliance with the Bedfords which might result in Townshend's becoming prime minister. The plot did not succeed, but it did upset harmony; and new troubles ensued.

Various conquests in India had been made under the direction of the East India Company who had carried on a series of intrigues with Indian rulers. British military forces had supported the company. Grafton, with Chatham's backing, now proposed that the company should pay an annual rental to the government and that the dividend policy of the East India Company should be regulated by the government to prevent speculation in the company's stocks. This bill was carried, but Townshend and Conway publicly opposed their colleagues. Chatham later held that revenues from the East India Company could have made up the national deficit and averted the taxation issues with the American colonies.

Townshend was rapidly becoming a major troublemaker. As Chancellor of the Exchequer he introduced a bill providing that the land tax should be continued at four shillings in the pound. This was the customary rate in time of war, but it frequently had been three shillings in time of peace; and the public was expecting the reduction. The Parliament rejected Townshend's proposal decisively. This defeat gave Grenville, now in opposition, a welcome opportunity. He promptly moved that the land tax be reduced from four shillings to three shillings in the pound. This motion was carried against the ministry by a majority of 206 to 188. It was the first money bill to be carried against any administration since the abdication of James II.

However, the ministry did not retire, for Townshend came forth with another proposal which he thought would be acceptable to all parties: he introduced a measure to impose new taxes on the colonies. He was aware, of course, of the tumult which had been created by the Stamp Act, but he tried to sweeten the present proposal by saying that the duties when collected would be applied to the support of civil government in the colonies and any residue would be sent to England. The bill proposed imposts on glass, paper, pasteboard, painters' supplies, and tea. The tea tax was made agreeable to the powerful East India lobby, as the measure cancelled out the duties which the company had previously paid in England. This bill was passed during the first half of 1767.

The ministry then introduced another revenue-raising scheme by way of a regulation requiring the colonies to provide certain additional supplies for the troops quartered in their midst. In time of war when the British troops were an asset in defence against the French and Indians the colonies from time to time had voted supplies, chiefly food and shelter. In peacetime the British troops were not welcome; and the new ruling that they must be provided additionally with salt, beer and certain other items was deeply resented. The assembly of New York declined to vote the new levies. In reprisal the home government ruled that no laws of the province of New York would be assented to until the assembly changed its policy.

Throughout the summer of 1767 Townshend suffered from what was called "a putrid fever", probably typhoid, and died on September 2, leaving the nation's affairs in a state of tumult. His participation in the ministry had at least been vigorous, though disturbing, but the shakeup which followed his death left things in a worse confusion than ever. The troubles of George III and his ministers kept mounting. Bisset describes the situation in a gem of understatement, saying, "Wise and liberal as was the policy of our King, which sought to govern by virtue and ability instead of a party confederacy, it had not hitherto attained the merited success."

Wilkes, who had a keen nose for smelling out discontent, now decided from his exile in Paris that the time was ripe for him to clear his name and re-establish his fortune. He had the effrontery to propose to Grafton to seek a general pardon from the king, a gift of £5,000 in cash, and a pension on the Irish establishment. Grafton was dumbfounded and asked Chatham just how he should handle this request, knowing that Wilkes's conduct would be unpredictable no matter what answer was made. Chatham advised Grafton not to reply at all.

It seems unlikely that Wilkes could have expected his petition to be granted, but he chose to regard his neglect as a grievance and took the chance of returning to London while Parliament was in recess. He was greeted by the populace with tremendous enthusiasm. He was promptly tried on the old charges and sentenced to imprisonment for two years. The mob forcibly rescued him from the officers who were conducting him to prison and carried him triumphantly through the streets; but as soon as the mob was dispersed Wilkes prudently surrendered himself to the authorities, lest he be accused of being a party to violence.

Later when the Parliament reassembled, a mob again gathered, thinking erroneously that Wilkes would be allowed to attend Parliament from his prison. The soldiers, unsuccessfully, tried to disperse the assembly. The riot act was read to no effect and finally the soldiers were ordered to fire. Several persons were killed, including a man named Allen who was an innocent bystander. Several days later George III, with the endorsement of the Privy Council, issued "a proclamation for suppressing tumults and unlawful assembly". This added further to the public unrest.

Lady Sarah Bunbury (the former Lady Sarah Lennox), hardly an impartial observer, wrote to her cousin Susan about the general situation. "Are you still politician enough to be eager about the fuss they make with Mr. Wilkes? If you are, I wish you would write an anonymous letter to His M. to advise him not to skulk in his den like—I don't know what, for I must not say what a *pauvre animal* I think him; but it really provokes me to see him so bullied; but you know *we* always prophesied he would never make a figure once he ceased being in our good graces, and *we* never were mistaken certainly. Do you know that he has made his brat [the future George IV] the proudest little imp you ever saw, just like himself."

Chatham now had a nervous breakdown though he was not actually insane. George III offered to waive protocol and call on Chatham at his home. Chatham refused. He reluctantly received Grafton, but seemingly was unable to make any decision either as to policy or appointments.

Northington retired because of ill health. Lord Weymouth and Lord Gower joined the cabinet. They were men of no great consequence, but friendly to the king. A man named Lord Hillsborough was appointed to the new office of Secretary of State for the Colonies, a move which was supposed to relieve the other members of the ministry from that unpleasant responsibility.

The new Chancellor of the Exchequer was a boyhood friend of George III, namely Frederick, Lord North. Conway added to the muddle by expressing the wish to retire.

George III wrote to Conway's brother, Lord Hertford, saying, "Indeed your brother now has it in his power to extricate me out of all my difficulties by lending himself at least for a time to my civil service. . . . If he thinks of his duty it must teach him that he must continue the chief minister in the House of Commons as it will encourage the Duke of Grafton to remain and consequently prevent every evil that otherwise may arise." The king then added that if Conway stayed on for a while His Majesty would give him the command of a "very lucrative and honourable regiment . . . whenever it shall become vacant", and also would create a Secretary of State for America which would relieve Conway of responsibility in that direction.

The general did stay on for a time. That was the circumstance which had led to the creation of the new Secretaryship to which Hillsborough was appointed; but it seems as though whatever was done only created more trouble. Shelburne looked on the creation of a new Secretaryship as personally insulting to him. He had been the one person in the cabinet besides Conway who was sympathetic to the American colonies and accordingly regarded himself as the personal representative of Chatham policies. Offended at this new situation, Shelburne resigned.

Chatham in his illness was prone to magnify fancied slights and he also chose to consider the appointment of Hillsborough as a slap at him.

Then there was a further incident which incensed the Great Commoner, namely the appointment of Norborne Berkeley, Lord Botetourt, to the governorship of Virginia in place of General Jeffery Amherst. Botetourt was a deserving citizen in the eyes of George III. He had been an official in the royal household for a number of years, was a Tory member of Parliament, and had voted steadily on the side of the Court. He had become involved in a copper company which had failed, seemingly through no personal fault of his, and needed to recoup his finances. Botetourt in fact had become involved in this disaster by a William Champion, a senior partner and an over-ambitious Quaker who caused the company to borrow large sums of money against expectations which did not materialize. As he had been a loyal member of the king's friends, George III desired to give him an appropriate reward.

General Amherst, on the other hand, on his return to England had declined to run for Parliament and stayed out of politics entirely. Hence from the political viewpoint he was undeserving. The Virginia appointment had been made in recognition of his conquest of Canada. Customarily the office did not require the governor to be in residence, and the Crown's business in this largely self-governing province was carried on by a lieutenant governor.

If Amherst had been provided with an equivalent compensation, his removal and the appointment of Botetourt would have seemed reasonable, since Botetourt was willing and eager to go to America.

However, the transaction was handled most untactfully. Amherst first heard of the change through rumour. When he went up from his residence in Kent to London to inquire about the matter from Grafton, he was asked if he were prepared to take up residence in Virginia. When Amherst replied in the negative, Grafton said that it was felt that a resident governor was necessary in the colony due to the current unrest and Grafton closed the conversation without suggesting that any substitute reward would be provided for the general.

Grafton's remarks had implied that if Amherst were willing to be in residence he could continue as governor, but the general learned in a few days that Botetourt's appointment had already been officially confirmed at the time of Amherst's conversation with Grafton. The "Junius" articles printed in a Whig-supported periodical and later Horace Walpole (who was skilful as a gossip and character assassin) tried to inflame public opinion by unjustified reflections on Botetourt's reputation. Amherst in this affair apparently was shabbily treated; but the records of Virginia indicate that Botetourt was a worthy appointment.

This incident created an uproar both in the press and in political circles. Though Amherst was not in politics, he had many friends among leading Whigs. Furthermore, he was a military hero, highly regarded by the public. The dismissal of the general was particularly offensive to Chatham, for Amherst had been the commander-in-chief chosen by him, who had achieved the conquest of Canada. This incident, coupled with the treatment of Shelburne, led Chatham to talk of resigning.

That threat threw Grafton into a panic. He went down to Hayes where Chatham was then living to seek a further interview. Grafton was told he could not see Chatham. Grafton then pleaded with Lady Chatham to listen to him for at least a quarter of an hour. He recited various events and problems of the ministry which she promised to convey to her husband.

Grafton's mission, however, was not successful. Three days later Chatham sent him a letter in his wife's handwriting which was courteous in tone, but said, "Though unable to enter into business, give me leave, my Lord, not to conclude without expressing to your Grace that I cannot but lament the removal of Sir Jeffery Amherst and that of Lord Shelburne." And he requested the royal permission to resign the Privy Seal.

The king was incensed and replied to Chatham, "I think I have a right *to insist* on your remaining in my service." George III never seemed to get it through his head, in spite of numerous incidents, that while he had the right to appoint ministers, he could not compel them to serve.

He now had one more proof of that fact, for William Pitt, Earl of Chatham, on October 14, 1768, resigned from the ministry.

24

GEORGE III's WIDER HORIZONS

George III spent so much of his time in correspondence about political affairs and in fussy interference with details of government that his broad interest in the arts and sciences has been obscured. His taste in art, with a few exceptions, tended toward the mediocre, but at least he gave diligent attention to painting, sculpture, and handicrafts, and lent practical financial assistance to those whose work he approved. He was willing to recognize talent even if it originated in the colonies. He showed a strong partiality to Quakers. Two American Quakers who benefited particularly from his patronage were Benjamin West and Mrs. Patience Wright.

Though West never became a member of the Society of Friends, he was born of a Quaker family living near Philadelphia in a house now on the campus of Swarthmore College. He had a special aptitude for representational painting and even as a boy achieved local reputation for his landscapes. He also took up portraiture to a limited degree, and his first commission at the age of fifteen was a portrait of a Mrs. Ross of Lancaster, Pennsylvania. Most of his art, however, was anecdotal, a style which appealed to His Majesty. West painted *The Death of Socrates, The Trial of Susannah,* and various other historical, religious, and classical subjects which rapidly spread his fame.

He moved first to New York and thence to Italy. At Rome he was an object of considerable curiosity since he was the first American artist of note to study there. From Rome he moved on to London where he had introductions to Sir Joshua Reynolds, the leading artist of England. He joined the Incorporated Society of Artists where he made the acquaintance of Robert Hay Drummond, Archbishop of York, who was an ardent amateur painter. Drummond took a fancy to West and introduced him to George III.

The king felt comfortable with West's noncontroversial style of painting, appointed him "historical painter to the Court" at £1,000 a year, and personally commissioned him to paint various scenes for Buckingham House and Windsor Castle. George also commissioned West to do a number of portraits of the royal family.

Possibly West's greatest contribution to the interest of art in Great Britain was his influence in founding the Royal Academy. Sir Joshua Reynolds, as well as West, was a member of the Incorporated Society of Artists. The society, however, became ridden with feuds which led to the resignation of both West and Reynolds, whereupon the society wasted away. The two artists realized that the lack of a strong artists' organization was unfortunate, and West prevailed upon George III to establish the Royal Academy of Arts in London, in 1768.

This was not accomplished without some difficulties, for His Majesty desired West to be the first President of the Academy. West was shrewd enough to realize that an Academy would need the prestige of Sir Joshua Reynolds. Furthermore, West owed a great deal of his initial success in England to the kindness and courtesy of Sir Joshua.

Reynolds, however, was unwilling to accept the appointment without some special sign of favour from His Majesty. He required that he be given a commission to paint the king and queen, and that favour was granted. Reynolds remained at the head of the Academy until his death in 1792 when he was succeeded by West.

The other American Quaker who made an impression on the king was Mrs. Patience Wright of Bordentown, New Jersey. She was the wife of a man much older than herself who died in 1769 leaving her with the support of three children. Except for her husband's death and her need to support a family, her talent for modelling dough, putty, and wax might have remained unknown outside of Bordentown, for she had been modelling ever since childhood without attracting more than local attention.

However, when she needed means of support a neighbour, the famous American painter Francis Hopkinson, gave her important introductions to potential customers who might like to have their

M

portraits done in wax, and she succeeded so promptly that she soon was able to establish a studio in New York. There Mrs. Wright became acquainted with colonial society and received numerous commissions which encouraged her to try her luck in London.

She was an intimate friend of the Benjamin West family through colonial and Quaker connections. He used the younger Wright daughter as a model in several of his historical paintings and it probably was West who introduced Patience Wright to the king and queen. One of her early commissions was a bust of Lord Chatham which after his death was placed in the Islip Chapel in Wesminster Abbey.

Mrs. Wright soon was commissioned to do busts of the king and queen and she claimed to be on terms of familiarity with them, calling them "George" and "Charlotte". Some have doubted this report, but it was consistent with her bluff nature and her upbringing as a Quaker. His Majesty allowed familiar address by Quakers, as he recognized it as a part of their religious belief. Possibly also he enjoyed the change from the excessive ceremony of Court life. The king and queen not only gave commissions to Mrs. Wright, but also came to her studio to watch her work. That, of course, set the fashion and soon Mrs. Wright had as much business as she could handle.

It has been said that she later lost favour with the king by scolding him for his attitude on the American war, and it is known that Mrs. Wright became an amateur spy for Franklin. She was left unmolested, however, and was still in fashion in 1784 when Abigail Adams, wife of the first United States minister to Great Britain, described her as "the queen of sluts", being offended by the hearty kisses which Patience bestowed on both the gentlemen and ladies of the Adams party.

For a time another notable artist, Romney, had patronage from the Court until he became touched with Unitarianism. The fact that Romney was a bitter enemy of Sir Joshua Reynolds made him *persona grata* to George, for Reynolds as the chief portrait painter in England was regarded at Court as too big for his breeches. Reynold's reputation required no support from the king. The same was true of Gainsborough, though all the leading painters of the day had an occasional commission from the royal house. But the more pliant Romney was the more acceptable.

Romney made portraits of several of the persons attached to the royal household, including several of Lady Pembroke. Also he did one of Mrs. Josiah Wedgwood. All this indicated the approval of George.

In spite of Romney's general success, however, he was regarded in some quarters as an eccentric. In 1773 he went to Rome and stayed for seventeen months, studying the painting of the nude. Now this was something rarely done by British painters. The owners of the great houses of London and the country estates paid large sums for the paintings of Rubens and other European artists displaying the human form, but for an Englishman to do that sort of thing was not quite sound.

This attitude was expressed by Romney's son John, a clergyman and a biographer of his father, who disapproved: "There was at that time (in Rome) a young female of fine form who lent herself to artists for hire as a naked model, and by this means supported herself and her mother. Notwithstanding this species of prostitution, it does not appear that her mind was actually corrupt. Her mother always attended her, so that she was never left alone; and as much delicacy and decorum were observed as the nature of the business would admit of. Had the slightest liberty been attempted, it would have been repelled with indignation; so, at least, it was generally understood."

This Roman expedition, added to Unitarianism, dimmed Romney's prestige at the Court.

The king's most favoured portrait artist was Allan Ramsay, a Scot who had done an excellent full-length painting of Lord Bute and had opened a studio in London in the late 1750s. Ramsay had great technical facility and might have reached the stature of Reynolds and Gainsborough if he had not been appointed "portrait painter to his Majesty", a stifling occupation. This honour was conferred upon him in 1767 upon the death of his mediocre predecessor, John Shackleton.

Ramsay, on the other hand, had done some beautiful painting prior to his Court appointment, but from then on his studio became a factory. The royal commissions alone drew heavily on his time, for George III was fond of presenting full-length portraits of himself and Charlotte to those whom he favoured and Ramsay also was called upon to paint others of the royal family.

Wealth and fashion smiled on Ramsay. He had more orders than he could execute singlehanded and hence hired assistants to do all but the heads of the sitters. Perhaps he did not realize what was happening to his creative work, or didn't care, or was unable to escape. George himself was not discriminating and probably felt that he was doing Ramsay a favour by piling work on him.

The king's attitude toward the Royal Academy was evidence of a diligent interest in artistic activity. He personally had supervised the draft of the Academy's Constitution, he had provided free quarters for it in the royal establishment and he made up its annual deficit for twelve years until it was able to operate profitably, a support which totalled more than £5,000. Considering His Majesty's native thriftiness this was support indeed.

George III approved of the arts and sciences, but his judgment was influenced primarily by the attitude of the individual toward royal authority.

In Josiah Wedgwood, the famous manufacturer of ceramics, the king found a comfortable companion. Wedgwood was a highly successful businessman. About 1762 he had been appointed official potter to Queen Charlotte. He was not disturbed by political notions and he deferentially submitted various designs to the king and queen who occasionally paid him the compliment of visiting the Wedgwood studios and works.

George, though not an artist, was a handicraftsman of no small ability and a competent artisan. He was able to take watches apart and reassemble them. He was a maker of buttons. In agriculture he had a green thumb, showing a gift for landscape gardening. Anything that was clearly utilitarian appealed to him. Possibly he appreciated the beautiful designs of much of the Wedgwood pottery, but he was particularly fascinated by its usefulness and by the ingenious manufacturing process invented by Mr. Wedgwood.

Wedgwood was but one example of the creative genius of the era. In 1764 James Watt developed the application of steam to power machinery. In 1767 James Hargreaves invented the spinning jenny applied to the weaving of cotton whereby eight threads could be handled in the same time as one. Then in 1769 Richard Arkwright perfected the spinning frame based upon a cruder attempt by John Wyatt who had laboured thirty years earlier. Crompton then invented the mule jenny and Cartwright the power loom. In the aggregate these inventions virtually displaced hand-weaving and led to the large-scale production of low-cost fabrics which was the start of the industrial revolution. They were an ultimate boon to man, but at the start brought wealth only to a few and led to extensive unemployment. The changes added to the tumults in

George III's reign and there is little evidence that he comprehended their significance, though as a young king he had sympathized with the plight of the Spitalfields weavers.

He understood and encouraged the genius of handicraftsmen. This was the period of three men who probably were England's great designers of furniture: Thomas Chippendale, George Hepplewhite, and Thomas Sheraton.

An unexpectable phase of George's better nature was his toleration of various religious sects, in spite of the fact that the king was titular head of the Church of England. Since he took a personal hand in the appointment of bishops and lesser clergy and was punctilious in examining their qualifications, he might well have thought that any criticism of the Establishment was obnoxious. Nevertheless George not only favoured Quakers, but a variety of dissenters who sought to reform the church from within or without. One of the new evangelists was James Hutton.

Hutton established a congregation at Fetter Lane Chapel in London and became known as the founder of the Moravian denomination in England, an early reformist sect.

When the Wesleys founded Methodism, John Wesley had urged Hutton to join them, but meanwhile the Wesleys had introduced Hutton to Peter Boehler, an eminent member of the Moravian faith on the Continent; and Hutton became converted to them, a fact which estranged him from the Wesleys for many years.

Hutton for a time became one of the most prominent dissenters in England. He was received on intimate terms by the king and queen. He knew Benjamin Franklin and had cordial relations with Lord Shelburne, one-time cabinet member. Hutton's close contact with Shelburne is indicated in the discussion which he had with his lordship on a project to found a Moravian mission in Labrador (a mission which still is thriving in modern times). Shelburne asked: "On what footing are you with the Methodists?" Hutton replied, "They kick us whenever they can."

Later he became reconciled with the Wesleys, but he had long since made his place both in missions on the Continent and in the upper echelons of London. Cosway, a favoured painter of the nobility in the late eighteenth century, painted Hutton wearing his famous ear trumpet. Hutton was a friend of Dr. Burney (father of Fanny Burney) and of the intelligentsia who surrounded them; and he continued to be an intimate of the royal household.

George III's acceptance of various shades of religious belief

among English subjects may be interpreted as a desire to understand the diverse views of his subjects. To the same end, he also
read widely in English literature. He assembled a notable library
at Queen's House. This was in charge of a full-time librarian, a Mr.
Barnard. Samuel Johnson had assisted Barnard in organizing the
library and frequently visited it. Johnson was an ardent monarch-
ist and looked upon the colonials with disdain. Hence he was
doubly welcome at the library and the king asked Mr. Barnard to
let him know sometime when Dr. Johnson was present.

James Boswell is the authority for what took place in the famous
colloquy between Dr. Johnson and the king, a conversation which
revealed a more spacious mind on George's part than he usually
disclosed.

Dr. Johnson was reading by the fireplace in the library when
George III entered the room by a private door, followed by Barnard
carrying a lighted candle. Said Barnard to Johnson, "Sir, here is
the king." Johnson leaped to his feet, surprised, confused, but
greatly honoured. George quickly put him at ease by talking on
subjects on which Johnson was an authority.

The interview was a revelation of the thoroughness with which
the king kept in touch with the intellectual scene even though he
himself was not the philosophic type. He asked Johnson's opinion
of several esoteric magazines including the *Journal of Savans,
Philosophical Transactions,* the *Monthly Review,* and *Critical Review.* He inquired whether Oxford or Cambridge had the better
library (Johnson opined that Oxford did but that Cambridge made
the better use and volunteered that the Bodleian Library at Oxford
was the largest).

George complimented Johnson on his vast learning, asked his
opinion of various scholars and of Lord Lyttelton's *History,* and
said that he would like to see Johnson undertake a literary biography of England. The learned doctor was much flattered and
became a lasting advocate of the king.

George III, in addition to his interest in literary and philosophical matters, had a favourable attitude toward science, "pure"
science as well as mechanical developments. As usual he applied
the political test to his treatment of the individual. Dr. Joseph
Priestley, chief discoverer of oxygen, a Unitarian, and an opponent
of the ministry's American policies, desired to use the royal library.
George III agreed reluctantly, saying, "If Dr. Priestley applies to my
librarian, he will have permission to see the library as other men of

science have had; but I cannot think that the Doctor's character as a politician or divine deserves my appearing in it at all."

In spite of this attitude, the king had some of the milk of human kindness in him, for some years later Priestley was the victim of a riot during a Bastille Day celebration and the mob burned his house including its chemical apparatus and scientific manuscripts. On hearing this, George wrote to the Home Secretary, ". . . though I cannot but feel better pleased that Priestley is the sufferer for the doctrines he and his party have instilled, and that the people see them in their true light; yet I cannot approve of their having employed such atrocious means of showing their discontent."

Students of the flowering of genius in this era may be surprised that it occurred in the reign of George III if they have been conditioned to think of him solely in terms of the American conflict.

George III reigned in the greatest age of exploration for England since Elizabeth I. The conquests under William Pitt had been over lands already settled, rather than exploration. George III deserves credit for the vast territory added to the British empire, fully as much as Elizabeth I does for the explorations of Sir Walter Raleigh and others which led to subsequent colonization. In fact, the area explored under George III was even greater. George III not only approved and encouraged explorations undertaken under his reign, but also defended the explorers from jealousies in the cabinet.

The two chief explorers of this time were the famous Captain James Cook (1728–1779) and the hardly less important Joseph Banks (1743–1820) who was knighted after his major work was done. Close on their heels in accomplishment were Philip Carteret, Tobias Furneaux, and Samuel Wallis.

In 1768 Cook was commissioned a lieutenant by the Royal Society and given command of the *Endeavour* for an expedition to the South Pacific to observe the planet Venus. This was the start of an extraordinary career which, together with that of Banks, planted the British flag in many parts of the globe. On the trip, which lasted until 1771, Cook sailed thousands of miles. He visited Tahiti, charted the coast of New Zealand and the east coast of Australia.

Joseph Banks, fifteen years younger than Cook, accompanied him on the voyage of 1768. Banks had inherited a huge fortune and a large estate; but his great passion was scientific discovery which overruled any desire for ease and safety. He made an expedition to Iceland and was preparing to explore the South Seas when he encountered the jealousy and sluggishness of Lord Sandwich and other officials in the Admiralty. They assigned a vessel to him which he thought was unfit for the purpose. The Navy Board declined to agree and sent a note to George III complaining about Banks's attitude, but George upheld the explorer.

Carteret was among the greatest geographers in history. He sailed through the Straits of Magellan and mapped thousands of miles of hitherto unknown areas of the Pacific. He discovered Pitcairn Island (later occupied by the mutineers of *The Bounty*). He also discovered and named Queen Charlotte's Islands and the Sandwich Islands.

Furneaux, another Cook alumnus, mapped Tasmania and recharted parts of New Zealand while Captain Samuel Wallis sailed around the world and added materially to the knowledge of geography and navigation.

Most of this activity took place in the 1760s with the loyal encouragement of George III as evidenced in various of his letters. He had a keen interest in astronomy, navigation, and the physical sciences. This devotion unfortunately was overshadowed in the public mind by his family troubles and his incessant meddling in politics.

As a result of the work of these explorers and others less well known, the British flag was established in Australia, in New Zealand, throughout most of the Pacific Islands, in the South Atlantic, and in Antarctica.

It is ironic that if George III had not driven the American colonies away from the British flag, his reign might have been known as the Era of Great Exploration.

25

TWILIGHT OF THE CONSTITUTION

Despite the extraordinary display of British genius in the arts, sciences and exploration, the government of the nation had fallen into disrepute, and widespread disorder prevailed in many quarters. George III was largely responsible for the civil breakdown, for it was his stubborn insistence on unwise policies which caused general unrest: a ministry subservient to the Crown, corruption of Parliament whereby large majorities voted under direction rather than by conscience, continued persecution of Wilkes which threatened the liberty of the subject, haughty discourtesy to the officials of the Corporation of London, continued expensive attempts to coerce the colonies.

The chief redeeming feature of the king was his wisdom in foreign affairs on the Continent, for George III, while bullying the colonies, was a distinguished influence in preserving peace in Europe. For whatever reason, the king vented his spleen on the American colonies, possibly because he was continuously misinformed on that situation.

The king's character was continuing to deteriorate, perhaps imperceptibly even to himself. Now, in 1769, he indulged in an orgy of corruption which continued for the next dozen years. He asked Parliament for an increase of £500,000 in the civil list, a fund at the disposal of the Crown for secret service and other undisclosed purposes. At an almost full house of Commons, when 451 members were in attendance, there were 192 who were on the government payroll. The administration held that a man should not be ineligible for a legislative seat by reason of holding a government job. Not all civil servants were king's men but they lived under fear of dismissal if they displeased the Crown.

In addition to the number of placemen-votes were those swayed by cash payments. It was reported that at one dinner 250 banknotes of £1,000 each were distributed. Though the exact statistics may be debatable, the general fact was not denied. George III, the erstwhile purist, appeared willing to wallow in corruption if it would make Parliament obedient to him.

Grafton reluctantly continued as First Lord of the Treasury after Chatham retired and now became publicly recognized as chief of the ministry. He continued in office for about a year, and became an object of widespread abuse heaped upon him by the anonymous *Letters of Junius*. While the fact has not been proved conclusively, it now is generally believed that Junius was Sir Philip Francis. Though Francis held a minor government post, he was a staunch Whig. The Junius letters at this point laid the failures of the throne at Grafton's doorstep, for a minister of the Crown was considered fair game for criticism, whereas to vilify the king might bring a charge of treason.

In this critical era, Wilkes emerged again to agitate the king's men. Though he was jailed for two years on the old charges of libel and pornography, Wilkes ran for Parliament from Middlesex (a constituency lying partly within metropolitan London) and was elected. George III regarded the Wilkes victory as a personal affront to the dignity of his Crown and demanded action by his minions. Accordingly, on February 2, 1769, the government-controlled Commons expelled Wilkes by a vote of 219 to 137. Wilkes was re-elected again and again debarred by a majority of 235 to 89. He was elected a third time on March 16 and on this occasion the Commons, instead of expulsion, declared the election null and void. On April 13, 1769, Wilkes made a fourth try.

Obviously by now the principle had became greater than the man. The freeholders of Middlesex agreed to underwrite Wilkes's election expenses *ad infinitum*. The ministry, nudged by the king, entered a military candidate, a Colonel Luttrel, on the hustings, thinking that his prestige with the support of the Crown would carry the day. Luttrel was endorsed by the most conservative elements, in the narrow sense of Crown supporters. He was defeated by 1,143 votes for Wilkes and 296 for Luttrel. Then the Commons once more called the Wilkes election void and seated Luttrel. It may be assumed that George III momentarily was pleased, for he probably did not know that his brother, the new Duke of Cumberland (the king's uncle having died), was courting Colonel Luttrel's sister, a commoner by the name of Mrs. Horton.

Grafton had had no desire to persecute Wilkes or anyone else. He was one of those occasional accidents of politics which may emerge in any country: a pleasing character, not seeking money or power from his post, friendly in temperament, indolent and not nosey, an ideal compromise candidate. Grafton in his private conscience was much superior to his public repute. He was quite out of sympathy with the measures thrust upon him. He remained a Chathamite, having most of his friends among the Whigs. He had no affection for Tories. He wearied of the abuse brought upon him by the errors of his fellow ministers; and on January 28, 1770, he suddenly and firmly resigned from all goverment employ.

The Princess Dowager Augusta had boasted some years earlier that her son at last was king, but George never had the reins wholly in his hands until the appointment of Lord North's ministry, which immediately succeeded that of Grafton.

North, himself, had some abilities, but most of the cabinet were nonentities or worse. The three Secretaries of State, Weymouth, Rochford, and Hillsborough, were obedient ministers. Halifax, now Privy Seal, owed his career to the Crown. Barrington at the War Office was incompetent. Edward Thurlow, "a thug in robes", was named Solicitor-General. Conway was on the sidelines in the non-political post of Lieutenant-General of Ordnance; and in the joint office of Postmaster-General were those two dissolute alumni of the Medmenham Abbey, Lords Le Despencer and Sandwich.

George III at last had nothing to fear from his new "servants" other than inefficiency. He now could be firm and resolute in tone without fear of opposition or "impudence" within his official family.

That was a new experience for George, as he had endured six administrations in his first ten years on the throne: first, the great ministry of William Pitt, the elder, a man whom the king had distrusted and hated. Then Bute, Grenville, Rockingham. Following that, George had wooed Pitt back to office under the title of Chatham. Grafton was the sixth, and now North. Even that did not tell the whole story, for in the putting together of cabinets and their principal staffmen there had been over five hundred changes in office during the ten years.

Frederick, Lord North, son of the first Earl of Guilford and boyhood playmate of George, was an amiable man. That fact is important to note, for North became a villain in colonial eyes. As in the case of Grafton, it was customary to attack the minister rather than the Crown. North was a charming fellow in the opinion of his colleagues in administration and Parliament, including his political opponents. Said Burke, "He was a man of admirable parts, of general knowledge, of a versatile understanding, fitted for all sorts of business; of infinite wit and pleasantry, of a delightful temper, and with a mind most disinterested," though Burke added that North lacked "something of the vigilance and spirit of command that the time required".

Even allowing for the fact that Burke must have kissed the Blarney Stone somewhere in his career (see his tribute to George Grenville, quoted earlier), there was some substance to his appraisal. North was not personally corrupt, though he understood the machinery of the Exchequer and allowed his friends to purchase government securities on terms which assured them an inside profit. Also, as a career man he was virtually harnessed to the throne in an era when an independent civil service was yet to be developed.

North's income had been chiefly dependent on government employ. He was a relative of Newcastle, who had provided North with a job in the Treasury in 1759 which he held for seven years. North then became a joint Paymaster of the Forces for a year and as we have seen accepted the post of Chancellor of the Exchequer, a relatively poorly paid if elevated position which Townshend formerly had occupied reluctantly.

North lived beyond his income, for he was required to maintain an expensive way of life, especially after he became prime minister. His debts ran into thousands of pounds which George III discharged from time to time.

North was grateful for the king's generosity, yet there was an irony in the situation, for George was never actually solvent in the sense that a private citizen might be. The king's whole income was whatever the Commons might agree on and it was the job of the prime minister, North, to steer the Crown budget through the Commons. The master, George III, paid the servant's debts and the servant saw to it that the master received a substantial wherewithal from the public funds.

Mercantile England was fully aware of the realities. Probably no one was crass enough to refer to His Majesty as a hired man, yet that was the essence of his position, as we have emphasized. His most valuable perquisites did not belong to him if he should abdicate, which he had told Bute he might do in his earliest days of kingship (not that the threat was taken seriously by anyone). The properties which George III used were lavish: St. James's Palace, Kensington Palace, Kew Palace, Windsor Castle, and other public quarters such as Somerset House, but not one was a personal possession.

But to return to the amiability of North before his worries as a prime minister began to mount up: his first impulse was a friendly approach, for he was acutely nearsighted and could not see a hostile expression five feet away. It was as well that he could not see himself clearly in a full-length mirror for his figure had the general contours of a six-months' baby, fat all over, fat hands, supplemented by bulging eyes and thick light eyebrows.

George III and Lord North had inherited a peck of trouble at the outset of the ministry, though in Court circles the team of monarch and prime minister bore the aspect of a honeymoon. The king's colonial policy notoriously had injured trade. The sale of British products to America had declined from an index of 110 in 1767 to 70 in 1768, to 30 in 1769, yet North was unsuccessful in trying to modify the king's attitude.

Petitions poured in from merchants and manufacturers to the Parliament, king and ministry. In the House these complaints usually were "laid on the table" without being answered or even read. Remonstrances on various subjects were delivered to His Majesty by the Corporation of London, which he either left unanswered or rejected in some formal austere prepared response. North occasionally tried to mollify the City by letting their Corporation know that there would be no reply.

What had happened to that one-time apparently gallant young king? What blindness afflicted him that he could not take heed to these ever-growing discontents? A king inevitably is surrounded by yes-men who may conceal the truth from him in a sweetened fog. Perhaps George lacked the fortitude to face unpleasant facts. Perhaps if earlier ministers like George Grenville had been more tactful George III would have been more willing to take strong medicine.

26

A PERIOD OF TRANSITION

On February 8, 1772, the Princess Dowager Augusta died after a lingering illness. Though her influence over George had declined of recent years, he and Charlotte had visited her regularly, and George was determined that the funeral rites should be of a magnificent order, a sharp contrast to the meagre obsequies of his father.

Augusta lay in state for a week, during which there was considerable trouble in making arrangements for the funeral. The first difficulty arose when the Lord Chamberlain, who was Lord Hertford and the brother of Henry Seymour Conway, asked to be excused and to turn over his duties to the Vice Chamberlain. Hertford's daughter-in-law had died on February 11th. He said that his son had made "the anxious request" that Hertford should not appear in public till after the daughter-in-law was buried. "As his petition is founded upon the common practice of the world," Hertford pleaded to the king, "I hope your Majesty will not think him blamable." Hertford added that he had already attended to the matter of drawing up the lists of participants in Augusta's funeral for the king's approval.

George was not in the least moved by Hertford's appeal; why should a death in the family of one of his subjects be an excuse from a duty to the royal family! He directed the Lord Chamberlain to carry on.

Poor Augusta had died as she had lived, with her typical virtues and faults. She had bravely endured cancer for the last several months of her life without admitting even to her children what was wrong with her, and on the very last night of her life she dressed to receive the king and queen and said farewell to them in a casual manner. After her fashion she had been devoted to George III; and she had feared that the dissolute habits of the royal house, George excepted, and its financial troubles, would seriously impair the influence of the throne. She had hoped to inaugurate some reforms.

In the past two years Augusta repeatedly had urged George III to have a royal marriage act passed which would control the weddings of his brothers, sisters and children; also, she had attempted to get her financial house in order. On the latter point she had sought to gain title to properties which she had inherited in Germany, but there were legal entanglements not settled before her death.

When Augusta died her estate amounted to only about £7,500 in jewels and £7,400 in bonds and stocks. Since she failed to leave a will the assets of the estate came under detailed scrutiny. The government had provided her with an income of £64,000 a year, but seemingly most of that was required to keep up the appearances of a palace occupied by the princess dowager, with all of the carriages, horses, servants, and other expenses related to that position.

George III named Lord North as executor of Augusta's estate. The king directed that the valuable jewels, after they had been properly appraised, should be sold at Christie's. His sisters and brothers were given the opportunity to select any family mementos (which he described as "trinkets"), such items as miniature portraits and semi-precious jewellery, before these were offered on the market place. Certain furniture and china which had come down to George from his father he decided to retain for himself unless there was some evidence that it was needed to satisfy indebtedness. The final proceeds of the estate, when all debts and fees were paid, were negligible.

Augusta's plan to control the purity of the family by a marriage act had a lasting influence, if not for morality at least for defining the limits of royal matrimony.

George III's brother Henry, Duke of Cumberland (the same who later married the sister of Colonel Luttrel), was involved in an amour which cost the king the round sum of £13,000. Cumberland had seduced the wife of a Lord Grosvenor, who was something of a rake himself and did not mind destroying his wife's reputation if he could make some money in the process. Grosvenor had brought suit against Cumberland and had won a verdict of £10,000 plus £3,000 in costs. Cumberland appealed to his brother Gloucester; and the two of them went to the king, saying they had no resources to pay any money of that size and what should they do.

George III then wrote to Lord North imploring him to find the money somewhere, presumably in the expense account of the Crown, as he felt that if the debt were not satisfied it would undoubtedly be brought to public attention and be highly embarrassing to the royal family. North quietly provided the funds which took care of that scandal.

The next exploit of young Cumberland was to carry on an intrigue with the wife of a wealthy timber merchant. In this case the husband was rather flattered by the attention paid to his spouse and the three of them were frequently seen in public society.

It was after these two and other adventures that the sister of Luttrel, Mrs. Horton, cast her eye on the prince. She had beauty, wit and was a skilful dancer. Her long eyelashes were famous. She had inherited considerable money from her late husband and she had no intention of being just a plaything of Cumberland. She involved him in marriage and kept him there.

George III was so infuriated that he forbade the couple admission to the Court and sent word to foreign ministries and other socially eminent folk that any attention paid to the Duke and Duchess of Cumberland would be offensive to him and would incur the penalty of being barred from the royal presence. There was an irony in that edict, considering George III's pious public attitude. When Cumberland had been an adulterer and a seducer, even though his peccadilloes were costly to the Crown, he was not banished from the Court, but for the prince to marry a commoner was to put himself beyond the pale.

George III besought Lord North to apply himself with all speed to the passage of a royal marriage act. During most of 1772 that was the chief subject which agitated Parliament and Court circles. The king demanded the right to approve all marriages of the royal family including all descendants of George II, as well as George III's brothers, sisters and children. After much debate in Parliament these provisions, with a few exceptions, were enacted into law.

Though harassed by family problems and bullied by a series of ministers, George III in the first decade of his reign had had a considerable influence on the peace of Europe. Anyone who would judge George III solely by his bungling policies toward the American colonies, toward whom he was a would-be tyrant, would hardly picture him as a prince devoted to peace. Yet George from the time of his accession to the throne was an influence for peace under various trying circumstances. He continued to be so through the early 1170s and virtually until the outbreak of the American war. Indeed he did not look upon his "punishment" of the colonies as a war until it was too late for him to recede gracefully.

After the Peace of Paris in 1763, George "meddled" for peace successfully on the European scene with a skill worthy of Elizabeth I and suggestive of her tactics. Like Elizabeth he kept both his ministers and foreign powers in confusion as to England's intentions. Though his "meddling" habits were offensive and disturbing to the stability of British internal affairs and to the colonial situation, yet his policies kept England out of European conflicts for more than a dozen years. Indeed if he had left American matters alone, George III might have gone down in history as a shrewd pacifistic ruler. His position as nominal king of Hanover, the British subsidies to Prussia and other German states and George's numerous royal cousinships on the Continent gave him an international voice over and above that of the British Foreign Office.

George III's handling of the international tensions in Europe in the early 1770s gave evidence that he was no longer an amateur in world politics. He proved to be a skilful operator whose diligent attention to affairs of state, backed by a widespread intelligence service, was reaping its rewards.

Prior to 1773 the king of Denmark had accused George III's sister of adultery. George had sent a navy vessel to rescue her, but did not declare war, and Denmark remained quiescent. Early in 1773, Prussia and Denmark formed an alliance against France. The Russian fleet meanwhile was attacking the Turks and despoiling both French and Spanish trade in the Mediterranean.

Consequently George III was in a forceps. As an ally of Russia, England was supposed to attack France if the latter became belligerent in any direction. Yet the king obviously was hostile to Denmark, was jealous of Prussia (who had never been a reliable ally) and mistrusted Russia. The chief problem was to keep France quiet. France had scheduled a "promenade" of her fleet, obviously for warning purposes.

The first step was a public declaration of policy, to be followed by action if need be. On April 6, 1773, the king wrote to Lord North, "The speaking out is the best method. . . . I think a firm language will prevent the Court of France from taking the step that alone seems to oblige us to take a part." George was somewhat optimistic on that score, though he learned through the secret service that the French were not eager for a fight. Firm language alone would not have been enough.

On April 20, 1773, the king ordered all the available navy ships to be manned and "always ready for immediate service". He added, "That will, I am persuaded, prevent many wars, for by that means we have over 20 large ships ready before the enemy can equip one; consequently, about the start of three months, which is an immense advantage in all military operations."

The firm stand of George III accompanied by the show of navy strength accomplished the desired result. Within a few days the French ambassador to England announced that his government had countermanded the proposed assembly of its fleet and hoped that England might do the same. Hence a major crisis passed which was not renewed until France joined forces with the American colonies about five years later.

Since George had been so adroit in handling this ticklish European crisis, why was he so insensible to American affairs? A prime cause was the misinformation which was fed to him. Persons reporting to the king and ministry and others returning from the colonies described the Americans in low terms. Even the lamented Wolfe had referred to the provincial soldiers as "the most contemptible, cowardly dogs that you can conceive".

N

Unfortunately those who were in a position to have the ear of the Crown were the least qualified to make an unprejudiced report. An American scholar who has been able to track down the personal history of numerous loyalists who rejected the American Revolution found that about seventy per cent were employees of the Crown. They were the governors, clerks, judges, tax collectors, clergy and vicars (not dissenters), various others whose pay came from England. Obviously it was no disgrace to them that they were loyalists, as almost none had their roots in the colonies.

The significant figure in this study was that fewer than six per cent were planters. The planters were the chief Englishmen of the Southern colonies. This survey was made in South Carolina. The percentage of loyalist planters probably was even less in Virginia where George Washington was a planter, as was Thomas Jefferson, and so was Patrick Henry on a smaller scale.

Nearly all Americans at that time were men of the land. The majority did not have the wealth or social status of a George Washington, but they had a New World citizen status which was impregnable. Many had come over as bond servants who after five years under their contract received fifty acres of land, tools and £50 capital. These were proud, independent men who had worked for their freedom, and would allow no one, king or government, by theory or force, to take it from them.

Further, the colonial shipbuilders, whalers, importers, storekeepers, bankers, who reaped their major income from enterprise, also were holders of real property. George III, aware of the perilous lot of the English tenant farmer and the London rabble, failed to realize the stalwart foundation of the American attitude. The Americans were owner farmers, country squires, men of property all the way up the line to the equivalent of landed peers. Most importantly, the majority were English freemen and their neighbours, German, Swedish or Dutch, had imbibed the same doctrine of the right of self-rule. They would not and could not be made to submit to an authority from across the seas in which they believed they had no voice.

PART IV

Ordeals of a Tyro Tyrant

27

THE GATHERING STORM

George III had been so occupied with the minutiae of politics, the dispensing of jobs, the troubles in his family, that he was seemingly unaware of the growing alienation of the American colonies. In the ten years preceding the battle of Lexington a long string of resistances had taken place. The king had steadily favoured various acts designed to punish the colonies and had shown no interest in conciliation.

It will be recalled that the colonies had resisted the Stamp Act so violently that the tax was repealed. However, the repeal was accompanied by the offensive Declaratory Resolutions which affirmed that Parliament had the right to tax the colonies even though not doing so at the moment.

"No taxation without representation" became the American slogan and the principle was heartily concurred in by Chatham, Burke, and others of the opposition. The ministry held the somewhat ingenious theory that Parliament had the right to legislate for the entire empire, and that there were numerous sections of the population at home as well as abroad which did not have direct representation in the House of Commons or the Lords. For example, only men of property could vote and there were certain counties which had no representation. The inference was that the colonies were not a special case and therefore had no grounds for complaint. This indifference of the administration and the Crown to the colonial complaints was a continuing source of irritation to the Americans.

Indeed George's attitude was worse than indifferent. He had championed the Townshend Acts of 1767 which put a tax on tea and other products. The House of Representatives of Massachusetts sent a circular letter written by Samuel Adams urging the other colonies to take action against the Townshend duties. The British government then sent an order to various colonial governors to dissolve any assembly which approved the circular. Several had already done so, including Virginia. Their assembly accordingly was dissolved, but met informally and by retaliation drew up a non-importation, non-consumption agreement which was adopted by other colonies also. Most of the Townshend Acts were repealed, but George III insisted that the tea tax be retained.

Before the acts were repealed an incident occurred in Boston which created furious resentment among the Americans. This was the so-called "Boston Massacre". Two regiments of British regulars had been stationed in the city, presumably to protect the governor "from the hands of a trained mob", as he expressed it.

The citizens deeply resented the presence of the military and the soldiers were jeered at from time to time, provoked with abusive language, and pelted with oyster shells. On a snowy night of March 5, 1770, a mob gathered around the barracks daring the soldiers to fire and threatening to kill the sentry. The soldiers did fire, killing four persons and wounding several others.

The soldiers undoubtedly had considerable provocation. When they were placed on trial for murder, John Adams and Josiah Quincy, who were ardent colonial patriots, nevertheless defended them and secured the acquittal of all but two who were convicted of manslaughter and branded on the hand. In spite of the acquittal the incident had an inflammatory effect up and down the land which was increased by a cartoon by Paul Revere depicting the redcoats charging and firing on a civilian mob.

The next violent incident occurred on June 9, 1772, when the British warship *Gaspée* was anchored in Narragansett Bay near Providence. The *Gaspée* had been sent there to enforce the revenue acts against smuggling. Smuggling was notoriously popular in the colonies and many a fortune was made through bringing in rum from the West Indies without paying tariffs. The colonies did not oppose these import duties in principle, but as they were imposed by the British government they were highly unpopular and enforcement was difficult.

The *Gaspée* had run ashore while pursuing a merchant ship suspected of smuggling. A party of well-armed citizens from Providence numbering sixty-five crept up in the night in eight boats and took the crew of nineteen by surprise. The attackers put the crew ashore and set fire to the vessel, completely destroying it. The identity of the raiders never was revealed and hence no one ever was punished for the crime. The chief significance of the affair was to give the colonies a taste of victory and to prove that force could repel force.

The next dramatic incident occurred on December 16, 1773, the famous Boston Tea Party. The tax on tea had been a continual irritant, and in May of 1773 the statute had been revised to give a virtual monopoly to the East India Company. The tax had actually been lowered slightly with the idea of sweetening the tariff in the eyes of the colonists, but it was regarded as highly offensive, for it took retail sales of tea away from the local merchants to the profit of the East India wholesalers.

Hence when three ships loaded with tea arrived in Boston harbour the captains were warned not to try to land their cargoes. Groups of citizens took turns keeping watch at the various docks around the clock. Then one night a body of men totalling about a hundred and disguised as Indians swooped down upon the ships and threw 342 chests of tea into the harbour. In retaliation the king approved closing the port of Boston and revising the constitution of the province of Massachusetts in a series of orders known as the Coercive Acts.

This action, which gave rise to the first Continental Congress and a determination on the part of the colonies to unite for their defence, was a personal policy of the king who regretted that he had been so easy with the colonies hitherto. George wrote to Lord North on February 4, 1774, saying that he had been conferring with General Gage who had recently returned from America but was willing to go out again if he could direct coercive measures. Gage thought that four regiments would be "sufficient to prevent any disturbance". He advised that the colonists would act like lions as long as the government behaved like lambs. On the other hand, "if we take a resolute part, they will undoubtedly prove very meek". This was the same Gage who had neglected to advance from Niagara in the Canadian campaign.

At this juncture George thought that the behaviour of the colonies had justified his attitude toward them. "All men seem now to feel that the fatal compliance in 1766 [repeal of the Stamp Act] has encouraged the Americans annually to increase in their pretensions to that thorough independency which one state has of another, but which is quite subversive of the obedience which a Colony owes to its mother country."

In that one sentence George seemingly had a glimmer of what might lie ahead.

28

THUNDER ON THE LEFT

"Among the notionable dictes of antique Rome was the fancy that
when men heard thunder on the left the gods had somewhat of
special advertisement to impart. Then did the prudent pause and
lay down their affairs to study what omen Jove intended."

Such was the observation of Sir Eustace Peachtree who lived
about 1640, in his *The Danger of This Mortall Life*; but like the
cryptic oracles at Delphi there was room for at least two interpreta-
tions of the "thunder on the left", one by George III and the other
shared by the opposition in Parliament and the colonies.

The drastic measures demanded by George under the title of
Coercive Acts included abolishing (or attempting to abolish) the
town meetings which had been a characteristic of free government
in New England. He also proposed that the judges, council members, justices of the peace, and all other officials be appointed by
the Crown. He advocated that persons indicted for violence and
armed resistance should be sent to England for trial, and he appointed General Gage as Governor of Massachusetts with both civil
and military authority, which in effect established martial law.

One other measure was greatly resented in the colonies, particularly New England, the passage of the Quebec Act which received
the royal assent on June 22, 1774. The Americans were quite unjustified in attributing the Quebec Act to the tyranny of George
III. The measure was intended to placate the French Canadians
who were a large majority in the province. Though the Crown
appointed the governor, the general laws and customs of the French
system were continued. They had been tentatively authorized by
General Amherst in the terms of capitulation and further recognized in a proclamation by the home government in 1763. In respect to civil and religious rights the Quebec Act merely gave
formal legal status to conditions already in existence.

George III in agreeing to leave the French Canadians undisturbed
in their religion was consistent with his attitude toward Quakers
and other dissenters, though he later disapproved of Catholic
relief laws in Ireland. The freedom-loving Americans should have

praised George for approving the Quebec Act and might have done so if they had not already been stung to fury by the oppressions visited upon them.

The French civil system did not comprehend trial by jury, habeas corpus, or elected assemblies. Though these were three practices dear to the Britishers there was no attempt to impose them on Quebec. To do so would have been profoundly difficult and foreign to the majority of the French-Canadian population at that time.

Both Pitt and some colonial leaders agitated against the Quebec Act because it gave formal approval to non-British procedures and to a religion supposedly debarred by the king's coronation oath. The real sticking point, however, was not in these philosophical arguments but in the fact that under the Quebec Act the authority of the province was extended to all eastern Canada. Further, the physical boundaries were extended westward to the upper Mississippi and southward to the Ohio, thus attempting to contain the American colonies to eastward of the Alleghany Mountains.

Understandably the American colonies regarded the new power and territory conferred on Quebec as wholly obnoxious, but it could not dispassionately be regarded as a grievance against the king. George made the effort to keep Canada within the empire by a highly generous recognition of Quebec interests; and his policy proved successful. Unfortunately for him, he did not exhibit a similar understanding toward the provinces south of Canada.

George, even in his own cabinet, did not have full support for all of his punitive measures against the colonies. Lord Dartmouth who had the cabinet office of Secretary for the Colonies[1] wrote the required instructions to General Gage, and Dartmouth put the entire responsibility on the king and Parliament.

Parliament had passed a bill for closing the port of Boston, and the Treasury Board had voted the necessary directives; but that purely legalistic procedure had not satisfied George III and he had instructed Dartmouth to spell out the situation precisely.

Under those orders, the Secretary advised Gage that "the sovereignty of the King . . . over the Colonies requires a full and absolute submission. His Majesty's dignity demands that until the submission be made the town of Boston where so much anarchy and confusion have prevailed, should cease to be the place of residence of its governor".

---

[1] Hillsborough had voluntarily resigned from that office as he, too, was out of sympathy with Crown policy.

Therefore the Secretary further instructed Gage to remove his administration and the General Court of Massachusetts to Salem, until the king instructed otherwise. Dartmouth also said that if it were apparent that the local courts would not convict offenders of certain specified crimes the only choice was either to transport them across the seas for trial or not prosecute them at this time, for "an ineffectual attempt would only be . . . disgraceful to government."

Dartmouth was not at all happy in his instructions and before many months he was replaced as Colonial Secretary by Lord George Germain, the former Sackville who had been cashiered for insubordination at Minden. Germain was a perpetual toady to the king and encouraged George III in his suppressive measures.

However, Dartmouth was in charge in the present crisis and on March 14, 1774, the king wrote a testy letter to Lord North saying that he had had a conference with Dartmouth who was in favour of a change in the charter of the Massachusetts Bay colony, but did not favour trying colonial offenders in Britain. Dartmouth thought that perhaps trying them in Nova Scotia might be a compromise and that the culprits could be punished adequately by barring them from holding any provincial office in the future. George refused to accept the suggestions.

Those who were not George III's minions drew quite other inferences from the "thunder on the left". They were greatly worried as to where the arbitrary actions of the king might lead. Horace Walpole wrote to Horace Mann (February 2, 1774): "There is an ostrich egg laid in America where the Bostonians have canted 300 chests of tea into the seas, for they will not drink tea with our Parliament."

Chatham, writing to Shelburne, on March 17, 1774, said, "I am extremely anxious about the measures now impending with regard to America, and I consider the fate of Old England as being at stake not less than that of the New." Chatham disapproved of the Boston Tea Party and various other violent demonstrations in the colonies, but held that the first step should be to demand payment for the tea before imposing the various drastic penalties. He said: "The whole of this unhappy business is beset with dangers of the most complicated and lasting nature."

Seemingly, Chatham understood the "thunder" best, for the next event in the drama was the action which took place on the Common at Lexington, Massachusetts, April 19, 1775.

During the spring the province had assembled a considerable quantity of military stores which were deposited at Concord, a town which by the roads of that day was about twenty miles from Boston and about five miles from Lexington. General Gage determined to send a body of troops to capture or destroy these stores. The colonial militia in the area were warned of the approach of the British troops by several messengers, including Paul Revere on his famous ride. The redcoats in turn realized that the countryside had been aroused because of the firing of guns and the ringing of bells. Hence Lieutenant Colonel Smith in charge of the British detachment ordered his men to fan out over the countryside and secure the bridges and different roads leading to Concord. A considerable body of the king's troops arrived about five in the morning at Lexington where they saw about ninety of the colonial militia assembled on the village green.

What happened next always has been a matter of dispute. Witnesses on both sides agreed that the British officers asked the provincial militia why they were there and ordered them to disperse. It was said by some that the colonists immediately retired in confusion behind a stone wall, into the meeting-house and other buildings. According to the British claim, the Americans then fired upon the redcoats from behind their protections and the latter fired back killing several and wounding others. The colonials insisted that the British had fired first and therefore the Americans were simply acting in self-defence.

Regardless of who fired first, the behaviour of the militia went considerably beyond mere defence. During the Lexington engagement other British troops had destroyed the military stores at Concord. Since the object of the expedition had been accomplished the British detachment at Lexington was ordered to retire. On the march back to Boston they were pursued by the provincials who kept firing on them from concealed situations.

Benjamin Franklin and others spoke proudly of the affair. Franklin wrote exultingly to the scientist Joseph Priestley, on May 16, 1775: "You will have heard, before this reaches you, of the march stolen by the regulars into the country by night and of their *expedition* back again. They retreated twenty miles in six hours."

This first battle of the Revolution was regarded by the Americans as a great victory of their militia over trained regulars. The event stirred the spirit of all the colonies. The report from Gage to

Amherst, however, was inclined to minimize the affair which he referred to as "a little action near Boston on April 19th. . . . Nobody would believe in this country, and I find you had all imbibed the same faith, that the people would put their threats in execution of resisting with arms. . . . I did not expect they would ever have attacked so considerable a force as was sent out . . . and indeed they took the advantage the country affords to undisciplined numbers to harass troops."

The action at Lexington did not appear to arouse the king's ire as much as had the Boston Tea Party and other early acts of defiance. There had been a few British casualties and the regular troops had been put in a poor light, but no one of consequence had been killed, which was an important point in the aristocratic society around the throne.

However, at Bunker Hill near Boston there was a second battle of far more serious proportions, on June 17, 1775. By this time top-grade officers of the British Army were in Boston, together with 3,400 rank and file. In addition to General Gage were Generals Sir William Howe, Clinton, and Burgoyne.

Bunker Hill was located on the Charlestown peninsula opposite Boston. Though there was an inlet separating the two places they were within cannon fire of each other. The immediate purpose of the colonial army was to contain the British troops within Boston. With that in mind they had devised the plan of fortifying the hill, placing large cannon on it (which could drive the ships of war to the lower part of the harbour and permit colonial bombardment of the city). They made a breastworks on all sides, strengthened with strong railings taken from the fences in the area. They also stationed troops in various buildings of Charlestown which served as improvised fortifications. Virtually all of this elaborate task had been accomplished during the night of the 16th and the British were not aware of it until the following morning.

The British were virtually obliged to attempt the destruction of this colonial fortification which would be a constant threat to their security and a focal point for any large-scale attack.

It fell to General Howe to direct the assault and he has reported on it in convincing detail.[1] The British were handicapped by their conventional ideas of warfare and undertook to carry the fortification by direct attack. In this the British infantry were at a great disadvantage as they were obliged to move from lower

---

[1] In official dispatches to the Home Office.

ground to the higher position of the fortifications, trying to climb the breastworks under heavy continuous fire. Their formations kept falling into disorder because of the number killed and wounded.

Burgoyne was ordered by Gage to stay in Boston at the main camp, but Clinton was allowed to come to the aid of the Howe forces with fresh troops which ultimately enabled the British to turn the tide and drive the rebels off.

It was a victory, but as Howe said in his report of the battle, "The success is too dearly bought. . . . I come now to the fatal consequences of this action—92 officers killed and wounded—a most dreadful account. I have lost my aide-de-camp Sherwin, who was shot through the body and died the next day." Even though it was still early summer, Howe opined, "We can do no more this campaign than endeavour to preserve the town of Boston, which it is supposed the rebels mean to destroy by fire or sword or both."

Howe through most of his career exhibited a sympathy for the American cause, but for a time after the battle where so many of his friends had been killed he was full of bitterness and said, "The intentions of these wretches are to fortify every post in their way, wait to be attacked at every one, having their rear secure, destroying as many of us as they can before they set out to their next strong situation." This was, of course, a shrewd appraisal of what the American strategy would be. It was a concept of the natural advantages of the American situation which George III seemed unable to comprehend.

Burgoyne likewise admitted the wisdom of the American strategy, saying, "Their retreat was no flight; it was covered with bravery, and even military skill, and it proceeded no farther than to the nearest hill, where a new post was taken, new entrenchments immediately begun, and their numbers affording constant relief of workmen, they continued working night and day."

The king, however, was merely at the beginning of his long stubborn pursuit of the American war. On July 26, 1775, he wrote to Lord North, "I am clear as to one point: that we must persist and not be dismayed by any difficulties that may arise on either side of the Atlantic; I know I am doing my duty and therefore can never wish to retract."

29

"A KIND OF DESTINY"

George III became increasingly stubborn in his insistence that the colonies must submit before any attention could be paid to reconciliation. The battles of Lexington and Bunker Hill merely served to stiffen his attitude in his instructions to General Gage.

The king also reaffirmed his policy in a note to Lord North: "The die is now cast, the Colonies must either submit or triumph. I do not wish to come to severe measures, but we must not retreat; by coolness and an unremitted pursuit of the measures that have been adopted I trust they will come to submit; there is no inclination for the present to lay fresh taxes on them, but I am clear there must always be one tax to keep up the right, and as such I approve of the Tea Duty . . ."

However, the hint that there might be some leniency had virtually no conciliatory effect, for the king conspicuously revealed himself as the power behind Lord North's ministry when on August 23, 1775, he issued "A Proclamation for Suppressing Rebellion and Sedition."

The proclamation charged that the disturbances had been fomented "by dangerous and ill-designing men". It also said that such rebellion was promoted and encouraged by traitorous correspondents. It affirmed that "all our officers civil and military are obliged to exert their utmost endeavours to suppress such rebellion and to bring the traitors to justice".

George's manifesto also appealed to loyal subjects to be informers, "to disclose and make known all treasons and traitorous conspiracies which they shall know to be against us, our Crown and dignity [George was always touchy about his dignity]; and for that purpose that they transmit to one of our principal Secretaries of State, or other proper officer, due and full information of all persons who shall be found carrying on correspondence with or in any other manner or degree aiding or abetting the persons now in open arms and rebellion . . . in order to bring to condign punishment the authors, perpetrators, and abettors of such traitorous designs."

Obviously, such a proclamation could only widen the breach between the mother country and the colonists. In the face of these threats, submission by the leaders of the Revolution would be equivalent to suicide.

Though the king's ministry now commanded ample majorities in Parliament, that did not necessarily reflect the sentiment of the public, for the royal control had been achieved by a ruthless exercise of rewards and punishment. George III had come a long distance from the days when he dreamed of being a virtuous Patriot King.

There still were able men in Parliament who opposed the policies of George III toward America, realizing that his measures were a threat to the liberty of the subject in old England as well as in New England. There were at least six eminent men who continuously championed the American cause: Richmond (who never forgot the affront to his sister, Lady Sarah Lennox), Rockingham, Chatham, Shelburne, Burke, and Charles James Fox. These men also had certain lesser followers such as John Wilkes, who had by then become almost respectable, and Wilkes's friend, Isaac Barré.

Even before the king's proclamation many of the leading men in America had become convinced that independence was the only feasible solution. For a time the colonials had called the redcoats "ministerial troops", rather than the king's troops, in the hope that these persecutions could be laid at the door of Parliament and the ministry, rather than of the king. Thereby His Majesty might have the opportunity to intercede. But the proclamation had put an end to that hope.

The agitation in the colonies had been carried on by diverse groups, by the Sons of Liberty, debtors, Tom Paine, and miscellaneous riffraff who hoped to benefit by the overthrow of the British authorities; but the cause had been led by various of the chief men in America, such as George Washington and Benjamin Franklin, who were well positioned and risked their fortunes and lives in this defence of the freedom of the subject.

George Washington won such outstanding fame as a military commander, as the first President of the United States, and as "the Father of his Country" that his position as a political philosopher prior to the Revolution has been largely overlooked. As early as July, 1774, he was counselling armed resistance to taxation, to the Boston Port Bill, and other oppressions. More cautious souls were in favour of further petitions to Parliament. Another suggestion was to decline to pay the large sums owing to British merchants, looking to them to put pressure on the home government.

Washington was against each of these measures. Like Chatham, he held that a first step of the ministry in dealing with the Boston Tea Party should have been to require restitution of the loss to the East India Company. The fact that Massachusetts was punished without being given an opportunity to pay for the tea dumped in Boston harbour seemed to him an evidence of hostility of the British government toward the colonies.

"Is there anything to be expected from petitioning after this?" he wrote to a friend of his, the future and last Lord Fairfax. "Is not the attack upon the liberty and property of the people of Boston, before restitution of the loss to the India Company was demanded, a plain and self-evident proof of what they are aiming at?"

Washington did not sympathize with the idea of withholding payments due to British merchants, "for I think, whilst we are acccusing others of injustice, we should be just ourselves; and how this can be, whilst we owe a considerable debt and refuse payment of it to Great Britain, is to me inconceivable."

However, Washington was convinced that the time for compromise was past. "Shall we . . . whine and cry for relief, when we have already tried it in vain? Or shall we supinely sit and see one province after another fall a sacrifice to despotism?"

He held to the position of "no taxation without representation" and in writing to Fairfax he used virtually the identical words of Chatham on this point, saying, "I think the Parliament of Great Britain have no more right to put their hands into my pocket, without my consent, than I have to put my hands into yours."

The King and Lord North showed no sign of relenting. The port of Boston remained closed. George III did not realize that Lexington was no temporary skirmish, but the first action of an inevitable war. The Second Continental Congress assembled at Philadelphia on May 10, 1775, now resolved to take concerted military action.

George Washington at this time was a colonel and had had experience in protecting the western border against Indian attack. Because of his military knowledge, because of his eminence as one of the first citizens of Virginia, and because of his deep and articulate conviction of the justice of the American cause, he was unanimously elected Commander-in-Chief to raise a Continental army and direct its campaigns.

The Congress also voted him a salary of $500 a month. Washington, however, declined to take any salary, saying that "No pecuniary consideration could have tempted me to accept this arduous employment, at the expense of my domestic ease and happiness. I do not wish to make any profit from it." He said that all he would accept would be his expenses, of which he would keep an exact account.

He was aware of the momentous nature of the task ahead and said to the Congress, "I beg it may be remembered by every gentleman in this room, that I, this day, declare with the utmost sincerity, I do not think myself equal to the command I am honoured with." But since it was the will of the Congress, he assented, promising "to exert every power I possess in the service and for the support of the glorious cause".

George III, rusticating at Kew Palace, might well have trembled to learn of the appointment of that other George across the seas, for Washington was the greatest asset the colonies had and was due to come down in history as one of the most notable generals of all time. The king, however, was concerned with other troubles. He had just received word of the death in Germany of his sister, Caroline Matilda, the ex-queen of Denmark. George III was occupied with making arrangements for the Court to go into mourning.

General Gage in Boston had his own worries. He was thoroughly alarmed at the development of American events and saw that he now faced the inescapable necessity of carrying on a war. He sent word to the ministry that he would need fifteen thousand men for Massachusetts, another ten thousand men to fight in New York, and seven thousand men to be posted along Lake Champlain. He also called for an augmentation of the fleet, including flat-bottomed landing craft, as he heard that the colonials were fitting out numerous ships in various places. "I see no prospect of any offers of accommodation," he said, and therefore he issued a proclamation of martial law.

Meanwhile, George Washington, who was in Philadelphia, wrote to his wife, who was home at Mount Vernon, telling her that he must proceed immediately to Boston to build an army there. Washington was deeply devoted to his wife Martha, whom he called "my dear Patsy". He assured her that he had by no means sought this appointment and had wished to avoid it, not only because of his unwillingness to part from her and the family, but also because of its being a trust which he felt was too great for his

o

capacity. He said that he enjoyed more real happiness in one month with her at home than he could find elsewhere in "seven times seven years".

Even though Washington had a sincere doubt of being equal to the task, he also had a sense of its inevitability, for in this letter to his wife of June 18, 1775, he wrote, "It has been a kind of destiny that has thrown me upon this service. . . . It was utterly out of my power to refuse this appointment without exposing my character to such censures as would have reflected dishonour upon myself, and given pain to my friends. This I am sure could not and ought not be pleasing to you and must have lessened me considerably in my own esteem."

General Gage at this point seems to have been the only principal character in the conflict who foresaw that he was entering upon a considerable war, though possibly he had called for the large number of extra troops and ships because of a temperamental caution which had been typical of him throughout his career. George III had no concept of the difficulties ahead. He still clung to his "firmness and resolution" and believed that after suitable "punishment" the colonies would submit. Washington, too, apparently thought it would be a short war, ending favourably for the colonies, for his letter to his "dear Patsy" said, "I shall rely therefore confidently on that Providence which has heretofore preserved and been bountiful to me, not doubting but that I shall return safe to you in the Fall."

Though these sentiments may have been written in part to allay Martha's fears, Washington's statement was not without reason. As a military man he knew that Great Britain would need to make extraordinary efforts to achieve a victory over the colonial forces. He knew that several of the leading officers in the British army, such as General Amherst and the Howe brothers, were sympathetic to America and were well aware of the difficulties that would be involved. He knew the attitude of Chatham and his chief colleagues who had powerful influence even though currently they were outvoted in Parliament.

All in all, it seemed reasonable to expect that a substantial show of force by the colonies would lead soon to an equitable settlement. But what George Washington apparently did not realize was the incredible stubbornness of George III.

30

LAST PHASES OF THE COLONIAL ERA

When General Washington wrote to Fairfax expressing the opinion that there was no further point in petitioning the Crown he had moved ahead of some of his prominent colleagues.

John Adams, though a stout advocate of colonial rights, believed that there was still a possibility of reconciliation. On June 10th, 1775, he wrote to Moses Gill, one of his chief political colleagues, "I find the general sense abroad is to prepare for a vigorous and defensive war, but at the same time to keep open the door of reconciliation—to hold the sword in one hand and the olive branch in the other."

Thereupon when some of the members for the Congress drew up a second petition to the king, which was especially championed by John Dickinson of Pennsylvania, the document became known as "the olive branch petition". It was signed by only forty-six members, not including Washington or Patrick Henry. The petition arrived in England late in 1775, obviously after the king had issued his Proclamation of Rebellion, and it was never officially received. George had established the general policy of refusal to receive any petitions from Congress. There had been speculation in some quarters that if the King had actually seen the "olive branch petition" he might have been moved by it to accept reconciliation, but his proclamation had made any compromise impossible.

Even before Lexington the spirit of resistance had been flaming high in the colonies. In 1765 Patrick Henry had made his famous "Give me liberty or give me death" speech. In New Hampshire in 1774 a small group of patriots captured Fort William and Mary at Newcastle and seized a supply of powder. In June 1775, the governor was forced to flee. In January 1776 New Hampshire established a provisional government and on June 15, 1776, the assembly declared for complete independence. The attitude of Virginia was paralleled by Maryland on July 26, 1775, when that state created "The Association of Free Men of Maryland" who were organized for defence. Though clear-cut irrevocable independence was not yet official colonial policy, it was clear that the trend was inevitably in that direction.

In May 1775 there was a convention at Charlotte, Mecklenburg County, North Carolina, which drew up documents pointing toward independence and forwarded them to the three North Carolina representatives in Congress. Mecklenburg has claimed to be the first area to declare for independence, but its action was robbed of any immediate effect because the chairman of the North Carolina delegation still had hopes of a peaceful settlement and suppressed the papers which had been sent him from Charlotte.

Throughout the thirteen colonies scores of towns voted unanimously for independence. For any single town to take such a stand, regarded in terms of modern communication, might seem futile if not silly; but the king and ministry had in effect made war on Boston, a community of only sixteen thousand. General Gage with his regular army troops was having difficulty in inflicting "punishment" there and Boston was on the seacoast. The towns were for the most part isolated, largely self-governing. To subdue Charlotte alone, for example, in its inland location would have been a major operation for the Crown.

Since the colonies were largely agricultural, the towns and town meetings were vital generators of opinion. Vermont was not officially a colony, for there was dispute as to whether its lands, known as the Hampshire Grants, belonged to New Hampshire or New York. Nevertheless the towns and countryside in that area were valiant for independence and fought as stoutly as any colony when the Revolution came.

Early in 1776 resolutions of independence began popping up on all sides. North Carolina on April 12, 1776, supported the earlier sentiments of Mecklenburg by authorizing their delegates in Congress, *in concurrence with the delegates from the other colonies,* to vote for independence. Though the king probably was unaware of North Carolina's disaffection and might not have cared about a single instance coming to the support of Boston, in less than a year the fever of independence spread and was infecting all the colonies.

On May 4, 1776, the Rhode Island legislature severed all ties with Great Britain. The enabling act declared that obligations between the home government and the colonies were reciprocal and that allegiance was no longer due to the Crown. It declared that all commissions for offices should henceforth be by the sole authority of the "Governor and Company of the English Colony of Rhode Island and Providence Plantations". It provided that the law courts would no longer be called the king's courts and that no instrument should be dated in respect to the year of the king's reign. Moreover, the conclusion of the minutes of the General Assembly of the province, instead of the customary "God Save the King", said "God Save the United Colonies". In the spring of 1776 the New Hampshire assembly declared for unqualified independence.

In South Carolina at the opening of the session at Charleston on April 23, 1776, the Chief Justice said, "It is my duty to declare the law, that George the Third, King of Great Britain, has abdicated the Government, that he has no authority over us, and we owe no obedience to him." That wording was significant. The colonies initially had been disposed to blame the Board of Trade, various of the cabinet, and the Parliament; but now George was rapidly becoming the villain of the conflict; as in fact he was. He had sought the leading role and it was his.

It is pertinent to recite the acceleration of events, for as George came to know more about them he became stiffer in his "firmness and resolution" and more determined in his policy of repeated punishment of offenders. Which colony was the first "offender" was not really significant for the several revolts occurred at almost the same time.

Virginia offended on May 6, 1776, when the House of Burgesses met at Williamsburg and voted that "since the ancient constitution had been subverted by the King and Parliament of Great Britain" they dissolved the session unanimously. Connecticut on June 14, 1776, instructed its delegates to the Continental Congress to favour independence and a permanent union of the colonies.

During these crescendos of revolt throughout the colonies George III acted like an amateur chief of staff rather than as the ruler of a kingdom. His letters to Lord North are full of military minutiae but without the concept of any grand plan. In a letter of April 1, 1775, he opined that General Gage might recruit officers for his staff from persons now resident in America, but George was not to give them equal status with those of the regular army. For example, they should not be entitled to half-pay upon retirement, though they could be compensated by grants of colonial lands.

Meanwhile George worked on his own plan for conciliation of the American colonies, quite drastically different from the ideas of

Burke, Chatham, Fox, or Richmond. The drafting of the document occupied much of the first half of 1776, for even the king's close advisers tried to modify his attitude; that was particularly true of the Howe brothers who were to act as commissioners of the Crown in presenting the royal proposals to the American leaders.

General Sir William Howe was the senior military officer of the British forces in America and his brother Richard Lord Howe was admiral of the British fleet stationed there (both were younger brothers of the Lord Howe who had fallen in the assault on Ticonderoga). The Howe family were close friends of the Lennox, Fox, and other Whig connections. They had considerable sympathy for the American position, were well qualified to act as peace emissaries but naturally desired to present a realistic document which would have some chance of acceptance and there were many erasures in the final paper which was sent to the Howes as a basis for discussion.

Even with modifications, however, the king's proposals were preposterous. The basic principle was that George would issue a general pardon, in return for repentance and submission by the colonies and their leaders. Rhode Island and Connecticut in particular must be punished for their declarations of independence—their charters were to be completely abrogated in favour of new ones to be determined by His Majesty.

The punishment of these small two colonies was intended to be an example to the large provinces so that they might seek pardon before it was too late. Though the other colonies could retain their charters, there was to be imposed a third chamber in colonial legislatures responsible solely to His Majesty. Before the proposed pardon would be granted, the colonies must disband all revolutionary troops, surrender all forts and other army posts, restore all officials who had been appointed by the Crown, require local assemblies to vote obedience, and disband all societies which had encouraged revolution.

General Howe opened negotiations by writing to Washington in the latter's capacity as a private citizen, as the king would not recognize the existence of Congress. Howe requested a conference but Washington declined, as he had not been addressed in his official status as an officer of the Continental Congress. Howe then sought an audience by sending an agent with a verbal request for a meeting.

Washington waived protocol to the extent of agreeing to a talk which would be merely a personal conversation. General Howe yielded to that demand and met for an informal discussion. Here Washington torpedoed the proposed terms of "conciliation" by going immediately to the heart of the matter. He said that the basis of the commissioners' instructions apparently was to grant pardons, an attitude which was unacceptable. The colonists merely had asserted their rights, had committed no fault, and therefore no pardon was in order. That position left General Howe flat-footed, for all his other proposals depended on the initial principle.

Admiral Howe then tried to negotiate with Benjamin Franklin who temporarily was back in Philadelphia after numerous visits in England. As Franklin had been a colonial agent in London, had numerous English friends, especially Lord Chatham, the admiral had reason to think that Franklin might be less rigid than George Washington. Franklin knew at first hand of the warm regard of the Whigs for the American colonies, with the exception that they did not approve of the idea of separation from the mother country. The admiral, however, was doomed to a sharp disappointment.

Franklin replied in terms which rocked on their heels the Howe brothers, Lord North and George III himself. Franklin was prepared to discuss peace on the condition that Great Britain acknowledge the independence of America, that Great Britain would defray the expenses of the war to date and would indemnify the colonists for the burning of their towns.

Thenceforth the North administration, directed by the king, determined on a full-scale war against the colonies to bring them to submission by the sword.

31

GAUNTLET AT PHILADELPHIA

George III more than any other single force may be given credit for the decline of royalty and the rise of the republican form of government. The Declaration of Independence adopted at Philadelphia on July 4, 1776, has been famous for its philosophy of government and its statement of the rights of man. The Declaration, however, would never have come into being but for the injustices of the king; and the bulk of its text was directed against George personally. The words were so stirring and the indictment so provable that George's reputation was ruined then and there and the good that he accomplished in various directions was permanently obscured.

George had brought the accusations upon himself by his Proclamation of Rebellion which he said had been drawn up "by and with the advice of our Privy Council". However, the Privy Council as stated earlier was chosen by the king, principally from among his strong supporters, together with the chief officers of the cabinet, the archbishops, the Bishop of London, princes of the royal family, certain judges and others. Since any councillor could be stricken from the list by the king, the body was primarily the master's voice.

The colonial leaders described in the proclamation as traitors were virtually forced into rebellion and independence and to destroy if possible the prestige of the king. Considering the situation in the world at that time, the task called for extraordinary boldness. Monarchy was the accepted form of government throughout the world. England had adopted a constitutional monarchy the conditions of which were notably irksome to George, but after the unhappy experience with the dictatorship of Oliver Cromwell, Great Britain was not disposed to abolish royalty as such. Hence such a decision by the Continental Congress in July 1776 was a novel and exceptional step.

Conceivably the Congress could have invited some other member of the royal family to be their king under an agreement similar to that by which the Hanoverians had been called to the British Throne and it is perhaps rather surprising that Congress did not do so. (Later there was talk of asking George Washington to serve as king, but he wisely rejected the idea). The Congressional leaders concentrated on the misbehaviour of George III as the focus of attack.

On that fatal day, July 4, 1776, the Continental Congress assembled at 9 A.M. The meeting was in the State House of Pennsylvania (later called Independence Hall). John Hancock of Massachusetts presided. The delegates from the thirteen colonies had met in continuing sessions since early June to consider how best to resist the oppressive treatment they had endured from the

British Crown. The chief business of the day was to pass upon a draft of a declaration of independence. The need for some definitive statement was imperative. A hostile British fleet was in New York harbour less than one hundred miles distant. There had been intermittent warfare between colonial and British troops ever since the clash at Lexington.

George had no idea that this was to be a dramatic moment in his career. On that day the king merely attended to minor official activities. On July 4 he was engaged in raising several of his henchmen to the peerage: Lords Lisburne, MacDonald, Westcot, Ongley and Templetown, none of them persons of great consequence and little known since.

The committee on drafting the Declaration consisted of Thomas Jefferson of Virginia, Benjamin Franklin of Pennsylvania, John Adams of Massachusetts, Robert R. Livingston of New York, and Roger Sherman of Connecticut. At least the first three of these men were widely read in political philosophy and the history of nations. All five had experience in governmental office. Jefferson, who was known to have the most skilful pen, was chosen to write the basic draft.

The ideas, however, were a composite of the accepted thought of various writers who had supported the constitutional rights of free men. The most notable influence, even in respect to certain wording, was that of John Locke, the English philosopher. Locke's *Treatise on Civil Government* was a justification of the British "Revolution of 1688" which had deposed James II.

The members of the Congress were men of distinction in the various colonies. Here was no rabble, no hastily conceived gesture of defiance, but a decision and documentation which had been a long time in forming. Now that the decision was at hand even the weather was auspicious. The temperature reached a peak of 76°. Only fourteen times in the 135 years of available weather records for Philadelphia has the thermometer stayed that low on July 4th.

While the weather was pleasantly cool in Philadelphia, the atmosphere at St. James's Palace was right chilly, registering 62°, and perhaps significantly the wind was recorded "from the southwest, fresh."

After a few minutes of routine business Benjamin Harrison was called upon to read the Declaration for the consideration of the Congress. Benjamin Harrison was a huge man, fifty years of age, ruddy-faced, with an imposing manner. He had frequently been the Speaker of the Virginia House of Burgesses. He was a fit choice to present this document to the assembled delegates.

The preamble discussed the rights of man and the function of government, including the immortal words:

We hold these truths to be self-evident, that all men are created equal, that they are endowed by their Creator with certain inalienable rights, that among these are life, liberty, and the pursuit of happiness. That to secure these rights, governments are instituted among men, deriving their just powers from the consent of the governed.

Harrison then came to the indictment of George which formed the main body of the document. It is significant that there was little reference to Parliament beyond the comment that "our British brethren . . . have been deaf to the voice of justice and of consanguinity". It will be recalled that a very substantial element in Parliament had supported the colonial position and it was no secret that Lord North and his servile majority in the House of Commons were tools of the king. (George, egged on by his mother and Lord Bute, had determined to rule and now was the day of reckoning.) Benjamin Harrison read the words of the various charges which were unequivocal.

"The history of the present King of Great Britain is a history of repeated injuries and usurpations, all having in direct object the establishment of an absolute tyranny over these States. To prove this, let facts be submitted to a candid world."

The document made a long series of charges:

He has forbidden his Governors to pass laws of immediate and pressing importance, unless suspended in their operation till his assent should be obtained; and when so suspended, he has utterly neglected to attend to them.

He has called together legislative bodies at places unusual, uncomfortable, and distant from the depository of the public records, for the sole purpose of fatiguing them into compliance with his measures.

He has obstructed the administration of justice, by refusing his assent to laws for establishing judiciary powers.

He has made judges dependent on his will alone, for the tenure of their offices, and the amount and payment of their salaries.

He has erected a multitude of new offices, and sent hither swarms of officers to harass our people, and eat out their substance.

He has kept among us, in times of peace, standing armies without the consent of our legislatures.

"He." The repeated use of "he", rather than a royal title, was a calculated insult, emphasizing that George was no longer regarded as sovereign.

He has combined with others to subject us to a jurisdiction foreign to our constitution, and unacknowledged by our laws; giving his assent to their acts of pretended legislation:
For quartering large bodies of armed troops among us:
For protecting them, by a mock trial, from punishment for any murders which they should commit on the inhabitants of these States:
For cutting off our trade with all parts of the world:
For imposing taxes on us without our consent:
For depriving us in many cases of the benefits of trial by jury.

Tucked in the midst of these charges was a protest against the Quebec Act, though not naming it as such. Neither did the protest refer to the religious section, perhaps out of deference to the prominent Catholic statesmen in Maryland. It charged the king, however, with "abolishing the free system of English laws in a neighbouring Province, establishing therein an arbitrary government, and enlarging its boundaries so as to render it at once an example and fit instrument for introducing the same absolute rule into these Colonies". It was the one clause in the Declaration which was an unjustifiable attack on George III. Doubtless the drafters thought it would appeal to their champion, Pitt, who had tried to make the Quebec Act a political issue in Parliament.
The charges continued:

For transporting us beyond seas to be tried for pretended offences:
He has abdicated government here, by declaring us out of his protection and waging war against us.
He has plundered our seas, ravaged our coasts, burnt our towns, and destroyed the lives of our people.
He is at this time transporting large armies of foreign mercenaries to compleat the works of death, desolation and tyranny, already begun with circumstances of cruelty and perfidy scarcely paralleled in the most barbarous ages, and totally unworthy the head of a civilized nation.
He has constrained our fellow citizens taken captive on the high seas to bear arms against their country, to become the executioners of their friends and brethren, or to fall themselves by their hands.
He has excited domestic insurrections amongst us, and has endeavoured to bring on the inhabitants of our frontiers the merciless

Indian savages, whose known rule of warfare is an undistinguished destruction of all ages, sexes, and conditions.

The colonies were especially bitter over the last three points: the hiring of mercenaries, the impressment of fellow citizens, and the enticement of Indians to wage war on the colonial forces.

Harrison came to the climax of the indictment: "In every stage of the oppressions we have petitioned in the most humble terms: our repeated petitions have been answered only by repeated injury. A prince whose character is thus marked by every act which may define a tyrant, is unfit to be the ruler of a free people."

Congress did not vote immediately. To commit the colonies to the point of irrevocable action was a soul-shaking responsibility. The debate continued intermittently through the day.

There were hours of other business to be handled before the next reading of the Declaration. A letter was received from General Washington who was in New York, on duty with the troops. A committee of delegates from New York, New Jersey, and Pennsylvania desired to plan for the best means of defending those colonies. Two commissioners were appointed for Indian affairs in the middle department. Franklin, Adams and Jefferson were named as a committee to devise a seal for the United States of America. John Hancock, the president of the Congress, was empowered to hire an additional secretary.

It was evening before the second reading was called for. The sun set at 7.25 P.M. Harrison read, by the light of a huge crystal chandelier, from the preamble of the Declaration to the final thundering commitment which said:

We, therefore, the Representatives of the United States of America, in General Congress assembled, appealing to the Supreme Judge of the world for the rectitude of our intentions, do, in the name, and by the authority of the good people of these Colonies, solemnly publish and declare

That these United Colonies are, and of right ought to be Free and Independent States, that they are absolved from all allegiance to the British Crown, and that all political connection between them and the State of Great Britain is and ought to be totally dissolved; and

That as Free and Independent States they have full power to levy war, conclude peace, contract alliances, establish commerce, and to do all other acts and things which independent States may of right do.

And for the support of this declaration, with a firm reliance on the protection of Divine Providence, we mutually pledge to each other our lives, our fortunes and our sacred honour.

The Congress voted approval without a dissenting voice and such was the dainty dish set before the king.

At first George III paid little attention to the Declaration, and neither he nor the cabinet were inclined to take the warfare in the colonies very seriously. It seemed incredible that a powerful country like Great Britain could be defied successfully by a group of provincials. Neither the king nor cabinet had ever served in America and they had little comprehension of the difficulties of maintaining an army in hostile territory nor did they have respect for the military ability of the Americans.

For the first year and a half of the war the fate of the issue wavered back and forth—colonial victories, British victories. Washington's army felt its way cautiously during the late summer and fall of 1776. He was encamped in the vicinity of New York but kept avoiding action, as his force was outnumbered more than three to one by the enemy. The bulk of the British army was stationed at New York (Manhattan Island) under General Howe, having fled there from Boston the year before when the colonials had laid successful siege to the city.

After Washington had effected a skilful retreat from the New York area he staged several successful attacks in New Jersey where there was another British army under Cornwallis which included Hessian mercenaries. On December 26, 1776, Washington defeated a small force at Trenton, New Jersey. There he took the enemy by surprise and captured about one thousand Hessians, with arms and ammunition. It was the first notable victory by the colonial army.

Again on January 3, 1777, Washington successfully attacked Cornwallis's base of supplies at Princeton, New Jersey, and engaged the British in a pitched battle in which the Americans were again victorious.

Meanwhile Sir Guy Carleton, who was governor of Quebec and commander-in-chief of the British forces in Canada, was planning to swoop down upon New York State, travelling by the waters of Lake Champlain, Lake George, and the upper Hudson River. For this purpose he needed a flotilla of light boats. Many of these he constructed in Canada and others were shipped knocked-down from England and reassembled in Canada. Carleton with several thousand soldiers finally set out on his mission and was able to capture Crown Point at the lower end of Lake Champlain, but the season was so far advanced that he was obliged to return to winter quarters.

The British generals realized that warfare carried on in terms of occasional battles was inconclusive. A general plan was needed and Burgoyne went to England to propose a campaign. The object was to surround the prosperous and populous north eastern states, thus breaking the country in two. According to this project, Burgoyne was to assemble an army in Canada (which had stayed loyal to the Crown under the governorship of Carleton) and to use the flotilla which had already been assembled by Carleton.

When all was in readiness, Burgoyne was to sail his army southward on Lake Champlain, take Fort Ticonderoga, and move on down into New York State where his forces would be met by a British army from New York City, led either by Howe or by his second-in-command, Sir Henry Clinton. Each army was to receive its starting orders from Lord George Germain to make sure of correct timing.

Several things went wrong with this interesting scheme. First of all, Carleton who previously had been feuding with Lord George Germain was insulted that Burgoyne had been appointed to this mission after Carleton had done the preparatory work, especially in building a flotilla. Carleton did not become disloyal, but soon asked and received permission to return to England.

Burgoyne had requested that Germain supply him with fifteen thousand additional men and a supply of artillery; and this seemingly was agreed to. Germain, however, had counted on hiring additional soldiers from the Prince of Hesse who proved to be unwilling to spare any more; and the expected amount of artillery was not forwarded.

Then Germain blundered appallingly in respect to the dispatches. He sent word to Burgoyne to start moving, but neglected to notify Howe. What happened in that circumstance has never been precisely determined because of conflicting testimony. One version stated that Germain went down to the country for a long weekend with the Howe dispatches in his overcoat pocket, that he wore a different overcoat when he came back to town, and forgot about the whole matter. Another account declared that when about to leave London for the weekend Germain signed the orders to

Burgoyne, but that a clerk had not finished those intended for Howe. Germain allegedly was impatient to get going, said that he could not keep his horses waiting and that he would sign the papers the following week, but on his return to town forgot to ask for them.

Burgoyne himself, however, was considerably responsible for his trouble due to overconfidence and ignorance of wilderness warfare. The accounts of the size of his army have varied from several thousand to eleven thousand soldiers. Testimony was also conflicting as to the adequacy of his military supplies. In any event, he started off gaily. In the manner of warfare on the Continent, the officers were accompanied by their wives and it was reported that Burgoyne drank champagne every day. The journey in the flotilla on Lake Champlain was said to be one continuous party. Burgoyne reconnoitred Fort Ticonderoga and to his joy the provincial army retreated down into New York State and all seemed to bode well. Burgoyne, of course, did not know that there was no British army coming up from the south.

Burgoyne began his advance early in the summer of 1777 and somewhere along the line General Washington became aware of the British plan, though Howe seemingly still was without instructions to march northward, and instead unwittingly played into Washington's hands. Washington had an army in the Philadelphia area and was determined to delay Howe or Clinton if they tried to march northward. However, Howe obliged by embarking eighteen thousand men on British vessels and sailing down to Elkton, Maryland, whence he marched into Pennsylvania to engage Washington's forces. Meanwhile he left Clinton in New York with a small complement of men.

Howe engaged the Americans both at Brandywine and Germantown, caused the withdrawal of the Continental Congress from Philadelphia, and took possession of the city. To the British general this seemed like an impressive victory, but it accomplished Washington's purpose of keeping the main British army pinned down.

For some weeks Clinton remained inactive at New York, though by this time he seemed aware that Burgoyne was marching southward. Meanwhile Burgoyne completely misinterpreted the withdrawal of the colonials from Ticonderoga as a sign of weakness and his scouts misinformed him into believing that the enemy had an inferior number of troops. Actually the New York army of the provincials numbered about twenty thousand under the command of Generals Schuyler and Gates. Their retreat was a strategy to draw in Burgoyne until they could surround him and cut off his thin line of supplies.

Clinton finally had received some additional troops from England and in response to some alarming messages from Burgoyne, he started north along the Hudson, capturing two American forts on his way, but his advance was too late. The colonial strategy succeeded, though the British troops fought gallantly for several days near Saratoga. The Americans had the British surrounded. Burgoyne's troops were short of water, food, and ammunition, and on October 17, 1777, he was obliged to surrender his entire army.

32

1778—A YEAR OF CRISIS

The year 1778 has long been recognized as a turning point for America in the revolutionary struggle, first the dark days of Valley Forge, followed by the success of Franklin in France.

For George III the year was equally one of crisis in which he twisted and turned, trying to make up his mind as to what to do about American policy.

The disaster of Burgoyne at Saratoga had seemed almost unbelievable to Parliament and the British public, and it caused an increasing storm of criticism of the conduct of the war. Burgoyne had been obliged to surrender more than 5,700 men as well as ammunition and other supplies. Burgoyne's loss in manpower was about one third of the active British forces in America. The material was a most welcome addition to the meagre resources of the American army.

George III was faced with the problem of whether to get tough or to conciliate. On the dark side were the reports of his intelligence service that France had been helping the colonies with supplies and also carrying on active commercial trade with the new nation. It was also reported to the king in January 1778 that there was a prospect of a formal treaty between France and America.

On the other hand, George was encouraged by rumours of discontent in America, plots to supplant General Washington,
desertions in the American army, difficulties of the Continental
Congress in trying to raise funds. On balance, George thought that
the colonies might be willing to listen to "some reasonable ideas".
He also thought that the American difficulties might "make France
reconsider whether she ought to enter into a war when America
might leave her in the lurch".

Before he could formulate a new policy the king encountered
trouble in his official family on the home front. North said that
both his mind and his body were too infirm to carry on in such a
serious situation and that there was danger of the ministry falling
at any time, unless it could be reconstructed. He would be perfectly
willing to retire and bring all new men into the government.

George told North that it would appear before the world and the
nation to be a sign of weakness to have a cabinet change at this
time. In fact, he decided that the first step should be to put additional pressure on the colonies, prosecuting the war more vigor-
ously. With that in mind he summoned General Jeffery Amherst
with the intent of offering him the command of the forces in
America. The general, who had been commander-in-chief in the
conquest of Canada, obviously was the most experienced man for
the present crisis.

To George's surprise the general declined. From the beginning
Amherst had believed that a land war against the colonies was
impractical. He now said that it would be necessary to have an
additional army of forty thousand men in America to make any
strong impression. Even these would be no assurance of a lasting
victory. He advised the king that a sea war "is the only wise plan",
that a blockade which would cut off their trade would distress the
colonies and might ultimately make them listen to reason. He
said, "At this hour they will laugh at any proposition."

George III understandably was resentful and frustrated at
Amherst's refusal. However, he instructed North to invite the
general to the next cabinet meeting and to sound out the opinion
of the ministry on what to do.

The king had heard that Benjamin Franklin was empowered to
negotiate for the colonies but was insisting on independence. The
king told North that such a concession was unthinkable. "I do not
think," he said, "there is a man either bold enough or mad enough
to presume to treat for the Mother Country on such a basis; per-

P

haps the time may come when it will be wise to abandon all North America but Canada, Nova Scotia and the Floridas; but then the generality of the nation must see it first in that light; but to treat with independence can never be possible."

George was particularly worried, however, about what the opinion of Parliament might be on the American issue. He said, "What is still more material to be settled is the plan on which Administration is to repell the different attacks of Opposition when Parliament meets", and he directed North to bring up this subject at the next session of the cabinet.

Confronted with growing opposition in the House of Commons, the timidity of Lord North, and the lack of strong military leadership, the king returned to the idea of conciliation of the American colonies, though he was uncertain as to what would be the best method and timing to bring this about. He took a completely new position by alleging to Lord North that his mind had never harboured "any absurd ideas of unconditional submission". In saying that, George III had a convenient lapse of memory, for both his Proclamation of Rebellion and his instructions to the Howe brothers in 1776 had demanded a most humiliating submission.

The cabinet meetings produced nothing constructive. Amherst reiterated his belief that a naval war was the only practical solution. Lord George Germain was insistent that the rebels should be dealt with firmly, but he had no practical military proposals. North had arrived at a completely defeatist attitude and had been working with the Solicitor-General and the Attorney-General in preparing a draft of peace proposals to lay before Parliament.

Briefly, the proposals would repeal all of the laws against the colonies which had been passed since 1763, including the tea duty and the Coercive Acts. The plan would authorize peace commissioners with power to settle any other concession short of independence. North was well aware that such a retreat would be highly embarrassing. He said, "Lord North is in such a situation that whatever he does must be attended with some disgrace and much misery to himself and what is worse, perhaps, with some detriment to the public."

George was astounded to hear that the Solicitor-General and the Attorney-General had been assisting in a peace draft, for that indicated that North's defeatist attitude was not due solely to his mental and physical weariness.

The king turned to Germain for an opinion, but the latter was unwilling to go on record beyond saying that if there was to be any repealing they might just as well go the whole distance without wrangling over particular measures. However, he couldn't say whether concessions would make the colonies less inclined to deal with France or conversely whether France would thereby hasten to make a treaty with the colonies lest they return voluntarily to the British fold.

In view of all this indecision in his official family George III was in a grim situation. He was not convinced that peace proposals were desirable at this time. He wrote to North, "Perhaps this is the minute of all others that you ought to be the least in a hurry to produce any plan of that kind."

George recommended waiting for some future favourable military event when the nation "would be in a better temper to subscribe to such terms as the Administration might think it advisable to offer America, who on her part will at such a time be more ready to treat than at the present hour."

The king agreed that at some point during the present session of Parliament it might be feasible for North to bring in peace proposals for America, provided she had not brought France or Spain into the war on her side. George told North, however, that before he offered any proposition he must state his ideas to all of the cabinet and report back their opinion to the king; then if the king approved, North should canvas the principal men in the House of Commons "both in office and those of weight with the country members" in order that the House be not taken by surprise and persons opposed through not understanding the subject. As to North's continued desire to retire, the king said, "You have too much personal affection for me and sense of honour to allow such a thought to take any hold on your mind."

All in all, for several weeks George steadied the ship of state. He had bucked up Lord North, had kept the ministry from breaking down, and at least had delayed any admission of failure before Parliament; but on February 9, 1778, the king learned that France was in the process of signing a treaty with America. George was thrown into a state of great perturbation and confusion. He originally had told North that a treaty between America and France or Spain would preclude any peace proposals, but now he was not so sure.

George decided finally that to make an offer would be worth the gamble. He had received no details of the Franco-American agreement and he thought it possible that the colonies might welcome reconciliation if their major grievances were removed. The very thought galled him, for his instinct was to carry on the war with vigour. Nevertheless, he authorized the pacific course.

Lord North on Februrary 17, 1778, brought his proposals before the Commons. As he had recommended to the king earlier the proposition was to repeal all the measures which had been obnoxious to the colonies and to appoint peace commissioners empowered to make any concessions short of independence.

North's speech lasted for over two hours and the Commons heard it in stunned silence. The members of various opposition factions were surprised to have these views advocated by the ministry and many feared that some concealed worse disaster had occurred which the government knew about but was not prepared to reveal. The bill passed with little debate as the opposition, taken unawares, was not prepared to criticize or propose alternatives.

For about ten weeks the king was in ignorance about the status of the American Revolution because of the slowness of transatlantic communication. During this period no one in England knew what reception was given to the peace commissioners and the Americans themselves did not get the news of the French treaty until mid-May.

George III still desired to retain the present administration in spite of its weaknesses for it had the cardinal virtue in his eyes of being obedient. The ministry was able to continue in power in spite of the criticisms in Parliament. There was a reluctance on the part of some to change the cabinet in time of war. Also the opposition was divided into two strong camps. While the Chathamites had strongly supported the resistance of the colonies to oppressive measures, they would not countenance independence; on the other hand, the Rockingham Whigs and the Duke of Richmond held that the only solution was to recognize the United States of America as an independent state.

North was not comforted by his continuance in office for he felt that the toleration of his ministry by Parliament was merely a temporary truce. He was convinced, moreover, that the cabinet in view of the critical circumstances should be reconstructed on a basis which would include all important factions. Without the knowledge of George III, he sent an emissary to Chatham's home to inquire on what terms he would be willing to lead a ministry.

Chatham was not enthusiastic. He lamented the situation of the country and said that he was afraid that it was too late to save it, but he added that no man would undertake "that perilous task" unless "a pretty general power" was put into his hands. Chatham said that if he accepted he must be "the real author and composer of public measures". He pointed to his strong credit with the American colonies which he believed would be destroyed if he were associated in any way with the existing ministry. Hence if he were to come into office, all members of the present cabinet must retire.

North was entirely agreeable to these conditions and drew up a list of proposed cabinet members mostly from the opposition and of course headed by Chatham. He presented this to His Majesty, pointing out that though Chatham had been active in opposition he was always "attentive to the appearance of the dignity of the Crown". That was quite true, for while the Great Commoner insisted on having the realities of power, he always was obsequious in the presence of the monarch.

George was dumbfounded as he reviewed the list saying:

As such [I] do not object to Lord Shelburne and Mr. Barré, who personally perhaps I dislike as much as Alderman Wilkes . . . but I declare in the strongest and most solemn manner that though I do not object to your addressing yourself to Lord Chatham yet that you must acquaint him that I shall never address myself to him but through you and on a clear explanation that he is to step forth to support an Administration whenever you are to be First Lord of the Treasury and Chancellor of the Exchequer. . . .

No advantage to this country nor personal danger can ever make me address myself for assistance either to Lord Chatham or any other branch of the Opposition. Honestly, I would rather loose the Crown I wear that bear the ignominy of possessing it under their shackles. I might write volumes if I would state my feeling of my mind.

The more George thought of this proposal the less he liked it. He swore that he would never consent to removing the members of the present cabinet and he demanded that North should not desert him. As George warmed to his subject, he was less inclined than ever toward a policy of defeatism and he expressed confidence in the resurgence of British power, saying, "The old Lion will be roused and must show that resolution and activity that alone can keep his wonted station and deserve the respect of other nations."

The debates in Parliament and the attacks on the ministry increased in a crescendo of criticism day by day. It seemed certain that North's prediction about his downfall would come true and that George III would be forced to retreat from his bold stand when a wholly unexpected event cleared the air.

Chatham appeared suddenly in the House of Lords on April 7, 1778, looking pale and ill. He rose to make a speech against "yielding the sovereignty of America". He forthwith collapsed, was carried from the room, and died a few weeks later. Once again George III's ministry had had a narrow escape because the chief leader of the opposition was now removed and because in his last words he had supported the administration on its cardinal point of refusing to recognize independence.

However, the king was now distressed by bad news from America. General Howe sent word asking to be relieved of his command, an extraordinary request in time of war. Possibly Howe was activated by a sympathy for the American position or by a sense of his own incapacity, or by the seeming impossibility of his task. At any rate, a new commander-in-chief had to be found and George named Sir Henry Clinton, Howe's assistant, a general who had had a record of conscientious service but mediocre ability.

Then came the humiliating news that the negotiations of the peace commissioners had broken down at the beginning. They had tried to deal with the officials of the United States as English subjects; and the Congress refused to meet with them on that basis. Then began a series of attempts to negotiate with individuals personally. One of the commissioners tried to enlist the attention of Robert Morris, chief banker for the Revolution, giving assurances that Washington and his colleagues would be treated "with dignity" in any system of reconcilement, but Morris declined to be involved in unofficial dealings.

Another approach on the part of British subjects was an attempt to win the support of Benjamin Franklin in favour of some compromise which would end the war. Franklin was still chief representative of America at the Court of France and it was thought that he might be able to negotiate without embarrassing Congress. Furthermore, he had numerous friends in England. George III, having been rebuffed, did not personally address Franklin nor did any of the cabinet, but there were several attempts by persons close to George who presumably were acting with his knowledge.

David Barclay (1729–1809), an eminent Quaker, made a serious effort to sound out Franklin. He was a son of the Barclay who had been host to George III and Charlotte at the time of the Lord Mayor's Day parade. Barclay may have made the approach with the king's knowledge, though the Society of Friends was so conspicuously committed to peace that Barclay conceivably acted on his own. However, the would-be mediator left the question of independence unresolved. Franklin knew Barclay of old and had respect and affection for him, but the attempted negotiation failed since there was no agreement on the central issue.

David Hartley, a member of Parliament, was one of Franklin's earlier English friends. Franklin had been a guest at the Hartley home and the latter now wrote urging that Franklin consider some means of reconciliation within the framework of the empire. Hartley seemingly was sincerely convinced of the justice of the government's position, namely relief of grievances but no independence. Franklin's response was friendly but he regretted Hartley's blindness to the real situation, saying that Hartley had "a mist over his eyes".

John Adams and Silas Deane were two major colleagues of Franklin also stationed at the American legation in Paris with status as commissioners. Adams in later years, when writing of his Paris days complains that Franklin was very secretive, frequently failing to take Adams into his confidence or again telling him only part of a situation.

According to Adams, Franklin received a letter from a mysterious stranger signed with the admitted pseudonym "Charles de Weissenstein". The only evidence that this was a genuine letter is the fact that Franklin stated so to Adams. The letter made handsome offers to the American leaders if they would abandon independence and accept reconciliation with Great Britain. The letter also attacked the good faith of France.

Franklin was a staunch friend of Vergennes, the French Foreign Minister, but there were those who had an interest in trying to breed distrust between France and America and a schism obviously would be welcomed by George III.

Franklin showed the document to Adams, alleging that the phraseology was similar to that of George III but went into no details. He wrote an elaborate answer and gave both the Weissenstein original letter and the Franklin reply to Vergennes as an evidence of good faith. His reply had spoken highly of the reliability of France as an ally and haughtily rejected the Weissenstein proposals.

While some have assumed that George III was responsible for the letter, there never was any proof to that effect and it is more probable that Franklin invented the incident as a means of declaring his loyalty to Vergennes and France. Franklin never sent his reply to anyone except Vergennes who filed the papers in the French archives; and Franklin neglected to inform Adams that the reply was not sent.

There is one fully authenticated approach, however, which may have originated with George III and was carried on by James Hutton, the Moravian leader and printer. Franklin in the postscript of a letter to Hartley refers to Hutton as an old friend. He also mentions Hutton's intimacy with the royal family, which was referred to in an earlier chapter. Franklin tells that Hutton came to see him in Paris seeking to develop what terms of peace would satisfy the Americans, but he did not claim to have a commission to do so from either king or ministry. Nevertheless, in view of Hutton's intimacy with George III it is highly probable that the king was aware of the man's intentions.

The Moravian leader took a different approach from that of other negotiators for he made no specific proposals, but asked Franklin to state what would be acceptable to the colonies. The American ambassador at first avoided answering, but after Hutton had posed the question several times in writing, Franklin sent him a reply which was striking in its boldness:

Passy, 1st February, 1778.

My Dear Old Friend,

[The letter begins with some preliminary observations on the folly of British policy, the enmity that it has aroused, the first requisite to peace being to drop "all your pretensions to govern us", after which Franklin recited his recommended terms.]

... Instead of honouring and rewarding the American advisors and promoters of this war, you should disgrace them; with all those who have inflamed the nation against America by their malicious writings; and all the ministers and generals who have prosecuted the war with such inhumanity. This would show a national change of disposition, and a disapprobation of what had passed.

In proposing terms, you should not only grant such as the necessity of your affairs may evidently oblige you to grant, but such additional ones as may show your generosity, and thereby demonstrate your good will. For instance, perhaps you might, by your treaty, retain all Canada, Nova Scotia, and the Floridas. But, if you would have a really friendly, as well as able ally in America, and avoid all occasion of future discord, which will otherwise be continually arising on your American frontiers, you should throw in those countries. And you may call it, if you please, an idemnification for the burning of their towns, which indemnification will, otherwise, be some time or other demanded.

I know your people will not see the utility of such measures, and will never follow them, and even call it insolence and impudence in me to mention them. I have, however, complied with your desire, and am, as ever, your affectionate friend,

B. FRANKLIN.

Franklin evidently chuckled as he wrote these terms which he knew would not be accepted. In order to make sure that his words would be known by the government he sent copies of his Hutton letter to David Hartley, M.P.

George III now returned to his original position of trying to compel the submission of the colonies by force of arms. The advice of his military experts who counselled limiting the war to a maritime basis had never appealed to him. He never had been happy over the proposal to offer peace negotiations by removing the source of what the colonists regarded as grievances, but he had been forced to consent to that route by the pusillanimity of Lord North and the action of Parliament.

The king found himself thwarted on all fronts. He had tried being flexible and it hadn't worked. The peace commissioners had failed, Franklin had proved to be arrogant, and the colonies had declined any negotiations short of recognition as an independent state. George III now was determined to punish and, if necessary, destroy these rebellious "subjects". Regardless of the mounting deficits in the national budget and in spite of the increasing criticisms in Parliament, George resolved to carry the conflict to the bitter end—an end far more bitter than he foresaw.

33

GEORGE AGAIN TAKES CHARGE

George took upon himself the conduct of a world-wide war, a responsibility for which he was singularly unqualified. Parliament was prevailed upon by North (at George III's instigation) to vote the unprecedented authorization of more than 200,000 fighting men: 85,000 for the navy, 110,100 for land, and 24,000 mercenaries. The word "authorization" is used advisedly, for the total was never raised, but a supporting loan of twelve million pounds sterling was voted and spent.

George III had placed himself in a position where he was obliged to prove, at least to himself, his superior gift for leadership. He had refused to allow Lord North to resign and held to that position for the next several years though North repeatedly sought to be set free. George would accept no one in the cabinet who would not follow his orders and he wished the aid of no one from the opposition who would not recant former views, including criticism of the administration.

This inflexibility was perhaps the greatest of the king's failures as a leader, yet he had tried to be flexible and that had failed. North had pointed out to his master that in certain instances just a little tact and respect would win loyalty more effectively than bribes. However, North's advice on conciliation had proved to be bitterly disappointing. George still wished North to stay on as prime minister, but now solely as a useful servant.

Another handicap in George III's personality was a mind instinctively devious and distrustful. Shelburne said of him: "The King . . . by the familiarity of his intercourse . . . obtained your confidence, procured from you your opinion of different public characters, and then availed himself of this knowledge to sow dissension." This regrettably was true. While North was being urged by the king to stay in office, in the most friendly manner, George was corresponding with others in the cabinet who were disloyal to North. Such an attitude was not new in history, but it was not a quality which produced the ardent devotion needed in this crisis.

A further fault of the king was his ignorant self-confidence. While he invited the comment of military advisers and occasionally requested the views of one minister or another, he customarily went ahead on his own, frequently interfering with staff activities. Had he the genius of a Marlborough, Pitt, Amherst, or Wellington, this playing on the checkerboard of destiny might have been justified and desirable, but George was inept and an amateur. Protocol was the *sine qua non* for him, whereas formality is always expendable in the eyes of any great commander.

Protocol was highlighted in May 1778 when George decided to inspect the British fleet at Portsmouth where most of the major ships were being made ready for active service and still others were in the process of construction. George quite rightly believed that the power of the British navy was the chief defence against France and her allies. The British fleet had adopted the practice of protecting the hulls with copper sheathing and that proved to be a ready defence against the superior numbers of the Bourbon ships.

However, George's method of inspecting the fleet was a fantastic waste of time when time, as events proved, was vital. Instead of a personal, or even incognito, visit the king set forth with an entourage. He did arise before six and arrived at Portsmouth seven hours later, but he had commanded virtually all the top military and naval authorities of the government to be on hand. Moreover, he brought the queen and a train of her attendants.

The whole business, however, gave prestige to the navy. The king, aside from attending many official luncheons and dinners, inspected every aspect of the shipyards and wrote to North that his interest, as may well be believed, promoted "alacrity", a matter in which he took an understandable pride. Sir Hugh Palliser, vice-admiral of the fleet, told the king that his visit would enable the ships to sail "many days sooner than they would else" and George added in a letter to North that Keppel, the ranking admiral, had confirmed that opinion.

At that moment the spirit of the fleet and its copper-sheathed hulls seemed equal to any emergency and the king wrote from Portsmouth: "The affection I have received from all ranks of people at this place deserve every degree of activity for the good of the service, and no one is more hearty in the cause than myself." The king's good temper was augmented by news from Germain, Secretary for the Colonies, who sent word that "the desertion in

Washington's Army continues . . . they are sickly, in want of clothing and not above six thousand in camp".

That was all too true, but there is a verified account of Washington which helps to explain the ultimate triumph of the American
cause. During that bitter winter at Valley Forge, where Washington
had his dismal headquarters so well reported by Germain, the
American commander-in-chief lodged at a modest farmhouse
owned by Isaac Potts, a plain man, but a leader in the Quaker community. Potts when walking around his farm one day heard a voice
and discovered Washington upon his knees, his cheeks wet with
tears, praying for the deliverance of the American cause. Potts on
returning to his house said to his wife: "George Washington will
succeed! The Americans will secure their independence!"

"What makes thee think so, Isaac?" asked his wife.

"I have heard him pray, Hannah, out in the woods today, and
the Lord will surely hear his prayer. He will, Hannah; thee may
rest assured He will."

Such was the spirit which sustained most of the American patriots
through their darkest hours while the king and various parties in
Parliament were torn by political dissensions.

George, though still flushed with his happy and successful reception at Portsmouth, was profoundly annoyed to receive a pessimistic
letter from Lord North. North reported that the government had
been "violently attacked" in the House of Commons because the
fleet had not yet sailed. Again North sought to retire: "Every hour
convinces me more and more of the necessity your Majesty is
under of putting some other person than myself at the head of
your affairs. . . . I feel myself losing every day the good opinion
and confidence of the House of Commons."

George replied that the navy authorities were better qualified to
determine when the fleet should sail than were critics in Parliament. He brushed aside North's desire to quit, reminding him that
previously he had promised not to resign. His Majesty tried
repeated exhortations to buck up Lord North. In a typical moralizing letter George wrote: "It has ever been a certain position with
me that firmness is the characteristic of an Englishman." He went
on to say that the independence of America should never be
admitted. He urged North to see the "beauty, excellence and per-
fection of the British Constitution". North should not "allow
despondency in his breast . . . but will resolve with vigour to meet
every obstacle".

The king continued to need Lord North, for the extravagance of the royal household was fantastic and could be sustained only by grants from Parliament which were engineered by North's management of the bloc indebted to the Crown plus whatever trading of favours he might arrange. In 1778, with the national debt at a high point, the Commons nevertheless agreed to annuities on the six sons of George totalling £60,000 and on his five daughters amounting to £30,000.

The behaviour of the royal children was reckless, especially that of the older boys. The oldest son, the future George IV, while not yet of age, had written ardent letters to a female who threatened to publish them unless she were paid £5,000. According to His Majesty the young prince had made the woman "very foolish promises". The lady was the famous actress Mrs. Robinson, known as Perdita.

The king was greatly perturbed. He already had produced £13,000 to protect a brother from public scandal. Now similar trouble was beginning in the next generation, nor did the king know that more trouble of a similar nature would not recur later. Right now the problem was to keep this matter quiet. Only a year previously the Commons had voted an increase of £100,000 for the king's civil list. That supposedly was for secret service, but it had been severely criticized, and exposure of the current proposed expense could be highly damaging to the royal prestige.

North as usual was the bagman. George in a pious tone ordered him to pay the amount and wrote ruefully in capital letters: "I AM HAPPY AT BEING ABLE TO SAY THAT I NEVER WAS PERSONALLY ENGAGED IN SUCH A TRANSACTION." That comment has been interpreted in some quarters as evidence that George never was scandalously involved with any woman, but it might merely mean that he was too prudent to put his sentiments in writing.

Now that England was engaged in a large-scale war a vast increase in the public debt was inevitable and the enormous spending appeared to affect George III's once prudent nature. George was notorious for keeping a sharp eye on the royal kitchens to see that the help did not waste or steal food. Now, however, king and the Court lived lavishly, comparable in expense to that of Louis XVI, though not as picturesquely. George embarked on a series of visits to the vast English country houses, those of certain cabinet members and others. It was a social honour to be allowed to entertain royalty; but these expeditions were on a scale costly to the travelling expense of the Crown and well-nigh ruinous to any host. His Majesty was not content to bring merely his consort and a few servants, but brought with him a swarm of courtiers.

A typical occasion of this sort is described by the Earl of Pembroke when the king came to the family estate of Chilmark. Eight separate dining rooms were needed for the king and his official party, another dining room was required for the queen and her attendants. In addition there were tables for the servants in remote quarters of the house.

If the royal visits, supposedly bringing social prestige to leading families, were meant to increase loyalty to the throne, the plan was a failure in the Pembroke instance, for not long afterwards the earl went into opposition and resigned his place as a Lord of the Bedchamber. He possibly had strong personal reasons for the break, as George looked with longing eyes on Elizabeth, Countess of Pembroke, probably never seduced her, but raved about her in his later years of insanity. Pembroke disliked the whole Hanoverian connection, anyhow. He was the tenth earl and his family had been of consequence when George's ancestors were nobodies, as far as England was concerned. The earl resented being patronized by Germans, particularly Augusta, the sharp-tongued sister of the king. "I don't think I was ever in Augusta's good graces. She knows, I believe, that I know her: a b-tch, as she was in the beginning, is now, and ever will be."

The king's inspection at Portsmouth in July 1778 had borne fruit, for Keppel sailed from Portsmouth with thirty-four vessels and a complement of over nineteen thousand men, seeking to engage the French fleet off the coast of Brest. The results of the ensuing engagement were disappointing, not a defeat, but indecisive.

The worst feature of the affair was the dissension which resulted in the British naval command. Though Keppel was politically in opposition he had assured Sandwich that he would do his duty for the service if called upon to do so, and the fact that Sandwich had placed him at the head of the fleet despite his political views was eloquent testimony to Keppel's repute. In the battle off Brest, however, Palliser saw an opportunity to advance his own career and refused to obey Keppel's orders to advance to his support. Thus a possible victory was lost through dissension in the high command. Palliser, confident in his political adherence to the government, took the initiative of charging misconduct and incapacity on the part of Keppel and published his accusations in the press.

Keppel naturally demanded a court-martial and was completely acquitted. London went wild with resentment against his apparent persecution by the government. Mobs stoned the houses of North, Germain and Sandwich. The king debated whether Palliser should be cashiered or allowed to resign and decided for the latter. George did not condone Palliser's behaviour in this instance, but held that his earlier services "make him deserve a little indulgence". Keppel resigned also. The navy thus lost two of its top commanders and the followers of each admiral continued to feud. The Spanish government encouraged by this contretemps now openly came to the aid of France.

The king in mid-June 1779 still fatuously thought that America must sue for peace "unless this summer supported by a Bourbon Fleet". In any event, he would approve no more concessions to the colonies. If they should realize that they had not gained by the contest "I would show that the parent's heart is still affectionate to the penitent child".

Amherst had been by no means as sanguine as Germain about the state of the loyalists in America vis-à-vis Washington's conditions. Amherst had a report from a Mr. Galway at Philadelphia listing over twenty-five thousand British army personnel and dependents which alleged that they were supplied with "all manner of fresh provisions", which Amherst doubted, writing to the king, "I imagine that they all received salt provisions, and I suppose Mr. Washington's army was starving at the same time, or in great distress."

Amherst still felt that there was no use in trying military operations in the heart of the colonies or attempting to keep possession of any place that "cannot be maintained". He also enclosed an opinion from a Major-General Robertson who had served with him in the French and Indian War. Robertson also believed that interior fighting would be impractical and "the hope of forcing Washington over the Susquehanna is too sanguine". Amherst believed that a friendly declaration by the king was most important; but in the last analysis the judgment of the commander on location (Clinton) should prevail. "As the whole hope of success depends on the address and abilities of the commander-in-chief he should be vested with every power and at liberty to form and execute his own plans."

The king's pride obviously would never permit him to allow a subordinate in the field to determine strategy or policy. Hence most of 1779 was occupied by conferences in the king's "closet" or in cabinet meetings at which George and his equally stiff-necked associates made decisions on navy and field operations of which they were incompetent to judge. For the Americans, of course, the royal perversity was fortunate; but in England all except the Court followers were in a state of shame, rage and despair, for with a few exceptions Britain appeared to be getting nowhere in the American conflict.

Toward the end of 1779, George's ineptitude as a would-be saviour of the nation became increasingly apparent. The combined French and Spanish fleets were drawn up in the Channel. John Paul Jones, who had set fire to ships in the harbour of Whitehaven a year previously, returned in September 1779 to sink the *Serapis* which was protecting a merchant convoy. The battle was valiant on both sides but the loss of the British vessel was a blow to national pride.

The king was becoming desperate. In September 1779 he wrote to Sandwich that boldness was the only salvation. He was willing to risk neglect of home defence in order to pour all available naval force to hold the West Indies. "If we lose our sugar islands it will be impossible to raise money to continue the war." Again, "It is by bold and manly efforts Nations have been preserved and not pursuing alone the line of home defence." In that view, George III had a sound grasp of realities, for the rich sugar plantations of Jamaica were a major source of wealth for the leading men of the Corporation of London. They were already hostile to the Crown and if the throne failed to protect their interests on this score its days might well be numbered.

By November in fact George had come to a humbler mood. He wrote a memorandum to the Lord Chancellor (Thurlow), saying that he would forget past prejudices against individuals and would accept into his ministry any who would "keep the Empire entire" (presumably excluding independence for the colonies), who would prosecute the war, and that His Majesty should be "treated with proper respect and that no blame be laid on any past measure".

For George III this was a conciliatory statement though it came too late to produce national unity. Indeed, but two events saved the administration. Admiral Rodney at Gibraltar defeated the Spanish fleet. Sir Henry Clinton won a series of battles in the

Southern colonies. Neither Rodney's nor Clinton's successes were conclusive, but they were a tonic which gave strength to George's determination to hold onto his present subservient ministry.

In the early months of 1780, however, criticism of George and his policies rolled up like thunder. York and many other counties held meetings in which they deplored the vast current expenses which were bleeding their resources. One of these meetings was attended by six hundred substantial merchants and manufacturers who, according to Sir George Savile speaking in Parliament, represented a total wealth greater than that in the House of Commons.

Richmond in the Lords advocated universal manhood suffrage instead of the existing property qualifications. Burke moved a review of the numerous perquisites of the Crown so that its possibilities of corruption would be minimized. The bill passed, though North was smart enough to include numerous amendments which drew the teeth of the measures.

North kept trying to persuade George that times had changed and the ministry must modify its attitude; but as late as March 1780 the king wrote to the prime minister, "I can never suppose this country so lost to all ideas of self-importance as to be willing to grant America independence." Further, on May 6, 1780, the king deluded himself with the supposed weakness of America, writing to North, "Every account of the distress of that country shows that they must sue for peace this summer if no disaster befalls us."

North had tried repeatedly to warn the king about the rising tide of public opinion, the resentment of military failures, the great expense of the military establishment, but in vain. Then, in the House of Commons on April 6, 1780, there was thrown a bombshell from which George III and the whole theory of absolute monarchy never recovered. Mr. Dunning introduced his celebrated resolution "that the influence of the Crown has increased, is increasing, and ought to be diminished". Despite all of the votes supposedly dependent on the king's pleasure, the motion passed 233 to 215.

34

REVOLT IN ENGLAND

Call it revolt, rebellion, revolution, or by any name you may wish when mobs, for more than a week in June 1780, terrorized all London, prevented meetings of Parliament, and burned to the ground homes of chief ministers of the cabinet. Though the chief action was in London the infection spread throughout the realm; and indeed had been fostered in Scotland.

The trouble started because George III had had the grace to champion freedom of worship for Roman Catholics. Opposition to this view had simmered for two years. On June 3, 1778, George III had given his assent to a bill for the relief of adverse laws which had been imposed on Roman Catholic subjects in England. Catholics could not hold land or transfer it. Army officers could not be Catholics. Catholic religious services were illegal (though normally held without molestation). Catholic parochial schools were forbidden. The son of a Catholic who turned Protestant could denounce his father and take over the paternal lands.

The religious issue had been quiescent in England during George III's reign, for he had always stood for liberty of conscience. That must ever be added to his credit, not only in 1778 when it was politically advisable but at all times. George III had protected the Quakers, the Methodists, the Moravians, and all other sects in their freedom of worship.

The Catholic Relief bill was especially necessary to national policy at this time for reasons which will appear. Possibly it would not have caused any trouble of consequence but for the unexpected emergency of the hitherto weakling Lord George Gordon.

On June 3, 1778, when George III signed the Catholic Relief bill, Lord George Gordon was still a nobody in politics. He was a handsome young man, with a fine profile, a brother of the Duke of Gordon, a heavy drinker, a bachelor and an avid patron of prostitutes. He was a good mixer, fluent in speech, and had a seat in the House of Commons where he occasionally made himself heard, but where he was not seriously regarded. That annoyed him profoundly and led to his ultimate hostility to the government.

Lord George, though a lightweight personally, had various important connections. As brother of a duke he could demand an audience with the king. He was the third son in the family. The second son, Lord William Gordon, had eloped with Lady Sarah Lennox. In short, Lord George Gordon was born into the upper social and political circles, and he could not be ignored if he found some platform from which he could insist on being heard.

The Catholic Relief bill had passed unanimously in both the Commons and the Lords, and obviously had the support of the ministry. As George III had the controlling majority in Parliament at this time, the public rightly assumed that the bill had his personal sanction. Justice aside, there were practical reasons which favoured the measure. Ireland was being depopulated. Charles Carroll of Maryland, a province notable for its protection of Catholics, had had handbills distributed throughout Ireland, offering both land and freedom of religion to Irish emigrants. The British army had failed in recruiting in Ireland, in part because the anti-Catholic provisions gave no opportunity for a Catholic Irishman to rise in the service.

Further, various top men of the government, both in and out of the immediate ministry, had sizable estates in Ireland: Rockingham, Shelburne, Hillsborough, Sir George Savile and others. If Ireland lost its manpower the estates would diminish in value. It is significant of the Rockingham economic interests that his associate, Edmund Burke, an Irish Protestant, drafted the Catholic Relief bill.

In this crisis, George III's poor tutoring in his youth left him unprepared for the underlying, ready-to-be-inflamed feeling of English Protestantism. True, the anti-Catholic laws of England were unjust, but there had been a long history of persecution of various Protestant sects which had not been forgotten. The time was ripe for tolerance only if George III had the dynamic ability to make it so.

For a short time after George III had signed the Relief Act all boded well. The anti-Catholic laws had been passed before the Union of England and Scotland and the latter still had its own prohibitory acts not affected by the English repeal. Since the Relief Act had passed so successfully for England it was now logical for the Crown to favour supplementary legislation for Scotland, and Henry Dundas, the Lord Advocate, announced his intent to bring in such a measure in Parliament.

The effect of this notice was to arouse immediate and intense opposition throughout Scotland, a sentiment surprising to the king and ministry. In spite of the surface symptoms of unity, the Scots had a deep-seated distrust of their southern neighbour. The difference in the official religion was a cause of friction. The Church of Scotland was Presbyterian expounding a more militant Protestantism than the English Church, rejecting the latter's ritual and having a different system of organization. The Presbyterian theology also differed from the Anglican in detail, though not on major articles of faith.

Early in 1779 riots broke out in many parts of Scotland. In Edinburgh rioters tore down the house of the Catholic Bishop Hay and set fire to a newly built Catholic chapel. The Catholic prelates in Scotland addressed a letter to Lord North asking that the government forego its intended repeal in their area lest it subject their believers to violence. North agreed, but no appeasement in attitude was effective at this stage, for the ferment throughout Scotland was furiously agitated by none other than Lord George Gordon.

The Gordon family, of Scottish origin, had been now Catholic, now Protestant, through the centuries. The current generation was staunchly Protestant and Lord George was active in the Protestant Association of London in February 1779. Accordingly certain Scotch Protestants invited him to come there to lead a similar association and to direct its campaigns. Lord George accepted with alacrity, for here was an opportunity for the power and recognition which he craved. He displayed talents as an actor, an organizer, and a mob leader. He discarded the fancy investiture of a playboy, the jewels, the wig, the red morocco shoes and all that, for the dour habit of a Presbyterian leader.

He now directed a frantic campaign which penetrated into all corners of Scotland. The Presbyterian synods one after another passed anti-Catholic resolutions. Handbills and posters on the same theme were distributed throughout the land. Lord George went on a speaking tour, where he was elected the head of various local societies and was treated almost with adoration. His followers were legion and they believed that a new prophet had arisen in Zion.

On November 12, 1779, Lord George Gordon was offered the presidency of the Protestant Association of England. Swollen with success in Scotland, he accepted. In England the issue was big: to repeal an act which had been voted unanimously by Parliament and approved by the Crown.

Almost immediately Lord George moved into action. In mid-December the Association voted resolutions seeking repeal of the Catholic Relief laws. On December 31, the agitator sent copies to North requesting an audience. North was not in the least sympathetic, but did agree to receive a delegation at 10 Downing Street on January 4, 1780. Thereat North declined either to support the petition or to present it in Parliament.

The dour Lord George, with his pale tense face and his dark lanky hair, now embarked on a personal campaign to achieve his ends and that of the Protestant Association. In contrast to Scotland where he had had the machinery of the Presbyterian Church at his disposal, he was disapproved of by many dissenters who also had suffered under certain adverse laws and were sympathetic to the relief now afforded to the Romanists.

The agitator took the route of placing advertisements in newspapers saying that copies of a petition for repeal of the Relief Act would be available at stated places. The signature sheets were of parchment; ultimately they totalled hundreds of pages, and finally were collated by a tailor who was engaged to stitch them together.

Meanwhile Lord George was haranguing Parliament in threatening terms. He referred to the king's ministers as "odious", alleged that he himself was backed by 120,000 men, said that he would deliver the petition personally to His Majesty and asserted that the Scots "are convinced in their own mind that the King is a Papist". The last statement obviously was false; but it was a rabble-rousing sentiment which caught the popular imagination and was a troublesome misapprehension all through the domestic revolution of June 1780.

Lord George Gordon now demanded an audience with the king and in January 1780 George III received him. Gordon had his first interview alone. He read a pamphlet to the king for over half an hour, until George III desired to be excused, promising that he would read the remainder himself.

George III was now drawn into a most difficult situation from which only drastic action on his part could have rescued him. The agitator soon had a second interview with George III and bore down on the embarrassing fact that "the resolute opposition" of the Scots soon had been yielded to by government.

In a third conference with the king, Gordon complained that as president of the Protestant Association he was entitled to respect which he did not receive from Lord North or his associates, that the president had "something more to do" than exchange compliments with the monarch and he unsuccessfully demanded that the king define his position on "Popery". Gordon had a fourth audience with George III in which he alleged that Edmund Burke and others of the current opposition were not true Protestants.

There is no evidence that George III took this man seriously in these conferences in the spring of 1780, but unfortunately the king did not realize the man's hypnotic power to rouse the masses. Either the king or Lord North at this point tried to buy off Lord George Gordon. North called on Gordon at his London residence and in the name of the king (George III may or may not have known of this specific incident) offered the agitator a large sum of money and a leading position in Parliament if he would desert the Protestant Association. Lord George bluntly refused, saying that he would accept no favour of any sort whilst North was chief minister.

The incident was typical of a prime error of George III, namely his belief that every man has his price. He had found that to be true of many a man, but also not true of the chief colonial leaders, nor was it true of this strange fanatic. Certain Catholic leaders also had tried to buy off Lord George Gordon, to no avail. These attempts proved to Gordon the intrinsic strength of his position. He was feared by all the powers in the kingdom including the throne itself and he revelled in the situation.

Lord George Gordon on May 29, 1780, called upon the Protestant Association to march upon Parliament with twenty thousand citizens to present the petition for repeal. He gave directions to his followers through paid notices placed in the *Public Advertiser*, May 31, June 1 and June 2. His supporters were advised to assemble in four different divisions, each to wear a blue cockade to distinguish him or her from a mere accidental or curious follower.

Friday, June 2, was to be the big day for the march on Parliament and the mobs responded. Though the weather was oppressively hot, many thousands thronged into St. George's Fields from all sections of the city and its environs. Contemporaries estimated the number of marchers from twenty thousand to sixty thousand. There was no way of measuring who were Gordon's real supporters, as the throng was composed of Protestant Association members, onlookers, pickpockets, and other felons.

Lord George arrived that morning at St. George's Fields at eleven and was received as a hero. The crowd at first was orderly and evidently had been well organized by section leaders who directed a parade. The throng marched several times around the Fields singing hymns and displaying blue banners. About noon a man bearing the huge parchment roll of the petition with its thousands of signatures led the march on Parliament.

By mid-afternoon rioting began. Ruffians chalked "No Popery" on the carriage panels of arriving legislators. The mob pelted Lord Stormont and the Archbishop of York with mud. They snatched the wig of Lord George Germain and threw porter in his face. When Lord North drove up someone flung open his carriage door, seized his hat, cut it into scraps, and sold the pieces for a shilling each. Finally order was restored by the appearance of the guards.

Gordon had counted on a show of force to induce the Commons to receive the petition and vote for repeal. In this he was grossly disappointed. His motion was seconded by Alderman Bull, for the City by this time was so strongly against the policies of king and ministry that the Corporation welcomed any measure that might embarrass the administration. Gordon's motion, however, received only seven votes in addition to his and Bull's. Among the seven votes was that of Sir James Lowther, a son-in-law of Bute.

Now Gordon was faced with an impasse whereby he must lose face with his followers, yet if he encouraged them to more violence he risked arrest for treason and rebellion. Hoping to find some middle ground, Gordon went to an outer gallery of the House to address the crowd. He told them that Lord North called them a mob; but he relied on the king to grant their wishes.

"His Majesty is a gracious Monarch," said Gordon, "and when he hears that the people ten miles around are collecting, there is no doubt that he will send his Ministers private orders to repeal the Bill." Gordon also warned them against evil persons who might "incite to mischief". Gordon here exhibited a shrewd cunning, trying to absolve himself from the criticisms against George III which he had made in Parliament and also trying to place himself on the side of law and order. The crowd, however, did not disperse and continued to rage and roar to intimidate the legislators within.

When Gordon returned to the House, General Conway warned him: "Do not imagine that we will be intimidated by a rabble," and a Colonel Holroyd added: "My Lord George, do you intend to bring your rascally adherents into the House of Commons? If you do, the first man of them that enters, I will plunge my sword, not into his, but into your body." From that point on, Lord George behaved with great caution, was not seen late at night when the worst of future disturbances took place and remained most of the time in his house on Welbeck Street. Meanwhile on that June 2 evening the unruly mob kept the Lords virtually prisoners until half-past eight and the Commons until eleven.

George III for the time being remained inactive. Thereby he missed a cardinal opportunity to assert the authority of the throne, a principle which he had stoutly championed. He showed by this inaction that he did not have the necessary audacity for leadership in such a crisis. George III's inadequacy was understandable. His grandfather had refused to let him enter military service. His mother and Lord Bute had crippled his initiative though at the same time urging him to "be a king". He had cultivated the theory of "firmness and resolution", but lacked the technique personally to put those principles in force when confronted with the necessity on his own doorstep. In fairness it should be said that the king was trying in this instance to behave as a constitutional monarch, recognizing laws which he thought were binding upon him, which supposedly prevented any positive action by him unless the civil magistrates co-operated.

Lord Amherst, commander-in-chief, had the troops of the nation under his direction but they were not allowed to fire on the mob until the riot act had been read by the magistrate, giving the crowd one hour in which to disperse. Amherst asked the government for authority to act but was told that the above restrictions applied. Hence while the general called in regiments from far and near to protect the city the soldiers were effective only in isolated circumstances. Where the general assigned guards to private homes which had been threatened the soldiers were a protection against casual marauders. Against large gatherings the troops were helpless, for the mob had found that it could jeer at and pelt them without fear of reprisal.

Stormont, a Secretary of State, displayed a courage and diligence more vigorous than the king. He sent messages to the civil authorities requesting that they act, and he stayed at his post for several days on end with virtually no sleep. The City authorities, however, apparently welcomed disorder and had no desire to protect the national government or its officials.

Brackley Kennett, Lord Mayor of London, was a friend of crooks and had motives for welcoming a continuation of disturbances. He had started his career as a waiter at a house of ill-fame, then had a brothel of his own, acquired a tavern, became a wine merchant, gained wealth, was elected alderman and finally Lord Mayor. He hated the supercilious dignitaries of the West End, also he had support from many merchants who hoped that the North ministry would fall, as the American war was continuing to hurt trade.

A reign of terror ensued for several days. The mob operated with a sinister selectivity, which indicated that its leaders had knowledge and purpose. The places particularly marked for attack were (1) Catholic chapels, homes and places of business owned by Catholics; (2) homes of members of Parliament who were known to favour religious toleration; (3) houses of any magistrates who dared to try to enforce the law; (4) jails. The last item was significant of the influence of Kennett, for freeing the criminals obviously had no relationship to a Protestant-Catholic dispute, but rather a desire to use anarchy for ulterior purposes.

Immune from fire and pillage were (1) the homes of leading families in the aristocracy known to be against or indifferent to the Relief Act; (2) the homes of the *City* authorities except those few who stood for order; (3) the residence of General Lord Amherst; (4) the royal palaces.

The two latter exceptions are understandable. Though the mob hated the military, they well suspected that the hero of Louisbourg, Ticonderoga and Montreal would not wait for any riot act if an attack were made on his home or family. Throughout the week or more of anarchy the general was not even threatened.

A similar caution kept the rioters from assaulting the royal palaces, either St. James's, the Queen's House, or the suburban ones. Though George III had incurred great unpopularity and was initially at a loss in this crisis, he never lacked for personal bravery. During most of these days he stayed up around the clock and was frequently in evidence among the soldiers guarding St. James's, providing them with hot beverages and other refreshments. The mob leaders could not know what was in the king's mind or even that he was deterred by legal considerations. If once they attacked St. James's, they must win completely and depose the government or be hanged for high treason. They did not risk such a gamble, in part because their titular leader, Lord George Gordon, temporarily was lying low.

June 3, Saturday. While Gordon was safely in bed in Welbeck Street, before midnight the rioters moved on to a holocaust in the early morning hours of June 3. They destroyed the Sardinian Chapel, which had been used for Roman Catholic services. The mob then moved on to the residence of the Catholic Bishop Challoner and seized his papers. They had hoped to take Challoner prisoner, but friends had heard of that and had prevailed on him to move a few doors away. There were many other offences that early morning, some witnessed by Kennett, who said to the rioters: "That's pretty well, gentlemen, for one day; I hope you will now go to your own homes."

June 4, Sunday. No major incidents.

June 5, Monday. The day began quietly, with many assuming that the tumult had spent its force. George III at 11 a.m. wrote to Lord North that every step had been taken to prevent future disturbances and that he had seen that "proper executive orders" had been sent out by the Secretaries of State. Said the king: "This tumult must be got the better of, or it will encourage designing men to use it as a precedent for assembling the people on other occasions." The "designing men" had been at the destruction for more than seventy-two hours.

The tumult was not "got the better of". Throughout the day and evening a mob estimated by some at ten thousand (probably an exaggeration) damaged Sir George Savile's house in Leicester Square and moved on to threaten other dwellings in the West End not far from St. James's.

June 6, Tuesday. The government at last decided that the military must be its salvation though it still neglected to give the troops a free hand. George III on that day wrote Amherst a "go-to-it" sort of letter. The king approved of bringing in regiments to reinforce those already in London. He deplored the lassitude of the magistrates and feared that order would not be restored "unless more decisive means are used". That vague phrase carried no authorization with it. George concluded by asking for more protection for homes of various cabinet members.

As the hours advanced, this June 6 became a crucial day almost as critical as the following one. The Commons met 220 strong (about half maximum strength), declined to consider any petition at this time, advised the recompense of foreign embassies for damages, and promised that on some later date after tumults subsided petitions could be considered.

At this point, in the evening of June 6, George III sent a message to Lord North which had a peculiar ring in the light of his actions in the next few days. George wrote at "25 min. past 9 p.m." as follows: "The allowing of Lord George Gordon, the avowed head of the tumult, to be at large certainly encourages the continuation of it." The king said that he did not think that the House of Commons had moved forward on the matter as far as they should have, that the magistrates had been remiss, and that more vigour was necessary.

One magistrate, Justice Hyde, had the courage to read the riot act in the Palace Yard and the mob were dispersed. Whereupon the crowd streamed to the south end of St. Martin's Street to Hyde's home, threw the contents out of the windows and burned the effects until two o'clock in the morning of June 7. On the day and evening of June 6 the mob destroyed Newgate and other prisons and released those confined. Nearby blacksmiths were enlisted to remove the prisoners' fetters.

June 7, Wednesday. On the morning of this day George III was confronted with an unexpected situation and his behaviour is difficult to understand. About ten o'clock he received the inner cabinet at the Queen's House, including North, Stormont and Amherst. A page scratched at the door of the meeting room and announced that Lord George Gordon sought audience with the king. The proceedings throughout were peculiar. Gordon could have demanded an audience, but evidently feared that his position was so compromised that he needed the protection of a voluntary reception.

Stranger still, where was the "resolution" of George III who only a few hours previously had deplored the fact that Gordon was still at large? Now was the time easily to take the culprit into custody. On the contrary, George III merely dictated a reply for Stormont to hand to the visitor which said: "It is impossible for the King to see Lord George Gordon until he has given sufficient proofs of his allegiance and loyalty by employing those means which, he says, he has in his power to quell the disturbances and restore peace to this capital."

Gordon was not impressed by this scolding message and rode off to join his friends in the city. Meanwhile Rockingham arrived at the king's conference in informal dress, with hair disordered, and in great consternation, for his house had been threatened and was saved only by having armed defenders, whose presence prevented direct action by the rioters. Rockingham, however, had been up most of the night in peril of his life and he was in no mood to deal delicately with His Majesty. He had heard that a Privy Council was summoned and he had complaints to make at once and ahead of time. Why did the king and ministry allow the assemblage in St. George's Fields? Was it a fact that unlawful assemblages could not be fired on or at any rate dispersed by force without waiting for reading of the riot act?

George III was stung into response by these questions. In fact, he presumably had coached his Attorney-General, Alexander Wedderburn, within the past few hours, for the man came up with the desired opinion while this conference was still in session. George III summoned Wedderburn, apparently waiting in the wings, and asked if an assemblage could be dispersed by the military without waiting for the riot act or other forms.

Wedderburn said yes.

"Is that your declaration of the law as Attorney-General?" asked George.

Wedderburn repeated his affirmation.

"Then so let it be done," said the king and instructions were sent forthwith to Lord Amherst that he could shoot, bayonet, disperse any unruly crowd at will.

George III could have called on his legal resources much earlier, but he preferred himself to the law. The Lord Chancellor (Mansfield) ultimately held that the common law protected citizens and their property and superseded any special law which might have to do with unlawful assembly. George III had not thought of that and it would seem that Mansfield himself arrived at the doctrine expediently.

The king now on June 7 issued a proclamation denouncing the rioters, calling upon all good citizens and their servants to "keep quietly within their respective dwellings" in order that the unruly might be more easily identified, and instructing the military to use the force "with which we are by law intrusted" to suppress "such rebellious and traitorous" activities. As a further precaution the navy was ordered to patrol the coast lest France take advantage of the civil confusion to attempt an invasion.

In a few places where the king's proclamation was heard it had a calming effect, but obviously when mobs were in all parts of the city many did not know of the change in public policy and the soldiers repeatedly were called upon to fire before a crowd would disperse. Indeed the night of June 7 was perhaps the most hideous of all. Lord North watching from the roof of 10 Downing Street counted seven large fires.

The king's friend James Hutton, the Moravian, was in their chapel in Fetter Lane that evening and his diary describes the scene. "The flames ascending and rolling over our heads in vast volumes from the King's Bench and Fleet Prisons and New Bridewell, from the toll gates at Blackfriars Bridge and from houses in every quarter of the town, presented a scene horrible beyond description. . . . The violent burning of the houses of an eminent distiller in Holborn and at Fetter Lane, which contained vast quantities of spirituous liquors, brought the danger nearer." Only the fact that there was very little wind saved the City from destruction, for the fire apparatus was primitive and some of the engines were in possession of the rioters.

The behaviour and experience of the Fetter Lane congregation exemplified the fact that the tumult was not wholly due to a religious issue. Like the great majority of Protestant churchgoers, the Moravians had taken no part in it. Nevertheless they were threatened and felt obliged to send some of the women members to suburban regions carrying the records of the church into safe hiding.

Elsewhere in the City the revolt was reaching a crisis. Lord Amherst now had some ten thousand men under arms including regiments summoned from other parts of England and such sailors as could be spared from the fleet; but the requests for guards at all points was such that progress in pacification was slow. In the forenoon the City Council had passed a resolution urging the government to favour repeal, but shortly after that a messenger arrived with the king's proclamation advising the Aldermen that the metropolis was now under martial law. The impetuous Wilkes moved that the messenger be detained and kept captive, but no one seconded the motion. The canny Lord Mayor was no idealist and he sensed the turning of the tide. Wilkes felt the chilly attitude of his colleagues, soon left, and quickly lined up on the side of law and order.

Wilkes took part in the defence of the Bank of England, which had been marked for destruction. The attack began after eleven o'clock on the night of June 7. A great mob gathered, led by a brewer's drayman astride a horse decorated with chains stolen from Newgate Prison. In his *Diary,* Wilkes claims to have fired on the rioters and to have killed several. Another unexpectable would-be defender of the Bank was Lord George Gordon. He approached the captain in charge, offered to persuade the people to disperse and to risk his life in that cause by standing at the officer's side. The officer declined to have anything to do with him and Gordon retired. By early dawn the rioters had given up and the streets around the Bank were silent.

It was essential for George III and the ministry that the Bank escaped destruction. It was the core of the finances of government and commerce. More than that, it was a sacrosanct symbol of English stability.

June 8, Thursday. Except for relatively minor disturbances London became quiet. All places of business except the Bank remained closed. The Bank bravely but unostentatiously conducted "business as usual". The report of officers to Lord Amherst totalled several hundred citizens killed while resisting the troops during the riots. Scores of other citizens had died from swilling raw liquor or were consumed in the flames which they had lit.

George III well knew that though peace had been restored, there would be an aftermath affecting his reputation. He called a cabinet meeting for the following day.

35

"THE THOUGHT WAS MY OWN"

The king held his meeting of the cabinet on Friday, June 10, at two o'clock, to decide what should be done next, especially in respect to Lord George Gordon. Those attending were the Lord President (Bathurst, hardly more than a figurehead), the Secretaries of State (Stormont and Hillsborough), Amherst, and several other members of the Privy Council. After a discussion of nearly four hours it was decided to arrest Gordon and take him to the War Office for examination. A warrant was drawn up to authorize the seizure.

The messengers accompanied by troops found the agitator at his residence. Gordon offered no resistance, saying, "If you are sure it is me you want, I am ready to attend you." An examination followed at the War Office conducted by cabinet persons who had been at the initial conference, but the king did not attend. After a questioning of over three hours, Lord George Gordon was charged with high treason and was taken to the Tower in a coach under an elaborate guard of infantry, horse troops and militia. However, there was no attempt to rescue him and the populace remained prudently within doors.

Here was the brother of a duke charged with the greatest of crimes, for which presumably he would pay the death penalty if found guilty, yet an exchange of letters on the subject between Stormont and the Duke of Gordon showed a typically British aplomb, an ability to face crisis without panic. Stormont wrote that evening to the Duke of Gordon:

My Lord—We think it a mark of respect due to your Grace to give you the earliest intelligence in our power of an event for which we feel the utmost concern. We have been obliged, from the indispensable duty of our office, to commit Lord George Gordon to the Tower for High Treason, of which he stands charged by information upon oath. We beg leave to assure your Grace that it gave us the utmost pain to be under this necessity, and especially as it relates to one so nearly connected with your Grace.

We are etc.,

STORMONT
HILLSBOROUGH

The Duke, who was in Glasgow, replied promptly:

My Lord—I had the honour of your Lordship's letter, which I shall always look upon as a very particular mark of your respect and attention to me. It gave me the deepest concern to hear that my brother Lord George Gordon stands charged with a crime of such magnitude as that of High Treason. My feelings for his most unhappy situation would have naturally led me to have set out for London immediately if I had not thought it my duty to remain with my Regiment. As soon as I am informed that I can with propriety leave I shall appear before his Majesty to testify my attachment to his person and Government and to implore his clemency in case my unfortunate brother shall be found guilty.

A wholly unofficial comment by Lady Sarah Lennox gives perhaps the best balanced view of Lord George's true character. She was torn by conflicting emotions. Though she was not in London during the riots, she feared for the safety of her brother (Richmond) who was with his regiment, now in Scotland, attempting to maintain order. She knew of the restrictions which had been placed on the military at the outset and remarked tartly in a letter to her beloved cousin Susan, "Government are not *famous* for their skill in the military line."

Yet she had a tie to Lord George Gordon as brother to her erstwhile lover William Gordon, who was father to their child Louisa. Though she had left William years previously at the insistence of her family she still wrote that Gordon is "a name I can never hear with indifference". She feared that Lord George's fate would redound adversely on her William's reputation. She added that she had never seen "the poor, deluded Lord George" and remarked, "I hear he is wonderfully clever but wrong-headed, and I suppose is carried away by imagination beyond all bounds of reason."

Meanwhile the state of anarchy which had prevailed, the widespread destruction, the criminals still at large and the fact of martial law placed the government and George the king himself in a double jeopardy, or dilemma. If His Majesty was the one who restored order, fine; but was he also then the one who now had the country quieted under an armed guard?

George and his ministers clearly were frightened. Right now they dared not take political advantage of a huge unexpected (and rare) victory which had been won by the British forces under Sir Henry Clinton in America. As previously noted, Clinton's troops had had notable success for several months in the campaign against the Southern colonies. Both the Americans and the European courts were shocked by the loss of Polish Count Pulaski, American ally, slain in the siege of Savannah, in late 1779.

Clinton continued his sweep through Georgia and both Carolinas. The valiant officers Benjamin Lincoln, Moultrie, Marion, Sumter, Pickens and Lee harassed the British repeatedly; but Clinton with vastly superior forces compelled the surrender of Charleston, South Carolina, and captured about five thousand troops as well as much plunder in military and civilian supplies. This was the greatest British victory in the entire war.

The news arrived in London on June 16. Under usual circumstances it would have been celebrated by saluting guns, processions, bonfires. Neither the king nor ministry could risk permitting such demonstrations. Bonfires! No celebration bonfires could equal those which had lately blazed in London.

Throughout all the tumult in London and especially as it subsided, George began to worry about how his conduct might appear to the public and on the record. He wrote a cautionary note to the personal secretary of Lord North, at "56 min. past 8 a.m." on Monday, June 13, the first thing on his mind as the new week began. George expressed the hope that North was "closely employed" in preparing the king's speech to Parliament which would set forth "the whole course of my conduct on the present moment". He advised that His Majesty's attachment to the laws and Constitution must be shown, but also that there was a need that "obliged me to step forward to save all from confusion!"

"The thought was my own," said George III in this note, namely the thought that he was obliged "to step forward to save all from confusion". "The thought was my own, but all see the propriety of it. Indeed I will once more try to set the people right as to my own conduct; if this does not succeed I shall never again attempt to follow any line but that of my duty, and expect no justice or gratitude in return."

The somewhat pettish tone suggests that the king was not quite happy about his behaviour in the recent crisis. Legend says that when Rome burned Nero fiddled. When London was aflame George III scribbled—and scribbled belatedly. Forty-eight hours after the rabble had marched on Parliament the king had written note upon note to Stormont and others making suggestions which had already been put into effect, such as placing guards at strategic points. Stormont courteously informed His Majesty: "The commands with which your Majesty has been pleased to honour me shall be most punctually obeyed. Before I received them the intention of them was so far fulfilled that I had taken every step that I thought could be of use."

George III's thought had been "his own" ultimately, but it had been anticipated on June 6th, when seven members of the cabinet, including North, Stormont and Amherst, had addressed a minute to the king. Its issuance at "11.45 p.m." indicated its urgency. The

R

message pointed to the growing disorders, saying "where the civil magistrate declines to direct the soldiery to act with effect, other methods must be taken to preserve the peace and protect the lives and properties of your Majesty's subjects". Only after such memoranda and the force of events had the king finally acted.

There was no evidence of physical cowardice on the king's part but an apparent sluggishness of comprehension, a lack of initiative. Even in his instructions to North regarding the composition of his forthcoming address to Parliament, George III apparently had been guided by an anonymous note dated June 9 which has been preserved in the Royal Archives.

The missive said: "The Proclamation issued by his Majesty, and which, I doubt not, was the suggestion of his own noble mind, has restored the Constitution of this country to its former energy and lustre from which it has been generally declining for many years, until it seemed to be irrecoverably lost. He is now a *King* and may it please God to continue him so."

That was the ticket! When the king's address had been polished and repolished the final form which he read to Parliament on June 19, 1780, included the following justification of His Majesty's conduct: "The outrages committed by bands of lawless and desperate men, in various parts of the metropolis broke forth with such violence into acts of felony and treason, and had so far overborne all civil authority, and threatened so directly the immediate subversion of all legal power, the destruction of all property, and the confusion of every order in the state THAT I found myself obliged by every tie of duty and affection to my people to suppress, in every part, those rebellious insurrections, and to provide for the public safety by the most effectual and immediate force intrusted to me by Parliament."

Never was there a clumsier piece of self-righteousness, considering the events which had gone before and the opportunity for clear leadership. Here was an attempt to cover in advance any criticism of the Crown's action, and the result was a dubious and unconvincing tapestry of half-truths or maybe-truths.

If George III or his ministers by such weasel words thought to appease the opposition or allay resentment of those whose property had been ruined, they were mistaken. Indeed, how belatedly can an action be called "immediate"?

The claim that Parliament had intrusted George III with force flatly contradicted the king's other contention that "the thought was my own".

Opposition to the address developed promptly by several peers in the House of Lords who contended that His Majesty had exceeded the royal authority. At this point Lord Mansfield rose and gave the sweeping interpretation of the law which cleared George's reputation and buried the issue beyond revival.

"Every individual in his private capacity may lawfully interfere to suppress a riot," said Mansfield, ". . . not only is he authorized to interfere for such a purpose, but it is his duty to do so."

By extension, the jurist continued, groups of citizens are entitled to act in the same cause, including constables, magistrates, soldiers, or others. Moreover, he pointed out that if any individual or group exceeded authority to the harm of innocent parties, the latter had recourse through the court. The riot act is merely a law related to the dispersal of a tumultuous assembly without "abridging the means which before existed for preventing or punishing crimes". "His Majesty and those who have advised him," Mansfield concluded, "have acted in strict conformity to the Common Law."

George III had squeezed through this crisis with his reputation temporarily intact, and even enhanced.

36

THE KING ALONE

Temporarily the king and his ministers had won a victory. The City mob had been defeated; and thanks to the king's foresight in seeing that his conduct was favourably presented to the public, George III was regarded as a hero.

In fact, praise of his behaviour in the affair continued for a number of years. Various contemporary writers, such as Wraxall, assumed that His Majesty had played a noble part. As more evidence has come out in recent years, however, through the availability of private correspondence and memoirs, it is clear that the king was something short of noble—not ignoble, but slow, a second-guesser, and indeed a blusterer when it was safe to be so.

George III, at this point, while standing high in the public regard, nevertheless was on the threshold of a crumbling reputation. The Declaration of Independence, as we have seen, wrote an adverse epitaph for future generations, a fact which the king could not realize at the time and possibly never did.

Actually, George now stood pitifully alone, unaware of the weakness of the royal structure. He was like the fallen Cardinal Wolsey, "naked to his enemies" who soon would be throwing more and more deadly and effective darts at him. He was like the legendary emperor who wore no clothes. It was not embarrassing as long as the viewers did not admit the fact; and George was in a slightly less drastic state, because the nakedness of his personality and policies was protected flimsily by the golden Mother Hubbard garment of his royal office which tended to blind the eyes of the beholder.

The chief cause of the king's weakness was that he had dismissed from his presence, one after another, all of the strong men who could have maintained a working government and left him free to strut about as monarch with all the honours of kingship and none of the worries. His grandfather, George II, had enjoyed just such a position.

George III no longer was protected by the brilliant administration of the elder William Pitt. Nor that of the able, if testy, George Grenville, nor Grafton, nor Rockingham. His mother, Augusta, as she was dead, no longer bossed him. Lord Bute, the dominating if unwise adviser of his early reign, had been driven from public office.

Everything was now in George's own hands, through his own intention, and those hands were incapable. The king always resented any criticism. He thought of himself as a strong and righteous man. He was inflated by the oxygen of bravado. From the earliest days of his reign, he repeatedly talked of "firmness and resolution". He thought of himself as doing brave deeds. At the cabinet meeting, when much of London was in flames, he had said that he would lead the Guards against the rioters in person, if necessary. "I lament the conduct of the magistrates, but I can answer for one, one who will do his duty." He had had forty-eight hours in which to do so, but had not taken such a step personally.

Shortly after order had been restored, George III had held a levee attended by one of the chief officers in charge of the troops, to whom he said, "You peppered them well, I hope—peppered them well, peppered them well," referring to the fact that several hundred citizens had been killed or injured during the riots. The officer was aware that the English public was traditionally opposed to the military, and he desired no part of being glorified in the action which had taken place. Hence he replied noncommittally, "I hope your Majesty's troops will always do their duty."

The king and his ministers were temporarily riding high because they had finally survived the crisis, yet apparently they did not comprehend the essentially easygoing temperament of the English people who approved of law and order but did not like to have authority shoved down their throats. A Rev. Thomas Twining, at this time, wrote to Dr. Burney, father of the famous Fanny, "Your true Englishman is never so happy as under a bad government. A perfect administration, could the experiment be tried, would dislocate the jaws of about half of his Majesty's good subjects with ennui."

Not many months after the Gordon riots, when the administration's majorities in Parliament became slimmer and slimmer, the king wrote a memorandum to himself, found among his private papers, which is revealing: "His Majesty, therefore, with much sorrow finds he can be of no further utility to his native country which drives him to the painful step of quitting it forever." That was a typical example of George III's self-dramatization. Of course he did not abdicate, and it is doubtful if he ever had any serious intention of so doing.

In mid-1780 the ministry temporarily was in a strong position, as opposition feared a recurrence of the events of June and accepted authority without much grumbling. Gordon soon removed himself as a popular threat. He wrote a pamphlet about the evils of Popery in Scotland, and sought to present this officially to the king. Technically, he had the right to do so, first as the brother of a duke, and secondly because any citizen supposedly was entitled to make a presentation to the throne; but the ministry wisely advised His Majesty not to receive the document lest Gordon use the audience as a means of recognition. Gordon did not attempt to appeal against the refusal.

Still seeking publicity, the erratic Gordon wrote another pamphlet in which he alleged that the British judiciary had erred in a certain case (not of historical importance). He published a third opus attacking the character of Queen Marie Antoinette of France. For these publications he was convicted of libel and sentenced to five years in Newgate Prison. Further, he adopted the religion of orthodox Judaism, grew a beard, and dressed in the black habit of that faith.

His brother, the Duke of Gordon, who had been willing to intercede for Lord George when charged with high treason, no longer came to the support of this strange character; and ultimately Lord George Gordon, who had been the scourge of London for a brief period, died in prison during an epidemic of jail fever.

The king, naturally, benefited by the fact that Lord George was proved to be an unstable character. After the king's brief popularity, however, the minority in Parliament tried to make capital out of the actions of the military during the riots. Richmond, for a time, attempted to prove that Lord Amherst had exceeded his authority, but finally dropped that when the proposal received little support in the House of Lords.

Charles James Fox, son of Lord Holland and nephew of Lady Sarah Lennox, was a more dangerous opponent when he attacked both the mismanagement of the East India Company and the financial policies of Lord North. North had engineered a bond flotation in which friends of the government had profited hugely, though he himself had not done so. Initially, the brilliant oratory of Charles James Fox did not win majorities, and the king brushed aside Fox's criticisms by saying that they did not come well from an individual who had such a dubious private character. The comment was not particularly impressive from a monarch whose own family were involved in notorious scandals, but as George III personally set an example of conservative conduct, the remark sufficed for the time being.

Fox, Richmond, Burke and other brilliant orators against the government policy for a number of months won little support. Had the British armies continued to be successful in North America, the king might have continued to ride triumphantly; but the successes of Sir Henry Clinton in the Southern states, which had so elated the government, had been dimmed by increasing bad news.

Clinton had left Cornwallis in charge of the Southern area, and had retired to New York where he expected General Washington to stage a major battle. Washington, in fact, had prepared misleading dispatches which he hoped would fall into Clinton's hands. That took place and Clinton was completely fooled.

Meanwhile Cornwallis, then second in command, was left in charge in the Southern area. In England he had been led to believe that thousands of loyalists would flock to the British standard, but he was forced to report that this was not the case. His troops were under continuous attack from guerilla bands, and he found everywhere that the bulk of colonists were firmly attached to the cause of independence.

37

THE KING IN CRISIS

As the weeks rolled along without any conclusive victory in America there was an ever-spreading current of criticism against the government and its policies. There was a nucleus of idealists who believed that the colonists were fighting for the principles of free men. Then there were those who desired to oust North and the king's men in order to get the political plums for themselves. Further, the City of London, whose officials had been treated with repeated hauteur by the king, seethed with resentment against him.

Initially there had been general indifference to the American war, especially in the rural areas of Great Britain, but now many segments of society were being hurt. France was profiting by the American trade formerly enjoyed by England. There was increased poverty and depression, the public debt was constantly rising and the tax burden was increasing. Burke introduced a bill into Parliament for reform of the civil list, which was a stinging commentary on the extravagance of the ministry and the Crown. North urged His Majesty to consider bringing some of the opposition into the government.

George agreed to that conditionally, saying, "I am as anxious as ever for strengthening of Administration, if it can be obtained without a violation of my principles." He added that any newcomers "must give assurance that they do not mean to be hampered by the tenets they have held during their Opposition". North, through an intermediary, sounded out Rockingham and came back to the king with a series of proposals of which at least two were acutely distasteful. While Rockingham wished no office for himself he would not lend his support to a new alignment unless the Duke of Richmond and Charles James Fox were considered.

George III recoiled at the name of Richmond who, ever since the slight to his sister Lady Sarah Lennox, had repeatedly attacked the king. George said to North that after the duke's "unremitted personal ill conduct to me, it cannot be expected that I should express any wish of seeing him in my service". Further, George recalled that Richmond had proposed that the property qualification for voting be changed in favour of universal manhood suffrage. George considered that to be "a strange conceit" which would alter the Constitution. Again, "the Duke of Richmond has not put his foot into my apartment for above seven or eight years". Obviously, His Grace would not be acceptable and Rockingham doubtless knew that.

Though Fox was one of the Richmond-Lennox-Fox cousinhood, George regarded him with less resentment, though sneeringly. The king was willing to give him a "lucrative" office not of ministerial rank, "provided he will support the measures of Government". George added, "He never having had any principle can certainly act as his interest may guide him."

As long as the king insisted that ministers must agree in advance to accept his programmes and policy there was no chance of winning over any strong men in the opposition. As late as June 1781 he was resentful of a motion for a committee to consider the American war, and though it was defeated, George referred to the "impudence of the minority in again bringing it forward". He judged rightly that the current military posture of Great Britain would not produce the sort of peace acceptable to the Crown, but "it is by steadiness and exertions that we are to get into a situation to effect it". George felt with undoubted sincerity that on the defeat of America, especially on the independence issue, hinged "whether we are to rank among the Great Powers of Europe or be reduced to one of the least considerable".

North was in an agony of frustration over the king's policy which he saw to be unrealistic, whether desirable or not. Moreover, there were political thinkers of the time, including Adam Smith, author of *The Wealth of Nations*, who held that Great Britain would be better off economically without the colonies and that trade with America as a young, vigorous nation would be beneficial to all parties; but George III persisted in his views.

Through information obtained by a North agent, the king heard that France was having financial troubles and that Franklin was not able to borrow as much as the colonies sought. The news was greatly cheering to George: "I think it has the appearance that this long contest will end as it ought by the colonies returning to the mother country and I confess I will never put my hand to any other conclusion of this business."

His Majesty as usual laboured under the difficulty of rarely discussing his governmental policies with any except his inner cabinet, or those he set to spy on them, and he was not receptive to men who disagreed with him. The bulk of his communications were with Lord North whom he regarded as a subordinate, rather than as an adviser. In short, the king was self-insulated from the opinion of all except courtiers who told him what he liked to hear.

As late as November 3, 1781, dispatches arrived in London from General Clinton at New York headquarters which assumed that Cornwallis would move from his encampment at Yorktown, descend upon and beat Lafayette. In that case the two British generals could combine to fight the main American army under Washington. The king was elated: "if such an event can be effected I think success must ensue." He referred to the British forces in America as "such excellent troops"; he expressed confidence in the valour of the navy and army; he felt that France would be ineffective because of her "duplicity"; he affirmed "the justness of our cause" and expressed faith in the assistance of Divine Providence. "The object is certainly worth struggling for," George said in a lengthy message to Lord North, "and I trust the Nation is equally determined with myself to meet the conclusion with firmness."

In spite of all the favourable considerations which he mentioned, the king was seriously worried. Immediately after his reference to Divine Providence, he had written: "The moment is certainly anxious." His Majesty, indeed, had cause to be concerned, for against those hope-producing possibilities which he had recited was the weight of numerous disasters. Holland had declared war on England, which added a powerful fleet to the already superior numbers of enemy vessels. France had blockaded Gibraltar and a Bourbon squadron continued to threaten in the Channel. Russia's Catherine II instigated a so-called armed neutrality pact of European nations whereby any vessels not officially at war with England would be free from visit and search. Up to that point Britain had been stopping neutral ships suspected of carrying arms or other war material to her enemies. France and Spain scored several naval victories in the West Indies, including the capture of fifty richly laden British merchant vessels in a single battle.

No wonder that the king needed a stiff upper lip, and had needed one for some time past. The nation was becoming sick of this unsuccessful firmness and determination.

"*Firmness* is the word, let the nation sink or swim," the Earl of Pembroke wrote to his son. The earl was the same Pembroke who recently had been of the king's household. "Everybody pities him, and us. We are going to the Devil & beat too in the West Indies. How wonderfully this vast (and till now glorious) edifice is crumbling away to nothing under our feet."

As will be recalled, George Washington had fooled Clinton into expecting a major engagement in the New York area, while Cornwallis had remained in the Yorktown peninsula on Chesapeake Bay expecting to receive a load of supplies from British vessels coming from New York, England and the West Indies. Cornwallis was not wholly foolish in this move. Not only had he been disappointed in the failure of most colonials to support him with supplies or manpower, but also the relatively few loyalists were impoverished and besought him for aid of all sorts, including food, which he was unable to provide. If his supplies had been replenished by the British fleet while he encamped at Yorktown he might have been able to carry out those manœuvres predicted by Clinton in his dispatches.

In retrospect it is obvious that Cornwallis took a fatal risk in staying at Yorktown; but both he and Clinton evidently underestimated the resourcefulness of General Washington. Of necessity throughout most of the war the American army had avoided major battles, as in the retreat from White Plains, repeatedly waiting to counter the next British moves. Hence the swift attack which Washington now made on Cornwallis was unforeseen, as was the speed with which the French fleet moved into Chesapeake Bay well ahead of the British fleet, preventing relief from that quarter.

Several weeks before the uninformed George III had been relying on Divine Providence to assist him, Cornwallis had been under siege from land and sea. The serious bombardment of his encampment began on October 9. He defended his position as best he could for ten days, losing more than five hundred and fifty of his men in the process; but, surrounded on all sides, his situation was hopeless. On October 19, 1781, he surrendered his army of seven thousand soldiers and nine hundred seamen.

As the British army musicians marched onto a field near Yorktown for the ceremony of capitulation they played a then popular tune: "The World Turned Upside Down."

38

ABASEMENT OF THE KING

Despite the surrender at Yorktown, George III could not bring himself to face defeat. Like an animal at bay he struggled desperately to escape the inevitable; and his mental convolutions as he retreated step by step were a revelation of his character.

Though the king was badly shaken by the surrender of Cornwallis, he was by no means ready to yield. Though North saw clearly that the ministry must resign, there still was much work for him to do. Because of the slowness of sailing ships the news of Yorktown had not reached London until November 25, 1781, and Parliament was to meet within two days. The prime minister's immediate task was to revise the king's speech radically. His current draft had virtually ignored the American war. Under George's instructions the new speech deplored the unfortunate circumstances, but called upon the country to make fresh efforts in order to maintain the integrity of the empire.

The nation and Parliament were stunned by the news and the opposition did not immediately pull itself together for action. Hence approval of the king's address was voted with the usual majorities of the ministry. Though this temporary victory did not fool Lord North into thinking that the storm would be averted, George III chose to look upon it as a good omen. He directed Germain to write out his proposals as to the most feasible measures for conducting the war and instructed that each member of the cabinet should pass upon the proposals and add any thoughts of their own. "If measures are well connected," George III wrote to North, "a good end may yet be made to the war, but if we despond certain ruin ensues."

That comment was made at 8.40 in the morning of the second day of Parliament, November 28, 1781. The discussions in the House of Commons were still inchoate and desultory, for the nation indeed had a problem of what would be the best thing to do next. The king again felt that absence of attack in Parliament augured well. That evening he wrote to North, "I have no doubt, when men are a little recovered of the shock felt by the bad news . . .

they will then find the necessity of carrying on the war, though the mode of it may require alterations."

On December 13, 1781, Sir James Lowther in the Commons moved to put an end to the American war. Though the government defeated the motion by a margin of forty-one votes, the issue forced North to declare what the ministry had in mind. He told the Commons that he was ready to concede that it would not be "wise or right" to go on with the war according to the prior plan of sending armies into the interior of the provinces, "which had failed of producing the intended and desired effect". He was embarrassed to be so definite, but upon studying the estimates for army expenditure, which were then on the table for the perusal of the members, it was clear that the cost of raising larger armies would make such a procedure impractical.

George III told North that he approved of that explanation, as obviously something needed to be said, but the king still did not recede from his intent to carry on the conflict. Meanwhile His Majesty and the ministry had a brief reprieve as Parliament adjourned for the Christmas holidays, not to return until late January.

During the recess there was a growing disposition on the part of the cabinet to get rid of their colleague, Lord George Germain. As Secretary of State for the Colonies, he had failed to produce victory, had grossly misjudged the temper of the provinces, and had made various notable bungles.

North was of uncertain mind on this subject. He knew that to make Germain a scapegoat would not save the ministry. It will be recalled that several years previously George III would have welcomed the retirement of Germain, but the latter had solidified his position with the king by repeatedly clamouring that the colonies must submit and come to the mercy seat in a proper mood of penitence.

In spite of George's current regard for Germain, he was willing to dispense with his services if necessary. Germain had pointed out the necessity of naming a new commander-in-chief for the American scene. The king thought that Sir Guy Carleton, who for a brief time had been chief British official in Canada, would be the best choice. Carleton had made it clear that under no circumstances would he serve under Germain. The king, who normally gave orders to Lord North rather than seeking his advice, was in a quandary on this one and asked that North give his opinion as soon as possible. North delayed answering, because the question was irrelevant if the government was going to be forced to abandon the war or even to revise strategy drastically.

Meanwhile Germain had wind of the opposition of the cabinet to him and called upon the king to find out where he stood. He put the question as to whether he was or was not to look upon himself as Secretary of State for the colonies and said that his messenger to Lord North on the subject could get no definite reply. George III said that "as yet" certainly no step had been taken to remove him, but what was his own feeling about remaining?

Germain said that he was ready to stay "if the war was carried on with vigour, if steps were taken to strike a blow in the West Indies and . . . the separation with America was not adopted". Failing those conditions Germain said that he would retire, but he urged that he be raised to the peerage as a viscount so that he would retire with honour. He held that it would not do to make him merely a baron. "Should I only be raised to the dignity of a baron," he observed, "my own secretary [Thomas de Grey], my lawyer [Alexander Wedderburn], and my father's page [Jeffery Amherst], will all take rank of me." Though all of the three men named by Germain had had notable careers compared with his, he could not forget that he was the son of the Duke of Dorset.

Two aspects of this colloquy were distasteful to George III. First of all it really decided nothing and secondly it was a piece of cheek for a subject to nominate himself for the peerage, let alone specifying the degree. On the other hand, the Dorset-Sackville connection was a large one and it would not be prudent to make new enemies in view of the declining government margins in Parliament. On the plus side, too, the king still approved of Germain's position on the war.

A day or two after this interview the king still had not heard from Lord North and wrote to him, in a testy tone, complaining that Lord North had chosen "to keep this affair above six weeks in the same state of indecision". Then he added, "I shall ever co-incide with Ld. G. Germain, that is, against a separation from America, and that I shall never lose an opportunity of declaring that no consideration shall ever make me in the smallest degree an instrument in a measure that I am confident would annihilate the rank in which this British empire stands among the European States, and would render my situation in this country below continuing an object to me."

There were two phrases in the king's comments which indicated the beginning of weakening in his hitherto immovable position. There was no longer the confidence that he could make the colonies submit, for he retreated to the point of saying that he would not be *an instrument* in acknowledging separation. Again, instead of his familiar threat of preferring to lose his crown, he made the more temperate statement that his situation would no longer be an object to him.

The Germain matter was cleared up quickly as North was able to find a replacement in the person of Welbore Ellis, whose anti-colonial views coincided with His Majesty's, and the king in turn bought peace with Germain by making him a viscount.

North, who had sought so frequently to resign, was well aware that his ministry was doomed to fall. He preferred to get out gracefully and with His Majesty's approval. George, however, showed no disposition to be relieved of his hitherto pliant servant, though North now kept making himself a subtly annoying character. He must have known that a proposal which he made to the king on February 9, 1782, would be unpalatable, namely that Lord William Gordon be appointed to the dignified office of Vice-Admiral of Scotland—Lord William Gordon who was brother to the Gordon of the Gordon riots, former lover of Lady Sarah Lennox and father of her child. George rejected the suggestion on several counts and remarked dryly that the private character of Lord William was not much in his favour. (The appointment later was forced upon the king, after the resignation of the North ministry.)

When Parliament reassembled toward the end of January the opposition was in full cry and it was joined daily by increasing numbers of those who formerly had voted with the government. Throughout February the only clear-cut victory of the government was the approval of a loan to carry on the affairs of the nation. There were numerous votes of censure offered on one detail or another and the government margin in defeating these was increasingly slim.

On February 25, 1782, the government was able to block a resolution to discontinue the American war only by one vote. George was now thoroughly frightened. His boldness weakened to the point of being satisfied with having done his duty. His words to Lord North are memorable: "Undoubtedly the House of Commons seem to be wild at present, and to be running on to ruin, that no man can answer for the event of any question. I certainly till drove to the wall [will] do what I can to save the empire, and, if I do not succeed, I will at least have the self-approbation of having done my duty, and of not letting myself be a tool in the destruction of the honour of the country."

Though the king seemed almost willing to give way on the American issue, he was by no means prepared to abandon the North ministry *in toto*. He would be willing to part with North if necessary, but only if a satisfactory substitute of the king's own choosing could be found. He repeatedly said that he would not put himself into the hands of "faction", as had been his lot in the days of George Grenville. In short, he affirmed that he would not accept a cabinet made up of the opposition.

As the government majorities kept declining George realized that if the government should lose its majority in Parliament, Lord North would feel that the ministry must resign. Aiming to forestall any such action he said to North that there would be no need for the administration to quit solely because of adverse votes in the Commons. George proposed to reign with a cabinet of his own choosing, whether or not he had the confidence of Parliament.

North normally was respectful to his master, but this doctrine shook him to the depths of his being, and he laid down the law to the king in no uncertain terms: "Your Majesty is well apprized that in this country the Prince on the Throne cannot, with prudence, oppose the deliberate resolution of the House of Commons." The prime minister tried to save face for the king by pointing out that there were cases in the past where the monarch did not have his own way: "Your Royal Predecessors (particularly King William the Third and his late Majesty) were obliged to yield to it much against their wish in more instances than one: They consented to changes in their Ministry which they disapproved because they found it necessary to sacrifice their private wishes, and even their opinions, to the preservation of public order, and the prevention of these terrible mischiefs, which are the natural consequence of the clashing of two branches of the Sovereign Power in the State."

North pointed out that concessions by the throne were never thought to be dishonourable, but were considered as marks of wisdom. He praised George for steady support of the ministry and for adhering to what appeared "essential to the welfare and dignity of this country". However, North observed that the Parliament had altered its sentiments and "their sentiments whether just or erroneous must ultimately prevail".

This was bitter medicine indeed, but North had even worse news. He said that he was aware that the king would like to form a ministry "on a broad bottom", namely not beholden to any party except His Majesty, but this North held to be impossible. He was aware that the king had authorized Thurlow, the Lord Chancellor, to see what he might do about putting together a cabinet of the sort the king desired, but Thurlow and North in a private conference reached the conclusion that there were no persons willing and capable of forming a new administration "except Lord Rockingham and Lord Shelburne with their parties". Those two gentlemen were willing to have Thurlow continue as Lord Chancellor which would give the king one friend in the ministry, but that was all. North went on to say that the new group would constitute a strong ministry able to handle the great problems of government. Said North: "Your Majesty's goodness encourages me to lay my poor but honest advice before you."

George was absolutely furious. On the night of March 19, 1782, he wrote to Lord North, "Till I have heard what the Chancellor has done from his own mouth, I shall not take any step, and if you resign before I have decided what I will do, you will certainly forever forfeit my regard."

The king, who was at Windsor when he wrote this tart message, was unaware of certain events that were already taking place. The opposition in Parliament had found that they now had a clear majority ready to overthrow the ministry and on the 19th there was a large attendance at the House licking their lips over the intended political assassination of Lord North. Most of them were in their seats by early afternoon and most of them had dismissed their carriages until late evening, for they expected that the debate would be lengthy, as there were some skilled orators on the government side as well as in the opposition.

The very colour of the day was appropriate to cloak-and-dagger deeds. It was raw and chilly and snow was falling. As time passed by North did not appear and the Parliament became restive, occupying itself with routine business. Finally at 4.15 North entered in formal dress with the blue ribbon of the Garter across his breast, looking as chipper and cheerful as you please.

Immediately there was an uproar. Lord Surrey, who had been chosen to move the vote of censure, sought to get the floor, but so did Lord North. In fact the latter had turned to address the chair immediately he reached the Treasury bench. Neither man would yield and the members kept shouting for "Surrey" or "North" according to their respective preferences.

At last, in a momentary lull, North was able to shout that any motion which the opposition might have in mind was unnecessary as the ministry had ceased to exist. This was such an unexpected move that everyone was eager to hear what North might have to say. He was most gracious, thanked the Commons for their long support and forbearance, expressed regret that their confidence was now withdrawn, but said that they probably soon would have a leader of greater abilities and qualifications. The resignation and North's attitude torpedoed the speeches that Surrey and others had planned to make.

There were a few abortive growls about the need to look into numerous deeds of the administration which had just been concluded. But North put a stop to that line of talk by saying that he had no intention of running away, that he would continue in Parliament, and added, "I am perfectly conscious I am responsible for my conduct, and whenever my country shall call upon me to answer, it is my indispensable duty to answer for every part of that conduct."

The House soon adjourned and the members straggled out into the cold, facing a dreary delay while they sent for their coaches. All were in that situation except Lord North who had not dismissed his carriage. "Gentlemen," he said with a smile as he stepped into his coach, "this is the first time I have ever had any advantage from being in the secret."

George III was completely undone. "At last the fatal day has come," he wrote to North, "which the misfortunes of the times and the sudden change of sentiments of the House of Commons have drove me to." He did not throw in his crown or retire to Hanover, as he had often threatened, but surrendered gracefully, for the time being. He instructed North to have the old cabinet at St. James's Palace to go through the ceremony of formal resignation. "I shall hope to be there if possible by one, and will receive them before the levee, as I think it would be awkward to have the new people presented at the levee prior to the resignations."

S

PART V

Final Reckoning

39

A NEW UNWELCOME ROLE

George III now entered upon a new period of his life in which he was virtually a prisoner of successive cabinets. Only in a few instances in the next dozen years was he able to break loose and assert his own initiative. The change was a drastic contrast to the years of the North administration when the king had ordered both policy and an infinite number of details. Now his assignment was to do virtually nothing and he occupied his energies in domestic fussiness and rural pursuits.

George had been stampeded into accepting the second Rockingham ministry and for a few months he was stunned by the change. The new cabinet pointedly ignored him and sincerely believed that the proper role of the king was to be a cipher, a dignified but powerless head of the state.

The new Rockingham ministry included various men who were singularly distasteful to the king. There was the Duke of Richmond as Master General of Ordnance. The Duke of Grafton, whom the king regarded as a man who had deserted him, was Lord Privy Seal. Dunning, who had moved that the power of the Crown ought to be diminished, had an honorary post. General Conway, who had obtained the repeal of the Stamp Act, was now Commander-in-Chief. The Howe brothers, who had been seemingly lackadaisical in their pursuit of the American war, had minor posts, as did Edmund Burke, who had steadily advocated conciliation of the American colonies. The two Secretaries of State were Lord Shelburne and the hated Charles James Fox. As mentioned previously, of the king's friends only Thurlow, the Lord Chancellor, remained. Included in a minor role as Lord Lieutenant of Ireland was the inconspicuous Duke of Portland who was due soon to come into prominence.

As Thurlow was the one official close to the king for the next decade, his personality was of considerable importance. He has been described as a "thug in robes". He was large, ruddy-faced, beetle-browed, and overbearing. He was a thorough student of the law and could speak brilliantly, but enjoyed making his point with invective and shouting down his opponent.

George III, who normally resented any opposition, appraised Thurlow's rugged honesty at its true worth and reported an incident to a cabinet member who had come down to Windsor on government business. Said the king, "You are not acting correctly; you should do one of two things, either bring me down the Acts for my perusal, or say, as Thurlow once said to me on a like occasion: having read several, he stopped and said, It was all damned nonsense trying to make me understand them, and that I had better consent to them at once."

Even toward the end of his life when Thurlow was out of office, old and in poor health, he retained his vigour of expression. On being told that someone was planning a biography of Lord Bute, Thurlow observed, "The life of a fly would be as interesting!"

The second Rockingham ministry had come in in March 1782 and on July 1, 1782, Rockingham unexpectedly died. Fate repeatedly had entered into the king's affairs, changing the direction of his ways. Grenville was gone, so was Chatham, so was George's loyal uncle the Duke of Cumberland. If Rockingham had lived, his ministry might have lasted a number of years. Though the king heartily disliked the group, they constituted a strong government and might have gradually become more gracious to His Majesty. At any rate, with the death of Rockingham George was temporarily released from his thraldom, because the different Whig factions fell to quarrelling among themselves, and the king now had the satisfaction of trying to put together a cabinet of his own choosing.

George III hoped to have Thurlow as prime minister and instructed him to see what he could do about forming a cabinet. Thurlow was willing, but had honest doubts about the possibility. He was not a party man. He had voted both for and against Whig measures from time to time. If anything, he was a Tory. He had shouted loudly against "the rebellion" of the colonies and had sought to frame punitive laws against them, until a colleague pointed out that "rebellion" as such was not included in the criminal code. Thurlow, normally a persistent man, did not pursue the matter further, for the chief motive in his anti-colonialism was to support the king. Nevertheless, his record on the American issue was a political liability in the current temper of Parliament.

In short, Thurlow was obliged to report back to George III that he could not summon enough followers to form a cabinet.

George saw that he must placate the Whig connection, in some way, and he proceeded to do so with a bit of shrewd strategy. Charles James Fox, a Secretary of State, was perhaps the ablest man in the cabinet and expected to succeed Rockingham. Another logical choice would have been Edmund Burke, who had been the political brains of the late minister; but the king offered the post to Shelburne, who accepted. This aroused the fury of the Foxite Whigs who resigned. That left Shelburne with a thin line of support, though Grafton and Richmond stayed with him and a new star came into the firmament in the person of William Pitt, Chatham's son, who accepted the office of Chancellor of the Exchequer.

Shelburne found himself the target of abuse. General Conway, kinsman and favourite of Horace Walpole, was a non-Shelburne Whig and hence Walpole has left a vitriolic description of Shelburne's character which has tended to colour history.

Shelburne was a somewhat mysterious person, in part because he was independent and in part because he chose to speak in riddles or in vague terms. This often was done with a purpose, as in the case of his negotiations with America in favour of a generous peace which would ensure long-term tranquillity between the two countries. Shelburne saw no advantage, only liability, in retaining the string of British forts along the western frontier. A forthright declaration of his intentions at this juncture, however, would have defeated his cause; but he succeeded quietly in bringing about a peace treaty favourable to the United States.

Shelburne's ministry lasted for less than a year, from July 1782 to April 1783, but it deserves a permanent place in history because of the peace treaty between the United States of America and England which was negotiated under his direction. The provisional draft was signed at Paris, November 30, 1782; and as indicated above it ceded the vast Central Plains area to the United States, contrary to the geographical terms of the Quebec Act. This was an unprecedented action in the history of nations for there was no *quid pro quo* involved and a much less favourable settlement could have been forced upon the United States; but Shelburne had the genius to look toward the long-range relationships of the two countries.

The king did his best to help Shelburne to strengthen his administration, consulting with two new adherents. One was Dunning, author of the anti-monarchical motion; and the other was Thomas Pitt, a cousin of the younger William. Dunning had become hostile to certain Whig factions because as the chief lawyer of the opposition he had had good reason to expect that he would be made Lord Chancellor. The Thurlow deal had made that impossible and Dunning was *not* appeased by a place in the cabinet, a handsome sinecure, and a peerage (he was created Lord Ashburton). There were numerous conferences between Dunning and His Majesty, but they came to naught as Dunning had no important political influence, on top of which he died on August 18, 1783.

The royal conversations with Thomas Pitt at first appeared more promising. Thomas was urged to persuade William, who was only in his early twenties, to be prime minister. That would have been an excellent solution, bringing in the support of influential Whig elements and having the merit in George's eyes of being his own selection. William Pitt was much interested in the suggestion, but felt that he must be absolutely assured of a sizeable support in Parliament, lest he be discredited at the very outset of his career. He said that he must consult his mother before giving a final answer.

The relationship of Hester Pitt, widow of Chatham, to her children and to public affairs was quite different from that of the late princess dowager. In the numerous sick spells with which Chatham had been afflicted in his later years, Hester was the intermediary between him and the cabinet. In such times she handled his correspondence and was interviewed by his callers; and she did all of this unobtrusively. Obviously her judgment in the present situation was valuable and she advised her son to wait.

While these discussions were in progress other plans were being hatched without George's knowledge. Lord North still had a sizeable personal following in the Commons and Charles James Fox continued to be the favourite of one of the Whig factions. Hence friends conceived the idea of bringing the two together with the purpose of throwing out Shelburne and getting possession of the plums of office. The political world was scandalized by the cynicism of this alliance. The two men had spent a decade in denouncing each other. North defended his action by saying that he was burying his personal feelings in the public interest. His *apologia* indeed was quite suave and might have been persuasive if there had been any crying public need for the services of himself and Fox.

There are certainly times and circumstances and emergencies when it highly becomes all honest men, of every Party and description, manfully to relinquish their personal feuds and temporary animosities, and unite their serious efforts by one generous exertion, in the common interest. It is, then, that mutually convinced of the integrity and honour of each other's intentions, however much they may have differed in the carrying those intentions into execution, [they] could fairly meet in one cordial body for the public good. Every individual inspired by the genuine love of his country would then think it his duty to abate somewhat of the violence with which his former opinion was maintained, and form a junction at once honourable to himself and serviceable to his country. . . . Our union is on public principles; and to the public we shall always be ready to give in a just account of our stewardship.

North previously had been able to be prime minister because he had the support of the Crown and all its patronage, but neither he nor Fox had the financial strength or prestige to serve as first minister. The Whig aristocracy never felt quite secure in a ministry unless it were well larded with men of wealth. Accordingly the two plotters prevailed upon the Duke of Portland, a very rich man, to take the chief office, namely First Lord of the Treasury. They made themselves Secretaries of State, ousted Thurlow, and won the support of Parliament. Hence the king was forced to accept them.

George was beside himself with astonishment and anger. Not without reason, he looked upon North as a traitor and an ingrate, for he had provided handsomely for the former prime minister upon the latter's retirement; but North evidently welcomed the opportunity to exercise his independence.

The king contemplated the possibility of refusing to recognize Portland, regardless of consequences. The only solution that George could evolve was to abdicate in favour of his eldest son and he privately broached this idea to the ousted Thurlow who apparently gave him no encouragement. Thereupon George in his own hand drafted a message ostensibly to be sent to Parliament, proposing abdication and giving the reasons why, in which he said he was "communicating to you my intentions, not asking your advice".

George III said that "selfish views are so prevalent" that they had destroyed patriotism; that the real object of the American war had been destroyed by the actions of Parliament; and that he had failed in his effort to bring together an administration of the efficient men of all parties who might make definitive treaties.

Then the draft added: "A long experience and a serious attention to the strange Events that have successively arisen, has gradually prepared my mind to expect the time when I should be no
longer of Utility to this Empire; that hour is now come." He went
on to be more specific: "I am therefore resolved to resign my
Crown and all the Dominions appertaining to it to the Prince of
Wales, my Eldest Son and Lawful Successor, and to retire to the
care of my Electoral Dominions the Original Patrimony of my
Ancestors."

He then expressed the hope that "this personal sacrifice will
awake the various parties to a sense of their duty". He said that
he was resolved "forever to quit this island", but hoped that the
nation would give his son every assistance.

Before making his resignation public, however, George III consulted Thomas Pitt who produced a practical if unpleasant solution.
In a lengthy memorandum Thomas Pitt proposed that His Majesty
not abdicate and that he accept this new regime; but that the king
should let it be known that he did so unwillingly and would with-
hold any favours at the disposition of the Crown.

Thomas Pitt averred that the disfavour of the throne would so
weaken the Portland ministry that it would soon fall apart. Those
who were disappointed in their expectations of office would abandon the Fox-North men. "Those who were attached to them from
principle would disclaim them for deserting their principles . . .
reaping the fruits of their perfidy." Thomas Pitt pointed out that
the new administration would have the unpopularity of arranging
new loans and burdensome taxes and advised George "to yield his
Government and the *responsibility* of it into those hands".

George III welcomed this solution. It would have been a grim
end to his life to retire to Hanover, especially as he had never even
been on the Continent. The line of conduct advocated by Thomas
Pitt worked. The ministry came into office in April 1783 and
ended in December. The king announced that he would create no
new peers and he would not distribute any of the small amount of
patronage still left at his disposal.

Charles Fox had proposed a new bill for the control of the East
India Company. This had been one of his pet fields of legislation,
though opinion on the subject was closely divided. At this juncture
the king took an unconstitutional step, but he was beyond caring
about that. He sent a card to Lord Temple in the House of
Peers authorizing him to say that the king would regard as an

enemy anyone who voted for the East India bill. The act failed of passage by a narrow margin and that was the end of the Portland ministry.

The king instructed Thurlow to approach young William Pitt again. This time Pitt accepted and began a long ministry in which Thurlow was reappointed as Lord Chancellor.

George, however, never regained the authority which he had assumed in the days of North. Pitt was studiously courteous to the king; but he was aloof and conducted the affairs of state, like his father, according to his own wishes and sought merely the formal approval of His Majesty.

George might have had a comfortable twilight to his life except for his increasing ill health and the continuously scandalous actions of his sons, similar to those of his brothers described earlier. George raved about the evils of the times such as the gambling houses to which his sons were attracted. Charles James Fox was part-owner of one of these establishments and an inveterate gambler. Fox engineered through Parliament a bill to provide an allowance of £100,000 annually for the Prince of Wales. The king blamed Fox for the debauching of the prince, though that had already been accomplished. Moreover, the prince openly campaigned for the Foxites against Pitt in elections which the Pitt supporters won (though Fox won his seat in Westminster); and George III in rage cancelled the customary birthday celebration for the prince.

When Frederick, Duke of York, the second son, returned from several years of military duty in Germany, George III was moment- arily delighted, but Frederick soon came under the influence of his older brother and helped to found a gambling club. He became involved with the Countess of Tyrconnel, a woman of doubtful reputation, and he enjoyed unusual and shocking games. For example, he and his brother staged street races at Brighton between partially clad females, offering smocks as prizes.

The third son, William, Duke of Clarence, presented a different type of problem. He loved a commoner. George III had assigned William to the navy at the age of thirteen. He had served credit- ably on various vessels except for the fact that he resisted discipline. In defiance of his commanding officer at Quebec he sailed back to Plymouth where he arrived early in 1788. The king ordered William to stay at Plymouth in disgrace which proved to be no punishment at all as the two older princes joined him there and engaged in a round of parties. Then William fell in love with the daughter of a local merchant and proposed marriage. That was too much for the king who sent his son to sea again.

These incidents preyed upon the royal mind. He confided to his brother, the Duke of Gloucester, that after hearing of one of his sons' escapades he had not been able to sleep for ten nights.

40

HOME LIFE OF A MONARCH

Just before Pitt took office George III displayed an unusual bit of enterprise. On an evening in March, 1784, occurred one of the most bizarre incidents in British history: the Great Seal was stolen.

The Great Seal customarily was in the custody of the Lord Chancellor who was the highest officer of the Crown, outranking everyone except the king, the royal princes, and the Archbishop of Canterbury. Thurlow, having been reappointed Lord Chancellor, obtained the seal from the Commissioners thereof and took it home for safe-keeping. It was enclosed in an inner silk case and an outer case of leather. He then left it in a room next to his upstairs study and retired for the night.

While the Lord Chancellor slept, thieves jumped over the garden wall, forced two bars from the kitchen window, found the Great Seal in the room adjacent to the study, took it from its cases, took also a pair of swords and a small sum of money, and absconded without rousing anyone.

The king suspected that Fox was responsible for the job, as Fox might have thought that the loss of the Great Seal would stop the wheels of government. The Great Seal customarily was used in the dissolution of Parliament and if that could be delayed for several days or weeks while a new seal was being prepared, there might be a change in the trend of opinion in the Commons which had been running against the Foxite party.

George III moved into this situation with vigour. Thurlow had discovered the loss of the seal promptly upon awakening. He called upon Pitt who had moved into 10 Downing Street, and they both waited upon the king who fortunately was in town at St. James's

Palace. George III immediately summoned his chief engraver and sketched out directions for the design of both sides of a new Great Seal. Within twenty-four hours the new seal was ready (though a more finished replica was made later). Then on March 25, 1784, the king proceeded to the House of Lords and the Commons were summoned. The Lord Chancellor stood at the king's right hand holding the new Great Seal in the old purse.

"My Lords and Gentlemen," said George III, "on a full consideration of the present situation of affairs and of the extraordinary circumstances which have produced it, I am induced to put an end to this session of Parliament." The young Pitt was now officially in charge until another Parliament came in.

The first eight years of Pitt's administration were characterized by peace and prosperity. John Adams in 1785 was presented to the king in his role as American minister to the Court of St. James and was agreeably surprised to be received in a courteous and friendly manner. George III asked that it might be understood in America that his actions in the late contest reflected what he believed to be his duty. He said that he had been the last to consent to the separation, but since it had come about, he would be the first to meet friendship with friendship.

Since the young Mr. Pitt relieved the king of all routine business, George spent much of his time with his family at Windsor Castle where he acted like an absolute monarch at a petty German court. The atmosphere of the royal household was appallingly stultifying. In the presence of the king and queen no one was supposed to speak until or unless spoken to, not even the princesses. When Fanny Burney was called upon to read to the queen and guests she was expected to read straight ahead; no one was to interrupt and no one must comment. Fanny Burney, who was for several years on the household staff at Windsor, had this to say of the required decorum in the presence of the king and queen:

In the first place you must not cough. If you find a cough tickling in your throat, you must arrest it from making any sound; if you find yourself choking with the forebearance, you must choke—but not cough. In the second place, you must not sneeze. If you have a vehement cold, you must take no notice of it; if your nose membranes feel a great irritation, you must hold your breath; if a sneeze still insists upon making its way, you must oppose it, by keeping your teeth grinding together; if the violence of the repulse breaks some blood-vessel, you must break the blood-vessel—but not sneeze.

The king insisted that his judgment must prevail even in matters of taste. The Princess Royal, the oldest daughter, had no ear for music and even disliked it, but George insisted that her birthday celebration must consist of a concert.

The king's own taste left much to be desired. In talking to Miss Burney he said, "Was there ever such stuff as the great part of Shakespeare? Only one must not say so. But what think you— what? Is there not sad stuff? What, What? . . . I know it's not to be said, but it's true. Only it's Shakespeare and nobody dare abuse him, but one should be stoned for saying so!"

He disliked Voltaire and Rousseau (though he had consented to a pension for the latter), thinking their ideas to be subversive.

Of James Boswell he had a better opinion, though Boswell was something of a buffoon. The king had heard that Boswell was going to publish a life of Samuel Johnson and predicted that "perhaps he will devise something extraordinary."

George had a ruling that none of his several daughters could marry before the age of thirty, and he refused offers of marriage for them without their knowledge. The result was that one or another were afflicted with hysterics, illnesses, melancholia, and epilepsy. One princess, Sophia, is alleged to have given birth to a child without benefit of clergy, by an equerry in the household. The sadistic tyranny of George III over his daughters is difficult to understand except possibly as a symptom of his growing mental instability.

The king and queen also were inconsiderate of their household staff, even those at the upper levels such as the equerries of the king and personal attendants of the queen. Whereas the royal apartments were comfortably heated, the quarters provided for the staff were remote and meagre. Colonel Goldsworthy, an equerry, commented on the physical discomforts of Windsor in the following terms:

Bless us! I believe in my heart there's wind enough in these passages to carry a man-of-war! . . . Let's see how many blasts must you [addressing Miss Burney] have every time you go to the Queen. First, one upon your opening your door; then another, as you get down the three steps from it, which are exposed to the wind from the garden door; then comes another, fit to knock you down, as you turn to the upper passage; then, just as you turn towards the Queen's room, comes another; and last, a whiff from the King's stairs, enough to blow you half a mile off!

In spite of the discipline which George inflicted on himself as well as others, his physical condition was deteriorating. Though he was only forty-eight years of age and exercised furiously on foot and horseback, he had become fat. His eyebrows had turned white and stood out conspicuously on his ruddy face. The cartoonists continually made fun of him, unfairly attributing his heavy weight to gluttony, whereas it was an hereditary affliction.

These were unhappy years for George as he was aware of his growing unpopularity, which was occasioned in part by the public's awareness that there was a need for many reforms toward which the king was generally indifferent, if not opposed.

In 1786 occurred the first of several attacks upon his life, as he was entering St. James's for a levee. A young woman by the name of Margaret Nicholson approached him holding out a scroll, as at that time any subject had a right to present a memorial to the king. With her other hand she made a direct thrust toward his heart with a knife. On the second attempt the blade broke and in fact it had not gotten through his clothing to his body. A crowd gathered about, whereat His Majesty said, "The poor creature is mad. Do not hurt her; she has not hurt me."

The woman was a domestic, a barber's daughter who had the delusion that the Crown was hers by right and that if she did not get it England would be washed in blood. After an examination she was committed to Bedlam and remained one of the sights of that institution for the next forty years.

Word of the Nicholson attempt reached Windsor before George's return and the whole family were greatly perturbed, some of them in tears; but the king arrived in a quite cheerful mood. He hastened up to the queen and said, "Here I am—safe and well—as you see!" He tried to impress on the family that the event was a mere trifle but they remained badly shaken.

George as usual was brave in the face of physical danger, but the experience was disturbing. He said, however, that he was perfectly well aware that anyone who was willing to risk his own life could take the life of the king at any time. He refused to travel about with a guard and when riding horseback normally was accompanied only by a single equerry.

The strained events of these years bore heavily upon the king and may have accelerated the return of his insanity. He had spells when his speech became confused. William Grenville, son of the late prime minister, wrote his brother that he had called upon the king one evening and that from eleven until one George III had rambled on incoherently. He denounced Fox, spoke against the Duke of Portland, and blamed Lord North for all the disasters of the country including American independence. By 1788 his mental condition had become serious.

41

THE MAD YEARS

The lunatic spells of George III had a profound influence on the future status of the Crown. Never before in British history had the problem arisen of what to do in the case of the insanity of the monarch and it has not arisen since; but the ease with which public affairs were conducted in the absence of His Majesty demonstrated that there was no need for a king to attempt to rule and that the limitation of a constitutional throne to be a patriotic and social symbol was well founded. A monarch need not act in person.

The mental difficulties of George III lasted from the spring of 1788 to the spring of 1789, with a few interludes of sanity. Insanity recurred again in 1801 and reached a high pitch of violence in 1804. Each time George had similar delusions and similar symptoms of incessant rapid talking, hasty eating, inability to sleep, and violence. He kept saying, "I shall never lay my last pillow in peace and quiet as long as I remember my American colonies." He had persistent memories of past romances and his passionate desires at times were such that it was not safe for a woman to go near him.

His most persistent obsession was his love for Lady Pembroke who for twenty years had been attached to the queen's household, though his infatuation went back to the days when he was only seventeen and she, of the same age, was Elizabeth Spencer.

At times now George believed that Elizabeth was his queen and told Charlotte to go away from him. At other times he realized that he was not married to Elizabeth and said that he was going to become a Lutheran in order to get a divorce, which he could not do as long as he was head of the Church of England. All of this was said sometimes with a crazy cunning and sometimes in a wild delirium.

He also dreamed of Sarah Lennox and asked a certain Mr. Clements if he was the man who had run away with Lady Sarah Bunbury when he the king was in love with her. Apparently he mistook the man for Lord William Gordon.

Lady Sarah Lennox in turn preserved memories of George III which had somewhat mellowed with time. She had married General Sir Charles Napier who was stationed in Ireland during 1789. Sarah, however, kept posted on politics through her nephew Charles James Fox and others. In May 1789, writing to a friend, she said that she heard that the king had recovered from his illness "and very sincerely rejoiced I am, as all people of humanity *must be*, to think that he is relieved from misery".

The Foxites had spread the false rumour that Queen Charlotte had maltreated the king and Sarah had some acid comments to make on that score: "I see she was chosen to punish the poor king's faults by her ambitions and conduct, instead of *me* by my faults, and I *still* rejoice I was never Queen, & so I shall to my life's end; for at the various events in it, I have regularly cathechized myself upon that very point, & I *always* preferred my own situation, sometimes happy, sometimes miserable, to what it would have been had that event ever taken place."

Sarah said that upon reading the medical reports of the king's condition, "I did for a moment wish I was his wife. . . . Willis[1] says all mad people are better for the kindness of their friends, when they see them *often*; I own I did almost exclaim, 'Poor soul, if I was yours, I would never leave you an instant, but try & calm your suffering mind!' But then I soon forgot my pity, & rejoiced in the reflections on my own present happy state, which no poverty can lessen."

On some occasions George was less than romantic in his thoughts. He attempted to attack a housemaid. His language became obscene and profane which never had been the case in his sane condition. In a supposedly lucid interval he was allowed to hold inspection on a royal yacht. While there his eye lit upon an attractive woman guest. He went up to her and said, "My what a pretty bottom, I'd like to slap that bottom," while the crew who overheard it nearly choked with suppressed laughter.

---

[1]One of the attending physicians.

T

The incident was reported by General Sir Robert Wilson, a guest on board the yacht, who said that actually the king's words were so obscene that they could not be printed. Another instance of George's unbalanced mental state was his voracious appetite to which he gave way. Aware of the tendency toward obesity in his family he had always been most sparing of food and drink, but now he ate at a furious pace.

At times it was most difficult to cope with the king's illness because he would become quite sane for hours or even days at a time, even having a comprehension that he had been suffering from "nervousness", as he called it. He realized that he had spells of being an incessant talker, saying, "I am getting into Mr. Burke's eloquence, saying too much on little things."

It was not easy to detect just when George left or returned to the plateau of sanity. However, one day he suddenly became incensed at one of his younger sons, grabbed him by the throat and flung him against the wall. Charlotte then sent for a doctor and it was from this point forward that the ravings described above took place.

The various treatments were enough to kill anybody. The physicians, for soon there were several, alternately compelled the king to take purges and then gave him opiates to dull the intestinal pains. They shaved the top of his head and blistered it on the theory that this would remove the poison in his brain. They sent him to Cheltenham to drink the supposedly curative waters; but while there he ran a race with a horse and behaved generally in such a daft fashion that he was recalled, lest the fact of his illness become widely known.

Pitt and others in the ministry were eager to keep the king's condition a secret. They feared lest it undermine public confidence and set the opposition into agitating for a regency. It was well known that the Prince of Wales was an intimate of Charles James Fox and would try to bring about a change of administration if he could. Rumours of George's condition persisted as there were many persons necessarily in the know. The government consols declined sharply and Pitt finally on October 19, 1788, wrote to the king asking if he could come into town for a conference and show himself to the public at a levee.

George with the permission of his doctors agreed to do so "to stop further lies at any fall of stocks". Miraculously he was able to pull himself together and hold a levee for a brief time at St. James's

Palace on October 23, 1788, but the strain caused a bad reaction. On his return home to Windsor Castle he had an hysterical fit, though he was lucid enough to say to an equerry, "I return to you a poor old man, weak in body and mind." He then was taken with a high fever and again was afflicted with incessant talking in a hoarse and vehement voice.

It became impossible to keep the king's condition from the public. On November 5, 1788, the *Morning Herald* published a brief report revealing that George III had a malady and was under the care of physicians. It was a very guarded notice, saying, "Owing to the want of repose some slight derangements have been mentioned; but these have not excited much alarm." The queen and the Prince of Wales were unduly incensed at this news item. The prince insisted that his friend Richard Brinsley Sheridan (the dramatist) complain to the editor and warn all the press that if they said anything further, unless authorized, about His Majesty's health, the prince would "prosecute with the utmost severity". Regardless of this attitude, the royal family and the administration finally realized that it was inadvisable to keep silent and an information office was established at St. James's Palace where frequent bulletins were issued.

The Prince of Wales in the early stages of his father's illness was a devoted son and did not press the question of a regency. He spent most of his time, day and night, in a room near the king's bedchamber and early one morning, within a few days after the newspaper incident, the prince witnessed an appalling scene. He and his brother the Duke of York, together with friends, were in a sitting room when the king suddenly appeared in his nightshirt and addressed the Duke of York, saying, "Oh, my boy, I wish to God I might die for I am going to be mad." Then Dr. Baker, who was present attempted to lead the king back to bed, but as he did so George III grabbed him by the throat and pinned him in a corner. George then denounced the physician severely, calling him an "old woman" and saying he knew nothing of nervous disorders.

This violence obviously created a new problem. Would it be treasonable to lay physical hands on His Majesty no matter what the circumstances? The Prince of Wales consulted Lord Chancellor Thurlow on this point and Thurlow held that the use of a strait-jacket to prevent the king from committing a crime and in the interest of his health would be justifiable. The strait-jacket had at least some physical benefit as the king fought violently for two hours against being put into it and several attendants had to sit on him. At the end he was so exhausted that he fell into a much needed sleep.

Fortunately for the king one of his physicians believed in hydrotherapy and kept the patient in a hot bath for fifteen minutes at a time. This had a soothing and relaxing effect and George frequently asked that the treatment be repeated.

Several physicians were called in from time to time to treat George's malady, and there was considerable difference in opinion between them as to the proper course. The most famous of these practitioners was a Dr. Francis Willis who has been compared to a modern psychiatrist in his methods, though it might equally be said that he was a faith healer. At any rate, he had had notable success in the cure of unbalanced persons and George at first was resentful of having someone with that reputation brought in to attend him. Willis in fact was an ordained clergyman without formal training in medicine. George somewhat resentfully asked the man why he didn't stick to his original profession, but Dr. Willis replied, "Our Saviour Himself went about healing the sick."

"Yes," answered his patient, "but he did not get £700 a year for it."

The king had long clear stretches of intelligence between the end of 1789 and 1801 and again in 1802 and 1803. His strength, however, never returned in full force and his eyesight was failing. Nevertheless he was able to give support to the young William Pitt on most issues and even had enough remaining influence to defeat the prime minister's desire for a more liberal attitude toward Roman Catholics, especially in Ireland. Also, as George III became less assertive his popularity increased. When he was officially declared cured after his 1789 spell the nation was jubilant and it was said that on the evening of his return to London all the houses in town were illuminated.

George's physicians, however, were not optimistic about a permanent cure. They recognized that he was a manic depressive and one of the characteristics of that malady is that it usually recurs.

Hence when he was taken ill in 1804 the ministry as well as the doctors were most apprehensive and the case was complicated by the fact that the queen had had enough. She had tolerated his difficult personality for a lifetime. She had not interfered in his abuse of the children though from time to time she comforted them with special privileges without the king's knowledge; but to be a loving companion to a madman was more than she could endure.

Tension was increased by the fact that George renewed a passionate interest in the queen while at the same time, not content to rave about Lady Pembroke, he made her handsome offers if she would be his mistress. One of the ministry said that his pursuit of Lady Pembroke was renewed "with so much ardour and such splendid offers that I tremble for her virtue".

Elizabeth was tactful in dealing with George, but his proposal was repugnant to her. George continued intent on finding a mistress and made proposals to Lady Yarmouth; but she declined, and he boasted that he would make love elsewhere. He formed the habit of coming into the queen's room late at night and talking for hours, hoping in vain that Her Majesty would tell the ladies-in-waiting to withdraw. The cabinet was greatly distressed at this situation and tried to effect a reconciliation between George and Charlotte, pointing out that it was very important to preserve their reputation of having had for over forty years an ideal domestic life.

Their Majesties' forty-third wedding anniversary occurred on September 8, 1804, and the ministry urged the queen to resume relations with George, who had been barred from sleeping in her apartment for several years; but Charlotte was obdurate. She took the precaution of having two German women stationed in her bedroom early in the evening and two of the princesses attended her in case the king should appear. Even in the daytime she would never see him alone, no longer dined with him, and made no reply to his conversation. George moved to a private dwelling in the Windsor Castle grounds, declaring that he would never have a separate bed in the same residence as the queen.

The king recovered periodically from his insanity and was considered well enough to address the opening of Parliament in January 1805; but as he was driving to the hall he turned to a companion and said gaily, "I shall begin my speech today by saying, 'My Lords and Peacocks'." He did not carry out this threat and went through the speech; but afterwards he paid a call on Caroline, the Princess of Wales, his daughter-in-law, who alleged (though her words were often unreliable) that he threw her down on a sofa and would have ravished her except for the fact that the sofa had no back and she escaped on the far side.

George had had reason to hope that the princess would prove to be fair game. From the time of her marriage she had been treated disgracefully by the prince. The match had been forced on him by the king who declined to help the prince pay his staggering debts unless he would agree to marry his cousin Caroline. The prince was so drunk at his wedding that two attendants had to hold him upright. Caroline said later, "He passed the greatest part of his bridal night under the grate, where he fell and where I left him."

Caroline later had sought consolation elsewhere and George III instigated a private investigation into her character. She was cleared of a report that she had an illegitimate child, but it was established that she had been indiscreet with at least three lovers. However, she drew the line at the advances of her father-in-law.

42

ACTIONS IN THE INTERLUDES

When the king returned to sanity in various interludes between 1789 and 1811 his personality appeared to have undergone a mellowing change. He no longer had violent quarrels with his cabinet officers and with few exceptions did not try to influence government. He even had occasional touches of humour.

Many were surprised when George III supported William Wilberforce in his campaign to abolish slavery, for the king was habitually opposed to change, especially in any direction of reform. However, the bill had the backing of Pitt; and Wilberforce, who dedicated his life to the cause, was a man of talent, wealth, and social aplomb, characteristics which appealed to the king.

The proposal to abolish the slave trade was opposed in various respectable quarters. Many contended that the slaves under English masters were better off than in their native villages, that they had the advantages of civilization and that they were happy in their lot.

The Grenville brothers took a cautious attitude on the measure, affirming that abolition should take place slowly, though it was not quite clear how that could be effected. The Grenvilles were generally humanitarian, but the attack on the slave trade offended their sense of property. They held that if England discontinued that activity the only result would be that France and Spain would monopolize the trade and the black man would be no better off.

Thurlow made known his opposition to abolition. The Lord Chancellor had become increasingly difficult, considering himself as above the ministry. He had opposed the liberation of insolvent debtors. He had regarded certain liberal societies as seditious. Now, in addition to his pro-slavery stand he also voted against one of Pitt's chief financial measures.

The prime minister justifiably held that such conduct was un-constitutional and intolerable. He represented to the king that the Lord Chancellor must go. George faced the situation with regret, for Thurlow, whatever his faults, had been consistently loyal to the king and Thurlow regarded George with great affection. Indeed on one occasion Thurlow had wept bitterly when he learned that the king was insane. Now that George had recovered it was painful to him to be obliged to dismiss his faithful servant, but no ministry could stand if one of its chief members were allowed to go into opposition and at the same time retain office.

Wilberforce had been a contemporary of Pitt at Cambridge and the friendship continued in London after college days. They both belonged to the Goostrees Club and had made a European trip together. Wilberforce was brilliant in his studies, had a notable singing voice, and was also an excellent mimic. He was fond of mimicking the mannerisms of Lord North and other notables, but gave up the practice when Lord Camden advised him that it was not politically prudent.

Early in his career, when Wilberforce inherited a sizable fortune, he felt it to be his opportunity and obligation to devote his life to good works. This feeling was intensified when he became a religious convert in 1784. He had been elected to Parliament in 1780 and now offered his services to Pitt for whatever worthy purpose he might suggest. The latter said that there were a number of men who were already championing abolition, but he asked Wilberforce to take the lead because of his personal popularity and disinterestedness.

Wilberforce continued to fight for abolition and he won in-creasing support among the masses of the people. Inherently slavery was antithetical to the concept of British freedom. The Quakers campaigned zealously for abolition as did the dissenters and many devout Churchmen, all holding that slavery was inconsistent with the Christian faith. At one point George III wavered in his attitude, for he heard that many abolitionists were sympathizers with the French Revolution and he did not wish to be associated with that type of company. But in 1807, the king gave his royal assent to the abolition act. Opinion had been so divided on this measure that it could not have passed without royal support. Thus George III deserves to share with Wilberforce the credit for abolition.

Another prominent issue in which George had a major influence during the sunset years of his life was that of Catholic toleration, only here his attitude was negative. Pitt was wholeheartedly for abolishing all restrictive measures aimed against certain religious believers, either Roman Catholics or dissenters. Specifically he advocated that Irishmen in the army should be allowed to rise to the rank of colonel and that in the proposed union of Ireland and Great Britain Roman Catholics should not be prohibited from sitting in Parliament.

George III surprisingly resisted Pitt on this issue. The king held that to consent to any such measure would be a violation of his coronation oath in which he had sworn to support "the reformed Protestant religion". That had not troubled him when the Quebec Act had been passed which had preserved both the religion and the laws of the French Canadians, but the French in George's opinion were a breed apart who had their own peculiar ways.

In justification of George III's view it should be remembered that the Roman Church was still a temporal power, that it was the official church of France and Spain, countries which were traditionally hostile to Great Britain; and the king held further that a subject who was loyal to the Pope could not be wholly loyal to the Crown.

Ordinarily the character and prestige of Pitt would have carried the day on any reasonable proposition both with the Parliament and George, but this issue was too touchy, especially if the king were opposed. The memory of the Gordon riots which had been touched off by similar legislation was still very much alive and even now "No Popery" signs began to appear.

Pitt resigned, since he had been defeated on a major proposal endorsed by his ministry. When later the Irish Union bill was passed all Irish representatives in Parliament were required to be members of the Church of England which then was proclaimed to be also the Established Church of Ireland.

The close of the eighteenth century and the opening of the nineteenth was a period of confusion in governmental affairs as well as in the life of George III. Following the first Ministry of Pitt, which had extended from 1783 to the end of 1801, there was a cabinet nominally headed by Henry Addington, an inconspicuous man, who was a close friend of Pitt, and the latter virtually ran the government from behind the scenes, though there were instances of disagreement between Pitt and Addington. As mentioned earlier, the opposition endeavoured to embarrass Addington by encouraging the Crown Prince to petition his father for high rank in the army. George III, however, was stoutly opposed and the move was not effective. Pitt was again named prime minister in 1803 but died in 1806.

George again had trouble forming a cabinet; but this time the difficulty was not caused by the competition of ambitious persons seeking appointment, but an unwillingness on the part of leading men to serve. The lustre of Pitt had been so great that men hesitated to expose their dim abilities for comparison.

Hence George III reluctantly turned to Sir William Grenville, the youngest son of the late George Grenville, Sr., to form a cabinet and he also accepted Charles James Fox as a Secretary of State. The king made the condition with Grenville that the Catholic question should not be re-agitated as it was too disturbing to his peace of mind; and Grenville consented, believing that his unstable government might well be upset if George III's insanity returned.

In 1807 the Grenville ministry fell, due to the unexpected death of Fox in 1806 who had been a strong factor in the House of Commons. There was difficulty in putting together a cabinet and the Duke of Portland again was called upon to take office. He at least had the benefit of having served once before as prime minister. Many of the men in his cabinet were new names, including a Mr. Perceval as Chancellor of the Exchequer. Perceval had moderate abilities, but he was one of Lord Egmont's family who had been close to the throne for about fifty years, and a loyal supporter of George III's father, Prince Frederick. Portland retired in 1809 to be succeeded by Perceval who continued as prime minister until June 1812 when on his way to Parliament an insane bankrupt came up to him and shot him fatally through the heart.

Again there was a search for someone to lead the government. Various Whig factions quarrelled among themselves and the choice fell upon the second Earl of Liverpool, a colourless man who had the singular ability to avoid controversial issues and stayed in office for the next eighteen years. Liverpool was the oldest son of Charles Jenkinson who had been a secretary to Lord North and an undercover man for George III. From his youth up Liverpool had been trained in political tactics. There were no aspersions on his honesty but no evidence of unusual merit.

By the time of Liverpool's appointment nearly all of the notable figures of the eighteenth century had passed away. The fact that from 1806 to 1812 there were four changes in the office of prime minister and many virtually unknown names as cabinet officers exemplified the lack of governmental talent in the Houses of Parliament.

Even before the death of Pitt there had been a surprising obtuseness on the part of George III and Parliament to the significance of world events. The fall of the Bastille on July 14, 1789, caused little attention, hardly more so than the mutiny on the *Bounty* which was reported in London at about the same time and offended the authority of the British Navy. The execution of Louis XVI understandably frightened George III, who said that if this type of thing were allowed to continue there soon would be no kings in Europe.

However, the Reign of Terror in France which led to the guillotining of many of the revolutionary leaders, as one faction after another came into power, was viewed with complacency in England, as it was felt that France was destroying herself. Burke even moved for a reduction of the armed forces on the theory that France was no longer to be feared. There was some temporary alarm when the French Republic had the effrontery to declare war on Great Britain in 1793, but on England's part the hostilities at first were limited to naval engagements in which the British fleet was greatly superior under the direction of the notable Lord Nelson.

George III had been correct in thinking that the execution of Louis XVI would tend to stir up anti-monarchists. There were several further attacks on George's life in the decade 1790–1800. The perpetrator of one of these was not apprehended and may have been a professional revolutionist. The other attempts were by men whose minds had been unbalanced by serious misfortunes.

In at least two of these incidents George III had a narrow escape. In 1795 mobs lined the thoroughfares on the route to Parliament to protest against low wages, unemployment, and the high prices of food. As the royal coach rolled toward Westminster where the king was to open the session someone fired at the carriage from an empty house. The king's two companions were agitated but George said to them, "My lords . . . there is One who disposes of all things, and in Him I trust."

On the return trip the mob stoned the royal coach breaking all its windows and the king was struck several times. Pointing to the first missile, George said to a companion, Lord Onslow, "That is a stone—you see the difference from a bullet." When another stone lodged in the king's sleeve he said, "My Lord, keep this as a memo-randum of the civilities which we have received."

The second nearly fatal attempt occurred five years later as the king was attending a performance at the Drury Lane Theatre. As George III came to the front of the box a man in the pit stood up and shot at the king. Immediately the audience was in an uproar, the would-be assassin was overpowered by the orchestra players and hauled backstage. At the report of the pistol the king had retired for a pace or two, but then moved to the front of the box, observing the scene through his opera glasses and without the slightest appearance of alarm.

The Lord Chamberlain tried to prevail upon George to retire to an adjacent room but he declined. The manager of the theatre quieted the crowd by saying that the culprit had been taken into custody and would be dealt with by the law. (He subsequently was committed to Bedlam).

At the end of the play the audience as customary sang "God Save the King". Thrilled by the personal courage of His Majesty, they desired to sing it again. Richard Brinsley Sheridan, who was managing director of the house, then handed out a verse which he had written on the spur of the moment; it was:

> *From every latent foe,*
> *From the assassin's blow*
> > *God Save the King!*
> *O'er him thine arm extend,*
> *For Britain's sake defend*
> *Our father, prince and friend,*
> > *God Save the King!*

This was sung three times with tumultuous approval by the audience.

The king had entered upon a mellow era. Apparently his sufferings had worn down his native combativeness and there were numerous instances of his approachability, including one occasion when he was accosted by a stranger in Quaker garb. Thomas Shillitoe, a missionary of the Friends, tells of happening to see George III and his escorts in a stable yard where Shillitoe sought to address His Majesty. It was customary of the Quakers to testify to their faith whenever the occasion offered. To address His Majesty was audacious, but if successful it would be a triumph.

The courtiers in the king's entourage strove to send Shillitoe away but George invited the preacher to stand forth. Possibly the king remembered Hannah Lightfoot, Barclay, Benjamin West, Patience Wright, and other Quakers. At any rate, the monarch, with hat removed, listened while the Quaker expounded for "about twenty minutes". At the conclusion the king courteously asked for the man's name and address.

According to Shillitoe, the king was reported to have abandoned his usual daily hunt for that day and returned to the palace to tell the queen about Quaker doctrine. On the latter point Shillitoe was probably mistaken as the queen apparently was not reconciled to George during this period, though it is doubtful that the estrangement was known to the general public.

From 1789 through 1803 the king kept reasonably busy on affairs of state, conducting reviews of troops, conferring with cabinet members on matters of policy, delivering speeches written for him for the sessions of Parliament; but conscious of his mental instability, he refrained from actions or agitations which might bring on a return of his malady.

Nevertheless he again had a serious relapse in 1804 in which his violence reached an acute stage. There had been considerable fear that his constitution would not be able to survive that attack and when he recovered the public greeted him with a sympathy and devotion that he had never before enjoyed.

On October 25, 1809, celebrating the fact that George III was now starting the fiftieth year of his reign, the City, which had once been so hostile to him, arranged a great jubilee. Thanksgiving services were held in the churches, debtors were freed from prison, the poor were feasted, and at night there were illuminations and fireworks.

A comment by Sarah Lennox, who had witnessed almost every stage of George's life, shows how she and the public had forgiven him. Sarah's voluminous correspondence with her devoted cousin has furnished a running obbligato on George's career. Now she wrote to Lady Susan, reminding her of the day October 25, 1760, when George II had died and George III had ascended the throne:

I fear when the next change takes place it will bear a very different aspect, for each individual will feel that their existence as a nation is tottering, & anxious fear will fill *every* heart . . . the decease of a good old King who certainly is altogether beloved by his subjects will leave a deep impression of sorrow. However let us hope it will not happen for many years. I cannot help thinking of the poor King to-day, what a crowd of thought will be impressed on his mind. I should think that altogether he will feel more pain than pleasure.

Sarah in referring to "more pain than pleasure" was alluding to the illness of the king's favourite daughter, the Princess Amelia, who was dying of consumption. She was the remaining comfort of his life. Nearly all of his sons had disgraced him or rebelled against him, or both, and in 1809 his second son, Frederick Duke of York, created the worst scandal that had yet afflicted the royal house.

The Duke had been appointed head of the army and lived in handsome style. He had mistresses on whom he loved to lavish riches and his favourite was Mary Anne Clarke. Mary Anne had conceived the profitable idea of selling army commissions on a graduated scale according to rank, which she was able to accomplish by using her wiles upon the Duke of York to approve the appointments.

Ultimately the duke grew tired of Mary Anne and took a new favourite mistress. Mary Anne in fury told what had been taking place as to the army commissions; and charges were brought against the duke in the House of Commons. Never had there been a scandal of such proportions involving the royal house in betraying the public trust. York was obliged to resign and give up all of his military honours; and George III was crushed with grief and humiliation. His sorrow so preyed upon him, coupled with the death of Amelia in November 1810, that in 1811 his mind again gave way, this time finally, and the Prince of Wales (subsequently George IV) was appointed Prince Regent.

43

HAIL AND FAREWELL

George from about 1811 was wholly blind, deaf and incommuni-
cative save for babbling about scenes past or imaginary schemes
for the future. With his manic stare, his shorn poll, his aged face
and a large white beard which had been allowed to grow, his
appearance suggested some ancient prophet, possibly Elisha at
whom irreverent children had jeered, "Go up, thou baldhead!"
Or again the king was a second Samson, eyeless in Gaza and helpless,
except that George III had already pulled down the pillars of the
temple and could not look forward to any future self-redeeming act.

Until nearly the end he was ambulatory and in a white tunic
haunted the corridors of Windsor at all hours. He had various
hallucinations, at times imagining happily that he was conversing
with the angels. Only in his frequent visits to the music room did
he establish a tie to his former real world. Though blind he could
play selections from Handel on the harpsichord and piped arias
on his flute.

Great events swirled around him, such as the Napoleonic wars
and the allied triumph at Waterloo, but he had no part in them.
His life for all practical purposes was ended, though he was not
actually and legally dead until 1820. When that occurred his
funeral took place with gruesome pomp, but he had no close friends
left to shed a tear, and his eldest son, George IV, was glad to be
king at last in his own right. For the public there was something
almost eerie in George III's final departure, a personality so long
absent from the scene and then suddenly and briefly in the news
again.

An era, a whole attitude toward life, had slipped into the past.
The eighteenth century has been called the Age of Enlightenment,
because of the expansion of man's mind in all directions—humane,
political, philosophical and scientific. It could accommodate without undue internal explosion such sinners as Lord Sandwich and
such ascetics as John Wesley. But now the nineteenth century, the
age of conformity, had begun, soon to be solidified under Queen
Victoria.

Lady Sarah Lennox, as might be expected, had the final *mot juste*. She wrote, "However good our next King may wish, and try to be, the times are against him." Moreover, she testified in a letter to her cousin that she herself currently was rebuked by her children and grandchildren as one who did not know how to behave in public. In her youth she had been one of the most eminent young ladies of the realm, the cynosure of all who wished to know what was elegant; but not now. She said wryly that her offspring told her that she would disgrace them if she belched in public and that she must never refer to her "belly", the correct word was "abdomen".

The reign of George III and the close of the eighteenth century nearly coincided and the behaviour of the royal family doubtless had an influence in bringing about the nineteenth-century revulsion against the excesses of the earlier period, for the sons of the king had stood for the worst aspects of that era without its redeeming nobility. George Grenville, Jnr., said of the royal children, "Good God, what a set they are.... Three kingdoms cannot furnish such a brood, so many and so bad, rogues, laggards, fools, and whores." The remark was a libel on the cloistered princesses but all too true of at least the three oldest princes. The life of George IV was notorious and his reign of ten years was conspicuous for its lack of dignity. The Duke of York had reached a peak of scandal in letting his mistress influence the sale of army commissions. It will be recalled that William Duke of Clarence, the third brother, was a wastrel and a gambler. He ultimately reigned as William IV for seven almost forgotten years.

The fourth brother, Edward, Duke of Kent, may have been respectable. He spent most of his life in Germany and little is known about him. He died before William IV. His older brothers had no surviving children and so it came about that his daughter Victoria succeeded to the throne.

It is perhaps unfair to blame George III for the rascality of his children, yet obviously there was something wrong in the pattern of the family life, even if perchance it was only an overpowering dullness. George III suffered from a strong taint of mediocrity. He had an instinct for choosing the less good, for example preferring Benjamin West to Joshua Reynolds; and his shortcomings might have been less evident if he had been less assertive.

Since he lived in the midst of the Age of Enlightenment, under happier circumstances he might have won credit for it. He supported vast and successful explorations, he encouraged handicrafts and agriculture, he founded the Royal Academy of Art, he stood for the abolition of slavery, and he was tolerant toward Quakers and other dissenters.

With all of that there was something not quite majestic in his reign, even though it lasted longer than any other in English history except Victoria's. He was a tragic figure, belittled in public opinion by the Whig historians, by his ill-fated policy toward the American colonies and his consequent ill-fame in American tradition.

How may George III fairly be measured, by comparison with other English rulers? In comparison with the days when kings were warriors, such as Richard the Lionhearted, George's opportunities for romantic fame were handicapped, but to measure him alongside of Elizabeth I may be enlightening. George III, in contrast to Elizabeth, could not quite accept in his heart the fact that in England the royal will like that of all other persons was subject to the law. The law was the supreme authority, not the Crown. The law could be changed and repeatedly was changed, but at any given time in its existing form the law prevailed.

Elizabeth had a sure instinct for the sanctity of the law, even where it curbed her wishes. Once when convinced that a loyal subject, Davison, had betrayed her confidence, she wished to have him hanged solely by her royal authority as the evidence against him seemed too slight to win a court verdict. Elizabeth, however, before attempting any action sought the advice of the judges of the Queen's Bench. She learned promptly that the authority of the Crown was by no means absolute. Burleigh, who had long been her faithful adviser, sent word to the judges, "I would be loath to . . . see a woman of such wisdom as she is to be wrongly advised . . . that her prerogative is above the law." Elizabeth, though strongly self-willed, did not press the matter further, for she had a shrewd flexibility which enabled her to surmount many crises.

In contrast, the temperament of George III after the early years of his reign became fatally inflexible. He was stubborn, tenacious, disregarded those of his advisers who were able to see that his continued attempt to subjugate the American colonies was a lost cause; and his concept of sovereignty obviously was contrary to the British tradition and constitution; and he seemingly forgot that his family had been called to rule under a limited and specific agreement.

George III fell short of greatness, for he never acquired the breadth and strength to achieve heroic stature; and he also lacked the intangible quality of exaltation, a devotion to something beyond self, associated with the world's heroes. Burke said of Conway when moving to repeal the Stamp Act: "His face was as the face of an angel." The Pennsylvania farmer who came upon George Washington praying in the woods near Valley Forge was convinced thereby that independence would prevail.

The early George III had such moments, but later he appeared to the public in many unfortunate roles. The testament of his father Frederick Lewis could have been a rule of conduct for George: "A wise and brave prince may often times without armies put a stop to the confusion which the ambitious neighbours endeavour to create."

And Frederick added, "I shall have no regret never to have wore the Crown, if you do but fill it worthily." Frederick, instead of hating his first-born male child as had been the Hanoverian habit, evidently hoped that young George had the potentiality to "follow the gleam". The tragedy of George III's life was that despite his conscientious energy his native streak of idealism was overborne by a weight of circumstances beyond his strength to control.

However, George was honest, diligent, and conscientious according to his own lights. He was no dolt. He had suffered frustrations enough to command the sympathy of anyone, even if much of his trouble was due to his own weaknesses.

It was inevitable that George's long reign would influence the status of the throne, and it did so usefully in a manner he could hardly have foreseen. By his singleness of purpose and purity of intention in attempting to restore the dominance of the Crown he dramatized the ill consequences of such a policy.

George III made a contribution to history by showing that the stubborn assertion of royal power was forever out of date and his would-be autocratic rule never has been re-attempted in the British realm.

U

NOTES

CHAPTER 1

The complete texts of the Declaration of Rights and the Act of Settlement are readily available in *The Law and Working of the Constitution* by W. C. Costin and J. Steven Watson.

CHAPTER 2

For the past two hundred years the character of Frederick, Prince of Wales, father of George III has been based largely on the letters of Horace Walpole and the *Memoirs* of Lord Hervey. Each man was a personal enemy of the prince and presented him in the worst possible light.

Hervey has such a brilliant literary style that the temptation to a writer to lift his material bodily has been very great. Thomas Carlyle and others did so—and without crediting the source.

The reader who wishes to know more about Frederick is referred to *Poor Fred, the People's Prince,* by Sir George Young.

As early as June 24, 1725, Sir Robert Walpole, prime minister, was instructed by the future George II and Caroline (who were not yet on the throne) to confer with the current Lord Chancellor on the possibility of naming William instead of Frederick as the successor. This is set forth in the *Journal of Lord Chancellor King* and reported in Campbell's *Lives of the Chancellors,* Vol. IV, p. 619. Lord Chancellor King did not pursue the matter.

CHAPTER 3

Cliveden is the estate occupied in modern times by the Astor family and is now under the National Trust.

CHAPTER 5

George Bubb Dodington (created Lord Melcombe in 1761) was author of a famous *Diary*. Virtually every historian who deals with the boyhood life and character of George III has used the *Diary* as a primary source, whether giving credit or not. Thanks to the political mudslinging of his era, Dodington frequently has been treated as a silly gossip; but his character was substantial. He sat frequently in Parliament and held various government posts.

An attempt was made in the mid-nineteenth century in the case of *Ryves v. Ryves* to prove that there was a marriage between George III and Hannah Lightfoot. Marriage certificates were introduced purporting to be authentic and endorsed or scorned by handwriting authorities for one side or the other; but the jury held the documents to be fraudulent and impounded them. Anyone reading the account of the trial in the *Annual Register* will note the contradictions in the plaintiff's case and be unconvinced by the claims set forth therein.

The biographers of Hannah Lightfoot are singularly vague. One of these, Mary Pendered, speaks darkly of certain letters which she has been privileged to see, but cannot use. Lindsey, another biographer, quotes an "unverified report" that George III wrote a letter to Bute rebuking him for telling Augusta about George's interest in Hannah. If so, the letter is no longer extant. But why the Society of Friends in Hannah's own time were completely foiled in trying to trace her remains a mystery.

CHAPTER 6

Waldegrave's *Memoirs* are useful for their personal observations on the Court of George II and of the household of the princess dowager.

CHAPTER 7

Lord George Sackville changed his name at the instance of a Lady Betty Germain who left him a sizeable fortune under the condition that he take her name. There was no suggestion of scandal involved; she was a woman considerably older than Lord George, who had known him from childhood and was a close friend of his parents, the Duke and Duchess of Dorset. He as a younger son did not succeed to the title. Germain is spelled by some authorities with a final *e* and by some not. Such freedom of spelling was typical in the eighteenth century. Many an individual was inconsistent in the spelling of his own name.

CHAPTER 8

The prompt timetable of the actions of Lord Bute and George III upon learning of the death of the king bespeak a well-conceived plan which was carried out smoothly.

There are two letters in George's correspondence with Bute which are dated October 25, 1760. The first tells about the arrival of the messenger, and the second tells of the news received from Amelia and in this note George writes to Bute, "I am coming the back way to your house."

It is probable that these two notes were composed at a later date for the sake of the record, lest Bute and George seem to be waiting too eagerly for the king's death. This suspicion is reinforced by a statement that George made many years later when he claimed that on receiving the news he had told his mother "in the warmest manner to say nothing on the subject to Lord Bute, lest he should entertain some notion of endeavouring to be placed in a political situation". That recollection on the part of the king obviously is inconsistent with the facts, since he himself alerted Bute and had insisted all along that Bute must be his adviser.

CHAPTER 9

The chief sources for this chapter are the *Letters from George III to Lord Bute 1756-1766* and the *Life and Letters of Lady Sarah Lennox*. We have also made use of the *Grenville Papers* which cover the same area and verify the story told by Fox. George Grenville was a serious literal type and a reliable witness.

Other source materials consulted are the writings of Horace Walpole, Nathaniel Wraxall and J. H. Jesse but no detail of their accounts has been accepted here unless corroborated by others.

CHAPTER 10

The king's attitude toward Lady Sarah Lennox and toward Charlotte of Mecklenburg-Strelitz is documented in considerable detail in the letters of Sarah and in the letters from George III to Lord Bute.

The details of the wedding are based mainly on the *Annual Register* 1761, the *Diaries* of the Duchess of Northumberland and comments by Horace Walpole.

The description of the coronation also is based on the *Annual Register* augmented by MacDonagh's *The English King* which covers the history of coronation services throughout several centuries.

CHAPTER 11

The king's first negotiation with Pitt desiring him to form a new ministry after his initial cabinet had deserted him on the war issue was in the fall of 1761. The details as to the two different conditions laid down by Pitt, which were unacceptable to the king, are described by the Duchess of Northumberland in her *Diaries* under the date of October 10, 1761. She was an intimate of the Butes' and her oldest son married a Bute daughter in 1764.

Two years later Pitt was again approached by His Majesty. This time Pitt did not seek to have Bute included in the cabinet; but he repeated his condition that the ministry should be composed of his colleagues from leading Whig families. This later negotiation is more frequently referred to than the earlier one, but it is clear that there were two separate attempts by His Majesty to get Pitt to form a government, after the fall of the Pitt Cabinet in 1761. There were still later approaches when Pitt no longer insisted on an all-Whig connection.

CHAPTER 12

There are numerous contemporary accounts of the coronation dinner and the visit of the royal family to the Barclay home. There are several intra-family letters written at the time which are reprinted in the *History of the Barclay Family* by H. F. Barclay and Alice Wilson-Fox.

The Quakers occupied a somewhat singular position in eighteenth-century society. Some of them were persecuted for their faith and yet they were honoured for their typical thrift and sense of property. The names of Barclay, Wheeler, Willets, Woolman, and many others of the "friendly persuasion" have been associated for many generations with successful trade and manufacture.

CHAPTER 14

The character of Henry Fox was vilified by the Whig historians of his day, but his personality appears in a gracious light in his *Memoir* contained in the *Life and Letters of Lady Sarah Lennox*; and his commentaries on events show wit and understanding.

CHAPTER 15

The summary of the characteristics of various members of the Grenville phalanx is based upon their letters, their actions, and comments of contemporaries.

CHAPTER 16

The confusion in the cabinet system is brought out clearly in the *Secretaries of State* by Thomson. He points out that the duties overlapped, that sometimes there were one, two or three Secretaries of State, and that one Secretary was usually considered to be the senior in authority. During the first administration of William Pitt, though he was prime minister in fact, it will be recalled that he held the office of Secretary of State.

In general, however, the principal Secretary of State was second in authority to the First Lord of the Treasury, who lived at the official residence, 10 Downing Street. The principal Secretary, however, occasionally succeeded to the office of chief minister, as in the case of George Grenville.

There are varying accounts of the Spitalfields riots, including the circumstances of the petition to the king. George Grenville in his diaries asserts simply that the mob went to Richmond, sending in a letter to the king, and that he sent back a sympathetic message without receiving the men in person. Grenville, however, was not present at the event. The fact that the king's interest in the weavers continued to be active lends probability to the reports that he did receive them in person.

The inexperience of the king was felt by himself even after he had reigned for two and a half years, for he wrote to Bute on May 2, 1763, "Many mistakes will be made by me for want of experience, though I will be most attentive to escape them as much as I can."

CHAPTER 17

Grenville inherited the Stamp Act problem from Bute's administration. Townshend when President of the Board of Trade had proposed an amendment to the Molasses Act to raise additional funds from the colonies but the ministry did not support him. Hence Grenville felt the need to reactivate the question of colonial taxation. For a useful review of this subject see "A Postscript to the Stamp Act" by Jack M. Sosin in the *American Historical Review*, July 1958.

CHAPTER 18

The *Grenville Papers (Including Correspondence of George Grenville and Lord Temple)* offer a fascinating portrait of George Grenville and his times. Grenville had a stout belief that he was always right and his positions of self-justification are revelatory and frequently unintentionally amusing.

CHAPTER 19

Grafton's abilities were viciously attacked by the writings of "Junius" and in Horace Walpole's *Memoirs of George III*. A dispassionate review of the main events of Grafton's career, however, reveals him to be a man of devotion to Pitt, loyalty to duty, and with a pleasing humility about his moderate talents.

CHAPTER 20

Though George III usually is blamed for forcing the American colonies into independence, being encouraged in his oppressive policies by Grenville, Germain and other autocratic advisors, his troubles almost were inevitable. R. R. Palmer in *The Age of the Democratic Revolution* has forcefully presented the view that the Western world was ripe for change, that the American Revolution was but one outcropping of general unrest, leading to the overthrow of the existing governments in France, Poland, and elsewhere. The view generally held in America that our Revolution set the pace for world democracy is accordingly subject to some modification. It still is a fact, however, that George III by his anachronistic ideas and actions accelerated the popular discontents.

CHAPTER 22

Bridget Henley, eldest daughter of Lord Northington, is the most elusive of the ladies in whom George III was supposed to have had an interest, and we do not find any letters from him to her. He apparently was too discreet to have any correspondence with women friends (quite a contrast to others in his family) and probably he was literally faithful to Queen Charlotte even though his fancy wandered.

CHAPTER 23

Botetourt's reputation like that of Grafton was attacked by both "Junius" and Horace Walpole because of his political connections. An impressive appraisal of the true character of Norborne Berkeley, written by Bryan Little, appeared in the *Virginia Magazine of History and Biography* in October 1955.

CHAPTER 24

Patience Lovell Wright has been confused occasionally with another colonial woman by the name of Mrs. Mehetabel Wright, said to be a niece of John Wesley. The confusion stems from a footnote in *Private Correspondence of Benjamin Franklin* published by William Temple Franklin, London, 1817. As the source was seemingly authoritative, the error was copied repeatedly in later works.

However, the known lives of the two women show that Mehetabel could not have been the noted sculptress. Dr. Manfred S. Guttmacher, writing in the *Johns Hopkins Alumni Magazine,* June 1936, has set the matter straight: "Charles Wesley had a sister, Mehetabel, who made a very unhappy union with a man named Wright from whom she parted. Patience Wright had no connection with the family."

Authorities agree that Patience Wright was a diligent spy for Franklin during the Revolution, but disagree as to her effectiveness. The fact that the British government did not arrest her has been interpreted to mean that she was ineffective, or again that British top society was uninterested in the American Revolution (an untenable theory). Her immunity most likely was due to her open espousal of the American cause which she dared to champion to the king and Lord North whereby she would not be suspected of being an undercover agent. Or possibly they simply regarded her as a harmless female who could become politically important only through martyrdom.

CHAPTER 25

Luttrel's name has been spelled with a final double *l* by various authorities; it is one of numerous examples of inconsistent spelling in the eighteenth century.

CHAPTER 26

The Royal Marriages Act of 1772 was 12 Geo. III c. 11. The complete text is given in *The Law and Working of the Constitution* by Costin and Watson (see Bibliography).

The statistics on loyalists were compiled by Ralph Louis Andreano and Herbert D. Werner and published in the *South Carolina Historical Magazine* in July 1959 under the title of "Charleston Loyalists: A Statistical Note".

CHAPTER 27

As stated earlier, Chatham had enunciated the principle of "no taxation without representation" in 1766. On the American side the principle was developed in considerable detail in a letter addressed to Chatham dated February 2, 1768, from the House of Representatives of Massachusetts. The letter is significant of the folly of George III's coercive attitude toward the colonies for it states that if the colonies "are charged with the most distant thought of an independency . . . the charge is unjust".

CHAPTER 28

An ingenious point of view regarding the causation of the Battle of Lexington is presented by John A. Barton in *History Today,* June 1959, under the title of "Lexington: The End of a Myth". The author doubts various heroic versions, saying "The affair at Lexington was a monstrous blunder". He also maintains that the action by the Lexington militia was fomented by Samuel Adams in order to provide an issue which would precipitate the war. The difficulty with that theory is that there had been many incidents prior to Lexington such as the Boston Massacre in 1770; and the first Continental Congress meeting in 1774 had drawn up plans for the defence of the colonies.

For detailed accounts of the negotiations in this period a most useful
work is *The Command of the Howe Brothers During the American
Revolution* by Troyer Steele Anderson (see Bibliography).

As in respect to the previous chapter, *The Command of the Howe
Brothers* is especially recommended for those interested in greater
detail.

All mentions as to the time of assembly and procedures of the day
are from *Journals of the Continental Congress,* Vol. V, edited by W. C.
Ford, Government Printing Office.

All prior petitions and addresses to the Crown had observed the formal usage of "his Majesty". For example, see: *Declaration and Resolves
of 1st Continental Congress,* October 14, 1774; *Declaration of the Causes
and Necessity of Taking Up Arms,* July 6, 1775; *Mecklenburg Resolves,*
May 29, 1775.

John Wade, *British History Chronologically Arranged,* Fifth Edition,
p. 504. Henry G. Bohn, London, 1847.

London Packet, July 4, 1776.

The July 4, 1776, temperature was recorded by Jefferson. London
temperature is from *Gentleman's Magazine,* June 1777 (including
weather report for July 1776).

Dumas Malone in his *Story of the Declaration of Independence*
reprints the Declaration and uses the phrase "endowed by their Creator
with certain *un*alienable rights". He uses "unalienable" because that
was the spelling used in the first printed copy, a form which persisted
for many years afterwards. However, Dr. Malone also reports and gives
a facsimile of Jefferson's written draft in which the word is "*in*alienable". Each form has appeared in present-day printing and obviously
a plausible argument can be made for each form.

CHAPTER 32

For the relationship of Franklin to James Hutton, the Moravian
leader, and of Hutton to George III, see the *Memoirs of James Hutton,*
edited by Daniel Benham. This book, long out of print and seldom
cited, gives an intimate picture of Franklin's numerous friendships in
England and it also establishes Hutton's considerable status with
George III.

The supposition that there actually was a person who called himself
Weissenstein and wrote a letter to Benjamin Franklin has been widely

accepted, on Franklin's say-so to Adams. Franklin also believed that the proposal emanated from George III, or so he told John Adams. Accordingly many have assumed that the letter was sponsored by George III (though Carl Van Doren in his biography of Franklin said that there is not "any evidence that this was a communication from George III"). Jared Sparks stated in a footnote to Franklin's Works that the writer was a "secret agent from England" and Sparks affirmed that Franklin understood that the letter proceeded "from high authority".

CHAPTER 33

Both the weakness of Lord North and his desire to modify the stubborn attitudes of the king are fully evidenced in the lengthy correspondence between Lord North and George III.

CHAPTER 34

There have been numerous accounts of the Gordon Riots. Dickens's description in *Barnaby Rudge* is true in atmosphere though inaccurate in details.

The reports of military movements under the direction of Jeffery, Lord Amherst, who was also a member of the cabinet at that time, are available today. An index of the documents is given in the *British Manuscripts Project* of the American Council of Learned Societies. In America the papers may be consulted at the Library of Congress on microfilm or at Amherst College. In the latter collection are photostatic copies of the 1780 period.

CHAPTER 35

For a fuller study of the Gordon riots and the after-effects we recommend *The Gordon Riots* by J. Paul de Castro.

CHAPTER 36

The citation regarding loyalists in the notes to Chapter 26 is again pertinent here.

CHAPTER 37

The letters and diaries of Henry, tenth Earl of Pembroke, and his circle reveal the growing opposition to George III and his policies.

CHAPTER 38

For a compendium of eyewitness accounts and recollections covering this period see Volume V of *Correspondence of King George the Third* edited by Sir John Fortescue.

CHAPTER 39

For a thoroughly documented study of Shelburne's role in the peace treaty with the United States see the Raleigh Address of C. W. Alvord before the British Academy, October 28, 1925.

In contrast to the three oldest royal princes, the three sons of George Grenville were public-spirited citizens and a credit to the state. Since they had better manners than their crusty father, the king had accepted them with confidence into various official offices.

The Lord Temple referred to in this chapter was George Grenville, Jr. (1753–1813) who had inherited the Temple title from his uncle. He later became Marquess of Buckingham.

Thomas Grenville (1755–1846) initially was a Foxite but switched his allegiance to Pitt.

William Wyndham Grenville (1759–1834) became secretary to George, Jr., in 1782 and was a Secretary of State in 1789. In 1790 he became Lord Grenville, with the rank of baron.

CHAPTER 40

Macaulay and others have wondered how Miss Burney could write so adoringly of George and Charlotte, whilst most of the specific examples which she reported showed them to be mean, narrow, stupid, and inconsiderate.

The explanation of the apparent inconsistency may be found in the comment of a colleague on the household staff who accused her of the technique of using excessive praise as a means of making an individual appear ridiculous. He called it "skating a man down". In short, by excessive praise she saw to it that "the poor dupe makes so many turnings and windings and describes circle after circle with such hazardous dexterity that at last he drops in the midst of his flourishes to his own eternal disgrace". Perhaps significantly, Miss Burney did not defend herself from this charge.

CHAPTER 41

The illness of George III and its effect on his family and the government are fully documented in various sources. We mention especially the *Diaries of Robert Fulke Grenville,* who was of the king's household, and the *Private Diary* of Sir Robert Wilson, an equerry to the king, which give many details of the king's behaviour when insane; also the *Diary and Letters of Frances Burney* (Madame D'Arblay) for scenes in the royal family at the time of the king's illness. The political problems are discussed in the correspondence of the three Grenville brothers in *Court and Cabinets of George III*, edited by the Duke of Buckingham.

A particularly illuminating discussion of the king's madness in the light of modern medicine is given in *America's Last King* by Manfred S. Guttmacher, M.D., psychiatrist at Johns Hopkins Hospital and Chief Medical Officer to the Supreme Bench of Baltimore.

Lucille Iremonger in *Love and the Princesses* has described the romantic and marital destinies of the daughters of George III, with especial attention to Sophia. She writes: "Like her sisters, Sophia suffered from her enforced spinsterhood. Like them all, she was desired. Unlike them—as I think we may say with some confidence—she bore a child. She died, officially at least, unmarried."

It is well established that there was a boy adopted by an equerry Garth and given the name of Tom Garth; and that the princesses resented his frequent presence at the Court without specifically saying just why.

CHAPTER 42

During one of George III's spells of illness Thurlow negotiated a verbal agreement with the Prince of Wales to support a bill making the prince sole regent provided he would continue Thurlow in office as Lord Chancellor. When Fox and others in the opposition heard of this commitment they were greatly incensed and treated the incident as a betrayal of His Majesty.

It is difficult, however, to put such a construction on Thurlow's conduct for if the king's illness continued beyond recovery it was obvious that some provision had to be made for a regency and it would seem perfectly honourable for Thurlow to protect his own interests. The issue proved to be meaningless as the prince did not become regent until 1811, five years after Thurlow's demise.

On the question of the abolition of slavery many have assumed a priori that George III was opposed to the measure because he was habitually against change. Lord Brougham in his book referring to statesmen and other eminent characters in the time of George III makes the unqualified statement that the king was opposed to abolition because it would be an innovation; and various other writers have accepted that statement. As a writer Brougham was an engaging amateur, but his work is full of historical lapses.

In *George the Third* by J. D. Griffith Davies, however, we find the statement that George III "was enthusiastic for Wilberforce's measure to abolish slavery"; and we are told that George III was "much grieved" when the Prince of Wales spoke against Wilberforce's motion for abolition. According to biographies of Wilberforce by his sons and by Coupland, the king was in favour of abolition up to 1795.

However, opposition in England to the liberal principles of Tom

Paine and the French Revolution increased; and because many of the
abolitionists were also supporters of these democratic movements, their
cause was soon identified with the Jacobin influence. An uprising by
the slaves on the Caribbean island of Santo Domingo in 1795 was the
turning point in George III's support of Wilberforce and he stolidly
backed the anti-abolitionists thereafter, although he did give his assent
when the abolition bill was finally passed in 1807.

CHAPTER 43

In conclusion we make a parting gesture to Lady Sarah Lennox (see
her *Life and Letters*), who perhaps understood George III best of anyone.

BIBLIOGRAPHY

The bibliography primarily indicates that works have been consulted. In some instances, such as the various books telling about Hannah Lightfoot, a moderate amount of fact is mingled with hearsay and conjecture. The inclusion of any book in the bibliography does not necessarily imply an endorsement.

In the more serious historical works there may be found wide divergences (even as in the memoirs of present-day generals). For example, there is considerable disparity in the accounts of Burgoyne's campaign ending in defeat at Saratoga as described by E. S. Creasy compared with F. J. Hudleston.

I have not listed here certain standard sources which inevitably were consulted, such as the *Dictionary of National Biography*, Hansard's *Parliamentary Debates,* and various public documents such as those of the Historical Manuscripts Commission and the *Journals of the Continental Congress.* Also, certain sources quoted in the notes, where they have dealt chiefly with a particular point are not repeated here.

Adams, James Truslow, *The Epic of America*. Little, Brown and Company, Boston, 1955.

Anderson, Troyer Steele, *The Command of the Howe Brothers During the American Revolution*. Oxford University Press, New York, London, 1936.

Andreano, Ralph Louis, and Werner, Herbert D., "Charleston Loyalists: A Statistical Note." *South Carolina Historical Magazine,* Vol. LX, No. 3, Charleston, July 1959.

Annual Register. Dodsley, London, 1791.

Arkell, R. L., *Caroline of Anspach*. Oxford University Press, London, 1939.

Bailey, Thomas A., *The American Pageant*. Little, Brown and Company, Boston, 1956.

Barclay, H. F., and Wilson-Fox, Alice, *A History of the Barclay Family*. St. Catherine Press, London, 1934.

Barnes, Donald Grove, *George III and William Pitt, 1783-1806*. Stanford University Press, Palo Alto, Calif., 1939.

Benham, Daniel, *Memoirs of James Hutton*. Hamilton, Adams and Company, London, 1856.

Bernheim, G. D., *German Settlements and the Lutheran Church in the Carolinas*. Lutheran Bookstore, Philadelphia, 1872.

Bigham, Hon. Clive, *The Prime Ministers of Great Britain*. E. P. Dutton and Company, New York, 1924.

Boswell, James, *Life of Samuel Johnson*. Hill-Powell edition, Clarendon Press, Oxford, 1934-1950.

Boswell, James, *Samuel Johnson's Letter to Lord Chesterfield; and Interview with George III*. Charles Dilly, London, 1790.

Boulton, William B., *In the Days of the Georges*. J. Pott and Company, New York, 1910.

Britton, John, and Braley, Edward W., *The Beauties of England and Wales*. London, 1801.

Brougham, Henry, Baron, *Statesmen in the Times of George III*. Charles Knight and Company, London, 1839.

Buckingham and Chandos, Duke of, *Court and Casbinets of George the Third*, 2 vols. Hurst and Blackett, London, 1853.

Burke, Sir Bernard, *Peerage and Baronetage*, Fifty-ninth edition. Harrison and Sons, London, 1897.

Burney, Fanny (Madame d'Arblay), *Diary and Letters*. Roberts Brothers, Boston, 1880.

Butterfield, Herbert, *George III and the Historians*. Collins, London, 1957.

Buxton, Travers, *William Wilberforce*. Religious Tract Society, London, 1833.

Carlson, C. Lennart, *The First Magazine*. Brown University, Providence, R. I., 1938.

Carlyle, Thomas, *Frederick the Great*. Harper and Brothers, New York, 1858.

Cecil, David, *Melbourne*. Bobbs-Merrill, Indianapolis, 1939.

Chamberlain, Arthur B., *George Romney*, Methuen and Company, London, 1910.

Chancellor, E. Beresford, *The Private Palaces of London Past and Present*. London, Kegan, Paul, Trench, Trübner and Company, 1908.

Clifford, J. L., *Johnsonian Studies: A Survey and Bibliography*. University of Minnesota Press, Minneapolis, 1951.

Colburn, Henry, *George the Third, His Court, and Family*, 2 vols. London, 1824.

Continental Congress, *Journals of the Continental Congress*, Vol. I, 1774, edited by W. C. Ford. Government Printing Office, Washington.

Costin, W. C., and Watson, J. Stephen, *The Law and Working of the Constitution: Documents 1660-1914*. Adam and Charles Black, London, 1952.

Coupland, R., *Wilberforce, A Narrative*. Oxford University Press, London, 1923.

Creasy, E. S., *The Fifteen Decisive Battles of the World from Marathon to Waterloo.* American Book Exchange, New York, 1881.

Curtis, Edith Roelker, *Lady Sarah Lennox.* G. P. Putnam's Sons, New York, 1946.

Davies, A. Mervyn, *George III and the Constitution.* Oxford University Press, Oxford, 1921.

Davis, Rosemary, *The Good Lord Lyttleton.* Times Publishing Company, Bethlehem, 1939.

de Castro, J. Paul, *The Gordon Riots.* Oxford University Press, London, 1926.

De Tilly, du Comte, *Memoires du Duc de Lauzun.* Librairie de Firmin Didot Frères, Paris, 1862.

Dickenson, John, *Life and Writings of John Dickenson.* Memoirs of the Historical Society of Pennsylvania, Vol. XIII, Philadelphia, 1891.

Dodington, George Bubb (Baron of Melcombe Regis), *Diary of the Late George Bubb Dodington, March 8, 1749 to February 6, 1761,* third edition. G. and T. Wilkie, London, 1785.

Dunlap, William, *A History of the Rise and Progress of the Arts of Design in the United States,* edited by F. W. Bayley and C. S. Goodspeed. Goodspeed, Boston, 1918.

Egmont, John Perceval, Third Earl, *Manuscripts of the Earl of Egmont* 3 vols. His Majesty's Stationery Office (Historical Manuscripts Commission), London, 1920-1923.

Fitzgerald, Brian, *Lady Louisa Conally.* Staples Press, London, 1950.

Fitzgerald, Percy, *Life and Times of John Wilkes, M.P.,* 2 vols. Ward and Downey, London, 1888.

Fortescue, Sir John, *Correspondence of King George the Third,* 6 vols. Macmillan, London, 1927-1928.

George III, *Correspondence with Lord North,* edited by W. Bodham Donne. John Murray, London, 1867.

George III, *Letters to Lord Bute, 1756-1766,* edited by Romney Sedgwick. Macmillan, London, 1939.

Grenville, George, *Grenville Papers* (including correspondence of George Grenville and Lord Temple), edited by William James Smith. John Murray, London, 1852.

Grove, Sir George, *Dictionary of Music and Musicians,* third edition (H. C. Colles, ed.). Macmillan, New York, 1944.

Guttmacher, Manfred S., M.D., *America's Last King.* Charles Scribner's Sons, New York, 1941.

Halsband, Robert, *Life of Lady Mary Wortley Montague.* Clarendon Press, Oxford, 1956.

Hamilton, Lady Anne, *Secret History of the Court of England,* 2 vols. L. C. Page and Company, Boston, 1901.

Henry, David, *An Historical Account of the Curiosities of London and Westminster.* Carnan and Newberry, London, 1772.

x

Herbert, Henry, *Henry, Elizabeth and George* (Letters and Diaries of Henry, 10th Earl of Pembroke and His Circle). Jonathan Cape, London, 1939.

Hervey, John, Lord, *Memoirs of the Reign of George II,* edited by Romney Sedgwick. Eyre & Spottiswoode, London, 1931.

Hibbert, Christopher, *King Mob.* World, Cleveland, 1958.

Hudleston, F. J., *Gentleman Johnny Burgoyne.* Bobbs-Merrill, Indianapolis, 1927.

Hutton, James, *Memoirs, see under* Benham.

Ilchester, Earl of, *Lord Hervey and His Friends.* John Murray, London, 1950.

Jackson, Henry E., *Benjamin West, His Life and Work.* Winston, Philadelphia, 1900.

Jenkins, Elizabeth, *Elizabeth the Great.* Coward-McCann, New York, 1959.

Jesse, J. Heneage, *King George the Third,* 3 vols. Tinsley Brothers, London, 1867.

Jesse, J. Heneage, *Literary and Historical Memoirs of London,* Vol. I. Richard Bentley, London, 1847.

Johnson, Rev. Samuel, *An Argument Proving that the Abrogation of King James by the People of England Was According to the Constitution.* Printed for the author, fourth edition, London, 1692.

Journal of the Friends Historical Society, Vol. V. Headley Brothers, London, 1908.

Knight, Charles, *London.* Charles Knight and Company, London, 1841.

Knollenberg, Bernhard, *Franklin Jonathan Williams and William Pitt: A Letter of January 21, 1775.* Indiana University Library Publications, No. 1, Bloomington, Indiana, 1949.

Knollenberg, Bernhard, *Origin of the American Revolution, 1759-1766.* Macmillan, New York, 1960.

Larkin, Oliver W., *Samuel F. B. Morse and American Democratic Art.* Little, Brown and Company, Boston, 1954.

Little, Bryan, "Norborne Berkeley: Gloucestershire Magnate." *Virginia Magazine of History and Biography,* Vol. LXIII, No. 4, October 1955.

Long, J. C., *Lord Jeffery Amherst.* Macmillan, New York, 1933.

Long, J. C., *Mr. Pitt.* Frederick A. Stokes Company, New York, 1940.

Lyman, Susan Elizabeth, "The Search for the Missing King." *American Heritage,* Vol. IX, No. 5, August 1958.

Macaulay, Thomas Babington, *Two Essays on William Pitt, Earl of Chatham.* University Press, Cambridge, 1900.

Malone, Dumas, *The Story of the Declaration of Independence.* Oxford University Press, New York, 1954.

Marchmont, Hugh Hume, 3rd Earl of, *Marchmont Papers,* edited by Sir G. H. Rose. John Murray, London, 1831.

Miller, John C., *Origins of the American Revolution.* Little, Brown and Company, Boston 1943.

Miller, John C., *Triumph of Freedom.* Little, Brown and Company, Boston, 1948.

Molloy, J. F., *Court Life Below Stairs.* Hurst and Blackett, London, 1883.

Muirhead, L. Russel, *England* (Blue Guides). Ernest Berne, London, 1957.

Mumby, Frank Arthur, *George III and the American Revolution.* Constable, London, 1923.

Namier, L. B., *Additions and Corrections to Sir John Fortescue's Edition of the Correspondence of King George the Third (Vol. I).* Manchester University Press, Manchester, 1937.

Namier, L. B., *England in the Age of the American Revolution.* Macmillan, London, 1930.

Namier, L. B., *The Structure of Politics at the Accession of George III,* 2 vols. Macmillan, London, 1929.

Namier, Sir Lewis (L. B.), *Personalities and Powers.* Macmillan, New York, 1955.

Nobbe, George, *The North Briton.* Columbia University Press, New York 1939.

Northumberland, Elizabeth Percy, First Duchess of, *The Diaries of a Duchess,* edited by James Grieg. Hodder and Stoughton, London, 1926.

Palmer, R. R., *The Age of the Democratic Revolution: A Political History of Europe and America, 1760-1800.* Princeton University Press, Princeton, 1959.

Pares, Richard, *King George III and the Politicians.* Clarendon Press, Oxford, 1953-1954.

Park, Joseph Henderson, *British Prime Ministers of the 19th Century.* York University Press, New York, 1950.

Pearce, C. E., *The Amazing Duchess.* S. Paul and Company, London, 1911.

Pine, L. G., *The Story of the Peerage.* William Blackwood and Sons, Edinburgh and London, 1956.

Plumb, J. H., *The First Four Georges.* Batsford, London, 1957.

Prior, Sir James, *A Life of Edmund Burke.* George Bell and Sons, London, 1891.

Rhys, Ernest, ed., *Letters From Lady Mary Wortley Montagu,* J. M. Dent and Sons, London, 1906.

Rose, George, *Diaries and Correspondence.* Richard Bentley, London, 1860.

Shillitoe, Thomas, *Journal.* Harvey and Darton, London, 1839.

Sosin, Jack M., "A Postscript to the Stamp Act." *American Historical Review,* July 1958.

Stevens, B. F., *Facsimiles,* Vol. VIII. Nos. 835-837. 1891.

Taylor, Deems, *Music Lovers' Encyclopedia.* Garden City, New York, 1939.

Thackeray, William Makepeace, *Works* (*The Four Georges*). John Wurtele Lovell, New York, N.D.

Thoms, William J., *The Book of the Court,* second edition. Henry G. Bohn, London, 1844.

Thoms, William J., *Hannah Lightfoot.* W. G. Smith, London, 1867.

Thornbury, Walter, *Old and New London,* Vols. I-II. Cassell, Peter and Galper, London, 1872-1878.

Tolles, Frederick B., *James Logan and the Culture of Provincial America.* Little, Brown and Company, Boston, 1957.

Trevelyan, G. M., *History of England* (one-volume edition). Longmans, Green and Company, New York, 1927.

Vulliamy, C. E., *Royal George.* D. Appleton-Century, New York, 1937.

Wade, John, *British History Chronologically Arranged,* fifth edition. Henry G. Bohn, London, 1847.

Walford, Edward, *Old and New London,* Vols. III-IV. Cassell, Peter and Galper, London, 1872-1878.

Whitley, W. T., *Artists and Their Friends in England, 1700 to 1709.* London, 1928.

Wilberforce, R. I. and S., *The Life of William Wilberforce.* John Murray, London, 1828.

Wilkes, John, *Essay on Women.* Privately printed, London, 1871.

Williams, Folkestone, *Domestic Memoirs of the Royal Family and the Court of England; Chiefly at Shene and Richmond,* 3 Vols. Hurst and Blackett, London, 1860.

Wraxall, Sir N. W., *Historical and Posthumous Memoirs,* edited by H. B. Wheatley. Scribner's, New York, 1884.

Young, Sir George, *Poor Fred, the People's Prince.* Oxford University Press, London, 1937.

INDEX

ABERCROMBY, GENERAL, 58-9, 60
Act of Settlement, 18
Adams, Abigail, 178-9
Adams, John, defended British soldiers, 198; conciliation, 211; Declaration of Independence, 217, 220; and Franklin, 231; received by king, 285
Adams, Samuel, 197
Addington, Henry, 297
Addison, Joseph, *Cato*, 34
Age of Enlightenment, 303-4
Aix-la-Chapelle, treaty of, 57
Albermarle, Lady, 73
Amelia, Princess (aunt), 64
Amelia, Princess (daughter), death, 301
American cause, champions in Parliament, 207
American colonists, independent character, 194
American Revolution, make-up of sympathizers, 151-2, 194; discontent on conduct of, 263-5. *See also* Colonies
Amherst, General Lord Jeffery, commander in America, 57-8, 62-3; replaced as Governor of Virginia, 174-5; Quebec Act, 200; and American Revolution, 203-4, 210, 225-6, 239; and Gordon riots, 248-54, 257, 262
Amherst, Captain William, 53
Anna, Princess, 18
Anne, Queen, 18-19
Annual Registry, 66, 94
Apology, 98
Arkwright, Richard, 180
Arne, Dr., *Alfred*, 26
Arts, George's interest in, 176-82
Augusta, Princess Dowager, 15, 260; marriage and life with Frederick, 20, 22-4, 26; domination of George III, 36, 39, 40, 74, 162; opposition to match with Sarah Lennox, 74, 77; baptism of grandson, 121-2; new regency bill, 132-3; loses influence over king, 147; and Lord Bute, 163, 165; boasts of George's dominance, 186; death and obsequies, 189-90; for a royal marriage act, 190; her estate, 190-1
Augusta (sister), 27, 77-8, 238
Austria, 55
Axford, Isaac, 46

BAKER, DOCTOR, 291
Bank of England, saved from Gordon rioters, 253-4
Banks, Joseph, explorations, 182-3
Barclay, David, host to royal family, 96-7, 98, 100; peace emissary to Franklin, 231
Barré, Isaac, 105, 114, 207, 229
Barrington, Lord, 187
Bastille, fall of, 298
Bath, Lord of, 121
Beckford, Alderman, friend of Pitt, 94, 97, 99
Bedford, Duke of, marriage, 21; political shrewdness, 116; silk tariff issue, 129-30, antagonism to Bute, 141; offer to resign, 148; for modification of Stamp Act, 151
Belle Isle, 63
Berkeley, Norborne. *See* Botetourt
Bill of Rights, 17
Bisset (historian), on Shelburne, 169; on Townshend, 170-1; on George's failure to govern, 172
Blackstone's *Commentaries*, 43
Boehler, Peter, 181
Bolingbroke, *The Idea of a Patriot King*, 27, 162
Bonnie Prince Charlie, 19, 20
Boston Massacre, 198
Boston Port Bill, 199, 201, 207
Boston Tea Party, 199, 208
Boswell, James, 182, 286
Botetourt, Norborne Berkeley, Lord, 68; Governor of Virginia, 174-5
Bounty mutiny, 298
Bradstreet, Colonel John, 58, 59
Brandywine, battle, 223
Bruce, Lord, 68
Bull, Alderman, 247
Bunbury, Sir Charles, 165
Bunbury, Lady Sarah. *See* Lennox, Lady Sarah

Bunker Hill, battle, 204-5
Burgoyne, General John, Bunker Hill, 204, 205; on strategy of colonists, 204-5; plans campaign, 222; failure at Saratoga, 223, 224
Burke, Edmund, 246, 298, 305; on George Grenville, 125; qualities, 150; sympathy for colonies, 158, 197, 207; on Conway, 158; on Pitt, 160; on Chatham-Grenville ministry, 169; on Lord North, 187; moved review of Crown perquisites, 241; drafted Catholic Relief bill, 243; attacked government policies, 262; bill for reform of civil list, 263; in cabinet, 277; logical choice for prime minister, 279
Burney, Dr. Charles, 181, 261
Burney, Fanny, 181, 261, 285-6
Bute, Earl of, 260, 278; relations with Frederick Lewis, 15, 30; tutor of Prince, 42, 43; ascendancy of, 49, 50, 52-63; and Pitt, 57, 154; influence over king, 66, 72, 73, 87, 88, 127, 131, 141; Secretary of State, 76; sought English peerage, 88; attacked by Wilkes, 107; unpopularity as prime minister, 117, 126; position on cider tax, 120; resignation, 126; and weavers' riots, 130; and Grenville, 141, 148; on continent, 147; selfishness, 159; scandal with Augusta, 163, 165; king breaks with, 166
Bute, Lady, 77

CABINET, STRENGTHENED POSITION, 65
Camden, Lord, 169, 295
Canada, campaigns, 56, 58; plan for conquest, 62, 63
Cantelupe, Lord, 120-1
Carleton, Sir Guy, 221-2, 268
Caroline, Princess of Brunswick-Wolfenbüttel, proposed marriage to king, 39, 79
Caroline, Princess of Wales, king's advances, 293
Caroline, Queen (grandmother), wife of George II, 20; hostility to Frederick, 22, 23
Caroline Matilda (sister), 27; scandal as queen of Denmark, 165; death, 165-6, 209
Carroll, Charles, 243
Carteret, Philip, explorations, 183, 184
Cartwright, Edmund, power loom, 180
Catherine II (Russia), armed neutrality, 265
Catholic Relief Act, 242-3; repeal sought, 245-6
Catholic toleration, opposed by king, 296
Challoner, Catholic bishop, 250

Champion, William, 174
Charles, Prince (Young Pretender), 29, 30
Charles I, 23
Charlotte, Queen (wife), engagement to king, 78-9; arrival in England, 80, 82; children, 81; wedding, 82; coronation, 83-4; household, 90-1; at Guildhall banquet, 94-5, 100-1; birth of first child, 120-1; estrangement from king, 163, 293, 300; and king's insanity, 288-91
Chatham, Baroness of, 93. *See also* Pitt, Hester
Chatham, Earl of. *See* Pitt, William (the Elder)
Chatham-Grafton ministry, temporarily with party, 162, 167; make-up, 168, 169; troubles, 174-5; fall, 176
Chesterfield, Lord, 27
Chippendale, Thomas, 181
Chudleigh, Elizabeth, 34, 35; relationship with king, 49, 162; scandals and marriages, 163-4
Churchill, Charles, 107, 111, 112
Cider tax, 118, 137-8; repeal, 150
Citizen, The, 45
Clarke, Mary Anne, and army scandal, 301
Clinton, General Sir Henry, Bunker Hill, 204-5; command in New York, 222, 223-4; failure to relieve Burgoyne, 223-4; commander in America, 230; victories in Southern colonies, 240-1, 256; later duped by Washington, 262, 266; predicted Cornwallis victory over Lafayette, 265, 266
Clive, Lord Robert, 59
Cliveden on the Thames, Frederick Lewis's Court, 26, 34
Cobham, Lord, 124
Coercive Acts, 199-200
Colonies, effects of Stamp Act, 139-40; worsening of situation, 152; angered by Townshend Acts, 172; "taxation without representation," 197-9; demands for independence, 211-14
Concord, Massachusetts, military stores destroyed, 203
Connecticut, for independence, 213; punished through new charter, 214
Continental Congress, First, 199
Continental Congress, Second, appointment of Washington as Commander-in-chief, 208; Declaration of Independence, 216-17; flees Philadelphia, 223; refusal to meet peace commissions, 230
Conway, General Henry Seymour, 277, 305; removed from command, 114; Secretary of State, 149; American sympathizer, 149, 152; king's man,

Conway (*contd.*)
149, 150; against Stamp Act, 156, 158; moves Declaratory Acts to appease Crown, 158; sent dismissal notes to old cabinet, 167; manager in House of Commons, 168-9; opposed East India bill, 171; wished to retire, 174; in North's cabinet, 187; on Gordon riots, 247; non-Shelburne views, 279

Cook, Captain James, explorations on *Endeavour*, 183

Corbett, J. S., 63

Cornwallis, General Charles, in New Jersey, 221; lack of success in Southern area, 262-3; at Yorktown, 265, 266; surrender, 267

Cosway, Richard, 181

Cotes, Humphrey, 130

Country Party, Bolingbroke's concept, 27-8

Court Gazette, 93, 94

Cresset (household treasurer of princess dowager), 41, 42

Critical Review, 182

Crompton, Samuel, 180

Cromwell, Oliver, 16, 216

Cromwell, Thomas, 23

Crown Point, 62, 222

Culloden, decisive victory, 29

Cumberland, Henry, Duke of (brother), 196; scandals and marriage, 201

Cumberland, William, Duke of (uncle), 22, 122, 141; popularity, 29-30; chairman of regency council, 39; commander of forces on continent, 57; position on Sarah Lennox affair, 73; and Pitt, 138; helps form cabinet, 144; colonial toleration, 149; death, 150

Curzon Street Chapel, 44

DARTMOUTH, LORD, replaced by Lord Germain, 201

Dashwood, Francis, 106

Deane, Silas, 231

Declaration of Independence, 215-24; effect on George III's reputation, 215, 216, 218-21

Declaration of Rights, 17, 18

Declaratory Acts, 158, 197

Denmark, king's enmity toward, 193

Devonshire, Duke of, king's distrust, 116; Lord Chamberlain, 122; death, 137

Dickinson, John, "olive branch petition," 211

Divine right, 17

Dodington, George Bubb, influence over prince, 39, 40-1; Hell Fire Club, 106-7

Dorset, Duke of, 59

Drummond, Robert Hay, Archbishop of York, 177

Drury Lane Theatre, 299

Dundas, Henry, 243

Dunning, John, Baron Ashburton, attacks Crown's influence on Parliament, 241; in cabinet, 277; death, 280

EAST INDIA COMPANY, 262; attempts to regulate, 171, 282; monopoly under tea tax, 199; and Boston Tea Party, 208

Edward, Duke of Kent (brother), 27; father of Victoria, 303

Edward VI, 23

Effingham, Lord, 85

Egmont, Lord, 27, 297

Egremont, Earl of, Pitt's successor, 93; action against Wilkes, 113; personality and career, 123-6; death, 126, 137

Elector of Hanover, 18

Elector Palatine, 18

Elizabeth, Princess (daughter of James I), 18

Elizabeth, Princess (sister), 60

Elizabeth I, 183; George III compared with, 192, 304

Elkton, Maryland, 223

Ellis, Welbore, 270

England, revolt and riots, 242-54

Europe, campaigns in, 55, 59-61, 63; king's "meddling" in affairs, 192-3

Excise tax, 118

Exploration, under George III, 183-4

FAIRFAX, LORD, 208

Fetter Lane Chapel, 181

Fort Niagara, 59, 62

Fort Ticonderoga, 58, 60, 222; taken by Amherst, 62; taken by Burgoyne, 223

Fort William and Mary, 211

Fox, Lady Caroline, 73

Fox, Charles James, American sympathizer, 207; attacks government, 262; sneered at by king, 264; Secretary of State, 277; resigned, 279; in Portland ministry, 281-2; attempt to regulate East India Company, 282; and Prince of Wales, 283, 290; implicated in theft of Great Seal, 284; spread rumours, 289; death, 297

Fox, Henry, 36, 94; on regency question, 39; influence, 49, 50; character, 69; tribute to Lady Sarah Lennox, 70; effort to promote royal match, 76, 77; attacked by Bute, 87; attacked by Wilkes, 109; effective party whip, 109; elevated to peerage as Lord Holland, 117-18; position on cider tax, 120; dismissal from Paymaster's office, 142-3

France, population, 55; peace offer, 92; "promenade" of fleet stopped, 193;

France (*contd.*)
Franklin negotiates treaty with, 224, 227-8; attempts to discredit good faith of, 231; naval threat, 240; naval victories, 265; at Yorktown, 267; Revolution and war with England, 298

Francis, Sir Philip, 185

Franklin, Benjamin, against Stamp Act, 139-40, 153; provincial agent for colonies, 152; on Lexington battle, 203; for independence, 207; repels conciliation attempts, 215, 230-3; Declaration of Independence, 217, 220; success in France, 224; negotiation for French loan, 264-5

Frederick, Duke of York (son), scandals, 283, 301, 303

Frederick, Prince (brother), 26

Frederick Lewis, Prince (father), popularity, 15; hostility of George II toward, 20, 22-3, 24; marriage plans thwarted, 21-2; marriage to Augusta, 22, 26; home life at Cliveden, 26-7, 34; political and social views, 28, 30, 35-6, 37; relations with Lord Bute, 30-1; testament and advice to George III, 37, 304-5; death, 38

Frederick of Prussia, 56

Freedom of speech, attempts to throttle, 106, 110-15

French Canadians, tolerance shown, 200

French Revolution, effect in England, 298

Furneaux, Tobias, explorations, 183, 184

GAGE, GENERAL THOMAS, 62; harshness toward colonies, 199; Governor of Massachusetts, 200; closed port of Boston, 201; troops in Lexington and Concord, 203; minimized Lexington to Amherst, 203-4; Bunker Hill, 204-5; stiffer instructions to, 206; planned for a long war, 209-10

Gainsborough, Thomas, 178

Gaspée affair, 198

Gates, General Horatio, 224

General warrants, debate, 133-7; prohibited, 150

"Gentle Shepherd," 119

George I, 16, 18, 19

George II, 15, 16, 17, hostility toward Frederick Lewis (Prince of Wales). 20-3, 25; unpopularity, 36; and Augusta, 40; control of education of Prince George, 42; and marriage of Prince, 47-8; death, 64, 66; descendants affected by royal marriage act, 192; status compared with George III's, 260

George III, contradictory elements, 15; birth, 24; early education and accomplishments, 27, 32-3; testament from father, 37-8; changes caused by death of father, 38-9; struggle to control, 39-42; tutors, 42-4; Hannah Lightfoot, 45, 46; devotion to Quaker persuasion, 47; romantic streak, 48-9; birthday ball, 49; Bute's influence, 52-5, 87; loss of sister, 60; attempt to enlist in army, 60-1; father's death, 64; appearance and nature, 67; first speech before Parliament, 67; disregard of precedent, 67, 88; and Sarah Lennox, 69-78; engagement and wedding, 78-83; coronation, 83-6; resentment of Pitt, 89-90; daily routine, 90-1; foreign affairs in 1761, 91; dilemma on resignation of Pitt, 92-4; entertained at Barclay House, 96, 97-9, 100; at Guildhall banquet, 94-5, 100-1; and freedom of press, 106, 110-15; air of distrust, 115, 116; "firmness and resolution," 115, 118, 119-20; position on cider tax, 119, 120; domestic life, 120; birth and baptism of first child, 120-2; and Spitalfields weavers, 122, 128-30; handicapped by early education, 123-4; difficulty in finding successor to Bute, 127-8; mental condition, 131; regency bill, 131-3; and the general warrants debate, 134-6; loss of familiar faces, 137-8; galling experience of dismissing Grenville, 141-4, 147-9; and the Rockingham ministry, 150, 152-3; position on Stamp Act, 154, 157, 158, 162; failure in moral leadership, 159, 161; women associated with, 162-5; scandals of brothers and sons, 165; act to regulate marriages, 166; break with Bute, 166-7; stand against colonies, 167; and Chatham-Grafton ministry, 167; has axis of power, 168-9; lacked ability to dominate, 170-1; tries to hold Pitt, 176; interest in arts and sciences, 176-84; visit with Dr. Johnson, 181-2; and Dr. Priestley, 181-2; deterioration of character, 185; dominates ministry, 187; ironic generosity to North on debts, 188; unheeding of growing discontent, 189; funeral for mother, 189-90; and Cumberland's marriage, 191-2; peace of Europe, 192-3; misinformed on American affairs, 193-4; anti-American attitude, 197-9; pushes Coercive Acts, 200-2; tolerance shown in Quebec Act, 200; "A Proclamation for Suppressing Rebellion and Sedition," 206-7; stubborness prevents colonial solution, 206-10; proposal

George III (*contd.*)
for conciliation, 214-15; decides on full-scale war, 215; Declaration of Independence focused on, 215-16, 218-19, 220; American policy 1778, 224, 225; considers conciliation, 226-7; fear of French treaty in America, 227; peace proposals, 228, 230; against new Chatham ministry, 229; distrust and self-confidence of, 234-5; fleet inspection by, 235; firmness on North's extravagance, 236, 237-8; inept personal conduct of war, 240; relationship with cabinet, 240-1; Dunning's successful attack on Crown, 241; Catholic Relief bill, 242; audiences with Lord George Gordon, 245-6; dispersal of rioters, 250-3; arrests Gordon, 254-9; dwindling reputation, 259-63; persists in pressing American war, 265-8; replaces Germain, 268-70; refuses North's and Thurlow's suggestions, 271-2; accepts resignation of North ministry, 273; asks Thurlow to form cabinet, 278-9; Shelburne, 279-80; accepts Portland, 281; proposes abdication, 282; Pit's advice on withholding Crown favours, 282; ill health and scandals, 283-4; Great Seal theft incident, 284-5; receives John Adams, 285; home life, 285-6; growing mental instability, 286-7; status of Crown, 288-9; obscenity, deterioration and nature of insanity, 289-90; trip to London to show self, 290-1; question of physical handling of, 291-2; support of Pitt, 292, temporary cure, 292; estrangement from Queen, 293; advances to daughter-in-law Caroline, 293-4; mellowing personality, 294, 299-300; backed abolition, 295; resisted Catholic toleration, 296; changes in government, 297-8; frightened by French Revolution, 298; attempts at assassination on, 298-9; recurrence of madness, 300; jubilee fiftieth year, 300; grief over York scandal, 301; final insane years, 302; death and funeral, 302; family scandals, 302-3; compared with Elizabeth I, 304; fatal inflexibility, 304; summary of failures, 305

George IV (as Prince of Wales), birth, 120-1; Lady Sarah Lennox quoted, 173; extravagance and scandal, 237; a gambler, 283; friend of Fox, 283, 290; and George III's insanity, 291-2; disgraceful treatment of Caroline, 293; application for army rank, 296-7; appointed regent, 301; king in own right, 302; notoriety and lack of dignity, 302-3

Germain, Lord George, insubordination, 59, 61; toady to king on colonial matters, 201-2; the orders for Burgoyne campaign, 221, 222; insistent on firmness, 226, 227; concerned with desertions in Washington's army, 235-6; over-sanguine concerning loyalists, 239; and Gordon riots, 245; proposals for continuing war, 267; replacement, 268-70

Germantown, battle, 223

Gill, Moses, 211

Gloucester, Duke of (brother), 284; married Waldegrave's widow, 165

Glover, Richard, 119

"God Save the King," 299

Goldsworthy, Colonel, quoted on drafts at Windsor, 287

Goostrees Club, 296

Gordon, Duke of, exchange of letters on brother's arrest, 255-6; ignored brother's later jail term, 262

Gordon, Lord George, agitation against Catholic Relief Act, 242, 245-6; audiences with king, 245; march on Parliament, 246-7; attempt to quiet mob, 247-9, 254; lies low, 250; king refuses interview, 252, 262-3; arrested and questioned, 254-5; later erratic career and death, 262-3

Gordon, Lord William, 256, 289; eloped with Lady Sarah Lennox, 242; Vice-Admiral of Scotland, 270

Gower, Lord, 173

Graeme, emissary to Charlotte, 79

Grafton, Duke of (Augustus Henry Fitzroy), on Prince's household staff, 49; Secretary of State, 149; colonial sympathizer, 150; youth, 150; abilities, 161; ministry with Pitt, 161-2; new ministry with Pitt, 167-9, 170, opposed East India bill, 171; troubles over Amherst's dismissal, 175-6; attempts to appease Pitt, 175; First Lord of Treasury, 186; resignation, 187, 260; Lord Privy Seal, 277, 279

Granby, Lord, 141

Granville, Lord, 92

Great Seal, theft of, 284-5

Grenville, George, and cider tax, 119; social and political background, 124, 125; prime minister, 128, 131; legacy of errors, 133; for general warrants, 134-6, 137; for Stamp Act, 137; newfelt independence, 141; terms for continuing ministry, 141-5; note of dismissal to, 144; final conference with king, 147-9; views on Stamp Act, 152, 156; tactlessness, 153; attacked by Pitt, 154, 155, 156-7; lack of flair, 159-61; views on Bute's dismissal, 166; opposed to land tax, 171-2

Grenville, George, Jr., 302
Grenville, Henry, 123
Grenville, Hester, *See* Pitt, Hester
Grenville, James, 125
Grenville, Richard, *See* Temple, Lord
Grenville, Thomas, 123
Grenville, Sir William, on the king's rambling, 287; prime minister, 297
Grenville, phalanx, an influential group, 122-4
Grey, Thomas de, 269
Grosvenor, Lord, 191
Guildhall, royal banquet, 94, 95, 100, 101
Guildford, Francis, Earl of, 34
Gunning, Elizabeth, 34, 81

HALDIMAND, COLONEL, 62
Hales, Stephen, 43
Halifax, Lord, action against Wilkes, 111, 112, 113-14; Secretary of State, 116; regency bill, 131-2; Grenville cabinet, 141; Lord Privy Seal, 187
Hamilton, Duchess of, 26, 81
Hamilton, Duke of, 34
Hampshire Grants (Vermont), 212
Hampton Court Palace, 23
Hancock, John, 216, 220
Handel, 302
Hanover (House of), 17, 18, 19-20, 21
Hanover, delivered to French, 57
Harcourt, Lord, 42-3
Hardwicke, Lord, 25, 138, 147
Hargreaves, James, 180
Harrison, Benjamin, reads draft of Declaration of Independence, 217-20
Hartley, David, peace emissary to Franklin, 231, 232, 233
Heights of Abraham, 62
Hell Fire Club, 106, 107
Henley, Bridget, 141, 162, 163
Henley, Robert, *See* Northington, Lord
Henry, Patrick, 193; on Stamp Act, 153-4; "liberty or death" speech, 211
Henry, Prince (brother), 26
Henry VIII Chapel, 67
Henry VIII, 23
Hepplewhite, George, 181
Hertford, Lord, 173; non-attendance at Augusta's funeral, 189-90
Hervey, Augustus John, 35, 164
Hervey, Lord, 22, 25
Hillsborough, Lord, Secretary of State for colonies, 174; dissension over, 174-5; Secretary of State, 187; resignation, 201; arrest of Gordon, 255
History and Adventures of Miss L-ght-f--t, the Fairy Quaker, 45
Holland, Lord. *See* Fox, Henry
Holland, declared war on England, 265
Hopkinson, Francis, 177
Howe, Lord (brother of Richard and William), death, 60

Howe, Richard Earl, American sympathizer, 210; Crown commissioner for conciliation, 214-15; cabinet post, 277
Howe, General Sir William, Bunker Hill, 204-5; sympathy for colonists, 205, 210; Crown commissioner for conciliation, 214, 215; commands British army in New York, 220, 221; not notified to meet Burgoyne, 222; takes Philadelphia, 223; asked relief of command, 229; cabinet post, 277
Hunter, Miss Kitty, 163, 164
Huntingdon, Lady, 27
Huntingdon, Lord, 121
Hutton, James, king's tolerance, 181; peace proposals to Franklin, 232; describes fires in Gordon riots, 253
Hyde, Justice, read riots to Gordon rioters, 251

Idea of a Patriot King, The, 28
Ilchester, Lord, 75
Independence, growing agitation of Americans for, 207, 208
India, Clive's victories, 59
Irish, repression of Catholics, 242, 243
Irish Union Act, 295

JAMAICA, IMPORTANCE, 240-1
James Francis Edward, Prince (the Old Pretender), 17-18
James II, 17, 18, 217
Jefferson, Thomas, 194; wrote Declaration of Independence, 217
Jeffrys, John, 46
Jenkinson, Charles, 297
Johnson, Samuel, 287; chat with king in royal library, 181-2
Johnson, Reverend Samuel, 19
Jones, John Paul, sank *Serapis*, 240
Journal of Savans, 181
"Junius" letters on Botetourt appointment, 175; attack Grafton, 186

KEARSLEY, GEORGE, 111
Keith, Reverend Doctor, 44
Kennett, Brackley (Lord Mayor of London), welcomed Gordon riots, 249
Keppel, Admiral Augustus, 235; in decisive engagement off Brest, 238-9; acquitted in court-martial and resignation, 239
Kildare, Lady, 71
Kingston, Duke of, 164
Kolin, battle, 56

LAFAYETTE, MARQUIS DE, 265
Lake Ontario, British operations around, 58
Lambeth Palace, 95
Le Despencer, Lord, 187
Lennox, Lord George, 74

Lennox, Lady Sarah, 207, 264, 270; affair with George III, 69-78, 162; affair with Newbottle, 76-7; bridesmaid at royal wedding, 82; marriage to Bunbury, 165; marriage to Lord William Gordon, 165, 242; on Wilkes, 173; comment on Gordon riots, 256; and king's insanity, 289-90; comments on king's fiftieth jubilee, 300; on change in the times, 302

Letters of an Elder Brother to a Fair Quaker, 45

Lexington, battle of, 203-5, 206

Library (Queen's House), 181-2

Lightfoot, Hannah, and George III, 45-6, 162, 163, 300

Ligonier, Sir John, 57

Lincoln, Benjamin, 256

Liverpool, Earl of, prime minister, 297-8

Livingston, Robert R., 217

Locke, John, exponent of constitutional doctrine, 8; *Treatise on Civil Government*, 217

London, Corporation of City of, banquet to George III, 100; remonstrances ignored, 188-9; hostility to Crown, 240-1, 247, 263

Lord Chancellor, duties, 142

Lord Mayor of London (and Lady Mayoress), Guildhall banquet, 99-101

Loudon, Lord, 56-7

Louis XIV, 17

Louis XVI, extravagance, 237; execution, 298

Louisbourg, campaign, 56, 59

Lowther, Sir James, 247; moved end of American war, 267-8

Luttrel, Colonel, 186-7

Lyttelton, Lord, 27; *History*, 181

MacDONALD, FLORA, 30

Mackenzie (Bute's brother), direction of Scottish affairs, 141; dismissal, 143, 147; restoration, 167

Mann, Horace, 202

Mansfield, Lord Chancellor, ruling on Gordon riots, 252, 258-9

Marchmont, Earl of, 27

Marie Antoinette, Queen of France, 261

Marlborough, Duke of, 59

Marlborough, Sarah, Duchess of, 21, 25, 48, 163, 289

Marriage Act (1753), 44-5

Mary, Queen, 17

Maryland, for independence, 211-12

Massachusetts, against taxation without representation, 151; objected to Townshend duties, 198; constitution revised under Coercive Acts, 199; repressive measures against, 201

Matilda. *See* Caroline Matilda

Mayfair Chapel, 44

Mecklenburg Declaration, 211

Medmenham Abbey, 106

Middlesex, Lady, 26, 59

Middlesex, Lord, 59

Monitor, The, 107

Montague, Lady Mary Wortley, 30

Montague, Mrs. Elizabeth, 34

Monthly Review, 182

Moravians, king's tolerance, 181; threatened, 253

Morning Herald, 291

Morris, Robert, declined peace proposals, 230

NAPIER, GENERAL SIR CHARLES, married Lady Sarah Lennox, 289

Napoleonic wars, 301

Nelson, Admiral Lord, victories, 298

New Hampshire, for independence, 211, 212, 213

New York, declines to vote Townshend levies, 172; Washington's retreat from, 220

Newbottle, Lord, 74-6

Newcastle, Duke of, 25, 27, 36; importance, 49-50; First Lord of Treasury, 51, 63; and Bute, 87, 88; deprived of funds for political use, 107-9; king's distrust, 116; Lord Privy Seal, 150; and Pitt, 159-60; dismissal, 167

Nicholson, Margaret, attempted assassination of king, 287-8

Norfolk House, birth of George III at, 24

North, Frederick Lord, 33, 42; Chancellor of Exchequer, 173; ministry appointed, 187; qualities and background of, 188-9; subservience to George III, 190; executor of Augusta's estate, 190; settled Cumberland scandal, 191; royal marriage act, 192; and French fleet "promenade," 193; harshness to colonies, 199-200, 206-9; "die is cast," 206; determination on full-scale war, 215; wish to retire, 225, 227; Parliamentary opposition growing, 226; peace proposals, 227; consults Chatham, 228; effect of Chatham's death, 229; repeated attempts to resign, 234-6; obtains greater Crown grants, 237; advises change in ministry, 241-2; Catholic Relief Act, 245-6; attempt to buy off Gordon, 247; attacked by rioters, 248; action in crisis, 250, 251, 252, 254; ordered to defend king in Parliament, 258-9; policies attacked by Fox, 262; urged some of opposition in cabinet, 262-4; agony of frustration, 265; foresaw fall

North (contd.)
of ministry, 267, 270; declared need to end war, 268; on replacing Germain, 268-9; tried to resign, 270; stood up to George III, 272-3; resigned despite king, 272-3; in Portland cabinet, 281-2

North Briton, 105, 107, 109, 110-12, 151

North Carolina, for independence, 212-13

Northey, Mr. W., 67

Northington, Robert Henley, Lord, Lord Chancellor, 141, 142, 144; holdover in Cumberland cabinet, 149; quoted on lack of giants, 153; failure to help king in Rockingham ministry, 158-9; in Chatham-Grenville ministry, 169; retires, 173

Northumberland, Duchess of, 83, 84, 120-2, 130

Northumberland, Lord, dismissal from government of Ireland, 143

Norton, Sir Fletcher, on general warrants, 134-6

Norwich, Bishop of, tutor to Prince, 42-3

Nuthall, Thomas, Esq., 99

OLD PRETENDER, 17

"Olive branch petition," 211

Onslow, Lord, 299

Orkney, Lady, 26

Oxford, Earl of, 67

PAINE, TOM, 207

Palliser, Sir Hugh, Vice-Admiral of fleet, 236; insubordination, 239

Parliament, contractual conditions imposed on Crown, 16, 17, 19; policy appointing a succession, 17, 18, 19; Declaratory Act emphasizes supremacy over colonies, 157, 197; corruption by bribes and placement, 185-6; rising criticism of king's policies, 226-7, 233, 236, 241, 242, 261-2, 270-1, 273, 274; passes resolution against Crown's influence, 242; and Gordon riots, 246-8; dissolved by king, 285

Parsons, Nancy, mistress of Grafton, 149

Peace of Paris, 109-10, 192

Peachtree, Sir Eustace, *The Danger of This Mortall Life*, 200

Pearne, Robert, 46

Pelham, Thomas, *See* Newcastle, Duke of

Pembroke, Earl of, 49; scandals, 163; king's visit at country estate, 238; on crumbling of the empire, 266

Pembroke, Elizabeth Spencer, George's interest, 48-9, 162, 238; scandals, 163; and king's madness, 164-5, 238, 289, 293; Romney portrait, 178-9

Pennsylvania, resolution against stamp tax, 139, 140

Perceval, Spencer, 297

Perdita (Mrs. Robinson), and Prince of Wales, 237

Peterborough, Bishop of, 43

Philadelphia, Declaration of Independence, 214-23; taken by Howe, 223

Philosophical Transactions, 181

Piozzi, Mrs. Hester Thrale, 45

Pitt, Ann, Keeper of Privy Purse, 39

Pitt, George, 67

Pitt, Hester, 93, 123, 124, 280; made Baroness of Chatham, 99

Pitt, John, 99

Pitt, Thomas, 280, 282

Pitt, William (the Elder), service under George II, 16, 37, 39, 50; friend of Frederick, 25-6, 27; leader of Commons, 50-1; Prince's distrust, 51-2; brilliant prime minister, 55-63, 87; informs Prince of death of George II, 64-5; Bute debases, 87; king's antipathy, 89-90; and foreign affairs, 91-2; resignation and pension, 92-4; public disapproval of pension, 94-5, 99; at Guildhall banquet, 99; political and social background, 94-5, 99; approached for prime minister, 129, 131; against principle of general warrants, 134-6; "village philosopher", 147; Grenville's jealousy, 148; American sympathies, 152, 197, 207, 210; speech against Stamp Act and influence of throne, 154-6; dispute with Grenville, 156-7; advocates repeal, 158; vanity and ill health, 160; and Newcastle, 159-60; appointed Lord Privy Seal and made Earl of Chatham, 161-2, 168-9; forms ministry with Grafton, 167-8; on East India bill, 170; nervous breakdown, 173; grievances over appointments and dismissal of Amherst, 174, 175; resignation, 176, 177; against Quebec Act, 200; against repressive measures, 202; against independence, 227; approached by North for cabinet, 228; death, 229, 260

Pitt, William (the Younger), Chancellor of Exchequer, 279; declines prime ministry, 280-1; appointed prime minister, 282-3; relieved king of administration, 285; kept insanity secret, 290; king's support in lucid spells, 292; backed abolition of slavery, 295-6; for Catholic toleration, 296-7; temporarily out, 321; return to power and death, 298

Portland, Duke of, in cabinet, 278; prime minster, 281; temporarily out of power, 282; second ministry, 297; fleet inspection, 235, 238

Potter, Thomas, 107

Potts, Isaac, story of Washington at Valley Forge, 236

Pownall, Thomas, 61-2

Priestley, Dr. Joseph, king's aversion, 181-2; and Benjamin Franklin, 203

Princess Royal, 286

Princeton, battle, 221

Prior, Matthew, 157

Privy Council, powers and functions, 19, 65, 66, 136-7, 215-16

Proclamation of Rebellion, 206-7, 211; a great cause of Declaration of Independence, 215-16

Protestant Association, and Gordon riots, 244-6

Prussia, population, 56; English aid to, 57; Peace of Paris, 113-14

Public Advertiser, 45, 246

Pulaski, Count, death, 256

QUAKERS, George III's partiality for, 45-7, 98, 176, 178, 300; for abolition of slavery, 296

Quebec, capture, 62

Quebec Act, 280, 296; resented in colonies, 200-201; protested in Declaration of Independence, 215

Quérouaille, Louise de, 69

Quin, James, 33

Quincy, Josiah, 198

RAMSAY, ALLAN, 179

Regency, established, 300

Regency bill, 39, 44, 131, 133

Revere, Paul, cartoon on Boston Massacre, 198; famous ride, 203

Reynolds, Sir Joshua, 46, 177, 179, 303

Rhode Island, for independence, 213; punished through new charter, 214-15

Richard the Lionhearted, 303

Richmond, Charles, Duke of, brother of Lady Sarah Lennox, 70; and regency bill, 132; Secretary of State, 165; dismissed 168; American sympathizer, 207; for independence, 228; for manhood suffrage, 241; attacks government policies, 262; distasteful to king, 264; in cabinet, 277, 278

Richmonds, one of leading families, 69-70

Riot act, 258

Riots, Gordon, 242-54

Robertson, Major-General, 240

Robinson, Colonel, 42

Rochford, Lord, Secretary of State, 187

Rockingham, Marquess of, 260, 272; ministry of, 144; liberal policy, 149; youth, 151; on changes in king's speech to Parliament, 152; moderate enforcement of Stamp Act, 153-4; obtains repeal, 158; lack of Crown

support, 158-9 dismissal, 161, 167; American sympathizer, 207; for independence, 227-8; threatened in Gordon riots, 252; new ministry of, 264; ignored king, 277, death, 278

Rodney, Admiral George, defeated Spanish fleet, 241

Romney, Reverend John, 178; king's patronage, 179

Rousseau, Jean Jacques, 286

Royal Academy of Arts, 177, 180, 304

Royal marriage act, 190, 191, 192

SACKVILLE, LORD GEORGE. *See* Germain, Lord George

St. James's Chapel, 22

St. James's Palace, 23

Salem, Massachusetts, government moved to, 201

Sandwich, Lord, 184, 302; Hell Fire Club, 107-9; in Grenville cabinet, 141; in North cabinet, 187; promotion of Keppel, 238-9; king advocates boldness, 240

Saratoga, battle, 223

Savile, Sir George, reports on uprisings, 241; home damaged, 251

Savoy, Duke of, 18

Schuyler, General Philip, at Saratoga, 223

Sciences, king's interest in, 176, 182-4

Scotland, riots because of Catholic Relief bill, 243-4

Serapis, sunk by John Paul Jones, 240

Seymour, Jane, 23

Shackleton, John, 179

Shakespeare, William, detested by king, 286

Shelburne, Lord, 272; Secretary of State, 169; resigns at appointment of Hillsborough, 173-5; close contact with Hutton and the Moravians, 181; and Chatham, 202; American sympathizer, 207; and king, 227, 234; in cabinet, 277; ministry of, 279-80, 281; negotiated peace treaty with U.S., 280

Sheraton, Thomas, 180

Sheridan, Richard Brinsley, 291, 299-300

Sherman, Roger, 217

Shillitoe, Thomas, 300

Slavery, abolition, 295-6

Smith, Adam, *Wealth of Nations*, 265

Smollet, Tobias, 38, 107

Society of Friends, *See* Quakers

Sons of Liberty, 208

Sophia, Princess, marriage to Elector of Hanover, 18, 19

Sophia, Prince (daughter), 286

South Carolina, for independence, 213

Spain, population, 55; Pitt's policy on, 91; naval threats, 240; defeat by Rodney, 241; naval victory, 266

Spencer, Lady Diana, 21, 48
Spitalfields weavers, demands, 122-3, 128-30
Stair, Lord, 26, 27
Stamp Act, 139-41, repeal sought by ministry, 150; concern of commercial interests, 151-2; as a symbol, 153-8; repealed, 158, 197
Stationers Company, 95
Stormont, Lord, 247, 251; bravery, 249; and arrest of Gordon, 255; measures to restore order, 257
Strangways, Lady Susan, 67, 73, 75
Stuarts, attempt to return, 29-30
Stuart-Wortley-Mackenzie, James Archibald. *See* Mackenzie (Bute's brother)
Surrey, Lord, 272

Talbot, Lord, 84, 85
Tariff on silk, 122, 128
Tea tax, 198, 199
Temple, Richard Grenville, Lord, 282; loyalty to Pitt, 92-3; at Guildhall banquet, 99; stricken from Privy Council, 115; king's distrust, 116; political and social background, 126; unwilling to play second fiddle, 160, 167-8
Thurlow, Edward, Solicitor General, 187; Lord Chancellor, 241; declines ministry, 272; a king's man in cabinet, 278; unsuccessful in forming ministry, 278-9; ousted 281; reappointed in cabinet of Pitt the Younger, 282; theft of Great Seal from his house, 284-5; on handling of king during spells of madness, 291-2; opposed abolition of slavery, 295
Toleration, of king in religion, 180-1
Tory, definition, 68
Tower of London, 113
Townshend, Charles, in cabinet, 169-70; a hatchetman, 170-1; opposition to his land taxes, 172-3; death, 173
Townshend Acts, 172-3
Trenton, battle, 220
Twining, Reverend Thomas, 261
Tyrconnel, Countess of, and Duke of York, 283

Valley Forge, 224; story of Washington praying, 235-6
Vane, Miss, 22
Vergennes, Comte de, French Foreign Minister, 229
Vermont, for independence, 212
Victoria, Queen, 15, 302-3
Virginia, assembly vote against taxes, 151-3; Botetourt replaces Amherst as governor, 174-5; assembly dissolved, 198; for independence, 211, 213
Voltaire, disliked by king, 286

Waldegrave, Lord, tutor of Prince 32, 43; king's personal agent, 49-51; death, 140; widow married Duke of Gloucester, 165
Wallis, Samuel, explorations, 182, 183
Walpole, Sir Edward, 165
Walpole, Horace, quote on George III, 67; tribute to Lady Sarah Lennox, 70; on mob of weavers, 129; on Grafton, 150; on Botetourt's appointment, 175; on Boston Tea Party, 202; vitriolic description of Shelburne, 279
Walpole, Sir Robert, 16, 17, 21, 25, 28, 139
Warburton, Bishop, 108, 109
Washington, George, 193, 304; early supporter of armed resistance, 208, 209, 211; appointed Commander-in-Chief, 209, 210-11; greatest asset of the colonies, 210; expected a short war, 211; failure of Howe's attempt at conciliation, 215; early campaigns, 216, 218; draws Howe off from meeting Burgoyne, 219-20; at Valley Forge, 235-6; duped Clinton, 262, 266; Yorktown, 267
Waterloo, 302
Watt, James, 180
Wedderburn, Alexander, 252, 269
Wedgwood, Josiah, king's patronage, 179-80
Wedgwood, Mrs. Josiah, Romney portrait, 178
Weissenstein, Charles de, peace proposals to Franklin, 229
Wesley, John, 181, 302
West, Benjamin, king's patronage, 176, 177, 300, 304; and Mrs. Patience Wright, 178
West Indies, importance, 240-1
Westminster Monthly Meeting of Friends, 45
Weymouth, Lord, 173, 187
Whig, definition, 68
Wilberforce, William, 299-300
Wilhelmina (daughter of king of Prussia), Frederick betrothed to, 20, 21
Wilkes, John, *North Briton*, 86, 108, 109, 110-11; libertarian and libertine; 105-6; *Essay on Woman*, 107-8; government action against, 112-16; in tower, 115; found guilty *in absentia*, 116; implicated in weavers' disturbance, 130, 133-4; sympathizers in England, 138; applies for pardon, 169; return and imprisonment, 173; continued persecution, 185; jail and election to Parliament, 186-7; American sympathizer, 207; and Gordon riots, 253-4
William, Prince (brother), 16

William IV (Prince William, Duke of Clarence, son of George III), scandals, 283-4, 304

William and Mary, invited to throne, 17, 18, 19

Willis, Dr. Francis, 289-92

Wilmington, Lord, 24, 28

Wilson, General Sir Robert, 313

Wolfe, Major-General James, 56, 204

Wolsey, Cardinal, 23, 259

Wraxall, Sir N. W., *Memoirs*, 45; on Bridget daughter of Lord Northington, 163; on king's part in Gordon riots, 259

Wright, Mrs. Patience, king's patronage, 176, 177-8, 299; amateur spy for Franklin, 178; and Abigail Adams, 178-9

Wyatt, John, 180

YARMOUTH, COUNTESS OF, 58

York, Archbishop of, 245

Yorke, Philip. *See* Hardwicke, Lord

Yorktown, Cornwallis at, 265-6; surrender, 267

Young Pretender, 29